Beyond Even the Stars

MAY YOU

ALWAYS WALK

THE WAY

HE WALKED

Beyond Even the Stars

A Compostela Pilgrim in France

KEVIN A. CODD

WIPF & STOCK · Eugene, Oregon

BEYOND EVEN THE STARS
A Compostela Pilgrim in France

Wipf & Stock
An Imprint of Wipf and Stock Publishers
199 W. 8th Ave., Suite 3
Eugene, OR 97401

www.wipfandstock.com

PAPERBACK ISBN: 978-1-5326-4191-6
HARDCOVER ISBN: 978-1-5326-4192-3
EBOOK ISBN: 978-1-5326-4193-0

Manufactured in the U.S.A.   FEBRUARY 15, 2018

To Caroline and Gene, who kept me walking.

Contents

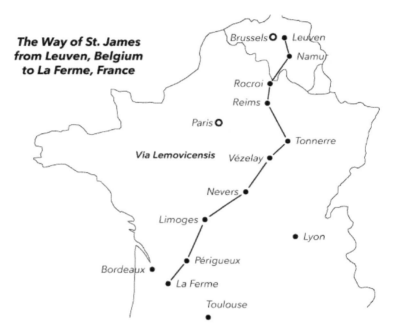

**The Way of St. James
from Leuven, Belgium
to La Ferme, France**

Brussels ○ ● Leuven

● Namur

Rocroi ●

Reims ●

Paris ○

● Tonnerre

Via Lemovicensis   Vézelay ●

Nevers ●

Limoges ●

● Lyon

Périgueux ●

Bordeaux ●

● La Ferme

Toulouse
●

Preface

I fear I am forgetting what it is to be a pilgrim. Some years back, I walked the Spanish Camino de Santiago from the French village of Saint-Jean-Pied-de-Port, just north of the Spanish border, and across northern Spain to the ancient city of Santiago de Compostela. It took a month plus a few days to complete the walk; well, it was more than a walk. It was, in fact, a *pilgrimage*, something much grander. I wrote a book about the experience and titled it "To the Field of Stars."[1] I now wish it could have been a deeper book, a truer book, one that captured not just what the walk was like, but how much that month-*plus* would affect me long after I had walked the last step. With the passage of months and then years, the pilgrimage experience quietly bore ever more deeply into my heart, and I slowly but surely found that it had changed me—and changed me a lot.

How did it change me? It is not so easy to put into words, but these are the best I've found so far: it humbled me. Which is to say that I came to know my own fragility as a human being as well as the goodness of everything beyond me: the whole big-banged universe, the tender earth, other people. I found I had my place in all this goodness, and I lost much of my fear of death, though certainly not all. After I had walked that last step, I promised myself that I would never lapse back into the person I had been before I had become a pilgrim.

Alas, of late, I am feeling myself more like that pre-pilgrim me and less like the person I thought I had become following my arrival in Santiago de Compostela. The power of that long, slow pilgrim prayer has diminished; the lessons have receded under the weight of life's quotidian duties. I have become increasingly aware that I have been slowly losing the memory of

---

1. Codd, Kevin A. *To The Field of Stars: A Pilgrim's Journey to Santiago de Compostela*. Grand Rapids, MI: Eerdmans, 2008.

those walking days. The particular memories have congealed into a generality; the specificity of each day, each hour, each moment of that previous pilgrimage is being lost to me. I don't like that feeling: of losing my grip on the *details* of the thing, for it is in the details that one finds the thing's meaning. Yes, that long walk was a prayer for me, now that I look back on it, and I don't want to forget the words to that prayer, the steps, the solitude, the community, the joy, and yes, even the pain of blisters and tendonitis.

One night not long ago, I awoke to a dream. It was one of those dreams that is clear and clean of mental clutter and easily remembered. Most of all, it seemed very real and felt very true.

So this was my dream.

I am walking. I am happy beyond words. I am on a gently winding road, a road that is rising. The sun is brightly shining, but it is not hot, and a breeze is cooling my face. My shirt is open to both wind and the shine of the sun. I have nothing on my back, and my feet are almost prancing, or maybe, dancing as I climb. The increasing elevation does not slow me; it *lifts* me. My smile is wide, my eyes are alive, and my heart is beating in time to my footsteps. I come over a final rise, look up from the road, and there is sea as far as I can see. And sky. The blue of one melding with the blue of the other along a hazy thin line that is the horizon. This is the very end of the earth and the beginning of the heavens, and I am walking into it. I am not afraid, for the road and the sea and the sky and all that is beyond is so beautiful. I lift my arms and soundlessly shout across the universe: *Ahhh!* And with that cry, as one does in dreams, I fly. Or better, I am lifted up and carried beyond the horizon, beyond the End of the Earth, beyond even the stars above, and . . . into . . . into . . . into . . . ? Well, I don't know—into God perhaps.

I awake. I am not flying at all, but altogether horizontal in my old bed. And this is old Leuven[2] in old Belgium where I have lived these past eight years. I climb out from under my blanket, walk to the bedroom balcony and step outside into the Belgian night. I can see only a few stars here for the lights of the city are strong, and there are clouds. In the few stars able to break through the halogen haze, I imagine the outline of the ancient apostle with his walking stick and floppy hat, a cockleshell tied to his breast. He waves his staff and invites me to follow him. I nod and say to the stars, "Yes! I shall come." And so it is that I make a pact with James the Great, Santiago, Jacques, Jacobus Maximus himself, to walk back to the Field of Stars, Compostela, and this time, to walk beyond it, to Finisterre, the End of the Earth, and to do my best to walk, then, into God.

---

2. Or "Louvain" as it is widely known in the English-speaking world.

1

The First Day of the Week

To this end, that is, to walk to the End of the Earth, I have a plan.
I have completed my work as rector of my old seminary in Leuven,
The American College; my trunks are packed, and I have made my goodbyes
to eight year's worth of friends. Tomorrow morning, Sunday, the First Day
of the Week, the first day of July, I will commence my second pilgrimage to
Santiago de Compostela, but this time I intend to walk from home, from my
home in Belgium: Leuven. From my front door, like pilgrims of old, I will
begin this new pilgrimage. I shall first walk in a southerly direction across
Wallonia, the French-speaking part of Belgium, then, in about a week, I
shall enter France. I will then hoof it across that country, north to south,
back to Saint-Jean-Pied-de-Port in the Pyrenees, and if all is still well, once
again cross Spain to Compostela. And then I shall walk three days more to
the eastern shore of the Atlantic, to medieval Europe's last bit of land before
there was nothing but unknowable sea and sky, *Finis Terrae*. All in all, I will
walk about 2,500 kilometers, a little more than 1,500 miles, *if all goes well*.

I spend a long night packing a grand new backpack that bears the
brand name "Gregory." At about four in the morning, I prod the last bits and
pieces into the pack and weigh it on my bathroom scale. I am disheartened
to see that it pushes the needle to just over forty pounds; that's about ten too
many. But it is now very late, and I am very tired, and I have to get up early,
so I leave it as it is, its broad seams straining to hold all that I have stuffed
within. In its heft, the mute bag seems almost to have a personality of its
own, so I dub him *Gregorius Magnus*, Gregory the Great, one of those grand
popes of times past.

In the two hours remaining to me before I must arise and begin my
new pilgrimage from this place to that of Saint James the Apostle, I barely
doze and certainly do not sleep. A voice within my brain calculates the

foolishness I have gotten myself into: "That Gregory is not just 'Great', he is *obese*! You can never carry that much weight across 2,500 kilometers!" *Somehow, I'll manage. I HAVE TO!* "But have you forgotten the last pilgrimage across Spain? Don't you remember the blisters? Are you ready for *that* again? And the ten days of tendonitis? That about killed you!" *Yes, I remember, only too well; but I made it, didn't I?* "But it is impossible!" *NO, I don't care if it is impossible!* My final words on the subject: *My job is to begin, just to begin.*

The alarm rings six o'clock; I jump out of bed and, ready or not, I begin.

I shower quickly, don my new pilgrim duds, all made of high-tech, sweat-wicking, artificial fiber stuff. I pull Gregory the Great up and swing him onto my back, shift his heft a bit to this side and then that, snap the various belts together, and decide I will be able to manage him just fine. There is no use being a pessimist on the day you begin a pilgrimage. I leave my old room for the last time, locking the door behind me. Ever so slowly, I lug myself, Gregory, and my trekking poles down the old oak staircase to the front foyer of the American College where a small crowd is waiting for me.

I've framed out this whole thing in my imagination for a long time, and it is happening just as I dreamed it would. I lead my early farewellers into the chapel for Lauds, where even more friends are waiting; we pray the appointed psalms, then following the final blessing, we all step into the small courtyard that opens into the street. A few bid me farewell here at the gate, but most follow me into the Sunday-morning emptiness of the Naamsestraat. These friends buzz about me, snapping pictures, gabbing, and cheering me on as we take possession of the traffic-less arterial radiating out from the Leuven town-center towards the city of Namur where I hope to land in just a few days. Our giddiness echoes off the brick walls of the buildings to either side. Everything is awash in morning light. We are a little parade of perky pilgrims ambling ever so amiably towards the Naamsepoort and our exit from Leuven proper.

Outside the city, we follow a shaded walk, separated from a woods to the right by a long brick wall. I lead the way through an open arch in the wall, and we leave Leuven's civilized streets behind, following now a damp path beneath a canopy of leafy linden trees. Along the mulchy way, the sound of our footsteps changes, becoming softer, milder, almost otherworldly. Small birds flutter, twitter, and tweet just above our heads. Only a few meters more and we arrive at a hillock topped by a twelfth-century chapel, that of Sint-Lambertus, now much renovated to contemporary sensibilities. The door is opened, and we all gather between the arcades of stone and glass that form its walls, and here I drop Gregory to the ground, stretch a bit, and prepare to celebrate Sunday Mass. I invite my friend, Gene, to read the first readings, and a priest-friend to proclaim the Gospel. I feel strange presiding with my dark Meindl boots incongruously sticking out from under the hem of my white alb. We sing an opening hymn with grand enthusiasm: *Morning has broken, like the first morning; blackbird has spoken like the first bird.* The scripture readings for the day hit the mark for this unusual liturgy: Jesus heads for Jerusalem. Along the way, he expects a less than hospitable reception; once there, we all know what will happen. He walks on anyway. This Jesus is a pilgrim. It is one of the things I have come to love about his story: this Jesus walks. I preach a simple homily then continue with the Eucharist: bread and wine, and we with them, becoming the Body of Christ; it seems more real than ever in this chapelled frontier between city and woods, past and future, the old me and the new me about to be reborn in walking. The Mass concludes with a final hymn: *I heard the voice of Jesus say, come unto me and stay* . . . As we end our prayer, I relish the echo of the last line of the hymn: . . . *and in that Light of Life I'll walk till traveling days are done.* May it be so.

Farewells and exuberant embraces ensue. I take Gregory in hand and hoist him onto my back, take my two trekking poles, dubbed last time around as Click and Clack, and I am ready to go. I will be accompanied this first day by Caroline, Gene's wife. Caroline and Gene walked the Spanish Camino the same year I did, and we have since become great friends. Having worked five years thereafter in the town of Los Arcos as *hospitaleros,* the kind people who welcome pilgrims into their refuges and clean up after them, they love the Camino as much as I.

We have just fifteen kilometers through the Heverlee woods to manage this first day. Easy. Caroline carries a very light pack, a little brother to my much bigger Gregory. We wave a final good-bye to our troop of friends at the chapel and heading into the Heverlee woods, Caroline and I begin our walk to the village of Tourinnes-la-Grosse.

These woods are not like anything I know from my hometown of Spokane. No pine and fir here. In these Flemish woods, oak, beech, and linden trees are generously spaced and perfectly ordered in extensive grids. There is little underbrush. Wide paths crisscross the whole and some even have names like streets in a city. There is nothing wild or woolly about them; they are absolutely civilized and designed for gentle family strolls on a Sunday afternoon. They are lovely as light filters through the leaves and branches above, speckling the soft, brown soil below with random flecks of light. At this hour it is mostly quiet except for an occasional bird chirp or crow caw. Fallen acorns crackle underfoot. It is just about as perfect a day as there could be for beginning a pilgrimage. Caroline and I wander down our chosen path at a leisurely pace; we chat as we go, talking about the beauty around us. My pack is weighty, but I seem to be managing just fine under its heft; my optimism rises as time passes and no disaster befalls me. *Easy.*

We stop for a brief rest on a couple of stumps beside the way. We take a few sips of water and talk softly about our friends and the unusual pilgrim liturgy at Sint-Lambertus this morning. We have been walking for an hour and a half: five or six kilometers under our belt with just ten more to go. *Easy.* We get up off our stumps to move on; I lift Gregory, swing him up onto my back, and begin buckling the straps and belts. *My, he is heavy!*

I stagger just a bit as I turn back to the road. I take a few steps forward, then it happens, faster than I could ever have imagined: my right knee gives way. I feel it sort of squash beneath me as I step forward. I have had problems with this knee for some time; some thirty years of jogging have taken their toll. I don't say anything to Caroline at first, but just take a few more steps; it is not getting better. I complain to Caroline that my knee is acting up. She suggests a few more steps; maybe it will ease up. I take the steps, but it becomes more painful. She recommends that I drop the pack for a few minutes and just walk about easily. I do, and it does seem a bit better now without the pack. I hitch up the pack once again, but with the new step, the knee gives way again. The pain is sharper than ever.

I stop and drop the pack, and we just sit and rest for a while. A dread thought strikes me: *This could be it; this could be the end of my pilgrimage. After only six kilometers!* I get up and walk about without Gregory and again, things seem a bit better. We load up once more but just a few meters down the road, I give in to the pain in the knee and admit to Caroline: *I don't think I can do this.* She responds that it is too early to give up. "You are meant to do this," she affirms, then suggests that as long as it seems that I can walk at all, I should walk. She calls Gene and arranges to have him meet us with the car so he can take my pack to Tourinne-la-Grosse; the hope is that if I walk unburdened I can get at least the first day done. We agree to meet about a kilometer further ahead where a paved road cuts through the woods, intersecting our dirt path.

When we finally get to the intersection, I ditch the pack, lie down in a grassy verge, and take off my boots and socks to air my feet a bit. Caroline, through repeated calls on her mobile phone, guides Gene to us. Once he pulls up in his shiny black Saab, the three of us talk over my situation. The pain in my knee notwithstanding, the plan remains: Gene will take the pack; Caroline and I will walk on. I'd rather get in the car and go home, but they are not paying attention to my cowardice, and soon enough Gene is driving off with Gregory the Obese in the back seat while Caroline and I hobble slowly back into the woods.

With Caroline to encourage me, I am doing it; I walk. It hurts, but with time and repetition, I slip into a sort of mental override and just give the ache less and less heed. I focus instead on the trunks of trees, so solid and sturdy and living, or the leafy ceiling above us, making this seem a world apart, a fairy tale kind of place where wolves pretend to be grandmothers and little pigs have their houses blown down. The softness of the organic topsoil under our feet reminds me of flesh; the earth's own flesh is what we tread upon now. We spot the Saab turning onto a nearby lane; Gene is tracking us. He approaches, and we give him a progress report. Again, we agree not to quit. I use my walking poles to take as much pressure off my knees as possible. It is slow going, but we are making progress. Nevertheless, my spirits remain dreadfully low; even if I get through *today*, what are the chances I can go on to walk 2,500 more kilometers to Compostela? Not much, I fear. To calm that fear, I return my focus to trees and leaves and flecks of light dappling our path.

After another hour and a half of walking, Caroline and I come to a rise in the road, at the top of which we leave behind the woods and are led through an open field of wheat. Above is a spectacularly blue sky with a few white clouds puffing along its hidden highways. A breeze cools us even as it rustles the wheat to our left and right. Up to this point, Caroline has been navigating our journey using a paper map of the Heverlee woods; we come to a T in the road, a large stone wall blocking our way forward, and have to make a choice of which way to turn with little help from her map. I pull out my handheld GPS loaded with digital maps of this section of Belgium and take a reading. I get longitude and latitude numbers, but no map shows on the small screen. *What?* I play with the various buttons to try to bring up the maps, but they refuse to comply. I turn the gadget off, and together we deduce the way forward picking our way down a stony road that drops us into a shallow valley. We come upon a paved highway with signs indicating that Tourrines-la-Grosse and its campground is about a half-kilometer to the right. We have almost done it; we have almost overcome the day's adversities, and though I am limping quite badly, leaning heavily on Click and Clack to move ahead, I feel a touch of pride in having gotten this far. I know also that I owe it almost entirely to Caroline's gentle but unbending insistence that failure is not an option.

Gene meets us as we approach the campground entrance. We drop into the campground cafe and take a table on the veranda overlooking a green field full of campers, caravans, and large family-style tents. We have left our wooded wonderland and reentered the ordinary world where everything is . . . well, *ordinary*. People buzz about, busy about many things, without seeing, hearing, feeling what is beneath and above and within. Yet, we, too, have slipped out of this Via, this pilgrim Way, as quickly as we slipped into it at the doors to that twelfth-century chapel a few hours ago. Gene, an engineer and a great one for fixing things, takes a look at my handheld GPS and finds that he can't get the maps to come up either. This is a topographical disaster, for my route forward from this point is laid out in those digital maps; I had punched in a hundred or more "way-points," marking the route to Namur across a variety of paths, roads, and even fields. I have no guide other than this to Namur. We order beers and sandwiches and size up my situation.

My plan had been to camp here, in Tourinnes-la-Grosse, tonight and continue cross-country south towards Namur in the morning. But there is much to dissuade me, at least right now. Gregory is just too heavy, we decide; that is almost surely the reason my already weak knee could not hold up. I need to drop ten pounds before I continue if I am to have a fighting chance of making it. The knee is bad and should be looked at by a doctor. Whatever I did wrong in loading the maps into the GPS has to be fixed. The campground is crowded and singularly unattractive; I really do not want to spend even one night here alone in the midst of this crowd of strangers.

We all agree; it is back to Leuven. I detest the thought of it, but there is just not much choice in the matter. My pilgrimage, after only fifteen kilometers, is already on hiatus.

We pack our stuff into the Saab and head down the rural highway that leads back home. A grey depression settles over me as we draw closer to the Leuven town center. My return to the front door from which I so recently departed is abject. I am a failure. After all the fanfare this morning, I go home like a dog with my pilgrim tail between my legs. Saint James: I'm sorry. I did not expect this. The worst possible outcome has actually happened; I have crashed and burned in less than a day of walking. Maybe I should just quit altogether. Maybe I should not have even begun. Like some fallen Greek god, I am paying for my hubris in thinking I could walk from Leuven, across half of Belgium, across all of France, across most of Spain, all the way to Santiago de Compostela and beyond. What a naïf to have thought my body could take this. We pull up to the stone portal of my old place, the place I just left, definitively left, once and for all left, but here I am again, right where I began. *Ah, hell.*

Caroline, Gene, and I agree that the first order of business tomorrow will be to see the doctor. After that, if there is still a chance to continue the pilgrimage, I will unpack Gregory the Great, ditch as much as possible in hopes of getting him back down to fighting trim. After that, I'll have to tend to my GPS and see if I can restore my digital maps and way-points at least to Namur after which my Grand Randonnée 654[1] guidebook will take over navigation south. At the doors of the American College I thought I had left forever, I get out of the car and return to my disheveled room for one more night, and sadly, maybe more.

1. Much of western Europe is crisscrossed by an extraordinary system of walking paths, the Grande Randonnée, or "GR" for short. Each path is numbered and mapped for safe trekking from five kilometer day-walks to months-long hikes like this one.

2

Reculer Pour Mieux Sauter

I sleep deeply through the night and wake up with the annoying realization that I am again in my former bedroom. Yesterday, Caroline tried to keep me focused on my mission by sharing with me a bit of French wisdom: *Reculer pour mieux sauter.* "Step back for a better jump." This morning as I begin this unexpected hiatus in my plans, those words express exactly my mission during the days ahead; I really do need to step back so that I can take a better shot at accomplishing the greater mission of the entire pilgrimage. I repeat to myself the saying: *Reculer pour mieux sauter!*

I wrangle an emergency appointment with an orthopedic specialist at the hospital across the Naamsestraat. Caroline asks if she might come along for the visit, suggesting that, as a doctor herself, it might help in discussing our options.

I am greatly afraid this guy in a white coat is going to say, "Stop! Walk no further." It will be good to have Caroline along for moral support if that happens. We meet at the hospital front door, go through the usual routine of getting checked in, then are sent up to the orthopedic wing. We sit nervously for what seems forever in the stuffy waiting room; finally, we are called by an aide into a consultation room. The doctor comes in, asks a few questions, extends and twists the leg and sighs. He is not particularly encouraging, and I suspect he thinks I am crazy for wanting to walk halfway across Western Europe, but he does not say the dreaded word, "STOP".

He puts me on the table, suggests the cortisone option, and we agree it is worth a try. He explains that for a day the pain may be worse but then it should get better. Its effects will last for ten days; after that, I will fall back on my own natural resources to deal with the troubled joint, for better or for worse. He unwraps a syringe and after loading it with the medication, injects it straight into the knee, twisting it like a dagger as he spreads the cortisone around inside the joint. It hurts like hell, and I grab hold of my gurney with both hands, my body going rigid as the seconds pass, then it is over. The doc prescribes a high-tech knee brace, then wishes me a good journey. Both Caroline and I are fairly rejoicing that this specialist did not tell me to walk no further. That's enough for one day, so we head back to the College where, standing at the gate, Caroline and I decide I should stay put for a couple days, get some rest, fix the GPS, then take up the road again, right where I left off on Sunday afternoon. Today is Monday; we pick Thursday as the re-*sauter* day. I hide out in my corner of the College, and tend to the business of *reculer*: resting, putting Gregory on a major diet, and fixing the GPS.

I take Tuesday morning to pull everything out of the backpack and spread it out on every available horizontal surface, then begin the process of ditching all that seems less than necessary. I get Gregory down to a manageable twenty-nine pounds. Terrific. Now to the GPS. It is a much more intractable problem, and it takes me the rest of the day to puzzle out the mystery of the lost maps, but by 10:00 pm, I have it resolved and with a sense of minor triumph, go to bed.

Wednesday presents a new challenge: finding lodging for my first night back on the road. From Tourinnes-la-Grosse, the most likely village at a reasonable walking distance is a place called Thorembais-Saint-Trond. Gene makes the arrangements with *Père* Paul, the local priest. He puts up pilgrims often and has plenty of room for me. I immediately feel much more secure knowing I have a bed awaiting me at the end of tomorrow's road. We plot our strategy for my return to the road; they will drive me out to the Tourinnes campground where we left off on Sunday; I'll use a small backpack while they'll keep Gregory the Great with them and carry it on to *Père* Paul's place twenty kilometers further on. If I need help along the way, all I have to do is use my mobile phone, and they will come to my aid. If all goes well, they will drive back down to Thorembais to meet me, and we will have dinner together.

Now that I've done all I can do to make this project work, I go to bed early and sink almost immediately into that deep place where pieces of dreams percolate inchoately like colors in a kaleidoscope until they once again come together into something fantastic. Almost as soon as I awake that something fantastic is lost to my consciousness.

Thursday morning, *sauter*-day, breaks grey, windy, and the threat of rain weighs heavy over Belgium. I am feeling determined to begin again; this time, though, with no parades, fanfare, or showy displays of pilgrim piety. I shower, dress in my high-tech walking togs, tighten up Gregory's various straps and cords, grab a bite to eat, then meet Gene and Caroline at the front door. "How's the knee?" I am asked right off. *Okay, I think. I've got the brace on.* Before long, rain has begun to splatter lightly against the windshield; the wipers go on and establish a beat to the drive back through the Heverlee woods: *wish-wash, wish-wash, wish-wash.* "The weather report is that you've got a couple days of this rain and wind ahead of you," Gene reports.

We pull up in front of the campground cafe, which is still closed, scotching the possibility of a warm morning coffee together; instead, we unload my gear. We take a few snapshots. I turn on the GPS. Gregory stays in the trunk awaiting delivery to Thorambais. I grab my hiking poles. Gene gives me a hug, Caroline a kiss, and as they get back in the car, I turn into the rain and brace myself against the wind. I take a look at the first way-point on my GPS and head down the street and around the corner leaving my friends behind. I am on my own now. The knee aches lightly but nothing like Sunday's dagger stabs. *Oh, please stay this way . . . at least for a while.* And so I begin again, hopefully having *reculer*-ed enough since Sunday to achieve today a better *sauter* on this 2,500 kilometer march to Compostela and Finisterre.

A quiet envelops me out here that absorbs the click-clack of my poles and accentuates the pock-pock-pock sound of substantial raindrops on my canvas hood. No voice is heard. No sound from the world of machines strikes me. Other raindrops, thousands of them, splatter on the surface of the road and upon the leaves of wayside bushes and broad blades of grass. It is the softest of hymns. My eyes focus on new details: The low clouds have billowy grey textures, some light, others dark. There is a small break in the distance where a brilliant stream of light slips through the clouds and angles down towards the earth below, illuminating the small segment of green field where it makes landfall. I've seen such knives of light a million times in this rain-inclined country, but this one today seems alive to me, like it has a mind of its own, saying to itself, "Ah, there, a green-veined leaf I wish to see better, so I shall dive down for a closer look. Yes, it is a beautiful leaf and all the more so because I illuminate it and see it and love it." And the fields all around, some dressed in the green of vegetables and sugar beets, others tilled and clumpy with clods of brown dirt piled in orderly rows, small pools of silvery water piling up in the rough troughs between those rows then trickling off where there is a break in the muddy dirt. This is a living, breathing, humming world I am walking through today, and it embraces me from all sides. I am in it, and it is within me, and a sort of communion in life is what I feel as I amble on, supported by Click and Clack, wrapped in Gore-Tex from head to toe, made free to walk by a shot of cortisone at work in my old knee.

The spell is broken by the ring of my mobile phone tucked within the small pack on my back, so now I have to stop and slip the pack off to retrieve the thing. It is Gene and Caroline letting me know that they've dropped Gregory off at the parish house in Thorembais-Saint-Trond where they had a delightful visit with *Père* Paul, a Flemish missionary priest who somehow has landed in Wallonia, the French-speaking region of Belgium. He will welcome me with open arms; "just a wonderful guy" is Gene's verdict. They ask how I am faring, and I am happy to report that though a bit wet, I am doing well. The knee is behaving, and my pace is such that I should make it to Thorembais by mid-afternoon.

3

The Missionary

I safely arrive at Thorembais. The place strikes me as more truck-stop than town, the busy N29 thoroughfare and the even busier E411 highway feeding a steady parade of motorists and truckers into its heart for fuel and snacks. Beyond its collection of eateries and petrol stations is the actual village, whose center is dominated by a twelfth-century church, providentially equipped with a steeple high enough to guide me in. I pass around and behind the church in search of the parish house; it is an easy find: white with blue trim, a two-story affair in a state of minor disrepair, a relic surely of the eighteenth-century. I mosey up to the front door and ring the bell. The grand *port* swings open, and there stands before me the smiling face of *Père* Paul, framed by a wool cap, wild grey hair jutting out from underneath, and a substantial grey beard equally untamed. Baggy clothes and a well-worn blue cardigan hang from his lanky frame. The man welcomes me in English and sweeps me out of the rain and into a hallway cluttered with gardening tools and a menagerie of beat up plaster saints. He ushers me into the kitchen, as untidy as the front hallway, and offers me a warm cup of coffee, a couple slices of homemade bread, and the condiments necessary for a healthy sandwich.

As with all good pastors, *Père* Paul asks first about me: where I'm from, what I've been doing, what I'm doing now. I then get some life details out of him: he spent most of his adult years as a missionary priest working in Haiti, until, as he says, "I got run out as a revolutionary." In his post-Haitian life, he preferred to settle in rural Belgium, which I can only imagine is less of a shock to his missionary system than big-city Brussels. Here in this small town, he can work like a missionary in a place where few still go to Mass on Sunday. He mostly spends time just hanging around with the folks, churchgoers or not. When not doing that, he has his garden and his pigeons to tend to. "Do you want to see the garden and my pigeons?" *Sure.* So up and out into the well-soaked back yard we go to inspect the expansive garden from which he gathers most of his daily food. And then there are the pigeons; as he goes about feeding them handfuls of grain he calls them his *kindjes*, Flemish for his "little kids." He shows me where I can wash the mud from my boots and then leads me back inside and up the oak staircase. He guides me into a large and austere room with well-worn floorboards partially covered by an equally well-worn carpet. Faded and water-stained wallpaper of a bygone design covers the walls. There is a washbasin in one corner and a bed across the way. Gregory the Great is waiting for me here, patiently leaning against the wall near the door. It is good to meet up with him again. All in all, it is a very good place to spend my first overnight on the Way, *le Chemin*, as it is called in French. I have *sauter'd* well this day.

After a bath, I find Paul busy in the kitchen snapping peas from the garden like an old grandpa. He is deep into the preparations for a fine meal he has planned for three guests he will be hosting at his table later in the evening. I am welcome for dinner, too, he says, but I decline since Caroline and Gene will be taking me out for our own "victory over the gimpy knee" supper.

They roll back into town in the late afternoon. Though it has been only a few hours since we parted at the campground entrance in Tourinnes-la-Grosse, greeting Caroline and Gene here some twenty kilometers of walking later feels like a grand reunion all the same. Paul welcomes them in, and we are seated in the parish house's living room. Beyond this *salle* is a very large dining room fitted with antique china cabinets and a table big enough to seat at least ten people. Paul asks if we'd like something to drink, a beer perhaps? A beer sounds great so I heartily accept the suggestion. Then he reveals that he is in possession of a case of Belgium's finest, rarest, most expensive Trappist beer, *Westvleteren*, something that can only be purchased directly from the monastery and is seldom found in any bar or cafe. In eight years of living in Belgium, I have never come across it, only heard of it. I heartily accept his offer to try the brew. Paul disappears into a storage room, shuffles about for a few moments, then returns with three of the precious bottles in hand. They are snapped opened and poured into wide-mouthed glasses made just for this kind of beer. Now for the taste test: I sip, I let it linger a while in my mouth, then savor it as it slips down my gullet, smooth and rich and deep as life. This beer is like nothing I have ever tasted before; it makes all other beers, even my other Trappist favorites, seem like poor pretenders and weak imitations of the real thing. How did those monks of Sint-Sixtus Abbey craft this malty taste of heaven? Is there prayer involved? The three of us rave about this special treat we have been given to share in this most unlikely moment and place, then I begin telling the day's tales from the road, while Paul returns to the kitchen to continue the preparations for his meal this evening.

As Caroline, Gene, and I finish the last drops of our *Westvleterens*, we talk about tomorrow. It will be a very long day for me: almost twenty-eight kilometers to Namur. I'll be carrying Gregory the Great again, all thirty pounds of him. Hopefully, the rain and wind of today will have passed. Even with good weather it would be a challenge. Caroline counsels me to stop if I need to stop and seek housing along the way. That is good advice; I'll keep it in mind, but I'm going to try to go for the whole route if I possibly can. After dinner in a local restaurant, these two guardian angels take their leave of me with a hug and a kiss. It is sad to see them drive off; I feel a touch of loneliness as I return to my refuge alone for the night.

As soon as I enter the foyer with its vanguard of deteriorating saints, Paul calls to me from the dining room, his voice accompanied by the hearty laughter of his three guests. I step in, take off my rain-jacket, and join the four at the big table. Paul introduces the gentlemen to me, and helpfully, all speak at least some English. They are in their forties, I would guess, and clearly have been enjoying the feast Paul has prepared for them. They are happy to welcome me into their circle and insist I try some of the dishes still on the table. I plead an already-full belly but take a small taste of the main course, a fine piece of pork roast prepared Haitian-style. It is delicious, and I wish I had the appetite to enjoy more than just a bite or two.

As Paul disappears into the kitchen to prepare dessert, these men's questions about my life and work make it clear that this day is far from over for me. They are very curious about my desire for pilgrimage. Just what kind of spiritual search am I on? They too, are searching, they tell me; that is why they gather here at Paul's every once in a while: to talk together about their search for meaning and a spirituality that will fit them. For my part, I do my best to explain what has motivated me to take on this old way of connecting with what is deep and holy in life. I share a few experiences from my previous pilgrimage in Spain. When I mention the sense that I often have on the road of walking with Jesus as a brother and fellow pilgrim, their curiosity is further piqued by my use of the present tense. Jesus? How? In what way? Why him? I go a bit deeper, expressing my belief that I feel him present and near, not so surprising really, since, as a Christian I believe in his resurrection. "So do you believe Jesus is a greater master than Buddha or Mohammad or other spiritual teachers?" I know this is a question, my answer to which, may well lead us into a debate I don't particularly want, but I answer honestly: *I do. I am a Christian, which means that I believe that though there are other revealers and prophets; he is the* most full *revealer of*

God. Incredulity shows on their increasingly serious brows. "So you believe Christianity is better than other religions? *Yes. But "better" in the sense of a fuller picture of God, not in a moral sense.* Do you really believe that Jesus is divine?" *Yes,* again. Then it comes: a barrage of opinions and further questions that make it clear these men find my faith to be anachronistic and disrespectful of the equal truth present in other religious traditions. I don't think I am being disrespectful of other religions; to the contrary, I believe there is tremendous good and plenty of God in other religious ways. Words start to be put into my mouth: "So you believe only Catholics can be saved?" *No, I believe that lots of people of many traditions can know much of God, and are good and holy people, probably holier than I am, and will certainly be welcomed by God into his eternal embrace; but, yes, I believe that those who know Jesus have the best picture of who God is.* "But surely you understand that the belief that Jesus is divine is just a myth, a sort of fable, don't you?" *No, I see Jesus as real, as real as you or me, more real than you or me. Without him I cannot be me, my real me, my truest me.* The conversation is all very friendly and animated; they are truly curious about my beliefs, but they clearly do not buy them. Particularly, the claims to a superior truth, the *most* superior truth, in Christ, are not washing with these seekers. Whatever spiritual journey they are on, my way is not one of the maps they are interested in using, at least not for the time being. Paul returns to the table with his homemade dessert, cigarettes are lit, small glasses of liqueurs are poured, and the conversation turns to other things. I excuse myself for I have had a long day, and I don't feel like defending my spiritual way throughout the evening, so I head upstairs for bed while their conversation below continues well into the night.

Tucked finally into my creaky bed, I am restless and nervous; a mosquito buzzes near my ear aggravating me further. The prospect of the twenty-eight kilometer march into Namur tomorrow causes me to fret about potential disasters that might befall me and what I would do to remedy them. I toss and turn. I do not fall asleep until sometime well after midnight.

Morning comes. The rain has stopped. The winds from yesterday continue to huff and puff. I get up feeling very tired. I prepare myself and Gregory, then I lug him down the oak staircase to Paul's kitchen where he is preparing coffee for us and setting out bread, butter, jam, and slices of ham for our breakfast. Paul explains that getting to the back-road to Namur is complicated and to keep me from getting lost, he will drive me to nearby Perwez where I can pick up the road more easily. At first, I consider declining his offer, wanting to preserve intact my commitment to actually walk every step of the way to Compostela, but my pilgrim bravado evaporates as I hear the rain start up again just outside the kitchen window. Accepting the ride, I quickly reason, is a way of accepting this good man's Christian hospitality to a stranger, especially on a day that promises to be particularly grueling for this recent cripple.

Paul pulls his small white Renault out of the garage, I carry Gregory to its trunk and throw him in and then get in myself. As Paul drives me the two kilometers to the outskirts of Perwez, I thank him for his welcome and his generosity to me; he responds with a happy shrug, "It is the regular thing to do." He pulls over to a side-road and tells me this is it; this is where I begin today. I step out of the car to a great gust of wind that ripples the cloth of my rain-jacket. I retrieve Gregory from the back, setting him down on the wet pavement, bracing him upright against my leg, and *Père* Paul, my missionary brother, drives off with a wave and a broad smile on his aging face.

Now it is just me, Gregory, Click and Clack, the road, and the wind. For the moment the rain has stopped, but I'm sure it will be back, so I pull out a light canvas cover on loan from Gene to protect Gregory from the inevitable downpour this day is sure to serve up, wrap it over Gregory, then cinch it up around the pack's extremities. As soon as I hoist Gregory to my back, a gust of wind rips the cover right off and sends it flying into the muddy ditch to my left. I drop Gregory, step down into the ditch, retrieve the cover, and stuff it back into a side-pocket of the pack. I will take my chances. *Okay, James and Jesus. I'm ready. Let's walk.*

The rain, mercifully, stays mostly at bay. I am buffeted by the wind, which, like yesterday, comes at Gregory and me from the right, making it necessary to compensate by leaning into it as I walk. This forces me to exert substantially more energy just to stay on course. When I come to my first crossroad, I check the GPS for directions and am once again both amazed and relieved that the gadget's screen coordinates exactly with the reality under my feet. With new confidence, I keep to the present heading towards the next way-point.

As I push on, my mind slips into a groove of thought over last night's discussion on religion. I remain unsettled by it. The disconcerted feelings call me to untangle the experience if I can. On the one hand, I am sorry that those men do not believe as I do, or more to the point, that the religious and spiritual tradition we all inherited in one way or another has lost its power to grab their spiritual imaginations. I am sorry, but I don't blame them. We Christians ourselves are mostly to blame for being out-of-favor in so many people's lives given our generally poor example in living the way of Christ the last two thousand years. The deep mysteries too often were not touched. Religion, as we lived it, lost its power to attract. The church's obvious faults and failings increased the sense that it was more a human institution than something sustained by the Divine: all the easier to walk away from it and just do something else on Sunday morning. Some just bumbled into effective secularism without much thought, with scientific advancement making the existence of God seem less likely and an ever-increasing social security making support from the heavens less necessary. Others, like these three wise-men in reverse, turned from the West and looked to the East, seeking out more exotic religious traditions and esoteric spiritual paths than the humdrum one in which their parents had brought them up. Their searching is a good thing, though I find myself aching that the star leading to Bethlehem doesn't seem to be on the table for these modern day searchers as a possible guide forward. The Christian claim that Jesus is the ultimate revelation of God, that he is God *en-fleshed*, is an extraordinarily bold, even audacious one, and who can blame anyone for finding it a spiritual mouthful. The surprise is that so many people *do* find it true and even with their faults and failings, still follow him as best they are able. This is what I hope I will be doing out on this Chemin: in a physical, peripatetic way, following Jesus down low, close to the earth, unencumbered by anything more than what I carry on my back. Even more, this is what I hope my mission out here might be: that I might point eyes towards God as Jesus did, in fleeting glances, simple greetings, eating and drinking together, an occasional touch, a multitude of small kindnesses.

My thoughts turn to the pastor of Thorembais-Saint-Trond. What is Paul up to with these discussions over his table with the three searchers? I suspect that what he is up to is what he has always been up to: he is a missionary, for years in faraway Haiti, but now a missionary in his own land, a land presently marked by as much skepticism and unbelief as any distant land of past centuries. This old priest has at least three things going on here that earn him the golden missionary seal: First, he maintains and supports the community of faith he already has, those few elderly parishioners who show up faithfully every Sunday and often enough during the week to pray, confess, be counseled. He is a good shepherd of his sheep. That is a big deal.

Second, he doesn't let himself get trapped in his church or parish house; he is out in the restaurants and cafes wherever folk, any folk, believers or otherwise, might be found. He talks with them about whatever they want to talk about: the rain and wind, for all he cares. He doesn't play the role of moralizer among them. He doesn't offer unasked for advice. He does not scold. He respects them, and they come to respect him. He earns their confidence as a good man among good men and women. He lives the example of Jesus and displays it to them not in any haughty, holier-than-thou, or pietistic way, but through kindness, hospitality, attentiveness, service. "It is the regular thing," he says of his generous gestures.

Third, and perhaps most importantly, from among these, a few begin to wonder what moves in this man: why is he so? They ask him. He gives them no lecture; he invites them over for dinner. Over the table he has set for them, he allows them to tell *their* stories. He listens. On the walls around them as they eat are the silent signs of what, or better, *who*, moves him: a small crucifix above the china cabinet. A print of some gospel scene near the door. An old statue on a small table. Most of all, there is the bread and wine on the table. None of it is pointed to. It is just there, the background of the conversation, subtle, silent, yet at play in the subconscious of a culture still residually Christian. These are the symbols these men's grandmothers loved. Some of that love must still be extant. These voices must still whisper, though perhaps only barely, of mysteries now almost lost to view. They search for ways, paths, new words that might lead them forward to know the sense of themselves and all that is. There are many paths so they wander down them a while, pick up some wisdom and grace along the way, and maybe, maybe, they wander back to the old way and its signs and symbols and ask what they mean. If and when they do, Paul the Missionary will be there, at the table with them. There are no guarantees, and Paul would never push to make it happen, but it *might,* and if it does, then *he* will tell the stories of Jesus as if they were new. The bread and wine they've been enjoying at his table over these months of discussions in his house will be easily taken in hand, blessed, and then what was in the background may find a place up front again. The mystery will have been entered. God will have been revealed as near. Perhaps. Paul cannot know where these men will walk, but he does his part as a trusted guide as gently and as patiently and as respectfully as possible. His way is much better than my profession of faith last night because, sincere as it was, it did not make sense to the searchers of Thorembais at this point in their journey.

This Paul is a fine missionary; I would like to be more like him. Maybe on this long walk I can improve my own practice of the missionary way he taught me last night. We'll see.

I leave behind the paved highway and take up a dirt road that will eventually meet up with another, smaller highway leading into Namur. With wind and the rain general over the land, there is little sign of life besides an occasional cow standing damp and dull-eyed in a closed-off field. An even more rare farmhouse, accompanied by barn and sheds mark the way with signs of human habitation. I approach one such settlement, the road taking me right through the center of it, old house to one side, barns to the other. I am taken by surprise by the unexpected presence of an elderly woman busy about something inside a small shed with the door propped open. She is as startled by me as I am by her. I smile and she smiles back, then she steps out of her tiny shed to talk. She is quite large and wearing work clothes: a worn dress, a moth-eaten sweater, and tall Wellington-style rubber boots. Her face is round, wrinkled, and set on either side of her nose are two great rosy cheeks. This lady is a classic European farm woman. She greets me in French, and I respond with a pleasant *bonjour*. She continues to size me up even as she asks me where I am going. I tell her, today: to Namur, but eventually: all the way to Compostela. "Where?" She obviously does not understand the Spanish name so I repeat in French, *Compostelle*. She frowns and asks me where Compostelle might be. I try to explain in my extremely limited French that it is in Spain, the home of *Saint-Jacques*. "Saint-Jacques?" she repeats, baffled still. I say that it is about 2,500 kilometers from here. "And you are going to *walk* there . . . with that *sac* on your back? She asks with complete incredulity. *God willing. I will try.* "*Pourquoi?*" Oh dear, the answer to this is way above my capabilities in French. All I can think of is to say, *à prier*, to pray. She wrinkles her brow into a frown, "2,500 kilometers *à prier?*" She calls loudly across the complex of barns; she wants to share this altogether ridiculous moment with someone. A thin old man appears from one of the barns carrying a bucket. He is wearing overalls and rubber Wellingtons, too. He ambles up to us and leans forward on an iron gate. He greets me simply then she explains to him that this *étranger* is going to walk to Spain, 2,500 kilometers, so he can pray. She is delighted by the silliness of the story so tells it with vigor. He nods but seems uncomprehending. He asks, "2,500 kilometers?" She says yes, that's right: 2,500 kilometers. "*À prier?*" he asks. She nods affirmatively. He takes this in then frowns himself in bemusement as if to say, "I don't get it, but to each their own." With a shrug, he adds, "*Bonne route, monsieur.*" The two of them look at each other with smiles that say, "Now this is something we've never seen before!" I can't help but smile with them, both at my ridiculous hubris in the matter, which they have made plain to me, and their enjoyment of my brassy plan, which clearly, they don't think I have a snowball's chance in hell of actually completing. In laughing together we have become friends, brief though our encounter has been, so we wish each other well, and I get back on the muddy road through their property. I turn to see them waving good-bye to me. I wave Clack at them in cheery response. I take off feeling like a man on a very ridiculous mission, but a mission nevertheless.

I continue on, eventually passing under the massive E42 expressway, then, bye and bye, pick up a hiking route through a light forest that leads me closer and closer to the metropolis of Namur. After the farm fields through which I have been walking the past two days, the cover of the trees above is a welcome change; it feels protective and reassuring to me. The sun comes out for longer periods now; the clouds are breaking up above my head. I stop at a bench and take off my rain jacket. I am sweat-soaked inside, but the sunshine warms me immediately. As soon as I walk under the shade of the trees though, I am chilled, but soon enough I am under the sun again and warm up quickly.

Signs of city life begin to make their presence felt. A street with houses and lamps lining it appears to my right, then side streets angling away from it. More traffic is evident. Bicyclists and then walkers begin to pass by. I feel like I should be close to the city, but the path continues with no sign that I am actually *in* the city. Kilometers slip by. I am getting tired. My knee is aching. I trudge on, using my poles more and more for support. I am limping rather seriously now. *Oh come on, Namur: appear!* And then, there it is: intersections, bridges, railway tracks, traffic-lights, *people*! Now I really have to rely on my GPS to get me across the city center and to the *Auberge de Jeunesse*, the local youth hostel at the south end of the city. I make a mistake and have to double back to catch the correct street that will lead me through the shopping district. I am really tired, and the buzz of the city as I go deeper into its busy heart only makes me feel all the wearier. I stop using Click and Clack because on the busy sidewalks they are making too much click and clack, and people are looking at me as if I were an alien from outer space. Teens go by with their ears plugged into iPods, sometimes bumping into me. A glamorous woman comes out of a glamorous store carrying a glamorous shopping bag. She doesn't see me as she passes right in front of me, forcing me to hold up for a moment. No one is looking at anyone. Anonymity reigns here.

I find my cross-street and head towards the Meuse river where the hostel should be located. I wander about the parallel streets near the river but don't find the place. I have been walking for seven or eight hours, and I am exhausted but have to carry on just a bit further. I ask for directions from a passing lady, but she shrugs politely, not knowing where such a place might be. I finally spot a small outdoor market, head for it, and discover that the *Auberge* is right here in front of me. I walk up the stairs, into the lobby, drop Gregory to the floor, then present myself to the lady tending the desk. She collects my fees, gives me a key, and sends me on my way to a room at the back of the modern complex. I open the door: two bunk beds, a window to the courtyard, a toilet and shower, and it all seems very clean. *Chez Kevin.* The lower bunk on the left side is already occupied by a man, perhaps in his early sixties. I greet him in French, he answers in French, but I detect a Flemish accent so ask him in Dutch if he is from Flanders. He responds in English that he is from Antwerp. We spot each other's pilgrim shells, and I feel relieved to be in the company of a fellow pilgrim for the night.

Meet Herman. He too is on his way to Compostela. He has been pre-paring for this pilgrimage for ten years, he says. He just retired as a police-man in Antwerp and now has the freedom to undertake the journey of a lifetime. Under his bed is a contraption that looks like a high-tech version of a Native American travois. With a small wheel on the pointed end of a V shaped tubular frame and a harness and clips on the wide end, this thing is clearly designed to take the place of a backpack. I ask Herman about it, and he acknowledges my good guess. He says he bought it by mail order from an outfit in Canada and was assured that it would work great on the way to Compostela: through the woods and over hill and dale, no problem. He has pulled it all the way from Antwerp, and it seems to be working fine, he assures me. I find myself a bit skeptical, but maybe he's got something there. I shower and wash my clothes, take a rest and then, with Herman, go to the small dining area of the hostel for an inexpensive dinner.

I am bushed from the day's work but have enough energy left to pick Herman's brain. From here on, I will be following the Grand Randonnée (GR) 654 route deep into France. It begins just a block or two from this hostel, but it looks from the maps in my GR guidebook that it will involve a steep rise and then multiple zigzags through the forest. This will probably provide some tough walking for a few kilometers. Herman agrees and says he is just going to follow the river south. He says that there is a perfectly good sidewalk bordering the Meuse riverbank at least until Dinant, and even better, it will be level all the way. I am pleased to hear this for Herman's route will make for a much easier walk in the morning. A small town called Rivière at a bend in the Meuse will be tomorrow's goal, less than twenty ki-lometers from here. Herman adds a serious note, trying to be clear without offending me: "It is fine to visit in the evening, but I prefer to walk alone." *As do I. Don't worry, I won't be a bother to you.*

4

Following My Meuse

I awake refreshed and ready. I dress, pull together my stuff, repack Gregory. I prepare my feet for the day's work: spreading antiperspirant on the soles to keep them dry through the day, next, thin Cool-Max socks are slipped on as liners, then heavy wool trekking socks, and finally, I pull on my hearty Meindl boots. Bavarian-made and tough as nails, they are supposed to be the best boot available for long-distance amateurs like me. They fit like gloves. Herman is way ahead of me this morning and disappears from the room with his travois and waterproof sacks. I eat a simple breakfast in the dining room and then head out into the morning light myself. The market outside the hostel is closed up at this hour. I walk past it and pick up the walkway across the street that follows the bank of the wide Meuse River south. The sun is shining brightly though still fairly low in the sky, making the surface of the river to my left sparkle like a flow of diamonds. Barges pass by, dividing the flow with their churning wake; a tourist boat full of school kids on some kind of day trip also passes. The kids wave at me and greet me, "*Bonjour, Monsieur! Bonne route, Monsieur!*" I wave back and smile across the water as broadly as I can. They seem delighted that I have responded to their greetings and laugh as they lean against the boat's rails. A boy calls back to me: "*À où?* Where are you going?" "*À Compostelle,*" I answer, but like yesterday's farmers, he doesn't seem to know the name. They continue waving as the boat passes.

As I leave urban Namur, the forested escarpment that the Grand Randonnée 654 would have had me tackling this morning rises to my right. It is steep, and I am very pleased not to be climbing around up there. The GR, I realize, has been designed for sightseeing trekkers, not really for pilgrims who generally prefer more direct routes between Point A and Point B, or actually, Church A and Church B. I guess I shouldn't speak for most pilgrims, but at least *this* pilgrim prefers the shortest and easiest way forward. It is going to be a long journey lasting several months, and I will see enough beautiful things along the way as it is. I do not need to zig here and zag there to see even more. I am no tourist out here. I have a mission. This is a prayer. I move both Click and Clack to my left hand, in temporary retirement, then pull my rosary from my pants pocket with my right hand. I begin fingering the beads with their attendant prayers: *I Believe . . . Our Father . . . Hail Mary . . . Glory Be . . .* The prayers and the beads and the steps of my feet fall into rhythm so that it is not just my mind that is praying, not just my heart, not just my lips, but all of me, the whole of me: body, soul, and mind. Thinking stops for a while. No pondering here. Just light and sparkling water and green hillsides and me and the author of all. *Glory be . . .* The world is flat enough along this river-walk that in the distance, perhaps a half-kilometer ahead of me, I spot the figure of a lean man pulling something silvery behind him. Of course, it is Herman of Antwerp. I am gaining on him ever so slowly, but I don't want to catch up because he wants to walk alone. I slacken my own pace just a bit out of respect for his will. He disappears for a while, then reappears, and now the distance between us is much reduced. I am gaining on him, like it or not. Luckily, we are both close to our destination for the day, Rivière. I do catch up to him and from behind, greet him. He turns and smiles as he recognizes me. I take up my position beside him, and we ask each other how it is going. It has been an easy and short walk, only thirteen or fourteen kilometers at most, so we are both feeling good. His travois is an interesting thing to behold: the yoke in front is harnessed to his body with a variety of straps and clips, he holds the two bars at the wide end of the V in his hands at about waist level, evidently distributing the weight of the packs behind him that way. The two poles come together low behind him and are supported by a single small wheel, a sort of reverse wheelbarrow. I suspect he has put a fair amount of money into this unusual replacement for a backpack, so it is not surprising that he is enthusiastic about its serviceability and practicality, though I continue to harbor doubts. I imagine pulling it over some of the mountains and along the rough paths that I encountered on the Camino in Spain some five years ago and cannot quite see it. I hope Herman's confidence in his gizmo is well placed when the going gets rougher. I am more than happy to carry my life-necessities on my back. Gregory the Great is no machine; he is more like a brother, heavy though he may be.

We amble on into the riverside village of Rivière and find the parish church situated part way up a hill near the road. Our hope was that we would find hospitality here from the parish priest, but the doors of the church are locked tight. Behind the church building is the parish house, but its gate is also locked, and there seems to have been no activity here for some time. Near the church I spot a red and white sticker applied to a steel post: it has a shell design and reads *Chemin de Compostelle*; it is the first formal indication I have seen that I am actually on the medieval route to Compostela. It gives me a small thrill, and I point it out to Herman who smiles at the sight. He speaks French quite well, so I leave it to him to make contact with a neighbor who gives us the bad news that the priest of the parish is elderly and has been in the hospital for several days. He will probably die soon. There is no chance of staying here tonight.

Herman is already on the move. I follow. The next substantial town downriver is Godinne, so we set our sights on that. There is a large Jesuit college there that should be able to take us in. Within forty-five minutes we are in Godinne, but the better part of the town lies on the other side of the Meuse. A wide bridge spans the river, and we begin crossing it, sharing its platform with the automobiles and trucks that whiz by.

Ahead of us on the bridge is the figure of a rather hunched old man dressed in black cassock and beret. Perfect! This aged angel will be our key to a good night's sleep. We greet the old priest, who smiles widely back at us. He immediately asks if we are pilgrims, and we acknowledge our identity. Though he is not a Jesuit himself, he assures us that we will certainly be welcome to stay with them at the Collège Saint-Paul, just over the bridge and up the hill. Herman and I take our leave of the sweet old priest and continue across the bridge and into the heart of Godinne.

The street to the Collège is the first uphill stretch I have encountered since Namur and though not steep, it leaves me slightly winded to climb it. We come to the entrance and enter the property in spite of signs saying only authorized persons are allowed. We amble through the front garden and climb the wide stairway that leads up to a grand porch of the building that is the centerpiece of the property. We ring the bell. No one answers. We ring again. Finally, another old priest comes down the path in front of the building, sees us on the porch, and slowly climbs the stairs. He listens attentively to our request for hospitality, but says he must defer to the superior, who will be away for an hour or so. In the meantime, he assures us, we can rest and relax in the garden. He shows us the way to the edge of a sports field where grass abounds and sycamore trees line the edge. He disappears. Herman unhinges his travois, and I drop Gregory, leaning him against a tree trunk. I settle in some shade, kick off my boots and socks allowing my feet some much-appreciated fresh air. It has been a good day. An easy day. After the twenty-eight kilometer march to Namur yesterday, I am grateful. Soon a shower and a rest and a pleasant evening in Godinne will make it a perfect day. I doze, and the noon hour passes.

The spry old priest returns to us. He looks grim. He has talked with the superior of the community, and our request for a place to stay has been turned down. I am crestfallen. *How can this be? You are Jesuits, for heaven's sake; you are in the business of welcoming strangers, no? My uncle was a Jesuit; does that not count for anything?* I tell the old priest that I am a priest as well; surely that would lead to a reconsideration for my pilgrim pal and me? The old man can hardly look at us. He feels our pain, and I suspect the inhospitality he is being forced to uphold is an agony for him. He just says he is very sorry, but we cannot stay here. He directs us towards the parish church across town.

Herman responds to the news with a plan for himself: since he has a tent he will go to one of the town's two campgrounds along the riverbank. He makes no allowance for me. "You'll have to take care of yourself," he says. I feel panic. Herman re-hitches his travois and takes off. I pull my socks and shoes back on, close up Gregory's open mouth and hoist him onto my back. *I guess it is just you and I tonight, brother.* I leave the Collège Saint-Paul not quite cursing the Jesuit superior of the Collège Saint-Paul for his lack of hospitality, but not far from shaking his Jesuit dust from my Meindle boots.

Alone again, the afternoon is growing increasingly warm, and the heat adds to my sense of being oppressed out here. I begin a search for the parish church. I have no map, and my GPS is minimally helpful. A small cross on the screen indicates an *église* across the train tracks, so I wander in that direction but find nothing. I come upon some teen-age Boy Scouts hanging around a schoolyard so ask one of them for the church. He explains, but sees that I am not understanding, so he jumps the schoolyard fence and with a smile waves for me to follow him. We cross a street, enter a courtyard of some kind of medieval palace and find ensconced in a small garden behind a diminutive stone church building, obviously once a chapel of the much grander palace.

Today is Saturday so, if I have any luck, there will be an evening Mass, and I will be able to ask the presiding priest for lodging. I enter the stone church through its main door set back in the nave wall. Instantly, I feel the cool of the interior as pure refreshment. A schedule of services hangs on a bulletin board just within. I read it: Saturday, 5:00 pm, Sunday Vigil Mass. It is now 3:00 pm, so I have two hours to wait. I am in luck. I wander towards the sanctuary but see no one. The door to the sacristy is ajar; sounds of someone fussing within come to me. I knock and say a tentative, *bonjour,* and a lady with rose stems in one hand and clippers in the other comes from within. *"Bonjour, monsieur."* she greets me. I apologetically try to explain my predicament and ask if the priest lives nearby. I tell her I am *un prêtre* also. She only partially understands but responds that the priest does not live in this town but some ten kilometers away. She is not sure which priest will be here for the 5:00 pm liturgy. She has no telephone number of the priests. She is clearly sympathetic to my situation but has little help to offer. I promise to return later, closer to the indicated Mass time, then dejectedly trudge back out the door to look for the campgrounds with the hope of finding a place, any place, to spend the night.

I make my way to the first campground. I find the manager in the front yard of his small caravan cooling himself in the shade. I ask about a place to stay, but he simply shakes his head and indicates there is no room in the inn, even if I had a tent to sleep in. I ask directions to the second campground, and he directs me back into town and across several streets. The second is much bigger than the first with actual streets wending their way through the caravans, family-sized tents, and mobile homes. I wander in but find no manager in this place and presume it very unlikely that it would accommodate lone pilgrims like myself so turn back to the arterial street that leads to the church.

My frustration level is now reaching very dangerous levels; I am feeling panic rise from my belly to my throat. I pass a school yard with a sports field next to it and take a good look at the grandstand: *I could sleep under that if worse comes to worse.* It is hotter than ever out here. *I hate this! I am no Boy Scout! I am not designed for camping in fields. What do I think I am doing pretending to rely on the hospitality of strangers out here? I don't even know how to properly ask for help. I should just catch the train and be back in Leuven in an hour and a half.*

Just as the aggravation in my guts is becoming unbearable, I am back at the church. The flower lady is still here. She greets me as if I were an old friend. She reports, as much as I can understand her, that she has made contact with the parish priest after all, and he will take care of me, but she should examine my documents assuring her that I am indeed a priest. I offer to pull them out from deep within my pack, but she then waves it off as silly. Again, I heartily thank her for her kindness and take my place in a back pew of the church. I drop Gregory and set him up against a pillar. Then I take off my boots and socks and let my feet enjoy the cool of the stone floor. I close my eyes for a while and simply soak in the dark silence of the place. I am still tied up inside with all the afternoon's worries and disappointments; like a bad drug, I can't easily get that stuff out of my system. I keep trying to rest and relax and most of all, *trust.* Trust is a virtue I terribly lack, I realize now. I do not take seriously Jesus' famous words about the birds of the air and the flowers of the field: if the Father so cares for them, how much more does he care for me? No, I am a fretter; I believe that the worst that could happen probably will happen. I suffer from cancer of the frets. *Okay, Jesus: I will try to trust.* I repeat over and over an old prayer from Julian of Norwich: *All things shall be well. All things shall be well. All manner of things shall be well.*

Time slips by quickly, and before long a few elderly people are arriving for the 5:00 pm liturgy. I slip my socks and boots back on and move Gregory to a position less likely to trip up some inattentive communicant on the way back to her pew. A forty-something man comes in and moves swiftly to the sacristy. Ah, the priest! I get up and follow him in. I introduce myself as best I am able, and without a second's pause, *Père* Bernard embraces me, assures me of full hospitality for the night, and offers me an alb and stole to concelebrate Mass with him. My cancer of the frets has been healed.

Bernard and I process out into the sanctuary to a melodic hymn sung thinly by the aging congregation. I am sweaty and mussed, but I am so grateful just to be here, to be welcomed, to be at home that I could care less right now how I might appear to the locals.

Bernard adapts his homily to include my pilgrim presence as a contemporary example of a disciple setting out to proclaim the Kingdom of God, with no money bag, no sack, no sandals, and to the homes where he is welcomed, saying, "Peace to this household."[1] "Today this household, this parish, has been blessed by the arrival of a disciple of Jesus who says to us: 'Peace.'" I know just enough French to understand this simple message. On this afternoon filled with aggravation over the lack of pilgrim hospitality, his message sinks deeply into me. Bernard does not know how recently I shook from my feet the dust of a household that did not receive me, but this pastor's reflection on the Gospel and his kind reference to me as a disciple blessing his household are particularly potent, and I almost cry. I straighten my back, take a deep breath, and resolve to live more truly what he says I am. In those hours after the Jesuit rejection, I was a very big baby. The superior there probably had good reasons for not welcoming two strangers he had only been told about and not seen for himself. Feeling sorry for myself has no place in the pilgrim way; this is what I am supposed to be learning on this Chemin, this long and winding Way.

Following the liturgy, Bernard closes up the church, shows me to his car and announces that he will take me to his parish house in the nearby town of Yvoir, where his grandmother's ancient bed is waiting for me. It is a brief ride, but Bernard takes advantage of it to ask lots of questions about my life and travels. His place is old, but it is clean as a whistle, and every little thing has its place, the exact opposite of *Père* Paul's house. After I settle in and clean up, he takes me out for a fine dinner at his favorite *bistro* situated near an old mill along a tributary of the Meuse. I enjoy a huge chunk of

---

1. Luke 10:1–12

roasted ham, spuds, and together we finish off a bottle of fine French red wine. That wine, together with the cool breezes rustling the leaves of nearby trees and the flow over stones of the small river nearby serve to restore my enthusiasm for my peripatetic life.

Bernard and I get along like brothers, as if we have known each other forever. We talk over the state of faith in Europe; I tell him of my conversation with the three searchers two days earlier. It is nothing unusual for him. He describes his life as a pastor in today's Belgium: besides Yvoir and Godinne, he tends six other communities. The shortage of priests in this land is now critical, so every priest does far more than "double duty" these days. I ask how he survives, where he finds support, what he does to keep himself enthusiastic about ministry. He prays. He has his family. And I add in my own mind: he welcomes ragged pilgrim priests into his home.

Bernard prepares a fine cup of coffee for me in the morning but needs to run: Sunday Masses await him. I put Gregory's innards back together, exchange my comfortable sandals for my big boots, then walk out the door, heading back to the banks of the Meuse for the hike to Dinant. It will be a day's journey hardly worthy of a pilgrim: under ten kilometers. I don't mind; after yesterday afternoon's difficulties, I feel entitled to an easy day. Besides, it is Sunday, the First Day of the Week, the Lord's Day, a day of rest. This morning marks the one-week anniversary of my grand departure from Leuven; after a major bodily breakdown and lots of frustrations during the past days, I am still out here on the road, still walking, still a pilgrim. I am proud of all this. The sun is shining. The river gleams. The morning air is fresh. My only problem is that, for some reason, Gregory feels particularly heavy. Has he put on weight? Perhaps I should dump the whole thing over the side of the riverbank and *truly* live as this Sunday's Gospel recommends, without moneybag, sack, or sandals. I am encumbered by too much stuff, even out here. I am not so very apostolic after all. This is my conclusion, but I am not courageous enough to do anything about it. The load remains heavy.

Dinant is a tourist stop for Europeans passing through Belgium. Even as I draw closer to the town, the increasing traffic on the riverbank highway I follow boasts license plates from Germany, France, and the Netherlands. It is a beautiful Sunday afternoon; the town will probably be packed. Will I find a room? Once again, I find myself fretting even before I have a problem. *Stop this!* I try to stop, but the worry returns. *What a pathetic pilgrim am I.* A man walking his dog overtakes me from behind, turns and says to me in French something about my *coquille*, my shell, then asks if I am walking to *Compostelle*. I respond with *oui*, to which he raises his hand in salute and says, "*Bon courage!*" His recognition of my mission and his well-wish in an instant restore my interior confidence as a worthy pilgrim. *Courage.* Yes, I need plenty of *courage.*

I spot a sign indicating that just ahead is the Abbaye Notre-Dame de Leffe, a Norbertine monastery dating from the twelfth century, more famous now for the beer that is sold under its name than for *Notre-Dame,* Our Lady, after whom it was named. I cross the highway and follow the side street indicated by the sign. I find the front door of the chapel open and walk in. Sunday morning Mass has already begun; upon entering I find myself immediately in the central aisle. The nave is brightly illuminated making the stone walls glow with warmth. People turn to look at me. I smile apologetically for disturbing them. The presiding priest makes momentary eye contact with me from his place in the sanctuary; clearly, I have distracted him as well. I take off my cap, drop Gregory from my back, and set him and Click and Clack on a small wooden bench, then squeeze past a few worshipers to take a vacant spot on a small pew to my left. I receive a kindly nod from the elderly man beside me. He, at least, is happy I am here. The gentle solemnity of the monastic liturgy envelops me as if a golden blanket were wrapped over my stooping shoulders. I rest under it. Glory from above and dirt from below subsume one another in an intimate embrace. I stand, follow the flow forward, extend my hands, welcome the gift, and just say *Amen.*

As soon as the presiding priest has commissioned us to go forth in peace, the same man who nodded to me earlier turns to engage me. Somehow he knows that I speak English and addresses me in my own language. He asks if I am a pilgrim to Compostelle, where have I begun, and if I would like to have the Abbaye seal placed in my credential. I answer his questions happily and assure him that I would *love* to have the abbey seal. I collect Gregory and Click and Clack, and he leads me through a passageway into the abbey itself. There, a few of the Norbertine canons are milling about, chatting with parishioners. He leads me to one, the abbot himself, and introduces me; it was he who had been presiding at the liturgy and who caught my eye as I entered. The abbot embraces me; as with Bernard's embrace yesterday afternoon, these arms wrapped around me are full of that *courage* I am so often wished. The abbot presents me to still another canon, directing him to retrieve the Leffe seal and stamp my *credencial,* all of which is accomplished post haste.

With fat Gregory on my back and my slender Click and Clack in hands, I head into the town center, a bustling mix of stone buildings, restaurant terraces, and camera-toting tourists. The town is the very image of quaintness, shoehorned between granite cliffs roughly excavated over millennia by the Meuse's passage to the north. I am jostled by the crowds as I make my way towards the bridge that crosses the Meuse to the other bank where the local tourist office is located. Luckily for me, it is open on Sunday mornings, and the attendant does in fact help folks like me find rooms for the night. She recommends a small bed and breakfast, what the French-speaking call a *chambre d'hôte,* just down the street on this same side of the river. I find the place, am welcomed in, pay my fees, wash up, then head back into the town center for lunch.

Without Gregory, my shell, my boots, Click and Clack, and now showered and wearing fresh duds, I no longer *look* like a pilgrim. As I wander Dinant's streets, I have become just another tourist; my pilgrim identity goes covert. Without its inhabitants knowing, I observe this world and its goings-on with the acute eye of the wanderer. What I see, at surface level, is every-day normal: Human beings of various sizes and shapes, from infants in strollers to the aged being supported by canes and walkers, milling about in typical tourist aimlessness, gawking, looking at maps, pointing to one sight or another. Most gab in one or another of the region's tongues: French, German, Dutch, British English. Others sit on the terraces of restaurants picking at plates laden with beef, sauce, *pomme frites,* a golden beer at hand. A very few are alone and seem content in their isolation, staring into the near distance or pouring over the grey pages of a tattered paperback book. Teens move in packs, earphones connecting them to their music, working hard to look as cool as possible.

I settle into the crowd by taking an outdoor restaurant table with a view of the river. High above, perched at the top of the great granite cliff is a balustrade with the tiny figures of human beings peering over the edge, viewing us as ants below, perhaps not unlike the way God must see us from above.

The melodic sounds of a young choir putting on a jazz concert drift by, so I follow the music to a nearby square and spend the next hour enjoying the show of these talented kids from somewhere in England. Finally, after the last bouncy notes of *It's a Wonderful Night for a Moonwalk,* I take my own moonwalk back over the Meuse to my *chamber d'hôte.* After these two days of following this wide river, I feel as if it were a sister faithfully accompanying me on my way. She is *my* Meuse now. *Teach me, Oh Meuse, the poetry of walking rightly and the music of traveling lightly across this great earth!*

The morning sun shines brightly, so I do not delay getting out the door for the day's effort. Before long I am crossing the Meuse so as to pick up my route on the abbey side of the river. I am feeling good as I leave town. My knee hardly hurts at all. This is remarkable. As yesterday, I am provided a level concrete sidewalk alongside the river road that leads south out of Dinant. It makes the walking easy, and Gregory seems to have lost weight overnight. I maintain a fine pace. I pray my rosary, then enter a grassy riverside park occupied by an occasional fisherman settled on the bank of the river with the tip of his long pole silently held far out over the water. I take a brief break at a picnic table, eat an apple, and continue my journey. The sidewalk disappears and before long, I am walking on a dirt path cut through increasing amounts of vegetation. The trail enters heavy woods, and I find myself negotiating a path thick with brambles, roots, and stones. It is all very damp and very slippery, so I manipulate Click and Clack to maintain my balance, making of myself something like a human 4x4.

I am following the GR 654 here; the red and white signs painted on tree trunks and fence posts are quite helpful in guiding me through this jungle-like forest. I come to a fork in the path with several immense granite stones blocking the way. I cannot decipher what the GR indicators are telling me; there seems to be no way around the massive obstacles before me. A couple of boys come down the trail. They know this place and see my confusion, so they direct me down to the river's very edge and point the way forward for me: the trail, it seems, passes along a small granite shelf with river water lapping up over its edge and above, a stone overhang that will force me to hunch deeply forward if Gregory is to pass with me. This is going to be delicate. I turn back to the boys: Is this the *only* way? *"Oui,"* they respond with a nod. *Okay, here goes nothing.* If I misstep, I'll be in the drink faster than I can say "my Meuse". I hunch down, retire Click and Clack from duty, and carefully set one foot forward, then the other. The river water laps at my boots as I go, but their soles hold firm to the stone ledge. It seems like it takes forever, but I do not slip. Once I make it to the far side of the granite ledge, I step back onto solid land, stretch back upright, and release a huge sigh of relief. No one said this was going to be easy, but *that* was just ridiculous.

The going stays rough for the next hour until I pass through a barbed wire fence into a large field occupied by dairy cows, then another fence crossing into another grassy field, this one empty, so I unload Gregory onto the grass above the riverbank, sit down, kick off my boots, nibble on some granola bars, and then just lay back and watch the cumulus clouds pass through their blue sea above. Tangling with those woods has tuckered me out, though my knee remains fine. I sense for the first time that I have now really left Leuven; there is no going back from here. I am far enough along the way, perhaps a hundred kilometers from where I began, that I now know: *that* world is not home anymore; *this* is home now. There is a new freedom in this for me. I am a real pilgrim again.

Ominously heavy clouds appear on the horizon, so I decide this real pilgrim had better get a move on. I continue traversing the fields, cuddling up to the Meuse towards the town of Hastière where I will have lunch. Once in town, I spot a small *café* just my side of a substantial bridge across the Meuse and head for it. I am sweaty, and my boots are muddy, so I settle at an outside table facing the main street heading across the bridge. A young man comes to take my order and spotting the shell attached to Gregory, asks if I am a *pèlerin*. I respond affirmatively, which leads to the next question: where did I begin? When I tell him Leuven, he sighs in wonder at the distance I have covered. I order a home-style omelet and a beer. The waiter returns with my order: a massive egg concoction filled with mushrooms, sausage and covered with melted cheese. I tackle it as best I am able; I am hungry but not *this* hungry. At the same time I sip my way through the beer and order a second. By the time I have exhausted my ability to eat and drink any further, I feel rather woozy and decide to call it a day; I've covered over twenty kilometers, most of them tough going. I ask the waiter if there is a *chambre d'hôte* in town. "Even better," he responds; "there is a pilgrim refuge next to the church just across the street." He indicates the way, but I don't clearly understand, so after collecting my payment, he leads me across the street, around and behind the church, into an enclosed garden and to the door of the parish house. He rings for me; the door is answered by an African, who greets me with a broad smile, and in English says: "Welcome, Pilgrim! I am Marcellinus! I am from Nigeria! And you are who?"

I introduce myself to my gregarious host, who then guides me within the house and up a stairwell to a large room equipped with two substantial beds. It seems the pastor no longer lives in this town, just one of several he cares for, so the house has been turned over to several purposes; a few foreign students or workers like Marcellinus reside here, and one room is set aside for pilgrims to Compostela. One or two pass through each week, I am informed. Hastière, with its eleventh century church next door, was a significant stop along the pilgrim way in medieval times. Marcellinus informs me that the church is open, and I can visit it this afternoon if I wish. I will visit it, I assure my host, just as soon as I have showered, napped, and laundered today's hiking duds. One thing at a time.

The church was once part of a much larger Benedictine abbey; it is a lovely Romanesque building with round arches and windows set into deep walls. It has been a place that has given shelter and succor to hundreds of thousands of pilgrims over a thousand years, and now I am one among that great throng of walkers. I am proud of this. The Meuse flows just beyond a stone wall a short distance from the church, so once outside again, I lean up against the wall to watch the river flow past, wide and powerful and in constant movement northward, not unlike us pilgrims flowing south.

Once back home, I settle into my wide room but soon hear clatter and voices from below. The door opens, and Marcellinus presents to me a second pilgrim for the night; in walks an exhausted Herman, dragging his packs behind him. We greet each other like long-lost brothers, but he is not in a good mood. He has had to manage his travois through the same wild and woolly woods I traversed today, and it has not gone well. He reports that he spent over an hour on one particularly tough kilometer. He has lost his faith in his rolling alternative to the backpack; it just does not work on these paths plagued with knotty roots, fallen boulders, and tangled branches. He had to ever-so-carefully guide the thing around the same ledge at river's edge as I and survived to tell the tale, but not without it terribly unnerving him. He is not ready to give up on his travois yet, but he is clearly shaken by today's experience.

We use the kitchen for an evening snack and a cup of tea, and then return to our room for a good night of sleep. I drift away to the sound of rain falling on the roof above our heads: things will be very muddy on the road tomorrow. What if I slip? What if I break something? What if I end up in the river? What if . . . *Ah, stop it!*

Marcellinus joins Herman and me for a simple breakfast in the kitchen. As we discuss our plan to follow the GR today to the town of Doische, Marcellinus interjects that we can save a lot of kilometers and several hours by taking a short cut to Doische from the next town downriver, Hermetton. This is great news since neither Herman nor I are committed followers of the GR 654; if there's a shortcut ahead, we're both in favor of taking advantage of it.

As before, Herman and I choose to walk separately; he departs a half-hour ahead of me. When I step out and head for the trail to Hermetton, the sky looks threatening again. The overcast has turned the silver surface of the Meuse into the steel grey of a battleship. I am developing a thing about rain; I rather dread it. Rain means not just wet boots and damp underwear; it also means mud on the trail, and mud is dangerous for its viscosity underfoot. It might as well be motor oil. Once again, I imagine a fall that leaves me covered in organic soup. The stuff clings to soles, and if not removed, hardens into something not unlike concrete. What I dislike even more about rain is that though hiking clothes need to be washed daily, on rainy days they seldom dry completely by next morning, or even next afternoon. If these clouds cannot dissipate altogether, then I wish them at least to hold their bladders until we have safely arrived at our afternoon destination.

I easily find the trail recommended to us by Marcellinus and make my way down its paved pathway without a root or rock to trip me up. It has broad shoulders of grass, and for much of the way, I walk on the soft grass, the better to avoid tendonitis. Instead of the six hours the GR would have taken with its zigzags across the countryside, I land in Doisch in three and a half. I stop in a small grocery store and purchase fruit, juice, and fixings for a nice sandwich: a *pistolet* of bread, slices of turkey and cheese. Upon leaving the store, I see no park or comfortable place to enjoy my picnic lunch so set myself up on a retaining wall between the street and the parking lot, Gregory perched against a light pole, thus serving as a backrest as I prepare my sandwich and nibble at my luscious little grapes.

I size up my guidebook: I can be in Mazee in two more hours, about an eight-kilometer walk. Very do-able. The map makes it clear that I am skirting the French border, though I will not leave Belgium for a couple days yet. A sort of horn of French territory pokes up into Belgium; I am coming down on its west side. I am encouraged by my closeness to the frontier; I am making real progress.

I clean up my mess from lunch and get a move on; the rain could begin falling at any time. I pick up the GR even as the Meuse disappears from view; I miss the river's sisterly presence and feel more alone in my mission without her at my side. The route climbs steeply then descends, then climbs again. These are the first substantial hills I have encountered since leaving Leuven, and I can feel the thirty pounds on my back dragging on me. This is substantially more difficult trekking than what I have been up against thus far; I huff and puff, but on I go.

The kilometers pass under my boots and by early afternoon, I find myself in the small village of Mazee. I walk into town along a back street that leads me down a gentle slope to a playground where I find a mother and a couple of children enjoying with happy laughter the swings and teeter-totters. In my broken French, I ask about a place to stay the night. The mother informs me that there are two *chambre d'hôtes* in town, one just around the corner and the other a half-kilometer up a steep street. I offer a smile and *merci beaucoup* in gratitude and head for the closest one. Its door is locked, windows shuttered, and no one answers my knock. I then notice a small sign hanging in the window indicating that the place is closed, forcing me to trudge up the steep street towards the second option. The name of the new place is written in wrought iron on the exterior wall: Point du Jour. A sign in the window gives me a phone number to call for service. The fact that no one actually attends these places is a sign of just how far from tourist country I have wandered. I dig out my phone and poke in the numbers. A woman's voice answers, and I make my pitch for *logement*. She asks if I am the pilgrim who called earlier. I am not, but presume that caller must have been Herman since we are walking the same road today, but why is he not already here ahead of me? His start this morning was considerably earlier than my own. There is some confusion between the lady and myself because of my limited language skills, but in the end, she tells me to wait here, and she will be by soon.

Within fifteen minutes, a shiny Renault pulls up and a middle-aged lady gets out, greets me, and begins rifling within her purse for a ring of keys. She leads me into a courtyard, up some stairs to a small garden, around to a back entrance, and unlocks the door to my haven for the night. She shows me the room, tells me the price, and asks if I want a beer. I do! So as I drop Gregory and begin pulling my toiletries and fresh clothes out from within his guts, she disappears through a door for a minute, and then returns with a glass of amber beer just for me.

Herman finally makes his appearance, perhaps a full hour after my own arrival; as yesterday, he is looking ragged and exhausted. He smiles wanly and enters. He immediately tells me he has had his fill of the travois; it is over. His contraption has become impossible to manage over the increasingly primitive trails we have been traversing. He rolls it into the courtyard, unloads it of its packs, and is then shown by our hostess to his room. After his own shower, he tells me that he has phoned his son-in-law in Antwerp who will drive down this very evening with a rucksack for him. His travois will make the return trip to Antwerp in ignominy while Herman continues on with the more conventional backpack.

Herman's son-in-law and a friend arrive late in the afternoon; the travois is packed into the back of the BMW and traded for the well-used backpack thus making the divorce between Herman and his fancy Canadian contraption complete. He moves his possessions to the pack to make sure they fit and puts the leftovers in the vehicle with the travois. The three then invite me to join them for dinner at a restaurant in the next town, Treignes, just a few kilometers down the highway. We eat simply and cheaply, then Herman and I are delivered back to the Point du Jour for the night.

The *madame* of the Point du Jour has a fine breakfast waiting for us at 7:30 am: cheeses, jams, honey, slices of ham, and breads of all kinds are spread across the table in her dining room. It is delectable and will surely provide me the energy to get through the morning. I notice that the *madame* has a parish bulletin from the local Catholic Church on her sideboard and I ask if, by chance, she knows the priest who serves the village that is my destination for the day, Oignies-en-Thiérache. She says she does know him well and that he resides in Oignies. At my behest, she gives him a phone call to see if we can arrange a place to stay in his parish house for the night. No answer. Well, at least I know there is a priest living there; once I get to town I can look him up.

Herman and backpack are on their way first; I don't want to intrude on his pilgrim solitude so dawdle about in my room for a half hour more before heading down the road myself. I follow the same route we took last night to the restaurant in Treignes; these few kilometers of pavement take about forty-five minutes on foot; last night in the car they took about three. In Treignes, I pick up the GR 654 again, pass through some hay fields, then enter the forest of the Belgian Ardennes. I pass through two villages with relative ease, then after some rest, tackle the nine kilometer stretch through deep woods to my destination for the day, Oignies-en-Thiérache, where I will spend my final night in Belgium if all goes well.

These woods become very dense and dark. I follow a small creek through a deep valley. I suppose this stream trickles its way eventually into the Meuse, which though unseen, cannot be far away. I am back in a land where moss and mud make for unsure footing. I clamber over roots and around rocks, dodging low branches, using Click and Clack for support and balance at every twist and turn, leveraging my top-heavy body through this wild and woodsy forest. With the poles, my arms walk this route almost as much as my legs. I have to cross the creek at several points, my boots kicking up splash as my jumps don't quite carry me all the way across. The red and white GR route indicators sometimes point in ambiguous directions, and the GPS is little help with the canopy of leafy trees blocking its connection to satellites above.

The rain begins. I hear it before I feel it. The drops falling onto the leaves above make a soft pelting sound that is beautiful. I stop, pull my Go-re-Tex jacket from a side-pocket of my pack, put it on, then cover Gregory with his canvas as well. The rain never grows heavy, then eases altogether.

With the sweet percussion of the falling rain having dissipated for the moment, I am feeling kind of jazzy out here by myself, so I take a rest, pull my iPod from the top pocket of Gregory, and plug the buds into my ears. This is the first time I use the iPod while actually walking. I twirl to an album of contemporary hymns, simply presented with guitar and solo voice in a folk style by a fellow named Fernando Ortega. The first hymn takes for its lyrics the opening words from Saint Paul's standard introduction to his letters in the New Testament: *Grace and peace to you from God our Father . . . and the Lord Jesus Christ.* That is the whole song, repeated over and over like a mantra, each repetition slightly different in tone and quality than the other. It is as beautiful as the rain on the leaves of a forest. The words are being sung to me, not so much now by Fernando Ortega, but by Saint Paul himself:

Grace and peace to you, soft and muddy and living earth.
Grace and peace to you, snails and slugs and worms that slither below.

Grace and peace to you, rain falling on leaves and into creeks.
Grace and peace . . .

The rain returns, and the hymn has changed it for me into a delicious grace. I do not mind it now. I thrill in it. I play in it like a kid outside in a warm summer shower. I splash in its puddles and throw back my head to let it drizzle down my face. I drink it in. Then I begin to slip and almost fall, and I am jerked out of the music; I have to pay extra attention again to the ground under my feet, but this extra care for well-placed feet does not stop me from enjoying the rain falling on leaves and stones and snail shells all about me. Nor does it keep me from singing aloud to myself as I am pattered by the rain: *Grace and peace to you . . .*

I scramble up an embankment and find myself standing on a ribbon of grey-wet concrete. It is a bicycle path traversing these same woods. The red and white GR signs on a nearby tree trunk tell me to follow it. I press on down this concrete way for another few kilometers until the GR path separates again, and I clamber up a muddy logging road that ascends to a spread of pine through which I pass, then descend the last kilometer in heavy rain into the town of Oignies-en-Thiérache. As I trudge into town, I find an old man working in the dry safety of his garage, so I ask him where the parish priest lives. My high spirits from the day's walk drop like a rock as he informs me there is no point in searching out the priest since he is on vacation. *Ah, crimeny!* For the first time today I feel chilled. At this moment, Herman appears on the street, as soaked as I. Together we walk towards the town center, mostly in silence. Other than the gentleman in the garage, there is no visible sign of human life here. It is mid-afternoon and the inhabitants of this village are safely tucked within their cozy homes. We are the only ones crazy enough to be bumbling our way through this present downpour, which no longer feels like grace in any manner. It is an affliction.

We arrive at the dreary town center and look for a place to eat and spend the night. The local post office is open so we step inside, and Herman asks the attendant if there is a pilgrim hostel in Oignies-en-Thiérache. Nope. She adds that there are a couple of *gites-d'étap,* but that they are very expensive and a ways outside of town. Our best bet, we are told, is the petrol station just down from the town center; its owners may have some available rooms. We trudge in the rain through the streets of the central square and down a steep hill to the fuel station but find it closed up tighter than a drum. From the looks of it, the place has been abandoned for some time.

We march back up into the center; we are being drenched out here, so I suggest a warm cup of coffee and a few moments out of the rain to sort things out. Herman is talking about moving on to the next town or camping in the woods in his pup-tent; he doesn't want to spend the money for a room. The next town is another eight or nine kilometers down the road, and after more than twenty already, many of them in the woods and under a shower of rain, I just can't consider it. I intend to stay here no matter what it might cost. Friends in Leuven gave me some cash just for days like this; if ever there were a moment to spend such a gift, this seems to be it. I spot a restaurant sign and signal to Herman that we should get our coffee there. On the way, I ask him how much he would be willing to pay for a night's lodging? He says he will not stay in anything that costs more than thirty euros. Okay; let's get our coffee and clarify our options.

We trundle over to the front door, and I notice the place is also a hotel. I take a look at the price list: fifty for one, sixty-seven for a double. Herman wants none of it. I make an offer: I'll pay fifty if you will pick up the other seventeen euros. He declines. He walks away announcing that he is moving on; he's not even staying for a warm drink. Well, I am not camping in the woods, and I am not walking to the next town, so I go inside to be greeted by the restaurant hostess. I ask her what it would take for me to stay the night; she answers that for me, *seul*, it will be fifty. And for *two of us*? "Twenty-five each", she says. Great! I drop Gregory and kick him out of the way, head outside and begin looking for Herman. He is nowhere to be seen, so I walk as quickly as my tired legs will carry me towards the church and what must be the road out of town. I find him passing by the church, already on his way. I call through the rain for him to come back: *it's only twenty-five for the night!* He turns around and together we take the room; it is just big enough to hold two beds, a small writing table, and sports a tiny loo in the corner. We take our turns in the shower, put on our dry sets of clothes, wash our soaked ones, and are pleased to find the radiator pumping just a bit of heat into the room: perfect for drying wet wool socks. After dinner in the restaurant, we call it a day.

Once in bed, I reconnect the iPod to my ears, and as I fade into sleep, the hymn from the woods softens the passage into dream: *Grace and peace to you . . .*

5

La Belle France

Today, I march on France!

I could not have ordered up a more heavy, misty and altogether grim day for my victorious entrance into *la belle France*. France is, in my pilgrim imagination, a magical place, an enchanted beyond, that holds within its grand frontiers both my past and at least some of my future. Out of this land came my mother's ancestors a century or two before me. The language of France is the maternal tongue of my Grandma Dufault, my aunts and uncles, and even my mother before she went off to primary school. I know so little about it; I have visited Paris numerous times, but only as a sightseer. I do not really know this country beyond the glitz of the Champs-Élysées and the Eiffel Tower, the masterworks of the Louvre and the Orsay, or the windows of Notre Dame and Sainte-Chapelle. I look forward to discovering the *real* France as well as the *belle France* of popular imagination.

Yesterday's cheery feelings concerning rain are lost to me as I leave Oignies-en-Thiérache; it is an ever-so-dreary drizzle that dampens my hood. I pass some farm buildings, begin climbing a slippery road of mud, and soon enough find myself in the midst of a vast spread of pines. Even as I walk, I am congratulating myself on how good I have gotten at using the Grand Randonnée's red and white stripes and the digital way-points in my GPS. I have a firm confidence that if one lets me down, the other will surely save me. No concern for failure afflicts me as I follow this well-used logging road, not even when I slide down an embankment and find myself standing on a road paved in concrete. I look right. I look left. The GR indicators are confusing me: they seem to point me to the right, but my instincts tell me to go left. I take a look at the GPS screen: it too tells me to go right to the next way-point. I still feel odd about it, but turn right and proceed a couple meters or so. I notice a signpost that sure looks like one I saw yesterday.

Something is not right here. I do an 180° turn and recognize a scene that makes my stomach sink in despair: I behold the signpost, the curve of the road, the embankment, the logging road, the woods exactly as I saw it all yesterday. I realize that I have just spent the past forty-five minutes retracing my way *out* of Oignies-en-Thiérache *into* Oignies-en-Thiérache. Obviously, I have followed both the GR and the GPS track in reverse, and I curse myself for such stupidity, for such idiocy, for such *hubris* in thinking I am now a master of pilgrim navigation.

Now, what do I have to do to fix this embarrassment? Option one: backtrack up the muddy road and over the hill to Oignies-en-Thiérache and start over. This means not only losing the forty-five minutes I have already been out, but also the forty-five minutes to get back; that is an hour and a half loss on the day, but it is also the most secure possibility. Option two: use my GR guidebook and GPS' digital maps to find a shortcut to some point on the actual road heading south towards France. The GR guide shows that road, and it is possible that this cement path will intersect with it fairly easily, but I cannot be sure for my present position is so close to the edge of the map that what I presume to be the route is off the edge, and so I will have a blank for most of the way to the presumed intersection. I begin fiddling with the GPS to see what it will tell me. I zoom out and look for the connecting roads that will get me where I need to be. I think I see a way: a grid of service roads run through the woods to the right, and I can pick one of them up just a short ways ahead of me. There are risks since I don't know what kind of terrain I'm dealing with here, and I can only estimate the distances involved. It may or may not be less good than the first option. For whatever reason I am feeling brave: *Okay, lets be adventuresome here, Kev; let's go cross-country and see what happens.*

My concern over unknown terrain is not misplaced. The road becomes more primitive, and the mud grows sloppier and gloppier. I have to pick my way over and around massive puddles of oozing mire in extended tracks made by 4x4s and other trucks. It slows me down to a crawl. Sometimes I can ditch the road and carefully walk through the forest itself, pushing branches out of my face and stepping over mossy logs. Other times I just have to slosh my way through the mud troughs, choosing whatever counts as high ground, supporting myself with Click on this side and Clack on the other. I start to slip but catch myself. My boots are covered with the muck. I get through one extended pit, walk a few meters, then find that I have to pass through another, then yet another.

I come finally to a better road, and the mud problem is alleviated for the time being, but now I have to climb steeply, and it is a long pull. I am huffing and puffing. I pause to catch my breath then continue on. I reach the crown of the hill and see several foresters busy trimming branches. Well, one is trimming branches with a saw attached to a long pole while the other three are directing the work. They take in my approach with dull bemusement. As I pass, the largest of the men, his face adorned with a massive mustache, asks if I am okay. I say yes. "You are not making a good way, you know." I tell him I know but will pick up the GR in a little while. He raises an eyebrow. I suppose he is mildly concerned that I might die out here of stupidity, and he will be the one who will have to retrieve my cold, lifeless body from a mud-filled ditch somewhere. He makes a gesture of passage onward that seems to say, "Well, if you are so smart, be my guest . . . " I nod and say, *bonjour*, to all four and continue on my way. I hope they are extraordinarily wrong and that I am not as extraordinarily stupid as they presumably presume.

Shortly, my path leaves the graded road and heads across a meadow. Within just a few meters, the roadway under my feet disappears into high grass and wild flowers. My pant legs are getting soaked. I have to lift each foot unnaturally high and force it forward with each step. A barbed wire fence paralleling me on the right and constant checking of my position on the hidden road according to the GPS screen keep me mostly on track, but this, too, is very slow going. *How, in heaven's sake, did I get myself into this morass?* Another kilometer of hip-high grass and glory of glories, just ahead I spot a GR arrow nailed to the trunk of a tree. I am back on the Chemin de Compostelle.

I have been supposing that once back on the GR, my situation would improve. That supposition proves to be far from the reality: the GR 654 here is as bad as anything I have been through yet this morning. Mud, mire, and drizzle alternating with downpour make my forward progress distressingly slow. The slop that this forest road has become under the abuse it has taken from 4x4s, quads, motorcycles and tractor treads makes it anything but a *grande randonnée* for a poor pedestrian like me. There is so much moisture in the air that the lenses of my glasses remain permanently fogged.

I come out of the woods to a paved country road with a few houses and barns scattered about the terrain on either side. I follow the road as it curves and descends, finally delivering me onto a four-way crossroad. I blink twice. This is it: *this is the border between Belgium and France!* I do not cross it quite yet. I want to savor this moment a while. Standing on this threshold between two worlds is not just a matter of geography; just a few steps more, and I will pass from baby-pilgrim to big-boy-pilgrim. This is where I grow up. This is where I leave pilgrim novitiate behind and make a sort of first vow to accomplish this thing. This is a frontier of heart and soul as much as of pavement or government.

Okay, Gregory, Click and Clack: Ready? Let's walk ourselves right into la Belle France!

There is no post, no line painted across the pavement, no sign whatsoever of the place where Belgium ends and France begins. Odd. We are denied our photo-op straddling the frontier, one foot in both lands. As if to make amends, at the next intersection a kilometer or two down the road and already in French territory, a finely crafted post is set into the angle of the crossroad. It boasts a large blue and yellow sign with a modern pilgrim shell logo that reads: *Chemin de Saint-Jacques: 2,600 kms. My, that is a lot of kms!* Even if the kilometers seem altogether too many, it is good to know that at least this road has an end: Compostela is really out there, and I will do my best to arrive there one of these fine months.

The red and white markers of the GR lead me off the highway and towards a dirt road, but it is not altogether clear to me which of two paths I am to follow. A farmer is at work in his nearby yard, so I ask him, *Compostelle?*, and point up the road. He nods back affirmatively and says, "Compostelle." Then adds: *"Bon courage, monsieur!"* I wave in gratitude and up the dirt road I climb. The GR marking in this region of France, it is already clear, is not up to the standards I have come to enjoy in Belgium. The red and white stripes are faded, ambiguous or altogether absent at crossroads and Y's in the trail. It is really annoying, especially after a very long morning of hard walking already under my belt. But I have one unexpected advantage: in France, the GR 654 actually shows up on my GPS maps as a distinct roadway so following it becomes easier as long as I often check my position against the GPS, which means stopping every few minutes for a gander at the small screen. Unfortunately, the trail is turning ugly again. Overuse by heavy machinery has chewed up the surface, and with the onslaught of several days of rain, the roads are more viscous than solid. With each step my boots are sinking into the muck up to my ankles, and when I pull them out, they make a most disagreeable sucking sound.

My destination for the day is the town of Rocroi, the first substantial dot on the map after the frontier. As I draw closer to Rocroi, I pick up a paved road for several kilometers. At one point, both the GR guidebook and my GPS indicate that my route cuts off the paved road and takes a short cut to the city through a heavy forest. I look for the road but can find no cut through the woods where it is supposed to be. I am not amused that my GPS seems to be lying to me: there is not even a hint of a trail where it says there is one. I press on a bit further down the pavement and find an opening; though it does not match up exactly, it may be it. I am concerned that there are no GR signs here either, but I decide to take my chances, and so I turn off the pavement and start down the wooded trail. Within a few meters, I once again find myself in some of the worst slop I have yet encountered on the road. At one point, the muck rides up over the tops of my boots and leaks inside. I curse. I continue another ten meters or so only to find that the trail ends. It just ends. It goes nowhere. I curse again, then turn back to traverse in reverse the same miserable road to nowhere that I have just walked. Upon exiting the morass, I check my maps, and it seems the paved road will also take me to Rocroi, though less directly. This could become a thirty-kilometer day. I am seriously crabby now. Everything is a burden. Everything is against me: the rain, the mud, the road, my Gore-Tex which doesn't work, even fat old Gregory the Great getting his free ride across Europe at my back's expense.

It is another three kilometers of pavement, running with rain, before I reach Rocroi; I step off the macadam as automobiles or trucks approach, both to reduce the possibility of being whacked by their front grill as well as being drenched by the spray from their whirling wheels.

Rocroi, as it turns out, is a fortified city, its walls designed like a five-point star with dry moats surrounding them and defensive towers at each city gate. I am grateful to walk through the battlements and into the town center where a brightly lit tourist office is situated. I enter the office dripping rainwater onto the spic-and-span floor but am relieved that after my self-introduction in French, the young lady behind the desk has detected my American accent and responds in cheery English. She is more than happy to help me find a place for the night, but unfortunately the cheap option, a three-bed pilgrim refuge, is already full. We then look over a brief list of *chambre d'hôtes*; with a sympathetic smile, she recommends one that is located just outside the city walls, an easy walk. But I am exhausted and do not want even an easy walk. Option two is the town hotel just across the street. She continues to recommend the *chambre d'hôte*, so I figure she knows something I don't and head back out into the rain to find the place.

I leave town through an ancient gate and bridge lined with the flags of the town's World War I liberators, the Stars and Stripes among them. I cross a busy thoroughfare and find the house: it is a two-story place mostly covered in ivy. I go to the door and knock. No answer. I walk to the side where there is a garage but no door. I peek in a window and see what looks like a very unkempt living room. I go back to the front door and knock again. I am just about to leave when the door is cracked open, and I am examined by the peering eyes of a very old lady. I begin with my usual French self-introduction: *Je suis pèlerin et je cherche logement pour la nuit.* I am a pilgrim looking for a place to stay for the night. She tells me to wait so I remain outside on the small porch. A younger lady, perhaps in her fifties and dressed in a colorful paint-splattered smock, comes to the door and exuberantly welcomes me into the front room, where I am invited to drop my pack, take off my drenched jacket, and enjoy a tall glass of *champagne américain,* as she calls it: Coca-Cola.

The place is rather a mess, and I immediately regret my choice of this offering over the hotel. The ladies, obviously mother and daughter, are friendly, though, so I resist the temptation to excuse myself and head back to town. *Je suis pèlerin,* I now say of myself, so I should take what comes with graciousness. This is a no-whine zone, I declare to myself as I suck up my disappointment. The daughter is an artist with a small studio filled with canvases in various stages of completion. She aspires to be a neo-impressionist with great swaths of colors and gloppy brush and knife strokes giving texture to the still-life images she is working on. Not a one of these would find a place in my living room, but *de gustibus non est disputandum,* as older priests used to say: no point in arguing over taste. She leads me up a small staircase that takes a double turn before arriving at the first floor. I have to wrestle Gregory and Click and Clack up and around the turns and am relieved to catch up to my hostess and walk into my bedroom for the night. It is painted in purple, pink, and green, dizzying actually, but it is dry and offers a private bathroom and shower. The artist leaves me in peace.

I drop a dripping Gregory to the tile floor and sit on the edge of the bed, then lie back. I am exhausted beyond words. I do not even want to untie my boots, the leather of which is completely soaked, and on the soles, there are cakes of hardening mud between the boots' rubber lugs. I force myself to begin the process of decompression. I sit up and pull off the boots and peel the soaked socks from my feet. I fish my clothes from Gregory's belly, and there is dampness in them, too. I hang them out to rid them of clamminess, drop my used clothes into a wet pile on the floor, slither my wet knee brace down my leg and over my foot, then drag my sorry self to the shower. The warm spray relaxes me and sets me up for a good rest this afternoon. I launder my clothes in the sink, then go downstairs to look for newsprint to stuff inside the boots, which, according to more expert trekkers than I, helps them dry more quickly without ruining the leather. I nibble on leftover snacks from my pack, then lie down for a deep sleep on an altogether lovely bed.

I awake in a daze as to where I am: the vivid colors in which the room has been decorated leave me disoriented, but pieces of reality fall back into place as I situate myself in time and space. My body refuses to respond to my weak will to get up and do something, so I just spread eagle across the bed and remain in a state of comfortable suspended animation.

I size up my situation: This has been my eighth day of walking. I have wandered across half of Belgium, through mud and mire, rain and shine, with a knee riding on the edge of disaster. I am tired physically and emotionally weary. This day's tough trek has bled me of my enthusiasm and washed out my sense of mission; my frontier vow now seems weak and ill considered. I just do not want to walk. These must be the signs that I am due for a day off. I had planned since the beginning to take one free day per week; tomorrow may be my first rest day. I'll think about it through the evening and see what I feel like in the morning; if after a good night's sleep I am still feeling low, I'll hold up here in Rocroi and let my heart catch up to my body.

As afternoon fades into evening and the rain moves on, I lazily head back into town. I try to find a way into the church, but it is closed tighter than a clam in cold water, so I go into the restaurant of the hotel that I didn't choose to stay the night in and have a beer and pizza with a crust more like cardboard than bread. As I get up to leave, who should pass by the restaurant window but my old pilgrim pal, Herman. For the third, or is it the fourth, time, we are reunited on the pilgrim way. I wave to him through the window; he smiles, comes in, and together we sit down and talk over the day's walk. For all my troubles today, his were far worse. He got much more lost than I and wandered helplessly in the Ardennes for hours this morning. I am grateful for my GPS and the freedom from such travails it mostly affords me. He has a room upstairs and is ready for bed, so we make our farewells, and I return to my ivy-covered haven outside the city walls for a little prayer, then sleep. If I stay in Rocroi tomorrow, Herman and I will be on a different daily program; it is probable that I will never see him again.

I awake to daylight and lethargy. I dress and head downstairs for my breakfast at the big table in the cluttered front room of the house. I ask my hostess if I might stay a second night, but my request is not received with enthusiasm. There is whispering back and forth between mother and daughter. The younger explains to me that they have a wedding on their docket this Saturday afternoon in another town. They are not so sure about leaving a stranger in their home while they are away. I must look particularly pathetic as I wait for them to resolve their doubts about my request. Their furtive whispering has stimulated my tendency to fret; I am sure they are calculating the chances I might steal them blind while they are away. I am sure they will say no. What relief then, when Daughter announces the results of their secret consultations: "*Oui*, you can stay another day." I thank them as thoroughly as I am able and return to my room upstairs to enjoy my first "day off" of this pilgrimage.

Just what does a pilgrim do on a "day off" is not something I have considered up to now. I come up with a "to do" list: Clean and polish my boots. Repack Gregory from top to bottom. Write in my journal. Mark my journey forward on the GPS. Visit Rocroi's star-shaped battlements. Eat. Drink. Rest. That's about it. And that is just what I do.

This being the fourteenth of July, Bastille Day, Rocroi begins celebrating shortly after I have gone to bed. Popping, hissing, and the crackle of fireworks pull me out of the sack. I stand on the bed to peer through a skylight at the fiery display of multi-colored galaxies unfurling across the black of night then dissipating, unfurling again, and dissipating. I can hear an unseen crowd cheering, applauding, oohing and aahing at each new explosion of stars illuminating Rocroi, the star city, below. Those oohs and aahs of wonder are beautiful sounds, more beautiful than the fireworks themselves.

With morning, I say goodbye to my Rocroi ladies and am on my way by 8:00 am. My prayers for good weather have been answered; the sky is rich blue, the sun is shining, and the air fairly sparkles with morning light. Leaving the stellar battlements of Rocroi behind, I am soon walking through rolling hills blanketed in wheat, always lovely, but especially so when unseen breezes send successive waves flowing across their silky surface. Other fields are planted in clover, vibrantly green and dotted by a plethora of small white flowers. Silver beads from yesterday's rainwater glimmer on the cloverleaves. The recent rains and the clarity of the morning light have made these green fields, balanced against the blue of the sky, feasts for human eyes. Occasionally, small squares of pine forest have been sewn into the tapestry adding more dimension, texture and a different tone, a darker, rougher green, to the whole. I am so grateful that I have the eyes to see this, the feet to walk here, a mind capable of taking it all in, and a heart able to give thanks for it all.

I am walking very well this morning: my knee is hardly aching, I have had not a single blister so far, no touch of tendonitis has bothered me, and after my day-off, I have oodles of energy. Now *this* is what pilgrimage is *supposed* to be like, I tell myself as Gregory, Click and Clack, and I almost dance down this happy little trail through a truly *belle* France.

With three hours of walking under my belt, I arrive in Rimogne. I cross the E44 highway that cuts through the town and decide to take an early lunch in a bar across the way. It is too early to quit for the day, so over a beer and *baguette* loaded with ham and cheese, I study my GR guidebook: in about two hours I can be in Remilly-les-Pothées. The question is: will I be able to find lodging there? The guidebook lists just one *gite* and no grocery stores or any other form of commerce. I ask the bartender about the place and am assured that there will be no problem in finding a room for the night in Remilly.

While I am sitting at my small table, a man dressed casually in shorts and t-shirt takes a seat at the table next to me; he notices that I'm reading an English language guide book, then asks me, in English, what I am up to. His light accent gives him away as a Dutchman. I explain that I am a pilgrim to Compostela and slowly walking my way south. He says he is traveling too, taking a year off from work just to drive wherever he wants and do whatever he wants. He explains that his wife has recently died of cancer leaving him bereft, so in hopes of assuaging his grief, he is wandering Europe in a VW van. I express my condolences and ask if the travel is helping him. He thinks so. He knows of Compostela since he is just returning from Spain where he visited his son. He asks how it is that I have so much time available for such an enterprise, so I explain I am a Catholic priest, on sabbatical for a year, having just finished a big job in Belgium. He gets up to leave, so I stand as well; we shake hands like old friends, and he says, "Have a good pilgrimage". For an instant, I am not sure how to respond; what do I say back: "And you, have a good grieving?" So I say simply, "You, too", which I feel instinctively to be about right: his present wandering following the loss of his wife must be a special kind of pilgrimage. He is traveling towards something new, letting the cavernous hole left by death be slowly filled by time, geography, and chance encounters like the one we've just had. He walks to his van, gets in, and drives off. I am sorry I cannot get to know him better; I didn't even get his name.

The way forward continues to be fairly easy, but the heat at midday is increasingly uncomfortable. I am tiring as the kilometers to Remilly slowly pass under my steady pace; I see off on the far horizon to my right what looks to me very much like a mountain range. Craggy alpine peaks softened by mists loom over the distant countryside. But there are no such mountains in this part of France. I take a second look and realize I am beholding instead nothing but clouds, fantastically sculpted by the forces of nature into the appearance of high mountains. They are on the move, coming closer as the seconds and minutes pass. Before long, the clouds are covering a sizable portion of the sky, and I feel a drop of rain hit my nose. I presume I am about to be drenched yet again, so stop, dig out my rain-jacket, put it on, cover Gregory, and continue down the road. Then I observe something very Wizard-of-Oz-like in the sky above: a large funnel cloud appears in the midst of the heavy-grey formations almost above my head, but this is the weird thing: it is a *reverse* funnel, the sweeping clouds about its mouth are tapering upward, its spout pierces ever more deeply the atmosphere above rather than twirling downwards towards the earth as it should. I am actually looking up into its mouth from below. I have never seen anything like it. A funnel cloud spouting up rather than down? Is such a thing possible in nature? I don't know, but I see what I see. And then my mind goes all goofy on me, and I ask myself: what, then, does such a cloud *do*? In the grand scheme of heaven and earth, what might it be *for*? Could it not be a celestial vacuum cleaner designed to suck up the dirt and dust of earth into the heavens for cleansing? Or maybe it is a heavenly horn through which the angelic choirs above trumpet their *alleluias* to us mostly unhearing humans below. Oh, if we only had ears to hear! Or maybe, more likely, it is a trumpet of a sort, but not so much for blowing as for hearing, like those used in olden days by our deaf elders. Might God not now be listening *to us* through this thing? And if so, what does he hear: the cry of the poor as the Psalms say? I don't know. I hope so.

My fantasy falters as does the funnel as it loses shape and turns into just another leaden cloud. Some moments later, I quite suddenly feel the warmth of sunshine on my shoulders. I look up again and am surprised that the great rain cloud has completely disappeared from the sky; the heavens above are as blue as blue can be, not a wisp of white or grey cloud remains. It has not been that long since I first saw the mountains, then the funnel. Well, *that* was weird. I stop, take off my rain jacket, and continue under an increasingly hot sun.

The final few kilometers to Remilly are an uphill pull. The paved road I follow offers no shade. I am cooking out here. I finally arrive exhausted at the first few houses of the village, all made of rough hewn stone. In front of one sit an aged couple enjoying the shade of a large garden umbrella. I stop to greet them and to ask about the possibility of *logement* in the village. They tell me that just a bit further on there is indeed a *gite*, located right next to the village church. I am overjoyed and can hardly wait to find myself settled for the afternoon and evening. The old fellow asks about my nationality and when I tell him, *je suis Américain*, he smiles broadly and tells me that he has family in Battle Creek, *Michigain*. I respond, "Oh, the home of Corn Flakes!" He catches my English and says excitedly, "*Oui, Corn Flakes! La companie Kellogg!*" That slim connection between us pleases him greatly and without getting out of his plastic lawn chair, he stretches out his hand to shake my own. I am touched by his touch; the old lady just smiles broadly at the encounter.

I trundle up the street towards the church but see no signs indicating a *gite* in the place. At the top of the hill where the old church stands, I see some young folks who very much look like vacationers, getting out of two shiny cars. I approach and ask if they know where I might stay for the night. They are indeed staying at the *gite* right here; the owner, they tell me, lives a block away so one of the group leads me to his front gate. I pass through the gate and knock at the front door. A burly man dressed in worn jeans and t-shirt answers. I explain to him as best I am able my need for a place to stay. His face remains serious. After I have finished, he begins with words I understand completely, "*Je suis désolé . . .* " "I am sorry; there is no room.

The *gite* is full for the weekend. It is Bastille week after all. You may find a place up the road a few kilometers." And that is that. The door is closed. I am devastated. I don't know what to do with myself. I am just too exhausted and too hot to go on. I *must* stop here. I have nothing left for more walking today. I wander to the church and look around for a parish house but find nothing. The place looks altogether abandoned.

I see a bus shelter so go there to see if there is any bus coming or going today. No schedule is posted, but at least I find a bit of shade. I set Gregory to one side, sit, and pull out an apple. I decide I really cannot go any further today, so I go back to the landlord's door and knock again. His wife answers this time and offers me an altogether more sympathetic response. I tell her I *cannot* go on further, and ask if I can spend the night in the church. She seems doubtful but calls her husband back to the door, even while she re-trieves a slice of rhubarb pie that is still warm from the oven. He tells me that if I want to stay in the church, I will have to talk to the lady who controls the key. He describes the way to her front door as I down my lovely slice of pie. The lady of the house returns with a glass of cool water, which I drink in just a few gulps. I then wander back to the road, then past the church and down a steep street to the church lady's house. The door is open, the TV is playing a French soap opera in the kitchen, but no lady is near. The house seems abandoned for the moment. I see a man painting his garage door at the next house so amble over to ask him about where I might find the church lady. *Bonjour, monsieur . . .* Would you know where the lady with the church key might be? He looks up from his work and gives me the friendli-est smile in the world. "She's not there? Well, let's just see." He sets down his paintbrush, stands, and asks what my problem is. I explain my present desolation, and he assures me not to worry; I will be taken care of one way or another. He invites me to drop Gregory off on his doorstep as together we walk back to the church lady's open front door. She responds to his call and comes to the door. He explains my situation, adding even that I am a priest, but she refuses to grant me access to the church overnight without permis-sion from higher up. Besides, she adds, it is no place for anyone to sleep. He accepts her refusal politely even as I sink once again into desolation. As we walk back to his house, he says to me, "Listen, I'll find a place for you to stay. Let's go see the mayor; I'm sure you can sleep in the town hall where there is a bathroom and a kitchen. He directs me to his old Toyota Land Cruiser, and up the road we go, right back to the home of the landlord I have visited twice already. The two of them discuss my situation for a while. Finally, the landlord-mayor hands over a key, and I am set. "Now," my new friend says, "I'll take you back to my place where you can shower, have a drink, and rest while I finish up my garage door." I finally ask his name: "Jean," he tells me as he shakes my hand, " . . . and my wife is Anne".

I am invited inside Jean and Anne's home, a major part of which is under renovation. Anne is busy priming new closets as Jean and I pass through. I am presented to Anne, then directed to a beautiful new bathroom, given a towel, and told I'm welcome to take my time. Once finished, I am given a cold beer, shown to the living room equipped with a large television, and invited to put my feet up. The television is hooked to a satellite, so for the first time since leaving Leuven, I catch up on the rest of the world through CNN and BBC World.

Some time later, Jean asks if I would like to see the village church. I welcome the opportunity, so he goes next door to secure the key from the church lady. It takes some convincing, but she finally allows him temporary custody of the key, so across the street we go. The oldest section of the building, the baptistery, goes back to the twelfth century, other pieces to the fifteenth and sixteenth. The late afternoon sun is illuminating the stonework of the tower and front *façade* in golden light, making it seem a proud and noble edifice that has withstood the ravages of time with its head proudly up. Within, it is a different story altogether. Jean unlocks the side door, and we step into a shambles. Jean tells me it is hardly used anymore; perhaps there is a funeral service within its walls, at best, once a year. Regular celebration of Sunday liturgies stopped some years back. The stain glass is shattered in numerous places. The statuary is cracked. The walls are peeling and turning green with mold. It is a sad sight to behold, not unlike visiting a friend in the late stages of cancer. I ask Jean why the government doesn't do something to stop its deterioration before it is too late; he responds with a shrug: "France has so many old churches in the same situation; where do we begin?"

Wandering slowly about this place saddens me. Death, it seems, is inevitable, even for a church. So many generations of believers have prayed within her walls, yet it is *our* generation that lets her fall to the ground. I suppose, in some ways, this church building is a symbol of the overall church in France and in much of the West. Its congregations have grown old. Its old faithfuls are dying. The prayer and piety that sustained so many for so long hasn't been effectively passed on to the younger generation, or at least hasn't been received. The church is not hated; it is just not important, which is far more devastating. From the outside, Catholicism still looks impressive, but from the inside, where are the people? They are out and away and perhaps, even "searching for meaning" in other traditions, like the three searchers in Thorembais. Religion has become an old-fashioned book of fables with no bearing on our new, sleek, secure lives of today. But, as the Dutchman in Rimogne gives testimony: we who are alive still die, and those who survive still mourn, and the fundamental contradiction of life and death is still felt as profoundly as ever. So maybe the old "fables" portrayed in these decaying windows might yet be rediscovered as having some light in them for our modern, self-sufficient generations, and maybe the old rituals that were celebrated within this building for so many centuries might still express our deepest experiences of loss and gain, and maybe, just maybe, one of these days, one or two youngsters will ask their tottery grandparents: "Who *is* that man on the cross, and why is he there?" Perhaps such curiosity will be just enough to moisten the dry seed so that out of its buried husk, a sprout might unfold, break through the surface of the hard earth, curl around the tire of a shiny BMW, and stretch out towards the sun above. Would it not then eventually drop more seeds to the soil below so that soon enough the whole landscape would come alive with the wheat of life being ruffled in waves by the breeze that is Spirit? And would that wheat not be ground and made into bread and that bread be broken, and the hungry of heart, like the Dutchman, be fed?

Jean and I wander out through the old door, lock it behind us, and take our places with Anne at the table of their garden terrace for a gentle evening under the stars enjoying bread and wine, vegetables and beef. After night has fallen, Jean drives Gregory and me up to the town hall, where I set my mat and sleeping bag on the concrete floor and lay myself down. It is not so comfortable, but it is better than sleeping in an open field. It is so much better because I have once again been cared for by strangers who became friends. They have done for me what Jesus did for so many, and that makes sleep come easy.

I leave the town hall at first light. Before going out the door, I write a brief note of thanks to Jean and Anne on the only piece of paper I can find: a v-shaped coffee filter. No one is yet stirring as I pass their house and slip the coffee filter in the gap between the front door and its frame. As I follow the road out of Remilly, the fresh memory of sitting at their table under the stars enjoying a fine supper nourishes me still. The road beyond their house is all up-hill. This pull is hard enough at this fresh hour of the morning at the height of my energy; how much more difficult it would have been yesterday afternoon when I was at the end of my emotional and physical rope! I could not have done it. Anyway, it is a lovely morning as the light of the sun brightens more and more of the earth's ancient face. The sunlight is also bringing with it new warmth; as I climb, I can feel the temperature rising. By afternoon, it will be, as my dad used to say, "hotter than a pistol out here".

I poke my way along some well-kept roads and trails. Then I enter a wooded area that goes on for about a kilometer; it is all mud. I pick my way through today's serving of brown glop, take one misstep and almost fall, but with the help of Clack, catch myself just in time, and come out the other side just fine.

The day is heating up quickly, and my trek towards Signy-l'Abbaye becomes heavier, but it is a very short walk today, only sixteen kilometers. As is most often the case on this way to Compostela, the first thing I see of Signy is the steeple of its church. Steeples of this and every church I encounter along the way are God's fingers for me: from a long way off, they rise up and gesture for me to come this way. What a joy they must have been to medieval pilgrims who had walked far more than I, under much more trying conditions. Those towers of stone and slate, many with rusted roosters riding high atop their peaks, were the medieval equivalent of a GPS way-point. After hours of walking, the screen of hill and field would drop away just enough for that rooster to come into view, then the slate tower itself, and sometimes, if the timing were right, the sound of the bells ensconced protectively within would reach the pilgrims' ears. "You are near!" they would proclaim as they drew the pilgrims into the very heart of the village where relief and welcome would surely be found. I yet feel some of that joy each time I first spy one of these same old steeples. To me, they feel like family, and the voices of their bells not unlike that of mom calling us kids back home from our evening play.

It is Sunday morning, 11:00 am; I walk up to the front door of the Signy church, directly beneath the steeple that has led me into town. I expect, well, at least *I hope*, I will arrive in time for Mass. The massive double door is shut tight, but I notice a hunched old man slowly leaving the church from a side door, so enter where he has just exited. The church interior is lit, candles are burning under the feet of Saint Jean d'Arc, but nothing else seems to be happening. I wander a bit with Gregory, find a bulletin board and read that Mass was celebrated here *yesterday*. On Sunday, the priest is in other villages.

I dawdle a bit, wondering what to do next, then spot a hotel-restaurant across the main street so head over, and ask the receptionist for a room. Luckily, she has one available: forty euros for the night. No breakfast. The room is small and hot but has a bath and toilet. Good enough. I change into my sandals, then head back into town to buy a few groceries and find some lunch before the shops close. The GR guidebook leads me to believe I will be entering a sort of no-man's land for the next two days: no services, restaurants or shopping along the way. To prepare myself, I pick up bread, tuna, sliced pork, fruit, some peanuts, a chocolate bar, and a bottle of wine.

After a big restaurant lunch, I return to my room, nap, then clear off a small writing table, pour a glass of wine, take a wheat host out of a small Tupperware bowl I have ensconced in my pack, as well as a paperback missal with the prayers and scripture readings within. I pull up a chair and set everything in its place. This is the Lord's Day, and I can't let it go by without the Eucharist as an essential moment of this First Day of the Week. Mass by myself is a very different experience than when celebrated with others; it is not my preference, for this prayer is by its nature a communal one. But it can be prayed alone because and only because, though alone in one way, I am not alone in another. I recognize Jesus with me at this small table in the breaking of the bread and the sharing of the cup. And the saints. And my beloved dead. And my family and friends. And the whole church, that is, my sisters and brothers in faith wherever they are in this big world of ours. This realization reminds me to go back to Gregory and fish around for a special waterproof wallet, hidden deep inside where I store my valuables. From within I pull out a small wooden box that holds two tiny locks of hair: one of my father, the other of my mother, both clipped from their heads before their burial by my sisters. I set the box on the table to remind me that Mom and Pop, in particular, are not far from me now. I savor the scriptures of the day, then take the bread, this unleavened morsel, this food of people on the run, and raise it and bless it in Jesus' words. The cup too is raised in memory of him. Peace. Grace and peace. My pilgrim hymn reappears, and I sing the words aloud to myself and to all who are gathered with me around this small table.

I go in peace, leave my room, and wander down the hot and empty main street back to the Signy church. I enter and find a place amidst the pious clutter and just sit in the cool for a long time with the grace and peace hymn playing in the far back of my mind. The late afternoon turns to evening and evening to night and another day along the pilgrim way is complete.

6

Reims

My new pilgrim day begins with some simple calculations. I figure I have walked just shy of 250 kilometers in the past two weeks. *Has it only been two weeks that I have been out here?* More encouraging still is my estimate that I should be in the very major city of Reims in just a few more days, certainly by the end of the week. Besides being 2000 years old and *the* city of royal coronations through the centuries, Reims has also been one of the major pilgrim cities along the French Chemin, and I am encouraged to be now marching on that great and ancient city. The new day's overcast skies do not diminish my determination to enter Reims soon.

I spend a night in the village of Justine-Herbigny with a grandparently farm couple who welcome the occasional pilgrim into their home. The following day I make my way to Château-Porcien where I pick up the verge of a canal that will lead me eventually to the outskirts of Reims, and there I begin following the canal south. My guide does not display on its flat pages the impossibly tall grass nor the thorny brambles through which I must slowly pick my way before arriving late in the afternoon at the town of Vieux-le-Asfeld, an altogether charmless place where I pass the rest of the day and the night in an equally charmless hotel.

The third day of my march towards the grand city begins with a major decision not more than five kilometers outside of Vieux-le-Asfeld. There I come to a Y in the road; the right arm goes back to the GR and its bramble-ridden canal, but the left is signed for Reims and marked at just 23 kilometers. Though this left branch is off my map, and I risk again unexpected troubles, I choose it, a small country road labeled D274 and along its roughly paved surface, I continue my march southward with the bright hope that I could be in Reims by night.

As much as the road allows, I walk on the grassy shoulder rather than the hard pavement. The grass is soft under foot and easier on feet, tendons, and knees, I presume, at least in the long-term, and this pilgrimage is almost the very definition of "long-term". I walk steadily, but I lack spunk this morning. My energy levels are diminished; too much fighting with the canal for too long yesterday is costing me today. My mind wanders to odd thoughts: Behold the lowly beetle; how can something be so exuberantly black that it shines with a brilliance that makes it almost emerald? Snails and slugs interest me, too: snails carry their cozy caracoles with them wherever they go, while slugs, bereft of house and home, are condemned by nature to slither across the face of the earth with no place to lay their heads. Why one and not the other? *It is just not fair.* And why are these European slugs painted orange, not exactly effective camouflage in green and brown woods like these? I am proud, at least, that I have never deliberately stepped on either slug or snail as I have walked this long and winding Chemin. Live and let live, except when it comes to mosquitoes: I happily murder them before they drill me for blood. Swat. *Sorry, Charlie.*

And so it goes until my mind fades to a pleasant nothing, and I find myself ambling down the road with my brain set on pause. I just walk. And be. And walk.

And so I walk myself into the town of Bourgogne. It is an agreeable little place in a way Vieux-le-Asfeld was not. Its main street is divided by a wide green park shaded by leafy trees. The steeple of the village church guides me inward. A left-turn takes me to the front doors of the church where a man is painting the wrought iron fencing in front of the building. I ask him if the *curé* lives nearby. He shrugs his shoulders and tells me there is no priest here, but that there are some people within at the moment; I should talk to them. I am not even sure what I intend to do: quit for the day and stay here, after only ten kilometers? Or just visit a while, look for a place to lunch, move on? I don't know. I wander to the back of the church, and an open door invites me in. Indeed, there are people here, principally a small group of ladies who spot me just as I spot them. With wide smiles and grand waves of their hands, they call me to their clatch. One asks if I am going to Compostelle. Even before I can say yes, she has a hand on my shoulder and guides me deeper into the church with an invitation to share in some homemade cupcakes and warm coffee. Upon learning that I am an American, another lady tries out her basic English on me, and conversation suddenly gets three times easier.

There are several men here as well: they are happily buzzing about the bits and pieces of a new pipe organ that they are in the process of installing. Chrome tubes are being fabricated and tested on the spot. New oak is being shaved and sanded. One of the workers is from Spain, so we converse in Spanish about the instrument he is building while I nibble on my cupcake. All seem just thrilled to have a pilgrim walk in on them. The lady who speaks some English asks me about my plans for the day: am I going to stay here or go on? Do I want to spend the night with the parish priest, a very fine man I am assured, who lives in the next village just down the road? She offers to call him for me. Now I have to decide: on to Reims today, only thirteen more kilometers, or listen to my weary body and take advantage of local hospitality, putting off my march into the great city until tomorrow? As I did at the crossroad this morning, I dither indecisively for a few moments, then say, yes, I'd be happy to spend the evening with the local *abbé*. She pulls out her mobile phone and makes the call. All is set up in a few minutes, then she tells me to put Gregory into the boot of her Volkswagen, and she will drive me to his home in nearby Witry-lés-Reims. As I settle into the front seat of the VW, I thank her for her warm kindness. She responds breezily: *"De rien. Helping pilgrims is une joie* for all French people. We *love* our pilgrims!"

As we speed down a back road, I realize that Witry and the parish house is further away than I expected, and kilometers to Reims are clicking by without me having walked them. This tugs at my conscience, but there is nothing to be done, and in the grand scheme of things, a few less kilometers are really not so significant; after all, already back in Thorembais I gave up on my commitment to walk *every* kilometer myself. My new friend takes me to the door of the parish house, where the pastor greets me, invites me in, and shows me a quite formal bedroom upstairs that is now mine for the night. The *abbé,* Gerard, is delighted I am here, proving the point that it is *une joie* for the French to care for *les pèlerins.* He asks if I'd like to join him for lunch. *Of course!* It is *une joie* for me to take advantage of French table hospitality. As we enjoy our pork roast and *pommes frites,* we chat amiably, and he asks how his people have treated me along the way. I report that I am coming to love the French people along the Chemin. They find *joie* in caring for me.

In the evening, Gerard takes me in his car on a tour of the walking route into Reims so that in the morning I will know my way. It seems easy enough, but I worry that it will look differently tomorrow from a pedestrian point of view than it does tonight from the interior of this automobile. I try to mark in my mind the places where I should turn left, and those where I will turn right. The increasing urbanization rather scares me; streetlights and brightly lit stores, sidewalks, and McDonalds restaurants do not seem like my pilgrim habitat anymore. I am glad that tomorrow's short walk of ten kilometers will end in one of France's most beautiful cathedrals, a pilgrim's haven for more than seven centuries.

Once back at the parish house, my phone rings. It is the voice of Gene on the other end. He and Caroline arrived in Reims from Switzerland earlier today and will meet me at the cathedral doors tomorrow morning. What time do I expect to arrive? I advise them that I suspect it will be about 10:00 am. They report that they have scoped out a pilgrim refuge for me located in the former Grand Séminaire of Reims. We are all thrilled at the absolutely perfect timing of our paths crossing here tomorrow; it is one of those coincidences that seems like much more than a bare hit of blind chance. It feels like we are *meant* to meet tomorrow. We all sense some kind of design at work here, some kind of grace, some kind of providence, and it is a very fine feeling to have at the end of this day.

I am served a light breakfast in the morning, then invited by this kind and generous *abbé* to join his small weekday congregation for *Laudes* and Mass, so I leave Gregory and Click and Clack in the foyer of the parish house and walk over with Gerard to the church for the morning liturgies. We are welcomed by no more than six or seven congregants, all elderly, mostly women. All is spoken in French, but since I know these same prayers so well in English I have no difficulty grasping what it all means; even the brief homily given by my host is almost completely intelligible to me. I find this remarkable, though not unusual. I have often experienced this reality in far away places: the language of symbols and the movements of the heart they make visible, rise above the limitations of particular grammars and specialized vocabularies; they suffer less from the effects of Babel's hubris than do our various tribal languages.

With the breathe of Gerard's final blessing at my back, I collect Gregory and company, and together, trying hard to remember the lefts and rights along the way, we click-clack through the mostly quiet streets of Witry, towards my highway for the morning, the N51, the shoulder of which, I will follow straight into the heart of Reims. After leaving the town proper, I stop briefly to fetch my phone from within Gregory's top pouch and send a text message to Gene and Caroline that I am on my way. My first forty-five minutes on the road are free and easy ones, then the moisture being held within this morning's heavy sky finally begins to spill, and I must retrieve my Gore-Tex out of Gregory's side pocket to protect myself as much as I am able.

My grand march seems less grand as the world around me becomes increasingly industrial, which combined with the rain and the low sky makes the walking less than enchanting. This is now just work, the work of just getting there. The industrial fades into the urban with shops of flowers, fruit stands, displays of delicate pastries, and Internet cafes lining the wet street. The sidewalk is filled with umbrella-hoisting pedestrians. Strangers remain strangers on these sidewalks; no one smiles or greets the pilgrim as he passes. The streets themselves are filled with automobiles, rainwater noisily spraying out from under their wheels. I am clearly in Reims proper now. The city blocks keep passing, but I don't seem to be making any progress. When will I see the lacy stone steeples of the cathedral? Shouldn't I be hearing its bells marking the quarter hours by now? *Come on: Appear! Ring! Draw me in!*

My straight stretch of major street into the city finally dumps me into a maze of minor streets going every which way; signs indicate the cathedral is near, but where? I don't see it. How could something so big be so invisible? Finally, I cross from one corner to another and catch my first glimpse of flamboyant stonework: *there it is!* I take a look at my watch: 10:25 am. I am approaching the cathedral from behind; the exterior of its apse is ahead of me, so I will have to walk the length of its nave to get to the front doors. Bells above me toll the half-hour. They are beautiful in the deep tones they produce with each clap. The towers fairly loom above my head and seem heavy and dangerous in the flat light of this rainy day. I turn the corner into the *place* that spreads out before the main porticoes of the cathedral, but any breathtaking display of public space is upset by the intensive reconstruction of the square presently going on; steel barriers block access to the heart of the *place* and orange signs and ripples of caution tape guide tourist and pilgrim alike through a narrow path to the front porch of the cathedral.

Je suis arrivé! Here I am finally at the wide-open portico of the Cathédral Notre Dame de Reims! I know I am supposed to meet Gene and Caroline outside, but I cannot resist being drawn within for just a moment. Alone I enter into darkness of the vestibule, but the gloom passes quickly as this foyer gives way to the nave, and all becomes height and light. The glory of this Gothic architecture lifts me off my feet, and the weight of *Gregorius Magnus* makes no difference; I rise in here. The run of columns holding up the nave's roof lead my gaze forward to the sanctuary, the altar, the focus of so much prayer for so many centuries. I feel a sudden burst of *joie*. What else can I say? *Thank you, LORD! I am here!*

I know that Gene and Caroline are waiting for me somewhere outside, so I turn and return to the porch of the cathedral, pull out my phone and text them: "On steps of cathedral now. C U here." While waiting for a response, I look up into the archway above my head. I am delighted to find myself being regarded with delight by an angel, the famous smiling angel of Reims. She is lovely. Her smile is more ineffable to me than that of the Mona Lisa. Though carved from stone and not having moved for centuries, for this angel, too, clearly, it is *une joie* to welcome pilgrims like me. I keep my eye peeled for some sign of Caroline and Gene, and then across the *place* I see Caroline waving excitedly to me. I wave back and wait for them to work their way around the obstacles and to meet me under the cheery gaze of my smiling angel. Suddenly, we are all embraces and greetings and happy jabbering about this minor miracle: I have walked to Reims!

We enjoy a warm coffee and croissant in a nearby café, then drive a short distance to the old seminary of the Diocese of Reims, converted now into a conference center, rooming house for students, and refuge for pilgrims. I am signed in and led to a fine little room, all spic n' span clean, with a view into the central cloister of the building. After cleaning up, I rejoin my friends for our day's tour. First on the list is a visit to the Basilica of Saint-Rémy, an odd building melding together a Romanesque bottom and a Gothic top. In spite of its mongrel architectural pedigree, it is beautiful inside. The soft light of our overcast day infiltrates the interior, softening the lines between Roman and Gothic and making the stone seem soft and deep. Saint-Rémy himself is buried here; a big-shot Gallo-Roman who became bishop of Reims in the fifth century while still a layperson; hard to figure out how Rome let that happen, but there it is. Anyway, he succeeded in converting Clovis, King of the Franks, to Christianity and thus guaranteed solid footing for the faith in France henceforward. I pass by his tomb and ask the old man to take good care of his French people – for whom caring for pilgrims is still *une joie*.

After a light lunch at a *bistro*, we return to the cathedral for a view of the dramatic stained glass windows designed by the Jewish artist Marc Chagall. They depict biblical scenes in a most fanciful manner, and I take them in with gusto; I breathe in their imagery and wild colors as if the sweep and flow of their intricate designs carry me, tumbling and laughing, from here to heaven and back.

Before supper, Gene, Caroline, and I take some time in their hotel room just to put up our feet and chat. I confess to them that I am losing my original enthusiasm for simply trusting in the kindness of strangers. Despite my mostly good luck to date, I am getting anxious about where I am going to be sleeping the next night or two. Caroline takes my weariness in hand and phones one of the *chambre d'hôtes* listed in my GR guidebook in the town of Verzy, a day's walk from here. With remarkably little fuss, the reservation is made; I just learned something: I don't *have to* suffer the daily stress of wondering if I'll end up sleeping in a rain-drenched field; the mobile phone is the perfect tool for advance planning. And whoever said I *had to* go primitive out here? From now on, I shall do what I should have been doing all along if I had not been so hot to prove what a humble pilgrim I am: *call ahead!*

My friends treat me to dinner on the rooftop restaurant of their hotel, which features a fine view of the cathedral's towers in the near distance and those of the basilica much further off. It is a beautiful place: this Reims. Looking down on its tiled roofs and busy streets from above, we see it as the sun sees it, or the stars, or God. This work of human hands, stone and glass, crafted with care and passion, and this latest generation of humanity now filling it with their voices and gestures and busy comings and goings, their joys and their cares, their blessings and their faults, are all easy to love from up here. It is a beautiful place: this Reims.

From my bed in the Grand Séminaire, I awake to the sound of rain and a room dark with the muted light of a stormy morning. After a breakfast of coffee and croissants with Gene and Caroline, we get in the Saab, and Gene begins weaving his way through the complicated streets of Reims looking for a suitable place to let me off near the canal and GR path that I will follow out of the city and to Verzy. The rain becomes a downpour, then the worst of all scenarios develops: lightning and thunder begin their flash and clap above the city. *Oh no, not this!* Rain I can endure; lightning I just won't walk through. Gene, ever the optimist, assures me it will pass soon, so we park and wait, then we drive further, following the canal southward. Four kilometers on, we find a small grassy area near the Saint-Léonard bridge with easy access to the GR, so here we park and wait some more. Eventually, the lightning passes, but the rain continues steady. I finally decide it is time to go, so we unload Gregory, dig out my rain gear from his various pouches, saddle the Great Pontiff upon my back, take Click and Clack in wet hands, then in the rain, kiss and hug my great friends farewell. They retreat to the Saab and drive to the crown of the bridge to watch me walk off. I wave goodbye with Clack and take up the slippery path south towards Verzy and perhaps, Compostelle. I go around a bend; we disappear from one another's view.

7

Champagne and Thunder

Walking again. Alone again. Just the road and me again. And it is a rather dangerous road as my boots keep slipping out from under me, Vibram soles notwithstanding. The dirt of this path is mostly clay and with this rain, it might as well be grease. Click and Clack save me over and over again. I re-stoke my determination. I will to do this! I will do this! I will . . . *Boom!* All it takes is one clap of thunder to undercut my fragile confidence this wet morning.

After an hour of careful walking, the path takes a jog to the right, letting the canal go its own way. With each step away from the canal, I enter more deeply into new country: vineyards make their appearance as green quilts draped over the rolling hills. Welcome to the land of Champagne! These are the fields that produce the grape that gives the juice that is miraculously turned not just into wine, but into Bubbly. It is not long before I am walking not just towards these vineyards, but through them. My one-lane road, now mostly paved, cuts between the fields giving me a worm's eye-view of the vines, laden now with small green bulbs that will soon enough fill with sunlight from above and moisture from below, be kissed by the night and greeted by the dawn, and then, just when the sugar is right, be ripped from their leafy branches and give us all, but mostly to the rich, the drink of monks and gods.

Small stones mark the fields' owners: Mumm, Taittinger, Veuve-Cliquot, Moët et Chandon, among others. Red, pink, and white rose bushes at the end of certain lines of vines indicate the variety being grown. The clouds have passed, the thunder has exhausted itself, the sky is now as blue as a child would color it, and I am in a new land. I am surrounded by the Champagne, and it is something grand for the eyes. A hill rises to my right and atop it sits a village; my GPS tells me this is Verzenay. The GR guide tells me to climb up the substantial hill to Verzenay, presumably to take in the windmill that stands guard over the village. I choose to stay on the lower road and continue thus to Verzy, my destination for the day.

I take a turn to the right to approach Verzy then wander into the center of the village, a tangle of streets diving or rising like arteries into its heart from various directions. I ask at the *Poste* after my *chambre d'hôte* and am directed down a steep street a block or two until I find a small plaque labeling a nondescript doorway as that of "Alain Lallement". This is it; this is where I have my reservation for the night. I knock, and the door is opened by a young woman. I step into a sort of shop or garage. A lone man is at work operating a machine that glues labels onto wine bottles. He steps from his work to shake my hand and introduces himself as Alain and his wife as Odile. She shows me to one of several cozy rooms above the shop, each opening into a common dining area and kitchen. I pick a room, unload, shower, then take a brief walk back into the center of town only to find the restaurants already closed for the afternoon. I return to my own place, open a small can of tuna I've been carrying as an emergency energy supply and spread it on a croissant I copped from the morning's breakfast table. Simple but sufficient.

My nap is disrupted by the beep of my mobile phone telling me a text message has just arrived. It is from Caroline letting me know that she and Gene are back in Belgium already. She writes that she felt so sad seeing me walk off down the canal road in the rain this morning, not because of the rain, but the feeling that I was walking out of their lives. I write back that, for my part, I feel like I am walking *into* their lives. This is the ironic thing: even as I have walked further and further from Leuven, our friendship has only grown. I doubt I would be here now if it were not for their care and encouragement all along the way every day. The strength they give me is, I realize more and more with each passing day, essential to the success of this mission, for its opposite, despair, is always lurking in the darker recesses of my heart out here. This temptation to lose hope, to give up, to *feel* like this is all very meaningless, is a shadow within that never completely goes away. It sneaks up on me and overcomes my spirit without reason or cause. Keeping despair at bay is my most subtle challenge in finding my way to Compostela.

I suppose that this interior struggle over despair on the Chemin is not unlike despair over death, or really, despair that there is any meaning to life. What my atheist friends tell me, that we are just organic creatures, products of cosmic or evolutionary chance, and there is no "other" to us or beyond us, subtly scratches at the faith of believers whether we admit it or not. Could it be that they are right, and this sense that there is more at work in this dance of life is just an illusion? Or worse: a delusion? I suspect that the fundamental propositions of faith also scratch at the unbelief of my atheist friends, but that is not the point *here*. Doubt and despair are always just a depression away, I suppose. But belief is also just a joy away. Friendship, love, *communion* really, like that of Caroline and Gene, or that of my family, or that of my church family, foster hope, and that hope fosters happiness and meaning and heals the scratch of despair. Hope presents God to me.

I take my journal and head downstairs to do the day's writing, but before I am able to exit to the street, the happy sounds of several people enjoying a *dégustation* wafts into the garage. The chatting comes from a garden between the garage and the family home; the door is open so I step into the sunlight. The language is a familiar one: the garden hosts several Dutch and Flemish guests, all sipping, swirling and nodding knowingly as they taste the *grand cru* on offer. Odile welcomes me to join them. I quietly ask if there is a fee and am assured that as a guest of the Lallement family, I am free to enjoy the work of their hands. I set down my journal and take up a flute which is promptly filled with bubbly. I sip, swirl and nod, but far less knowingly than the others. It *is* ever-so-good, even if I can't name the various flavors and tonalities that are enlivening my taste-buds. Wouldn't you know, it would be monks who would invent and perfect such a worldly delight as this! I say *goede namiddag*, good afternoon, to the folks beside me, but being considerate Flemish, they catch my accent and respond in perfect English. We chat even as I take another flute of a different variety of the Lallement produce. And another. Once I feel my head beginning to buzz, I excuse myself, take up my journal, and head out into the street to find a quiet, shady place in which to write.

I walk out of town to the edge of a vineyard that drops from the town's ridge to the broad valley below. I take a seat in the high grass, leaning against the wall of a once-great champagne warehouse, now seemingly abandoned. The vineyards of the Lallement family, my hosts for the night, and so many others stretch out almost from my feet, intersected in the distance by two highways running north–south and one railway line. The automobiles on both highways race by at what seems to me to be lightning speed. I hear a swelling swoosh; from the south a bullet train whizzes into view on the tracks, knives through the landscape in a matter of moments, then disappears with a whoosh. It has just covered in a few seconds what has taken me hours to walk. That very fast train reminds me that, as a pilgrim, travel for me is made holy in its slowness. I see things that neither the passengers of the train nor the drivers of the automobiles see. I feel things they will never feel. I have time to ponder, imagine, daydream. I tire. I thirst. In my slow walking, I find me.

Later, I locate a restaurant for dinner. The menu outside seems reasonable, but I am worried by the linen on the tables and delicate candles burning at the center of each. I take a seat and am handed the real menu. Oh dear. This is not going to be a night of cheap eats, but I ate tuna and a stale croissant for lunch, so maybe I deserve a little extra tonight.

The worry about the coming hit to my pocketbook is made less so by the guests at the table next to my own: they are an English-speaking family, the parents attentive, the children polite and well behaved. The mother has an American accent; the father sports the British original. It takes a while for us to begin chatting, but eventually we engage. They have heard about people like me and are delighted to encounter a pilgrim and a priest, She is Foursquare Protestant; he grew up Catholic but now goes to church with wife and family. The children want to know all kinds of details of my walk. I tell them about where I sleep and how much my pack weighs and that he has a name, Gregory, named after a pope. All four are entertained by all this. Then this happens: as we take our leave on the front stoop of our expensive restaurant, they promise to pray for me. I am touched almost to tears because they remind me of how prayer unites us all and just how many people around the world I am united to right now because they are praying for me as I make this pilgrimage. I promise to pray for them as well.

I sleep well, and after a simple but substantial *petit dejeuner* served by Madame Lallement, I am on my way: a thirty-kilometer hike into the next big city of the Chemin, Châlons-en-Champagne. My route is mostly pavement. The sky remains blue. A fresh breeze cools me as I continue wandering southward through the vineyards.

About noon, I enter the small town of Vraux. I am feeling now the growing heat of the day and would like to rest, or maybe even call it a day. I find the village church, an eleventh or twelfth century building; it is open but completely unattended. No poster near the door announces Mass times or the name and phone number of the local *abbé*. I come out of its cool interior and into the small churchyard. A lady tending the garden next door calls to me, *"Monsieur! Monsieur Pèlerin!"* She welcomes me into her garden. I ask about a priest, and she informs me that he lives in the next town, Juvigny, about three kilometers further along the highway. She invites me to sit in the shade of a leafy tree and brings me a glass of cold fruit juice. *Madame* Pauzie seems just thrilled to be able to welcome a pilgrim to her home and serve me as if I were a visiting angel. She tells me she welcomes many pilgrims this way, a few each week. Her husband comes through the gate and joins us. Bernard speaks some English from his years working as a flight engineer for Air France. He has been fishing, but leaving his equipment to one side, he joins us at the plastic table and delights in conversing with me, some English, some French. They show intense interest in where I have come from and what I do in life when not walking across France. She asks if I have a place to spend the night; would I like to stay the night with the parish priest? She offers to phone him right then and there and with a single call, makes all the arrangements with the *abbé* in Juvigny. I feel a little guilty not continuing all the way onto Châlons, but I am not a bullet train, and I am in no great hurry.

It continues to surprise me that this far from Compostela so many people like *Monsieur* and *Madame* Pauzie recognize us pilgrims and cheer us on. The pilgrimage of Saint-Jacques is a living thing here with all manner of people caring for us along our way, handing us along from one to the other. It is almost as if we are their surrogates; since they themselves are too old or have too much work to do, or for whatever reason, cannot leave home and family behind, they find in us the part of themselves that would love the pilgrim life. And if this be true, then is it not just possible that the faith that was at the foundation of the movement of pilgrims to the far reaches of Galicia of former times is not so dead in Europe as some presume, as I have too often presumed? A thought arises: For all our self-declared religiosity in America, I wonder how many of my fellow countrymen would, like *Madame* Pauzie, be so completely ready with a glass of fruit juice for whatever pilgrim might wander past her garden. If faith is best manifested in care, then I suspect that Europeans have more faith than they sometimes pretend not to have and Americans, for lack of ancient roads and pilgrims to walk them, may have somewhat less faith than we broadcast to others.

I make my farewells to the Pauzies and take on the final few kilometers of the day. I follow the plain-Jane highway to Juvinet, struggling a bit as the afternoon has become quite hot. The parish house is supposed to be along the main street, a few doors down from the church, left side, so I begin tracking house numbers, a difficult procedure in rural France where a numbering logic other than consecutivity seems to operate.

I come upon the house number given me by *Madame* Pauzie painted on a nondescript *façade* fronting the main street. I ring the bell, wait, ring again. Finally, the door is opened by a woman well into her sixties who politely invites me in, announcing as she does, as if to preclude any possibility of misunderstanding or scandal, that she is the niece of the *Abbé* Bouchet, and serves as well as his caretaker and cook. *Madame* Monique shows me to my room, invites me to leave Gregory there and join the *abbé* in the garden. Would I like a glass of water? Do I need something stronger to drink? Have I had lunch? Might she warm something up for me? I am peppered with the essentials of formal French country hospitality by the *abbé's* niece, and it is a pleasant peppering for indeed I am thirsty and hungry and looking forward to visiting with the local clergy.

I am led back downstairs and into the expansive garden, where the *pèlerin* is presented to the *abbé* and his assistant priest, the *curé*. They warmly invite me to take a seat at the garden table with them as they sip a spot of brandy, their own noon meal presently coming to its completion in a most civilized manner. The *abbé* is at least an octogenarian; the *curé* perhaps in his late sixties. Immediately, they further pepper me with questions of a different sort: From where have I come? How goes the pilgrimage thus far? How do I find France? What is the state of *l'église en Amérique*? I answer dutifully, as best I am able. Meanwhile, the niece returns with a plate loaded with warm pork, fresh green beans, and fried spuds. A bottle of red wine and a carafe of water follow, accompanied by a small basket of *baguette* slices. Then another glass filled with cider is placed before me. And finally, a plate of cheese slices of various colors and smells is offered to *le pèlerin*. "A little brandy, *mon père*?" Church-talk among priests is not so different from culture to culture, so the chatting that extends well past the meal covers a broad range of ecclesiastical topics. They inform me that in their own diocese, there has not been a single ordination to the priesthood in over ten years, and there is no prospect for improvement on the horizon since the diocese has not a single man in seminary training. What will the bishops do about this *crise*? The younger shrugs his shoulders, purses his lips, sends a puff of air through them, then piously folds his hands and bows his head as if to pray.

As if to pray. Implicit in the priest's response is the presupposition that the French bishops and their church with them no longer have any program, any direction, any great answer. They are left with shrugged shoulders, pursed lips, and their prayers. The church as they have known it is in its last days, taking its final breaths. I feel great sympathy for these men as they watch their church seemingly die, but the sense of plight that so fills this garden now also impels me, perhaps too much the optimistic American, to wonder again about the meaning of the trickle of pilgrims wandering through these villages southward, ever southward. Are we just ants on a single-file march to nowhere? Are we just doing this for our own satisfaction, or is there something else happening here that may be going unnoticed? Could we pilgrims and "the great cloud of witnesses" that encourage us as we walk not be something like small blades of green grass breaking through the concrete pavement of this most recent round of secularization? Are our footsteps not a kind of tapping at the tomb from within? Could it not be that this tapping and clicking and clacking and grumbling and stumbling and *courage*-ing and praying that we are doing out here, in itself so small and insignificant, when combined with that of numberless others, may be the gentle force that pushes back the great stone of ecclesial death? And so I walk. And so I too, with those bishops of France, pray. I join the younger priest for his Saturday evening Mass in the church next door. There are few people with us, but those few are devout and serious about this praying business, and so we pray and together tap at the tomb from within.

Later in the evening, I study the GR guidebook and my GPS screen. For the first time, I become conscious of what has been going on since the beginning: looking at these cold, geographically accurate maps in advance of a day's or week's walk, sucks *courage* out of me. Their representations on paper or via LCD screen are lifeless, their roadways and trails and place-names just lines and dots. They tell me the future in a way, but make it seem unachievable, the more so the further out I look. The actual walking, however, is quite different. It is adventure and discovery and encounter; it is all living. Sky and field, faces and smiles, twists and turns, rises and falls, these are the real world, my world. It is lovely to have them unfold each day, to *regard* them, to remember them with gratitude. I should look less at maps and consider less the future they portray and worry less about tomorrow and its many "might be's" and just revel in the present unfolding grace and trust that it is a grace that is quietly expanding and deepening so that tomorrow, I can trust, will somehow be well.

Madame Monique has prepared an ample breakfast for us and rushes back and forth to the kitchen talking non-stop. Her uncle appears weary under the verbal onslaught; for my part I am so distracted by her mostly unintelligible chatter that I pour milk into my orange juice instead of my coffee. No one says anything, but I feel like I have just farted in church.

Once out the door and freed from niece-chatter, I am delivered into a perfect pilgrim day. The sun is already shining brightly as I leave the Juvinet parish house. The air is fresh and warming quickly. It is about a twelve-kilometer walk into Châlons, one that is without great hills or valleys. I follow the GR and feel fine as I walk these first morning hours. By the time I arrive in Châlons well before midday, I am not even close to being ready to quit. The GR leads me into the town center where the *boulangeries* are wide open for their Sunday morning trade. I squeeze myself and Gregory into a tiny one, turning sideways to avoid knocking over a display of pastries, and order the daily take-out special for an early lunch; a chicken sandwich, a raisin pastry and can of apple juice, all for only four euros. I find a bench outside and eat my lunch, saving half the sandwich for later, watching the distinguished Sunday strollers and occasional gaggle of scruffy teen skate-boarders pass by.

I continue along the GR through a tony neighborhood oddly named "Madagascar", grand homes to the left, a deep canal to the right. In a lovely park, I spot a post marked with the pilgrim shell logo and the message: "*Compostelle: 2300 kms.*" The GR path leaves the canal and wanders off into level fields, but not before leading me into what must be the only mud between Reims and Vézelay. What is it with this Grande Randonnée, anyway? Is there not enough mud in life that it must intentionally seek it out and zig or zag me into its gloppy depths? I plod my way through the stuff, and then after fifty meters or so am free again as I continue through the bright countryside, now more wheat-laden than vine-laced. A lone jogger overtakes me, then stops to greet me. I respond to his *salut* with my cheeriest *bonjour* and as soon as he detects my accent, he continues in English, and we walk together for a while. Éric asks how far I have come, where I will spend the night, and when I expect to arrive in Compostelle, a place he knows well. With his curiosity sated, he salutes me again: *Bon courage, Kevin!* and off Éric jogs. It was so kind that he stopped his life and walked in mine for a while. A little communion was just shared here. I sort of miss him. I hope that in my post-pilgrim life, I do that for others once in a while: just stop my life and walk with them in theirs for a while.

A breeze cools me as I amble on towards the next town along this grand Chemin southward: Saint-Germaine-la-Ville. As I wander into its squared web of blocks and buildings at mid-Sunday-afternoon, there is no discernible life in the place. I head for what seems to be the town center but find little in the way of a town center. There is no *place* in this place, just a crisscross of hot and hollow streets. An old man in a small pickup comes my way, so I hail him down; he pulls up to me and listens attentively as I ask him if there might be a hotel in the village. He gives me directions: keep straight, then take a left, but which of several possible lefts to take remains vague in my mind. I ask, since it's Sunday, if there is a priest living here, but he has no idea, evidently not much of a churchgoer himself. I trundle forward, then spot a plump lady on a bicycle, so hail her as well and ask about a hotel. Her directions are more precise: take the left right here, there is a hotel further on and a *gite* beyond that. Take your pick. I shoot for the *gite*, bypassing the darkened restaurant windows of the hotel. I see the typical Gites de France insignia on a farmhouse gate and enter only to be welcomed by very large, very loud, and seemingly very aggressive dogs. *Oh great! That's all I need today: a big bad dog bite.* I'm not sure where to go, but I do my best to keep my movements nonthreatening. Just in case, I hold both Click and Clack at the ready. I am saved by a young woman who has heard the canine ruckus and comes to my aid from within the family home. She calls the beasts to herself, and at her command, they become overgrown puppies, wagging their tales and playfully bounding towards her. We exchange smiles and waves and so I ask her for a room, and she responds with a heartening, *bon!* She explains that I am really in luck; just minutes ago a customer canceled his reservation, so she has just that one room free; it's mine if I want it. Of course, I want it. How could I not want it after a twenty-six kilometer day! My hostess asks if I'd like dinner tonight with her other guests, and I readily agree; the twelve euro surcharge is a worthy expense in a town with almost no one stirring on a warm Sunday afternoon. I am shown to a cheery room decorated in the bright yellow wallpaper that seems to be all the rage in France's rural hospitality industry these days. I wash, rest, and notice something new: a tightness in the tendon running from the top of my foot up the front of my leg. I repeat my earlier words in this new context: *Oh great. This is all I need: a case of tendonitis.* I pop several ibuprofen tablets, run my legs and feet through a generous round of stretches, and hope that it just goes away. After a snack and a rest, I wander down the block to the local church, but it is closed up tighter than a drum. I return to my room, pull up a chair, and set up the small desk for a personal Mass. A little wine, a little bread, the Word, and nothing else in the world to do and nowhere else to go. Perfect.

The first reading for this Sunday's liturgy is the story of Abraham's encounter with the three visitors at Mamre.[1] It was a hot afternoon in Mamre, like this one. Abraham rushes out to tend to three passersby, perhaps pilgrims like myself. He offers to wash their feet, give them something to drink, and feed them. He not only gives them bread, but enlists his wife, Sarah, and his servants to kill a calf for the strangers, an extravagant gesture. And he offers them not just water, but milk and curds as well, also an act of hospitality beyond the social norm. Though Abraham asks for nothing in return, it turns out the three visitors are angels from God, and in return for the gift of his hospitality, he and his wife are blessed with the gift of a child in the womb of Sarah, his long-barren wife.

The reading gets to me. I sink into this story, and in finding within its layers so many echoes of my own pilgrim experience these past weeks, my eyes well just a bit. I look back down my road: how many Abrahams and Sarahs have hailed me, greeted me, encouraged me, fed me, given me to drink, and offered me a bed for the night? They are now almost countless. I review some of their faces, seeing again their smiles, hearing again their words, tasting again the delicacies they have set before me. May each of them be blessed for their goodness and have whatever emptiness in their life filled as was the womb of old Sarah! I break the bread and take the cup and remember and give thanks.

1. Genesis 18

Clouds are building as I join the other guests for a glass of local beer and a few *hors d'oeuvres* in the garden. The others are a *mélange* of Dutch and Flemish tourists including a couple from my own Leuven. We are all welcomed into the rustic dining room of the guesthouse for a four-course country dinner with all the wine we can imbibe poured for us by our own Abraham and Sarah. As the evening gently grows into night, I cannot but feel: here I find myself in my own little Mamre.

I awake to the sound of rain on the roof; that is not good. I listen attentively, but I hear no thunder. That is good. I prepare for the day, and after a breakfast shared with the couple from Leuven, I wrap Gregory in his rain gear and me in mine, and head into the drizzle of the new day. On my way out the gate, my host warns me that lightning is being forecast for later in the afternoon, and she advises me to be careful. The maps show a number of villages on the road ahead, so if things get too wild and woolly, I should be able to duck into a safe place along the way.

I make my damp way to the town of Saint-Amand, walking the twenty kilometers through recently harvested fields of wheat, now all mud and stubble. On these rainy days, I can smell the mud, and its earthy richness has a beauty to it. It is a particular smell that has grown so familiar to me that I feel like I *know* this mud, the way I might know an old grandfather by the stale odor of his pipe. When I arrive, it is almost 1:00 pm, so I tuck into a small convenience store and purchase the makings of a substantial sandwich, then consume half the thing outside under the store's dripping awning. I decide to push on to Vitry-le-François, which will make this a thirty-kilometer day when all is walked and done.

As I leave Saint-Amand, I pass by the village church but before trying the *port*, walk over to the once-stately parish house next door. It seems altogether abandoned, shutters closed and largely unpainted, tall weeds filling its once manicured gardens. This house feels familiar, but I can't quite place it. I have a *déjà vu* sense about it that piques at my curiosity. I take a second look, but still cannot call to mind where I might have seen it before. I set my curiosity about the house aside and amble back to the church. I try the door set in an ancient Romanesque arch and surprisingly, it gives way easily. The nave is pure Roman, but the transept and apse are as Gothic as Gothic can get in a small town, their flamboyance contrasting sharply with the heavy sobriety of the nave. I don't stay long within, just enough to breathe in some of its stale air; it too smells, but of damp stone and old wood. The bad breath of God. Heavenly halitosis or not, respects must be paid, so with Gregory on my back, I make a clumsy bow, say a Glory Be, make the Sign of the Cross, and return to the grey day outside.

As I step out from the church's porch, I get another view of the parish house. *That's it!* It suddenly dawns on me where I have seen this *maison* before: it seems to me to be a double for the tubercular young priest's rectory in the film from the 1950's, *Diary of a Country Priest*. It has the same look, the same feel, the same grim desolation about it. In this overcast and rainy weather, it even has the same *black and whiteness* about it. The two might as well *be* the same house. The memory of that house, that priest, calls up in me the great line of the film: "*Tout est grâce,*" the priest says in a moment of lovely clarity before his fairly miserable death. *All is grace.* After all his other miseries, some self-imposed, and others offered to him by his difficult parishioners, that simple exclamation is a miracle, and I love that he could say it and hope that I can say it when I stare death in the face. *All is grace!* I repeat it over and over as I walk away from both house and church: *Tout est grâce! Tout est grâce! All is grace . . . !*

My awareness of grace is tested even as I rejoin the GR 654 and head out of Saint-Amand; the rain intensifies, coming down in heavy drops, then in sheets. My gear does not protect me against this kind of downpour, so I am getting soaked to the bone very quickly. On I trudge. I notice a pain in the calf of my left leg; it's getting worse as I carry on. It is the same leg in which I felt the tight tendon yesterday, but this is different, this is not just ache, this is the beginning of pain. But this is what is important here: instead of exclaiming, *tout est grâce*, I am whimpering to myself: *what the hell am I doing out here?*

Something of an answer soon comes my way; I find myself in the midst of harvested sugar-beet fields, the dank smell of rotting vegetation filling the air. The clouds lighten for a moment, and then there is a break altogether with a stream of sunlight angling down to the earth in the distance. I behold and gaze, then spin about and take a 360° look at the world surrounding me: hills and fields and low clouds and one luscious slice of sunlight cutting through the whole. It is a miracle of a view! No, it is so much more than that: it is a miracle of a world and a miracle that I am alive within it *right here* and *right now*! *Tout est grâce*, indeed!

I continue through the beet fields for a few more kilometers, then abandon the GR and choose a more direct road to the village of Vitry-en-Perthois. From there, I take up my chosen route on to Vitry-le-François, a highway that will save me a few precious kilometers at the end of a rainy day. I almost immediately realize I have made a major miscalculation. This highway is not my usual "D-something" back road; it is a major route filled with rushing automobiles, swooshing sixteen-wheelers, impossibly thin shoulders, and enough water rolling off the pavement to make the tire of every passing vehicle a shower-maker for this humble pilgrim sloshing his way along. I double-check my map and GPS; I have no options. I have to brave this test of my courage and endurance. As always, I take the left hand shoulder so I can track the oncoming traffic; I watch every approaching vehicle to make sure it is giving me the room I need to stay alive. It is, nevertheless, plenty ugly out here. I can feel the wind coming off the roaring trucks and slapping me in the face. I am really quite afraid. I stop and turn my face down and away when I am sure I am going to be splashed mercilessly. *Crimeny! How did I get myself into this?* The highway never ends. Vitry-le-François never gets any closer. Industrial developments spring up, making the scene uglier still; the rain has made the lenses of my glasses almost opaque. Once again, *tout est grâce* utterly fails me. *This isn't* grâce *out here; this is pure* merde!

Finally, I come to some kind of intersection that looks like the beginnings of a city. Streets fly off in various directions, but I can't tell which one I should take to find the city center. I look and walk about from one corner to another, then spot the square steeples of a church; it must be the cathedral, it must be the center! I head off in that direction as best as I can approximate it, but do not find the church so quickly. I can hear the water in my boots sloshing about; my wool socks have become sponges. I take a turn to the right, then a left and find the apse of the cathedral, walk around to its main portal a block further on, and enter. A man is standing at an information booth within so I approach; he smiles, and I ask about lodging with the parish priests. "*Je suis désolé*," he answers. Those dreaded words. "You can't stay with the priests, but there is a convent of Polish nuns a few blocks away that will take you in." I object, *mais je suis prêtre aussi!* But I'm a priest, also! He shrugs his shoulders, purses his lips and puffs in the Gallic manner. *Je suis désolé . . . mon père*, he adds respectfully. He does give me the address of the priests' house, assuring me I won't be welcome there. I wander to find the place; I am sure that if I just present myself they will take me in. I ring the bell. I wait. I am welcomed into the front office. As prophesied, I am refused refuge. I sullenly accept the secretary's offer to stamp my *credencial*, then I wander out to find the convent of Polish nuns. I fume as I go.

I find the convent, the Maison de Doyenne, ring the bell, and am welcomed by a sister with such warmth and kindness that all my anger and disgust dissipates immediately; her smile works the miracle. She leads me to a bedroom set aside for pilgrims, not minding the trail of puddles I am leaving behind me with every step. The room is simple but sufficient. I thank her, close the door, unhitch Gregory, pull off my boots and socks, pour the dirty brown water from within into the sink, ditch the rest of my clothes, and lay myself down on the bed and close my eyes, naked and wet and listening to the roll of thunder.

Later, I notice that the rain has lightened up to not much more than a mist. I clean up, dress, and wander out into the city to look for my next meal. I pass again the massive church; it is of classical design but dowdy and showing signs of bullets and bombs having pocked and scarred her stonework. It looks like a great ship having run aground in this landlocked *place*. Above the main portal, the "I" of the "IHS" insignia has fallen away, making the Latin monogram for Jesus' name meaningless. Somebody should fix that.

I enter this ship of a church and wander about, meeting a young father with two young sons, perhaps six or seven years of age. One boy does not genuflect as he crosses the central axis of the church, as is the Catholic custom. His father gently calls him back, inviting him to make the gesture, which the boy happily and reverentially does for his father. It is lovely, and it makes me smile because the little boy is so happy to have bowed before God. It is a sublime testimony at the end of this wet day to, what else, the great lesson of that fictional country priest: *tout est grâce*.

Night follows. Then day. Even as I awake, I know that this cannot be a walking day. The thirty kilometers in the rain yesterday and the twenty-six kilometers the day before have left me without spirit or will. I will rest and rebuild today. While taking a light breakfast, Gene and Caroline ring me on my cell phone just to chat and see how I am faring. They are happy I am taking a day-off. Caroline tells me that she has been keeping a candle lit for me in front of the old statue of Saint James in Leuven, even after all these days.

The day-off passes lazily, then following a restless night of sleep, I awake and begin a new day, a special day: this twenty-fifth day of July is the Feast of the Apostle, Saint James the Greater: Jacobus, a Son of Thunder, my Saint-Jacques, my Santiago, my Sint-Jakob, my pilgrim patron of the Way.

All of nature celebrates the feast of Jacques by giving me a clear sky and the promise of a walk free of rain or thunder. I leave a twenty euro note for the sisters of the Maison de Doyenne and find a *boulangerie* down the street where I purchase my breakfast: the raisin and cream roll that I have come to love. I am on my way out of the city before 8:00 am. After the disagreeable experience on the highway *into* Vitry-le-François, I choose to follow the GR 654 *out* of Vitry-le-François. The GR is, as always, a frustrating choice. Its zigzagging ways have not been reformed. It is a route designed for Eco-tourists interested in gazing across grand vistas, and trekkers wanting great physical challenges, not pilgrims who just want to get to the next church. But today, this pilgrim feast-day, this Grande Randonnée is treating me to a bounty of beauty. I am led away from open fields and crawling vineyards into dreamy deep woods where light is dappled and diffused, and every big and little thing is softened by a million shades of green and brown.

I leave the woods and drop down into a village, the name of which I do not notice. A matronly woman is at work in her barn, across a sloping lawn, located a fair distance from the road along which I now pass. She sees me walking by, drops her tools and comes running, *comes running*, across the lawn to me. She could be my grandma, plump and jiggling as she hails me like a long lost grandson, or better: like her long lost *prodigal* grandson. Arriving at the low fence separating the road from her place, she is huffing and puffing, wipes a bit of sweat from her brow, and happily commences the now standard pilgrim conversation with the question, *"À Compostelle?"* If I read her smiles and twinkling eyes and waving hands correctly, she would like to join me on the way, but age and life circumstances prevent that, so I am her surrogate pilgrim. Her final *bon courages* are effusive as she waves me down the road.

On this feast of Saint James, I walk with the other pilgrims out on this Chemin in mind. Though I never see them, not since Herman and I went our separate ways weeks ago, I know these unknown pilgrim brothers and sisters, though not many, are ahead of me and behind me. Though I do not see them, I hear of them. Those who greet me tell me others are passing by too: a few every week, one or two every three or four days. I imagine we, together, are like the billions of water droplets of yesterday's rain, each plunging with a plunk into a million tiny streams tumbling ever forward into thousands of creeks, the water of those creeks plunging incessantly into hundreds of wide rivers, the water of those rivers finally spilling into the one great sea. We are doing this together. *"Les Jacquaires,"* the medieval French called their pilgrims. I am proud to be counted in these times among those *Jacquaires* of old and those with whom I walk today.

In far away Santiago de Compostela, there are certainly grand celebrations already taking place. I can almost see the crowds spilling out from the cathedral's *Puerta de Gloria,* down its baroque steps and into the sunny *Plaza de Obradoiro.* This river of pilgrims in their thousands and hundreds of thousands from the villages of Galicia, from across Spain, from France and Germany and Belgium and even Norway and Russia, they each take their moment behind the great statue of *Jacobus* above the main altar, to give him their *abrazo*, their pilgrim embrace. What is so intense there today, here in northern France is much more diffuse, like light in a wood. Diffuse though it may be, the light of Compostela here nevertheless lifts me: This road is not just a road; it is a *via* between the earth and the heavens, dust and stars, flesh and spirit. I am on something here that is of cosmological significance. This Chemin is one small lace among many tying together the starry way of God and the muddy way of humanity.

The day's walk ends in another ghostly village, that of Saint-Remy Bouzement. At this midday hour, the main street is mostly deserted. I go to the *mairie*, or city hall, but it is closed. I walk a bit further and notice a *chambre d'hôte* insignia on the wide gate of a farmyard. I knock, hear rustling inside, and have the gate opened by a husky woman in a sundress who introduces herself to me as Silvie. I ask for a room but am given the always distressing answer: *complet*. She informs me that I should not worry, for the town has a municipal refuge for pilgrims where I will surely find a bed for the night. Silvie then invites me to join her for the *table d'hôte* that she will be preparing for her guests later in the evening. I accept the invitation. She calls her husband, and he leads me to the refuge, unlocking its door and showing me around. It's not much, but it's home. I am hungry, but the small grocery store is closed until later in the afternoon, so I am reduced to retrieving a tin of tuna from one of Gregory's pockets, and making that my midday repast.

I while away the afternoon, notice that new, heavier clouds are developing, then at 7:30 pm amble down to the hefty lady's *chambre d'hôte* for my dinner. I am welcomed into the open area between the half-timbered farmhouse and the barn and invited to sit at a long table set for the occasion. I am joined by a cheery group of young Flemish students who have been kayaking all day.

The *pièce de résistance* of the meal is a strange one: a large squash baked with a dollop of spicy ground beef in the center. The Flemish kids are amused, while I am a bit disappointed. Actually, the *plat du jour* tastes just fine and is a healthy meal all in all. After friendly *bon nuits* and *goede nachts*, I prepare to return to my refuge; I ask Silvie about my bill for the meal, but she shrugs off the request and whispers so the others won't hear: "For the pilgrim, *rien,* nothing. *You* are blessing *us!*" I find my eyes well just a bit, express my gratitude as best I am able, and truly *feel* like a pilgrim as this feast of Saint-Jacques comes to an end over the remains of a humble baked squash.

The day after the feast of Saint-Jacques opens like every other day along this long way except that I skip breakfast on the presumption that I will soon be able to pick something up along the way.

At ten kilometers, I walk into Outines, which offers the wandering pilgrim a fine example of a church made in the *pan de bois,* half-timber, style, but to my disappointment, has nothing to offer me in the way of *pain au raisin.* There is no bar, no *boulangerie*, no store. I am left to snack on the nuts and dried fruit still in my pack. It is going to be a long and hungry walk on to the next town, Bailly-le-Franc. An hour more and Bailly, like Outines, has nothing to offer but another fine *pan de bois* church. *I can't eat pan de bois, people!* This is now getting serious. I consult my GR guide book: Lentilles, the *next* town on the route, is similarly lacking in all fundamental human services, though I imagine it too has a fine *pan de bois* church. I decide to change course: I will jog to the west and head instead for the town of Chavanges, which boasts at least some services for the visiting trekker. This means an additional couple hours of walking on a bare minimum of sustenance. It is either go on or slowly fold from hunger, so I choose to go on.

I land in Chavanges a few minutes before 1:00 pm. I follow the main street towards the *centre-ville*, keeping to the small sidewalk on the left side. I have no idea where I will stay tonight, and this always sets up an unpleasant fretting inside my mind. A number of houses look abandoned. There is little traffic. This place does not look promising. As I pass an undistinguished house just to the left of my shoulder, I notice a piece of paper tacked to the door. For no particular reason, I stop to take a look. I can hardly believe my eyes: as if in answer to my fretting prayers, it welcomes me: "*Cher Pèlerin*: This house is yours! Get the key from the neighbor and here rest and restore yourself as the guest of the parish priest."

I find the LaBlonde home a few doors down, ring the bell, and the *monsieur* who greets me is delighted to have a pilgrim to tend to. He grabs the key, leads me back to the refuge, and shows me in. After a brief tour of the facilities, he leaves me to myself. It is the former parish house, old and worn, now used for small church gatherings and an occasional service, from the looks of it. An ample kitchen is well-supplied with utensils and other pilgrims' left-overs. A small graveled garden off the kitchen is surrounded by a high block wall. A bedroom upstairs boasts two lumpy and musty beds. There is a toilet but no shower or bath. I eat what I have: one last can of tuna. I dig out of Gregory's guts a fresh set of clothes then retire to the garden to take my bath out of doors, naked as a jaybird, protected from prying eyes by the concrete wall. I pour water over my body with a bucket, soap up, then throw more water over my head to rinse. The combination of cold water, fresh air, and blue sky above invigorates me.

Later, I wander up to the village church; I am particularly attracted by the fiery stonework of the Gothic building, seemingly out of place in this small village, making its stone flourishes all the more delightful. The side door is open; a man is within busy varnishing the stone floor. He is proud to show the church off to me, pointing to its grand sixteenth century stained glass and its twelfth century Romanesque portico. On the way home, I find a small grocery store and purchase what I will need for supper tonight, as well as breakfast and walking food for tomorrow. The can of ravioli in tomato sauce that I purchase is way too big for one meal, but it is the only thing that looks remotely appetizing on the thin shelves of this village store. Bread, fruit, and a replacement can of tuna round out my purchases. I return home to my refuge so that here, I might rest and be restored, as the note tacked to the door commends.

I enjoy a fair portion of my ravioli, then sit in the garden to pray the psalms of Vespers and write in my journal. Evening comes on, and something wonderful happens in the bushy tree that partially shades my small garden. A flock of sparrows has settled into its branches. For a while they flutter about, playing with one another, some taking flight, others following, then returning and finding their places again. Little by little, they calm down. Peeps abound. A flutter here and a flutter there. Fewer peeps. Silence. Peep-peep-peep. Flutter. Silence again. Peep-peep. A momentary flutter. Silence. Peep. Silence, silence, silence . . . It so reminds me of our family of eleven at bedtime. Commotion, joke, laughter, a bit of story, slug, raucous laughter, then my dad yelling up the stairwell: "You birds, get to sleep up there!" Silence . . . then a slug, ouch, laughter . . . Then dad again: "If I hear another peep out of you birds, I'm coming up!" Silence, silence, *peep*, laughter under the blankets, more threats from below, silence, silence, sleep . . . I sternly speak to the sparrows: *If I hear another peep out of you birds, I'm coming up!* I laugh to myself at the sound of my voice sounding too much like that of my old man.

Now to bed: I pass on the musty beds upstairs, throwing instead a foam mattress I have spotted in a back room onto the floor of the small meeting room *cum* chapel. Unlike the sparrows outside, I cannot settle down but yet again toss and turn most of the night.

Days of walking through France's Aube pass; I am handed off from one church steeple to another, guided as well by the hourly peal of ancient bells. I meet no other pilgrims and walk day in and day out almost completely alone. I spend one night in the sizable town of Brienne-le-Chateau, then another in Amance; I pass through rain-soaked La Loge-aux-Chévres and finally on to Courtenot.

There is something I have come to love about walking these French roads, especially when I am far from town or village, in the midst of field or forest, especially at the crossroads; set along the verge or built into a grassy bank, there are small shrines. Crosses of wrought iron, crucifixes of stone, tiny stone chapels with statues of the Virgin or some patron saint stand guard over the Chemin. Each time I come across one, especially the more common crosses and crucifixes, I feel that Jesus has been waiting for me at that spot in the road; there he is: sitting, resting, nibbling on a blade of sweet grass, just patiently watching for me, waiting there for me to pass. As I do, surprisingly, we don't talk. I nod and smile, or if it is a tough day, maybe I wince more than smile. He winks back at me, a slow, silent wink, like that of an old cowboy, lifting just one eyebrow to encourage me on to the next wayside visit. In another kilometer or two, there he is again, waiting, winking, encouraging me down the road. Sometimes I do speak: *Hey, Jesus* . . . I walk on a kilometer or two or five, and there he is, yet again, and that is how the morning goes and how I get from A to B, day in and day out. *Hey, Jesus* . . . Hey, Kev . . .

I take a day-off in Courtenot. A good friend from Brussels, Mimi, has her summer home here and has invited me to make use of the chateau for a day or two. She and an American priest-friend serving the English-speaking church in Waterloo, Vincent, have driven down to greet me as I amble into town. From above the stone wall surrounding the chateau, they both wave and call to me, and then when I enter the garden through the gate, Mimi kisses me on both cheeks and Vincent embraces me. *I walked here! I walked here from Leuven!* "Yes, Kevin, you did walk here indeed," responds Vincent. I join them for a beautiful midday meal in the chateau's country dining room. Mimi must return to Brussels and leaves the place to us for as long as we wish. Vincent and I spend my day away from the Chemin by visiting the nearby city of Troyes, enjoying lunch, and stopping in a number of churches to see the medieval art and architecture that has inspired pilgrims like me for so many centuries. The following morning, I sadly leave my friend behind and pick up the *rue haute* out of the village, turning off to cross the Seine, hardly more than a garden stream here. I then follow the small D-32 through Jully-sur-Sarce and Villemorien towards Aviney-Ligney, about fifteen kilometers from Courtenot. Even as I walk through the patchwork of fields south of Courtenot, I am feeling an uncomfortable tightness in my lower left leg. In Villemorien, I take a rest on the shady lawn of the village church, take off my boots and socks, and go through a routine of stretches to ease the low-level ache. I continue on my way feeling a bit better and walking strongly, so I don't pay much attention to the ache.

By the time I arrive in Aviney-Ligney, I have been walking already for more than three hours, the day is becoming hot, and my frustration level is rising as the needle in the pain-o-meter below is also rising. What had at first been an uncertain stiffness is now getting sharper and more precisely located in the large tendon that runs up the front of the leg from foot to knee. With each new step it announces itself more insistently. It is slowing me down, but not critically so. After a snack, I find some ibuprofen in my medical kit and pop a couple of tablets for safety's sake. I know only too well what tendonitis can do to a pilgrim; I had a bad case of it four years ago while walking the Spanish segment of the Camino, and it took well over a week to shake. It was not pleasant. I do not want to repeat that experience. I sit down in a particularly grassy piece of highway shoulder, take off my boots, and go through my stretching routines once again. Then I pull myself together, take a look at my GPS map, and decide that I can manage another ten kilometers today, no problem.

The final three of those ten kilometers are a tough up-hill pull, followed then by a treacherous final kilometer down into Bragelogne-Beauvoir. As I pick my way down the extremely steep and rocky goat trail, I can feel that my carefully placed steps are aggravating my problem knee and, even worse, the tender tendon. I survive the hike down into the village and hobble into town, keeping an eye open for a place to stay. At the edge of town is a sign indicating that just ahead is a *gite*, so I head for that. I am quite tired now and ready for a quick end to this long day on the road. At the end of the street, I turn left, walk a few meters and am greeted by the *gite* sign again. A wide yard opens before me with a farmhouse to one side, a barn to another, and between them, what must be the *gite*. I limp in, call to a lady moving laundry from machine to clothesline, and am waved in to my home for the night.

My hostess asks if I prefer the *gite* or the *chambre d'hôte*; I ask what the difference is and she explains that the *gite* has a common bath and toilet, two beds per room, but is only ten euros for the night, while the *chambre d'hôte* is more private and exclusive, but goes for forty euros. I opt for the *gite* and am shown the way to my room, almost as good as any *chambre d'hôte* I have yet stayed in. Besides hospitality, the Collin family also specializes in champagne production. I may be close to the southern frontier of Champagne country, but not out of it yet.

I shower and wash and then tend to my tendon. I take a plastic sandwich bag, fill it with ice from the fridge and begin soothing it with the cold-pack. I take more ibuprofen. I stretch. I think I can beat this thing. It is just not that bad. I do not look forward to the healing process since it could take some days, but this is not going to stop me.

While I am sitting at the kitchen table icing my leg, two more pilgrims are shown in. The women are about my age and look as exhausted as I did an hour ago. They are shown to their room upstairs without ado. Later, after their own showers, they come down, and we introduce ourselves and tell our stories. Marie Claire and Mary Anne are from Wallonia, the French-speaking part of Belgium. They began their pilgrimage in Arlon, a small town situated on the Belgian frontier with Luxembourg. They are also sisters. They intend to walk the whole route to Compostelle together. They have had their share of blisters and tendonitis, but they are still walking. These ladies are more aggressive in their daily plans than am I: they are doing thirty-kilometer days quite regularly. I am a bit ashamed to admit that my program runs closer to a twenty-kilometer daily average. They invite me to join them for a spaghetti dinner, and I offer to pick up wine and bread at the local shop to accompany the homey repast. They are concerned about my tendon problem, give me a bit of advice, then show me a pain relieving cream that they've been using to take care of their problems. I write down the product name on a napkin and plan to purchase a tube in the next town big enough to sport a pharmacy. Tomorrow, they plan a thirty-kilometer hike into Tonnerre, the next major city on the route; I reveal my puny plan to do just twelve with the hopes of giving the tendon an easy day. I can afford to go easy tomorrow; after all, I did at least twenty-five today. Besides that, the weather report for tomorrow calls for rain, lightning, and thunder.

The spaghetti dinner is lovely; a woman's touch in the kitchen is something my homemade meals, or far worse, a lowly can of tuna, just cannot match. Following our animated dinner and washing of dishes, I bring with me the ice-pack to my room for one last treatment before bed.

I am awakened in the middle of the night by loud, crackling rolls of thunder. I open my eyes, and the room is illuminated for a second or two by the blue light of sheet lightning crossing the sky. Wind sends curtains flying and fluttering. More rolls of heavy-throated thunder shake the house. This bodes poorly for tomorrow, but what can I do, so I roll to face away from the window and fall back asleep.

I arise before 6:00 am; the storm has passed, though the sky beyond my window remains gloomy. I step out of bed and test the tendon; it seems okay. I tend to my morning chores, then haul Gregory and Click and Clack down the stairway to the kitchen, where Marie Claire and Mary Anne are already set for their departure. We offer one another polite hugs, and after a final round of *bon courage*'s, they step outdoors, while I remain to eat a yogurt and banana. I clean up the kitchen and set out. I am still a little hungry so walk a block back into town to buy myself a croissant at the local *boulangerie*. By the time I am passing the front gate of the *gite*, the tendon is aching again. I consider going back for another night to give it more rest, but think better of it: I've planned for a sub-fifteen kilometer walk today; I can certainly do that, even with an achy tendon. I follow the GR the rest of the way out of town and then climb a rather steep and rocky road uphill, using Click and Clack to take pressure off the left leg as best I can.

After two kilometers, I top the crest of a hill and can see Bragelogne nestled cozily in the valley below. The view tempts me. This leg is hurting pretty bad; I should go back. But if I go back, I will lose the hard kilometers I have already gained and will just have to repeat them tomorrow. No, it is not *that* bad. I should go on. The next village is only four kilometers up the road. I can do this. I support myself against my poles and do my best to give the tendon a standing and booted stretch. I drink to keep it lubricated. I continue walking, but the stretching and the drinking have not helped. This thing is beginning to really hurt, but I can do this. I did this in Spain four years ago and survived. I did not turn around then, I did not quit then, I will not fail this time either.

I carry on down the dirt road through the fields and vineyards and yet more woods, the road softened by last night's rain, giving me newly created puddles and mud to traverse, making things even more difficult. The road turns to graveled pavement and leads me up and down and around, closer and closer to Villiers-le-Bois. The final two or three kilometers are all up-hill and quite steep. My tendon is now really hurting me. I cannot mentally override this. With each step, I cry: *Oh Jesus! Oh Jesus! Oh sweet Jesus, help me!* I no longer believe I can do this; I decide that if a car should come, I will flag it down and ask for help up this hill. No car comes. I keep walking, lifting the leg carefully and setting it down even more carefully, hunched over my poles as I use them to pull me up this hill. A car comes from behind me, but I do not notice it until it is too late; it speeds around me, and I have lost my chance. *Oh Jesus. Oh Jesus. Oh sweet Jesus.* I am now almost in tears. *What an idgit am I! I should not have walked today. Why didn't I turn around when I had the chance? Your hubris, you ass, has gotten the best of you this time. Oh Jesus. Oh Jesus. Oh Jesus.* Villiers-le-Bois is now visible ahead and above me, but I feel no progress is being made. All I can feel is the sharp pain fully possessing my lower leg. Maybe there is a *gite* or *chambre d'hôte* up there; if so, I will go no further. If not, I will look for a ride to Tonnerre. *I cannot do this. I cannot do this.* The thought of it makes me wince, and I find myself crying. *Oh Jesus.*

I finally struggle into the village to find it almost abandoned like so many of these provincial towns. I come across a man in his garage at work and ask him if there is a place to stay here. He waves me up the street, telling me that there is a *chambre d'hôte* just ahead. I find the place, but its shutters and gate and front door are closed, and the place looks utterly uninhabited. I knock. Silence. I knock again. I hear a voice: *Bonjour, monsieur.* Can I help you? A man is sticking his head out of a window above me. I say yes, I am a pilgrim and not doing well. I need some help. He switches to perfect British English and tells me he will be down in a moment. *My savior.* He opens the door but has bad news for me as we face each other across the threshold. The place is closed today, and he and his family are on their way to Troyes for a much-needed day-off from the demands of hospitality. He is very sorry for me, but assures me I can find a place to stay in the next village and that surely I will be able to hitch a ride to the town once I'm back on the highway. With my luck today, I am not so sure, but what can I do? I cannot *force* myself into his living room. He sadly closes the door on me, and instead of crossing that threshold to relief and healing, I limp back to the highway to Tonnerre. *Oh Jesus.*

As I mount a rise just outside the village, a car does approach and even stops at a grassy area to the side of the road. I think I am in luck. My prayers have been answered. This guy is going to help me! I approach the vehicle and ask for a lift into Etourvy or Tonnerre. He tells me that he is not going to either place, or *any* place; he has just driven up here to get a signal for his damn mobile phone. I apologize for interrupting him, and continue limping down the highway. It is six more kilometers to Etourvy, as many as I've already walked. *I cannot do this.* But there are no options here; I just have to keep going until I can hitch a ride. No cars pass. This highway is deserted; ordinarily that is something I would relish, but not this day. *Come on, someone! Come on!* Finally, a black Volvo approaches from behind, and I attempt to flag it down. It bears British plates, so I am sure I am in luck, but it passes me by with a whoosh that feels like a condemnation to death. *Oh Jesus.*

I keep walking. The pain eases a while then returns worse than before. The kilometers to Etourvy pass slowly under my feet. I do not see the sky or the trees or the green fields around me. I am blind to all that is beautiful and gracious and lovely; this is what pain does to us. I have been so free of misery so much of my life; may this present scourge teach me compassion. *Oh Jesus, teach me. Oh Jesus, open my eyes. Oh Jesus, a little further, please.* I grab hold of a few lines from John Henry Newman: *Lead thou me on. Lead thou me on amidst the encircling gloom. Lead thou me on. One step enough for me. Lead thou me on.*

I am led on, my ribbon of pained pavement circling around a steep hill and finally leading me down into Etourvy. A sign advertising a *gite* greets me as I hobble into the village proper. I ask directions to the *gite* and find the place easily, situated amidst shady trees and near a fresh and clear brook. Its grounds and buildings are large and spacious. I am sure that I have now, at long last, found the end of this awful day's journey.

I find some women cleaning within one of the buildings. I ask for assistance and they, in turn, direct me to another woman in the next room, Laurène. She is the boss of the *gite* and immediately comes forward to greet me as I approach her. I let her know of my need for a place for the night and of my leg problems. Laurène is the very picture of compassion and sympathy for my predicament and assures me that, though there is a large group of cyclists coming in this afternoon that will fill the place, there will certainly be a bed for me, too. She makes a call from her mobile phone to whoever manages beds, and after some discussion in French, her side of which, I cannot understand, she hangs up with the bad news that her manager says there will be no bed after all. Even floor space will be completely occupied by the cyclists. I am decimated and cannot even think of how to handle this latest rejection. Laurène considers my predicament for a few moments, then tells me: "Look, I have things to do now. You wait here until this afternoon. I will return and drive you to Tonnerre where you can see a doctor and find a place to sleep. Do you have something to eat for lunch?" *I have a can of tuna and some bread left over from last night, so I can throw together a sandwich.* Her offer of help is so generous, but I am stunned by the reality of getting a lift the seventeen kilometers to Tonnerre; it is not what I planned or hoped for, but it is obviously the only solution. I cannot walk those kilometers tomorrow with my leg in this condition. Today's pain was enough. In Tonnerre, the doctor will surely identify my problem as tendonitis, give me some powerful anti-inflammatory drug, tell me to rest a few days, then I will be on my way. This is not a pilgrimage killer. No knockout punch delivered today. *Okay. I will see you after lunch, and we will go to Tonnerre by* voiture.

I kick off my boots and pull off my socks. I dig out my foodstuffs and make my lunch. I find a bench under a tree, eat, then lie down, close my eyes and drift away. I presume my Good Samaritan will be back shortly, but time passes. One hour, two hours, then three. I am wondering if I have been abandoned. Has she forgotten me? Now what do I do? Finally, just as the first strains of panic begin to play inside my head, her van roars through the gate and into the garden, pulling up beside me. Oh, I am so grateful! I put on my boots, retrieve Gregory and lug him into the back of the van. Laurène's daughter accompanies us. This busy lady has other things to do, so in a jiffy we are roaring out onto the highway and across the landscape to Tonnerre. As we go, I notice two figures on the verge of the roadway ahead of us. I look more closely: Marie Clare and Mary Anne are walking single file, at a steady clip. They are still on their way, even this late in the afternoon. I try to wave at them as we pass, but they do not notice me. They look very tired. How I wish I could be with them. How I wish I could be as good a pilgrim as they are. I look backwards mournfully as their images grow smaller then disappear altogether.

We drive into Tonnerre, and I am delivered to the Salle d'Urgence of the local municipal hospital. I am signed in, then left to wait my turn in a small receiving room, stuffy with too many people also waiting their turns. I am eventually led by a nurse to an examination room where I am interrogated, forms are filled out to make everything official, then I am left to wait some more. The minutes on the big clock above the door tick by ever so slowly. I am still absolutely certain that this pain in my leg is a temporary setback, that the doc will take a look, affirm with confidence my own diagnosis of tendonitis, load me up with some drugs, and I'll be outta here. The doc, complete with white smock and stethoscope hanging around his neck, comes in and without looking at me, reads quickly the forms that have already been filled in; he is rotund, has rheumy eyes, wears an untrimmed moustache, and speaks a French I cannot make anything of. Is he Slavic? Or Arabic? Or just good ol' country boy French? I have no idea. He bustles around the room, starts feeling around my leg with his pudgy fingers, continues to avoid any communication with me, making me feel like a side of beef on this examination table. I don't trust this guy for a minute. He issues a command to the assistant, who then pulls out a new form that he scribbles something on. With a rush, the doc leaves the room. I ask the assistant what's up, and she tells me that I'm going up to *radiographie*. X-ray? *Pourquoi radiographie?* She shrugs her shoulders, purses her lips, and puffs, which I interpret to mean: "How the hell should I know?"

A wheel chair is brought in by a male orderly. I'm loaded in, pushed into an elevator, and taken on a herky-jerky ride up to another floor. I am wheeled into a dark and cool room loaded with what seems to me to be pretty high-tech equipment, then told to lie down on a cold table. A technician comes into the room, asks me which leg is the problem and where, adjusts the massive ray gun above me, then leaves. I hear the gun whine and click, and the whole thing is over. I am left there to wait for developments, then after a few minutes the technician from behind a thick window asks if I have fallen recently. *No.* Hmm. *Fallen?*

I am rolled back to the examination room and told to wait. I wait. Again the minutes tick by as slowly as molasses in January, as my first grade teacher used to say about my work ethic. The rotund doctor, now set in my mind as a character out of a Monty Python sketch, bursts into the room and begins mumbling and gurgling and thundering what seem like orders to me. His fat hands are waving. Body odor is evident. I am doing my best to understand and keep saying, *Je suis désolé. Je ne comprends pas.* I'm sorry; I don't understand. He gets more excited, and finally I make out the word he is fairly spitting at me now: "*Fracture! Fracture!*" Fracture? As far as I can tell he has only now received the large brown envelope from radiology but has not even opened it. *How do you know there is a fracture?* All I can imagine is that he has either seen the x-rays outside, which seems improbable, or he is going on what the technicians have told him they found. New rolls of thunder issue from under his twitching moustache: "*Fracture! Fracture! Á Belgique! Retourner á Belgique! Pas de marche! Pas de marche!*" He attempts English: "Stop! Stop to walk! *Pas de* walk!" He writes up a long prescription sheet, hands it to the assistant, thrusts the brown radiology envelope into my hands, then waves the bill before me. I take it and quickly decipher the scribbles: fifty-three euros. Well, you get what you pay for. I got Doctor Thunder.

As the attendant wraps my tender tendon in gauze and soaks it with some kind of cooling liquid, I consider two possibilities: Those radiology technicians spotted the results of a ski accident more than thirty years ago and don't know enough to distinguish it from a new break, or more disastrously, they discovered something new in there, perhaps small stress fractures from the constant pounding my legs have taken the last month. I have no way of knowing which. I am put back in the wheelchair and taken to the lobby of the hospital and delivered to the cashier. I hand over the fifty-three euros; my bill is stamped and sealed and signatures are applied in various places, then I hobble out the door and head to the *centre-ville* of Tonnerre, this town of thunder, as the name means in old French.

As soon as I exit the hospital property, I am confronted with a *hôpital* of a very different type: the thirteenth-century Hôtel-Dieu founded by Marguerite of Burgundy, who, for a time was queen of France until her adultery caught up with her and led to her strangulation on orders of her husband, the king. Her grand *hôpital* served the sick and poor and pilgrims like myself and fortunately for me, now serves as the tourist information office for Tonnerre. I have no choice but to spend the night here in Tonnerre, so I hobble over, step inside, and am assisted in English by a young attendant. I tell her I am a pilgrim, ask for the town seal for my *credencial,* then ask if the town has a pilgrim refuge. I get my stamp and am told that, indeed, there is a new refuge in town, operated by the city government, and she would be happy to make the arrangements on my behalf. Her smiling kindness is an antidote to the miserable bedside manner of Doctor Thunder. I am asked to wait a few minutes for the arrival of a representative from the city hall. A man shows up to collect me and leads me around a block, past the city hall, and finally to a non-descript house on a non-descript street; the front door is unlocked for me, and up I am led to the second floor where another door is unlocked. I am shown into a simple flat, still a work in progress as paint cans are set about with lids askew, and the dust of newly sanded woodwork still covers every horizontal surface. The bedroom holds a metal bed-frame covered with a lumpy mattress; an old end-table completes the ensemble. The kitchen, toilet, and shower are hardly spic-n-span but not disgusting. Nothing fancy but serviceable.

I am left to myself. I set Gregory and Click and Clack on the floor and stretch out on the bed. I am numb. *Fracture? Á Belgique? That's it? The end? C'est tout?* I wonder about a second opinion, after all, my doc was a joke. But considering this town, where would I find a second opinion any better than the first? If I were to return to the hospital, I would most likely just end up with Dr. Thunder again. Maybe I should just keep walking anyway; I beat tendonitis four years ago, I can beat it again. But what if there really is some kind of stress fracture down there? What a fool I would be to keep walking. There is no way to know for sure. I feel foiled. It is time to call for advice, so I send a text message to Gene and Caroline asking them to call me when they have a chance. Caroline is a doctor, after all; she will see clearly what the next step should be. I shower and launder my clothes in the kitchen sink, then lay down to await a call from Leuven.

After a few more minutes of pondering my present misery, I get up and take my phone in hand again. I text my friend, Vincent. It feels like an admission of defeat even to write the words, but I ask, *just in case*, if he'd be free tomorrow to drive down here and collect me. As I punch the send button, I would like to have a good pilgrim weep, but my eyes remain desolately dry.

The phone rings and Caroline's soft voice greets me: "Kevin? What's happening?" So I tell her the whole sad story, and I can sense her own discouragement and perplexity. Though she is a pediatrician, she knows something about broken bones; she cannot understand how stress fractures could be seen in an x-ray taken only hours after the injury since there would be no calcium buildup to show them off. She offers to check the Internet and her medical books about the details, then offers a few suggestions for my consideration. Option One: Look for a second opinion in Tonnerre. Not likely. Option Two: come back to Leuven and get a second opinion here, get proper treatment, then return to the road. Likely. Option Three: Give up on the pilgrimage and become a normal person again. No, not yet. She also offers to call my brother in Spokane, Bill, the physical therapist; he deals with plenty of sports injuries so might have some good advice for us.

I slowly descend to the stairwell to street level and begin a search for a pharmacy to pick up whatever it is Dr. Thunder has prescribed for me. As I walk, the leg is hurting like crazy. I turn the corner onto the main business street, only to find myself face to face with Marie Claire and Mary Anne. We greet one another and give each other the polite triple cheek kiss of the Belgians, and of course, they ask how it is that I am in Tonnerre already. As pedestrians pass, we stand on the corner, and I tell them in brief my story, and they are all sympathy for my predicament. I ask about a pharmacy, and they point one out about a block further on. Before I turn to leave them, I ask if they would like to have dinner together tonight. They say they have already found the restaurant and happily invite me to join them.

In the pharmacy, I present Doctor Thunder's prescriptions. The pharmacist begins collecting the various items and stacking them in front of me. Pills and lotions and liquids pile up on the glass counter. *What is all this stuff?* I ask the pharmacist, and she begins explaining. Included in the pile is a ten-day course of antibiotics. *Antibiotics for a fracture?* I ask the pharmacist what is the point of that, and she shrugs her shoulders, purses her lips, and puffs: *"Je ne sais pas"*. I tell her I don't want them, nor the cream, nor the liquid, though I'll take the anti-inflammatory and pain-killer. With a roll of her eyes, she hauls the better part of the pile back to her shelves and drawers while I dig out the euros to pay for what is left.

Vincent calls to tell me he can be in Tonnerre tomorrow by noon if I need him. Caroline calls back as well; I ask her about the antibiotics. She has never heard of such a thing and now shares my low opinion of this doctor; I add cynically that there is most probably plenty of good reason he is practicing in Tonnerre rather than Paris. She confirms that stress fractures wouldn't show up in an x-ray for several days after the injury. I insist that the fracture seen by the technicians must be the relic of my ski accident as a twenty-something. It seems likely to us both that we are dealing here with a very bad case of tendonitis, not a broken leg or stress fractures, but there is no way to know for sure while I remain in Tonnerre. We agree that I should come home and see the orthopedist in Leuven, then go from there. I text Vincent: *Yes. Come get me.*

Marie Claire, Mary Anne, and I meet at a small restaurant on the main street that advertises steak and *pomme frites*. They are dying for a taste of their homeland. I order a salad and pizza. We have ourselves a lovely evening together, beer and wine warming our hearts and cheering my drooping spirits. They keep it all in perspective for me: "Kevin, you've come a long way; you've done your best. The most important thing is to take care of yourself. Yes, it is best to go home for now. A pilgrimage is not about kilometers . . . " I ask them to send me a postcard when they arrive in *Compostelle*. They take my address and happily agree. I limp back to my pilgrim flat, turn off the alarm of my watch since there is no reason to rise early, undress, crawl into my sack, and before falling into a deep sleep, whisper: *Oh Jesus. I am so sorry.*

I wake up late feeling strangely at ease. The sleep has settled me and planted me in this new terrain of return. I am not just resigned; it seems *meaningful* somehow, part of the plan. That miserable Doctor Thunder has not misdiagnosed this pilgrim into oblivion just yet. I pack up Gregory, store Click and Clack in his side-straps. Put on my big boots, tie them up, and head out into Tonnerre. With Gregory on my back, I wander to the city hall to pay the ten euros I owe for use of the refuge. I am greeted with lots of smiles, but it takes the better part of an hour to arrange the transaction, papers must be signed, invoices completed, seals applied, funds transferred. To an American, it all seems a ridiculous waste of time and energy for ten euros, but the smiles and courtesy make it somehow worth the bureaucratic silliness of it all.

I sit down at a sidewalk *café* and enjoy a fine cup of *café-au-lait* and a croissant so flaky and tender it must have been fabricated using a whole cube of butter. I dawdle and take my time: I have two hours before Vincent arrives. Having sat as long as I can stand, I take Gregory up again and hobble up the main street to the lovely Église de Notre-Dame. I step inside, set Gregory on the stool next to me, and the two of us find rest in the quiet amidst these stone pillars and arches. I find myself leaning against old Gregory, like friends who have been through a lot together. I know his every strap and pocket like my own body now. He is dirty and smells, but it is the dirt of faithfulness and the smell of perseverance. It is my sweat he bears, this pope of a pack. I rather love him. And so I lean. And so he supports. My old friend, Gregory: *merci.*

I pray a rosary, letting the beads slip through my fingers like small friends. We call the fifteen decades of beads "mysteries" in our Catholic world. I muse on that word, "mystery" even as the Hail Mary's pass like so many train cars on a silver rail. There are so many mysteries, or rather one mystery with so many faces. There is so much that is beyond scientific observation, such simplicity supporting all our complexity, such presences that our eyes cannot see or our fingers touch except in beads rattled through old fingers. I believe this now more than before. This earth is girdled with veins and arteries of which only pilgrims and mystics know. They are not roads exactly, but ways, *vias*, ethereal and unsubstantial, wafting like the feathery tails of cirrus clouds across the planet, wrapping it in strings of gauzy light. They are like the Milky Way, but not so far away. We walk them, or rather, they carry us along. They are formed of billions of smiles and greetings and words of encouragement, billions of hearts and souls and persons. They greet us as we approach, welcome us, feed us, care for us, then after the proper while, hand us on to the next. They are blithe spirits enfleshed in wrinkles sometimes, and other times in the fresh rosy cheek of a child. Their hands join, they sing, they dance, they make an unbroken chain from there to here to there. Oh, I am so grateful to have been traveling along this Via all these days. I have never been lonely, really. I have never been alone, really. This is a mystery I am happy to sit with now and for a while longer.

Two ladies are quietly arranging flowers in the sanctuary. The blooms do not seem professionally cut and have presumably come from their gardens. They poke and prod and adjust and step back and look and adjust some more, then set the great vases on stands under this or that saint before going on to the altar adornments. They are preparing the church for the weekend Masses, softening its hard and ageless stone with tender blooms that will wither and die within only a day or two. One of the ladies leaves the sanctuary, walks back into the nave then comes over to me: "You are welcome to rest as long as you wish, *monsieur.*" See what I mean? What kindness. What love. What mystery. What *vita* there is along this *via.* I hope I can return. I will do my best. I want to keep walking, keep being carried, keep being cared for, keep caring. It is all just too rich to leave already. There are no more words for this moment, so I slip into that lovely low-geared kind of consciousness where formed thoughts disappear for a while, and all is well, all is well, all manner of things are well.

It is almost noon, so I stiffly walk towards the open door of the church. Before stepping outside, I pick up a small brochure describing the Église de Notre-Dame and am touched to find that it was *the* pilgrim church of Tonnerre in medieval times. I step back into the bright light of day and head down the street; I will meet Vincent at Marguerite's *Hôtel-Dieu.* In fact, we arrive at almost the same moment, so I limp over to where he has parked; we embrace and smile and say we are fine. Then I throw Gregory in the back, take off my boots, exchanging them for my sandals, and together we go off to look for lunch in the City of Thunder. As we walk, Vincent asks me if I realize I have made it into Bourgogne already. Somewhere, after Etourvy, I crossed from Champagne to Burgundy.

Vincent directs the nose of the Honda northwards, and we leave Tonnerre. This is not at all what I expected or wanted to be doing today, but I am surprisingly lacking in distress. Through little effort of my own, I have been given peace about this; what a change from my frantic response to the knee breakdown a month ago on my first day of walking. This month on the Chemin has taught me an acceptance of whatever is around the next bend that I did not have before. That which is hard and cold in me has been both softened by the tender blooms that have blessed me so often along the Way.

We pull into Vincent's parish house in Waterloo, one of Brussels' more famous neighborhoods, made so by Napoleon finally getting his comeuppance in some muddy fields a stone-throw from here. I drag Gregory upstairs to the guestroom and lean him up against the wall. I return downstairs, and Vince is already pulling together the fixings for a barbecued steak dinner. I join him for the Saturday evening Mass in the parish church; it feels good to be a part of this great prayer again with a community I know. In the few minutes available to meet and greet following the liturgy, it is hard to explain to his parishioners what I am doing back here, so I keep it as simple as I am able. *Leg troubles. Probably tendonitis. Yes, I hope to continue after a few days of rest.*

Caroline phones; she reassures me that I have made the right decision to come back to Belgium. She will accompany me to the local hospital in Leuven on Monday morning; we won't bother with an appointment but will just go in through the Emergency Room. It should go better than it did in

Tonnerre. It will be so good to have Caroline with me for this next stage in this so far unpleasant medical adventure.

The dinner Vincent has prepared for us on the veranda is great. Accompanying the steak is a fine bottle of Bordeaux, which we drink to the dregs. The summer evening is fresh, and we dawdle at the table until night falls. Well fed and enjoying the warmth of the wine, I'm feeling quite tired now so retire to my new room, clean up a bit, record in my journal the events of the past two days, then lay down for my first night of sleep outside of the pilgrim Via that has been my only world over these past four weeks.

Saint-Jacques: if you want me to come, heal this leg.

8

The Days of My Confinement

I awake to the chirping of birds, a breeze ruffling the sheer curtains over the open window, and sunlight filling the room. I have slept late. No worry: I have nothing to do and nowhere to go this Sunday morning. Vincent is already away for his first Mass of the morning at the parish church. I shower. I wander downstairs and pour myself a bowl of cereal and fresh milk, set out a glass of orange juice, drop some bread in the toaster. It all feels like extraordinary luxury.

With my breakfast complete, I take my place on the sofa in the living room, apply ice to the tendon, and begin browsing through a pile of magazines neatly stacked on an end table until Vincent returns from his morning duties and prepares a light lunch for us. The afternoon runs along as I continue reading, dozing, thinking about where I am not. This first day of the week, my first day off the road, ends with Vincent and I sharing a gourmet pizza and bottle of red wine in a pleasant Italian restaurant in the business center of Waterloo.

Monday comes, and it is to Leuven that I am now carried. Vincent drops me off at the front gate of the American College, from where I began walking seemingly ages ago. From there I limp my way along the short block to the entrance of the Heilig Hart Hospital just down the street, where Caroline is waiting for me. We go in through the emergency entrance, and Caroline takes over negotiating my care with the attendants at the front desk. They are surprisingly congenial about taking me in; I rather expected there would be resistance to our gaining access to the Emergency unit with so little urgency in my situation. We are invited to take a seat in the waiting room, and there Caroline and I chat about the whole turn of events. Just being in this room sucks courage out of me, but as always, she restores my supply with her reminders that I have made the right decisions, and this is the best place to be if I am to get back out on the road soon.

As it turns out, the doctor who comes to tend to me is the very orthopedist who shot me full of cortisone a month ago. He smiles to see me back again and asks what is up: did the knee finally give out as he surely presumed it would back then? No, we explain: he did a fine job with the knee; the problem now, after almost five hundred kilometers, is the leg. Caroline explains the details of the situation in Dutch and hands him the Tonnerre x-rays. He examines the black plastic sheets and sees the break. At first, he agrees with Doctor Thunder's evaluation, but after Caroline objects, he takes a look at my leg itself, applying pressure where the break should be in the x-ray. "Any pain here?" No. Where is the pain, then? I place my hand on the lower leg, just above the foot. He feels for himself and asks me to extend then retract the foot, flexing the tendon. He can feel the crepitation, the grating of the tendon against its inflamed lining; he nods knowingly then speaks aloud his diagnosis: tendonitis, for sure. He gives me two options for care: take a full month of rest, as little walking as possible, apply ice and take ibuprofen a couple times a day. The second option may cut the healing time in half: immobilize the tendon and foot with a cast. It should be back to normal in two weeks. After that, I should be able to begin walking again. Caroline and I talk over the possibilities and decide to go for the quick fix. *Give me that cast, doc!*

Before long, my lower left leg has been wrapped in ample bands of gluey fiberglass, and I am on may way out of the hospital lugging this monster slowly up the Naamsestraat and then into town to meet Gene for lunch. I make light of the new situation as best I am able, and both Caroline and Gene are clearly positive about the treatment. The inconvenience of the cast is worth the two-week recovery. They promise that as soon as I am able to walk again, they will drive me down to Tonnerre to pick up the route, and take a few days of vacation themselves to accompany me as far as Vézelay as backup until I'm sure I am in shape for the rest of the pilgrimage. It is so much more than a good offer, it is a grand gesture of pilgrim support and friendship to which I joyfully say yes, of course; I look forward to it with all my heart.

The fourteen casted days in Waterloo pass. I write little or nothing in my pilgrim journal. I feel increasing distance from the pilgrim way, and it is a hollow feeling, something akin to those days in life after someone you love has departed and there remains a hole within you that makes you feel almost sick. The *Chemin* has become a friend, I realize more and more. I am bereft at this love lost. On top of that, something distressing is also happening: I am getting lazier as the days pass; the thought of walking again with all its discomforts and troubles becomes less attractive, more subtly obnoxious. I do not want this to happen to me, so I try to exorcise this temptation by refusing to fold and neatly place my clothes in the drawers of the tall bureau or hang my shirts in the closet of my room; I continue to use Gregory as my storage of choice. *Gregory, you are the guarantor that I am yet a pilgrim!*

On the seventeenth of August I return to the Leuven hospital to have my cast removed. Vince and I drive in from Waterloo, and just as before, Caroline meets me at the door of the hospital. The cast is buzz-sawed down each flank, then pried open; my old leg is revealed. The nurse declares: "You are free!" I am invited to stretch and stand. It is very stiff, and I feel clumsy without the cast as I slowly take my first steps around the examination room and then into the hallway. The tendon seems almost fine; I can feel only the tiniest little catch at the top when I extend my foot downward. We carefully walk together into town, have lunch with Gene and Vincent, and we agree, that if all is well, we might drive back to Tonnerre as soon as Monday, or even later in the week if we want to be a bit more careful. I then do a bit of shopping on my own, shopping for the road: I stop in the outdoor sports store in the center of Leuven and purchase a new pair of hiking socks and Cool-max liners. I drive back to Waterloo with Vincent and feel relief that all is going so well. I will give it a day to rest and slowly stretch the tendon back into resiliency, then, if all feels well, put on my boots and take a walk.

Sunday, the nineteenth of August, gives me a sunny first day of the week to take my first real steps back to the Chemin. After morning Mass at the parish, I pull on my trekking socks followed by my boots and head to Waterloo's main shopping street, taking it easy as I go. I turn south and feel no pain. I am walking again! I continue on for a half-hour, and all remains just fine. After forty-five minutes, I decide discretion is the better part of valor and cross the Chaussee de Bruxelles to return home by way of the other side of the street. This will be an hour and a half test, pretty darn good for my first day out. The cast has done its job.

Almost.

At the hour mark, I begin to feel the old tightness return ever so slightly to the lower leg. I stop and rest a bit, giving the foot some stretches. Probably nothing. No big deal. I continue walking past the display windows of the fancy stores, most closed for the day. There are plenty of bistros and cafes along the way, too. They are brimming with folks sipping creamy coffees and nibbling at fancy snacks while formally dressed *garçons* tend them. The stiffness in my leg is increasingly notable. I need to get back to the parish house and get these boots off. There is no point in hurrying; it is the same distance whether walked quickly or slowly. I carefully mosey down the busy street and then at the big church where Napoleon signed off on his

Waterloo defeat, I turn east onto Vincent's street, and in a few more minutes I am home. I climb the stairs to my room and feel it again. The crepitation is back. I have overdone it. *Ah, cri-me-ny!* I ditch my boots, return downstairs, dig ice out of the freezer and apply it to my leg as I sit on the sofa and curse my wretched self for not taking it easier on this miserable leg. Now I have to wait and see if it will settle down again. Maybe a little ice, some ibuprofen and a quiet afternoon followed by a good night's sleep will get me back on track.

I awake to a very tender tendon; the crepitation has returned in all its previous glory. I have just lost two weeks of cast treatment and am back to square one. The possibility of getting out of my Waterloo confinement and back to the Chemin seems much less likely than it did at this time yesterday. I kick my boots across the room with my good leg, take a shower, dress, and go down to breakfast with Vincent. I tell him the bad news and add that I hope he can stand having me hanging around for a while longer. He assures me that I am welcome here as long as I want, but I also know this: time is running out, autumn will be approaching. I will have to get on with my life *at some point*. I decide that if this leg is not better by the end of the month, I will quit altogether. August 31: that is my deadline. This morning delivers up a desolation far worse than at any time since the first day of July when my collapsed meniscus was the failure at issue. I may *never* get back to Tonnerre, may *never* walk into Vézelay, may *never* cross through Saint-Jean-Pied-de-Port and into Spain.

I wake up at 4:00 am; the tendon is pulsing, and I cannot go back to sleep. *Saint James, I repeat, if you want me, heal me!*

Thus it is that the days of my confinement continue. More ibuprofen, more ice, more books. At my brother's suggestion, I begin a six-day course of a powerful anti-inflammatory called Medrol. If this doesn't work, I'm finished. I work on my attitude: detachment is the key; these weeks in Waterloo, I tell myself, are not *apart* from the pilgrimage; they are *integral* to the pilgrimage. The Chemin takes many twists and turns and sometimes doubles back on itself; my job is to follow it, let it surprise me, let it lead me on. *Hang in there, Kev; you'll see the big picture anon.* Alas, I am not so sure I am reassured.

My third Waterloo week passes. The Medrol has not worked. The scratchy crepitation continues. My end-of-month deadline draws ever closer; my sense of mourning the imminent death of something I have loved becomes darker. Probabilities are stacking up against me. I contact my pilgrim friend, Toni, in Galicia and ask if he could check into the possibility of this almost ex-pilgrim at least staying in the pilgrim game by serving as an *hospitalero* in some refuge along the Galician Camino route. He writes back that it should be no problem; this is consoling: at least I can contribute to the pilgrimages of others even if I can't walk the Way myself. Yet even with that fine Plan B in the works, my grief deepens: in my daydream moments when I can read novels no longer, I imagine the green fields, the vineyards, the villages, the wayside shrines, the steeples, the kind French people saluting me with their *bon courages*. I cannot but mourn at the growing prospect that I shall never go back to any of this.

One sign that I am resigning myself to the unimaginable, that I know my walking days are all but done: I have stopped wearing my hi-tech pilgrim clothes and am back to good old cotton briefs, jeans and t-shirts.

On Saturday of week three, the twenty-fifth of August, I awake and check my leg first thing, as I have done every day for a month: a bit of ache when I flex my foot but no noticeable crepitation for the first time. I keep testing it to see if the grating is really gone. So far so good. I begin to hope against hope that maybe, just maybe, this tendon is finally healing. I follow my ice and ibuprofen routines through the day and join Vincent for the Saturday evening Mass at the parish. We enjoy dinner together yet again, then I head for bed . . . yet again. As soon as I lie down, I can feel the old throbbing come back to the fore. I sink again into my August-long discouragement. *This will never end. This will just never get better.*

On Sunday morning, I am acutely aware that this is the first day of my fourth and last week of waiting. If I am not ready to walk before this week ends, I will quit. I check my leg, and begin the final week of waiting. I don't take any ibuprofen this morning to see how much ache there might still be down there. As I head downstairs for breakfast, the tendon is feeling better even than yesterday and last night's pains are gone.

Gene calls later in the day and offers me his appointment with a local physical therapist on Wednesday. The man does a lot of work with sports injuries so knows plenty about tendonitis. "No harm in having a professional take a look at your leg and give you some treatment," he advises me. I take him up on his offer.

Tonight, I talk by phone with my PT brother, Bill, about my situation. He wants me to be cautious about jumping back in to the pilgrimage too quickly, even with the progress I have made over the weekend. My optimism level drops again. Okay, I'll be cautious, but on the other hand, the calendar is working against me. It is almost September. If I don't get started again very soon, I won't get started at all. He reminds me that he is not here; I am. I am the one who will have to judge if the leg is sufficiently healed to begin walking anew. I am almost sure my visit to the local PT will bring me no good news; almost certainly he will tell me not to take any unnecessary risks with this thing.

Monday and Tuesday bring further improvement. The crepitation has not returned, and the soreness continues to diminish.

Wednesday comes and so to Leuven Vince and I drive. I walk with a slight limp to the small office of Gene's therapist, Koen. Once inside, he greets me and asks me to take my place on his therapy table. He feels around the tendon as I flex it, stretches everything, doses it with electricity, then tells me he thinks in a couple of days more I'll be in good enough shape to recommence my hike. He warns me, though, that it could easily go bad again, and if it does, I must stop walking immediately; he reassures me that there is a better than even chance it will be fine, and I should be able to walk on with no serious difficulty. I can hardly believe what I have just heard. *Is it true? I can walk again?* Koen reiterates his professional verdict in the most clear fashion possible: "Go!" he says with a smile. I am thrilled, thank him profusely, then phone Gene and Caroline with the news. They are just as thrilled as I and invite me to come to their place, a short walk from the therapist's office. I practically dance down the street and hum in the elevator up to the sixth floor of their building. When I arrive at their door, it is open, and we are all smiles and hugs, and they want all the details, which I excitedly offer. Gene breaks open a bottle of champagne to celebrate, and before long we are enjoying a simple lunch, the skyline of Leuven with its red and black tile rooftops and many steeples looking as cheery as I have ever seen it.

We make our plans: Today is Wednesday. I still need a few more days to rest the tendon, so on Sunday we will drive down to Tonnerre. They will make reservations at a *chambre d'hôte* somewhere outside of the town, which we can use as home base for a couple of days. For the first few days, they will be available to fetch me along the road if I have trouble or just want to stop walking early. Even better, each morning they will drop me off exactly where I left off the day before. I will carry only the light day-pack, leaving Gregory with them, so as to give my leg an easier break-in period. We examine my GR guide; with Gene and Caroline so close and lodging assured, I choose to abandon the GR 654, which from Tonnerre goes straight west through Chablis, then cuts south to Vézelay. If I follow small departmental highways that cut diagonally to the southwest, I can save at least two or three days of walking. I should be in Vézelay in three days, maybe four. At Vézelay, we decide, Gene and Caroline will leave me on my own to continue south while they return home to Belgium. It is only now, as the reality of my march on Vézelay takes hold that I realize how little hope I have had in the past month of ever getting back on this ancient road.

Merci, Saint-Jacques, for wanting me to come, for healing me, for getting me back on your Chemin after all.

I find myself wondering about my fitness: How much weight have I put on in this month in which I have been almost completely sedentary? I know I have lost most of the calluses on the bottom of my feet, especially on the foot that was casted; am I in for blisters once I start walking again? More seriously: Have I lost my pilgrim spirit? Do I still want to tackle the challenges and overcome the obstacles of life on the road? There is a part of me now that really doesn't want to go back, that has gotten used to middle-class luxuries again, that is just plain lazy and would prefer to never walk with a backpack again. But, I force myself to override the doubts: *I am committed.* I *am* going back and *will* take on the challenges of the road, whatever they may be. As I did on the first of July, I remind myself: my job is to begin, just to begin. This I know: it is time to put aside the mantle of house-guest and take up anew that of pilgrim. Period.

Saturday is the final day of my confinement. I arise edgy and nervous-but go about my preparatory tasks as systematically as I am able. I launder everything I own in Vincent's wash machine and dryer. I would like to cut Gregory's overall weight by a kilo or two over what I was carrying in July, if for no other reason than to make up for the weight I have gained around my own waist. I sift through my travel packs, ditching odds and ends I don't think I'll need, things I haven't needed so far. I cut the number of pairs of wool socks I am carrying from six to three. I set aside a second knee brace that I had been carrying for back-up. I replace both a bar of soap and a bottle of shampoo with a single smaller bottle of body wash; that saves me a quarter kilo right there. I replace my half-full journal, 288 pages in all, with a much lighter notebook, just 120 pages in all.

I prepare for sleep for the last time in this, my Waterloo guestroom. Tomorrow at 8:00 am, Gene and Caroline arrive to carry Gregory, Click and Clack, and me back to Tonnerre, that city of unexpected and unwanted thunder.

9

My Angels

At ten minutes to 8:00, I am standing in Vincent's kitchen finishing up a tall glass of orange juice when Gene and Caroline's black Saab pulls into the driveway just below the kitchen window. They are a bit early, but I am ready. Gregory is waiting near the front door, ready to be hauled back to Tonnerre, with Click and Clack safely tucked under his straps. He is indeed a kilo lighter than before, even though I have added a pair of thermal long-johns and a long-sleeve t-shirt in case the coming autumn nights grow cold.

The first question from Gene is a robust: "Ready to go?" *I am as ready as I'll ever be. Let's do it.* After thanking Vincent for his unstinting hospitality this past month and sharing a final fraternal hug, I grab hold of Gregory and carry him out to the waiting Saab. In he goes, then we slip in as well, and in a jiff, Gene is driving us past the Waterloo battlefield with its mountain of a monument, the great lion atop roaring at the French to never come back. I, on the other hand, now return to the land of Napoleon to continue my own march across a fair chunk of this continent. Caroline is all smiles as we whiz south.

Our plan for the day is to take lunch in Tonnerre, then I will set off with the intention of walking not much more than ten kilometers, breaking myself in gently; when I'm ready to quit for the day, Gene and Caroline will pick me up from the road, and we'll spend the rest of the day at our *chambre d'hôte*. Soon enough, we sweep through the vineyards of Champagne-Ardennes, a bright blue sky making the green vines now tinged with red seem all the more rich. The hard little grapes that I walked among in July must be close to maturity by now, plump and juicy and preparing themselves for their next life as nectar to the gods.

We pull into Tonnerre and find the town virtually deserted on this Sunday afternoon; there is hardly a soul on its streets. Gene parks the Saab in the same lot that Vincent had used a month earlier, and we get out to walk around and look for a café or restaurant where we might take lunch. Everything is closed. No cafes or restaurants have doors open nor lights on. *This town just does not make life easy for me.* We give up on the restaurant idea when we find a very small grocer open. Its stocks are limited, but we find enough to make ourselves a picnic lunch. We pack our purchases down the street to the car and drive to a park in front of the Tonnerre train station. In the shade of a chestnut tree we take a bench and spread out our delicacies. Bread, ham, cheese, peaches, Coca Cola: except for the soda, a perfect French picnic.

We eat and chat, and I'd love to take a nap here, but it is time. I am afraid to begin. I trade my sandals for my boots, fit my hat to the top of my head, and take the small backpack that will take the place of Gregory for the day. Caroline makes sure it is stocked with water, fruit, and a few snacks for the road. I retrieve Click and Clack from Gregory's straps. Gene then offers to drive me closer to the starting point of the trail, back in the town center, very near the Église de Notre-Dame. We all get back in the Saab, the small pack resting in my lap, and up the main street of Tonnerre we go. After some difficulty finding the right street to lead me out of town, we park, step out, say good-bye for now, hug, and off I walk, up a hill, out of town, checking my GPS screen occasionally to make sure I'm headed correctly. And thus I begin.

Again.

Just begin; that is your job.

At the top of the hill, just beyond the town limits, I find myself once more among the varied fields of France. Wheat here, clover and alfalfa there, vineyards in the distance, stubble ready to be bladed under to my right. I am soon startled by the snorting and snuffling of a whole family of wild boars crossing the road ahead of me. These animals are about as ugly as earthly creatures can get. They make for a fine dinner, though, so they have been much prized by hunters and culinary chefs since long before Charlemagne. Alive and on the loose, they are also quite dangerous, especially when mama boar has baby boars in tow. Neither Click nor Clack nor I are ready for battle, so I give the strange country cousin of the domestic pig wide berth. They trample diagonally across the field ahead of me and settle on the very road I now wish to take, cutting off my passage forward. *You miserable sides of bacon!* I wait and keep still, not wanting to antagonize or threaten them in any way. An automobile approaches, and the sound of it sends the whole bunch humping it back across the field and down into a gully where they disappear completely into the underbrush. I may now pass.

Tonnerre recedes into the distance, then disappears completely. Out of sight of the city, the feel of walking revives me. I declare to the earth and sky: *I'm walking here! I am walking here! Oh, thank you, Jesus; I AM WALKING HERE!* I feel much like one of those gospel cripples who has picked up his mat and walks. I keep a close check on my leg's health: meniscus and knee are behaving. Right tendon is fine for now. In the shady village of Viviers, the Saab with convertible roof pulled back catches up to me. Caroline is so happy to see me on the road and asks excitedly how I am faring. Pretty darn well, I assure her. Gene asks if I want to call it a day. I respond that I'd like to go a while longer; they remind me that they will be very close by so call whenever I'm ready. I assure them I will, so with a *bon courage* for me, they pull away and disappear around a bend.

I hope to make it another six or seven kilometers to Poilly-sur-Serein, but after another forty-five minutes of walking through the hills of Bourgogne, I find my tendon beginning to stiffen. Now, I know, it is time to quit for today, but I continue on to a crossroad with woodland to one side and fields to the other. I find myself a place on the shoulder. I dig out my phone from my small pack, give Gene and Caroline the call, and wait for them to collect me. I munch on an apple and feel rather proud of myself. I expect I have walked about twelve kilometers this afternoon. Not so many, really, but the important thing, I assure myself, is that once again *I am walking.* I lie back in the wild grass of the embankment and take in the blue sky above me. A white cloud passes, part cumulus, but becoming cirrus, it looks quite like an angel on the wing. I call to him:

Hey, Gabriel or Michael or Raphael, or whoever you are, come visit with me! He responds: "Yes, let us visit!"

So, nice wings, I say. "Thanks." He responds.

What gives with you guys? Life must be pretty easy for you all: no bodies and all that. You don't have the travails and trials we have below. No death.

"Well, no bodies, yes, but for the rest, we're not so different from you. We still have minds and hearts. We still have freedom. We still must choose."

Choose what?

"Choose to adore, praise, reverence God. We can choose *not* to, if we so wish."

Really?

"Yup."

Then what happens?

"We tumble. I mean, *really tumble.* We take our spiritual eyes off God, and we lose our balance and go into free fall. Not a dive but a head over heals tumble. And the more we tumble, the worse it gets. It gets harder and harder to regain our balance, get our sight fixed again, straighten things out. And it can last forever, always getting worse and worse."

So what is it that leads to the tumble, the loss of sight?

"Well, that's easy: the same thing as for you. We begin to think about ourselves rather than just simply praising God, unselfconsciously, for the pure joy of praising God. It is like young love, how joyous and unselfconscious it is, one just gives of him or herself to the beloved without thinking about it, without thinking of him or herself. Then, just the tiniest bit of self-preoccupation sneaks in, a little bit of 'what about me' and 'me first' slips into the relationship, and that is where all the trouble begins. Angels too: some of us begin to think: 'Wow, I'm pretty good at this praise business . . . maybe better than he or she over there . . . I deserve a bit of praise myself here.' And you know what, that angel does rise above the others, and he thinks he's pretty cool as he gets higher and higher and lets go of the hands of the others, and then he's up there and flying on his own, and then he begins to burst with pride at his accomplishment, and God is lost sight of, and he loses his balance because he has nothing to focus on beside himself, and his head goes up and then his heels slide out from under him, and the tumble begins, slowly at first, but soon enough, it gets faster as he flutters in panic and then faster and faster, until he is falling, not like a leaf in autumn, but like a terrible bomb dropped from a plane with no rudder to guide it. Boom. Falling forever. Lost. We have a technical name for it: 'egoliptical seraphimatic descent.' ESD, for short."

And do they ever recover from this ESD? Doesn't God want to save them?

"Yes, God keeps calling out to them *to just look at him,* and all will straighten out; some do; some don't. The longer they tumble, the harder it is to return. It is sad."

So the trick is to praise, revere, serve, without even thinking about it . . . well, without even thinking about yourself doing it.

"Yup . . . same as for you humans."

Can I join you for a while and try it?

"Sure, come on up. Join the circle. Leave your body behind and just come up . . . take my hand . . . balance . . . you are lighter than air . . . look at God now and laugh with him and delight in him as he delights in you. That's it . . . gentle now. Whoa . . . thinking about yourself praising God right then, huh?"

Yeah, I guess so. "That's when you go out of balance and lose your natural float . . . refocus: just adore, like young lovers . . . There, you got it now. Relax. Float. Delight . . . "

Thanks.

"That's part of it also: giving thanks . . . it's a big help in keeping us up and aright."

I imagine so. Thanks, again. Bye now . . . fly high, Gabriel, or Michael, or Raphael, or whoever you are . . .

I come out of my roadside dream to see real angels approaching: the Saab pulls up, and Caroline and Gene invite me in, congratulating me on a day well walked. *Thanks,* I say in return. *It was my delight.*

We drive to our *chambre d'hôte,* an old farmhouse greatly renovated and restored. The three of us are sharing an ample room with a loft, Gene and Caroline upstairs, while I take the bed downstairs. We agree to join our host's other guests for the *table d'hôte* this evening and at the appointed hour are served up a fine supper. Three languages are at work as all of us around the table introduce ourselves and chat amiably: English, French, and German. This being modern Europe, the communication is not hindered by the variety of tongues; everyone translates for everyone. It is a wonder how it works so well.

I eventually excuse myself from the great table of European geniality, pleading sleepiness, and settle into my portion of our room. Gene and Caroline come into the room a bit later, then settle themselves upstairs. After a final "good night", the lights are extinguished, I overhear their own intimate prayer as a couple. They say the Lord's Prayer, pray for their children and grandchildren and nephews and nieces, and then pray for me: "Lord, be with Kevin tomorrow as he walks . . . " Their prayer lifts me into tumble-free dream.

A grand country breakfast awaits us downstairs. We take our time enjoying the meal and one another's company. We will return to this same *chambre d'hôte* tonight, so it is easy getting ready for today's road; I have to collect only Click and Clack and the small backpack loaded with fruit, granola bars, and water, and we are out the door and heading down the road to the very spot where Caroline and Gene picked me up yesterday. The Saab sails down the winding roadways of this countryside until we find the crossroad of the angels. I step out, adjust the pack, take Click and Clack in hand, and begin my second day on the Chemin.

Though I am glad for the convenience of walking with only a light pack on my back, I am a bit sorry that I don't have Gregory with me, for today, the third of September, is the feast of Saint Gregory the Great, Pope and Doctor of the Church. It would be nice to have him out on the road with me on this, *his* big day. I look forward to having his namesake on my back again. It is a privilege to carry him as he once carried the church.

The path we would be walking together is a very pleasant one as it wanders through some fine Burgundian countryside. Mostly, I have dirt to walk on, which is great for my legs and knees. It is not long before I pass through my original goal for yesterday, Poilly-sur-Serein. From there, I follow a path that takes me along a river and through a forest and then up and over some well-tilled fields. Here I encounter a farmer and his front-load tractor at work in one of these fields. He is busy removing large stones from the soft dirt, carrying them to the front-loader and dropping them noisily in. As I pass, he gives his head a shake as if to say, "Well, you know, somebody has to do it." It astonishes me that after 1500 years of cultivating here, such heavy stones still have to be removed from these lands. God bless the French for sticking with it.

Lichères-prés-Aigremont is the next village to be conquered this fine day. Here I stop for a snack from my pack, then continue on towards Sasy. I enter another woodland, follow a path through its heart, then pick up the D-144 running generally south towards the mighty E-15, beautifully named for whatever reason, L'autoroute du Soleil. I can hear the speeding traffic of the auto-route in the near distance and am figuring I've just about had enough walking for today when Gene and Caroline's vehicle comes over a hill and down the highway towards me. The car falls in behind me, we stop, and I accept their offer of a ride. They are planning on lunch in Noyers-sur-Serein, reputed to be one of the prettiest medieval villages in all of France. We drive through a great portal and into the town center just as the rain picks up, making its cobblestones shiny and slippery. It is a remarkable town, protected by towers and walls and filled with old houses, now occupied by cozy restaurants and shops selling trinkets to tourists. After walking about, peeking in windows and checking menus, we settle on a little place set in an old gatehouse very near the fortified port we drove through to enter the village. A fire roars in the hearth, we are given a table, and homemade bread is brought to us. The waiter/owner is a young Dutchman. He recommends the *plat du jour*, and we accept. Everything is delicious. The wine is fine. I am perfectly sated as we leave to head back to our farmhouse.

After another fine supper, Gene, Caroline and I retire to our room, discuss our plans for the next couple of days, focusing on an imminent arrival in one of the dream cities of the French pilgrim route: Vézelay. Tomorrow I should be able to reach Voutenay-sur-Cure, a little more than twenty kilometers and my longest walk yet since returning to France. From there, I will be set to enter Vézelay the following afternoon.

To be so close to this fabled city on the French Chemin is something that awes me. Though I have never seen it with my own eyes, I feel as if I know her, this lovely lady, Vézelay. I have read of her charms and seen occasional images of her grand basilica, dedicated to the great friend of Jesus, Mary of Magdala. Vézelay is for the pilgrim a sort of "little Jerusalem:"

a city set on a hill, a holy mountain the pilgrim must climb up to. *Aliya,* the Jews would say: "Let us go up!" Once there, the pilgrim passes beyond its defensive walls and is enfolded into the city's protective womb, those great stone walls wrap themselves around the defenseless pilgrim, and then within, deep within, there he finds the temple, the sacred place, the holy of holies where the divine and the earthly draw close, where all that is common and everyday and opaque to the realities beyond time and space grow thin and where the things of God become visible, sensible, *feel-able* to us who are so mortal. Arches, naves, colonnades, diffused light filtering in from high windows of alabaster, liturgy with its processions and bells and bowing, chants and incense, these things wash away our tiredness, sweep away the ephemeral, and gently usher us into the City of God. This is why we walk, walk to the earth's Jerusalems: to approach the threshold of the heavens and be ushered into the City of God.

But first I must walk. Day Three on the Way to Vézelay leads me into the village of Sasy which boasts an imposing church, but I cannot enter; like so many others, it is locked tight. I continue on, my eyes treated to expansive vistas of the Bourgogne countryside: fallow fields on one side, squared forests of oak in the distance, rolling hills covered in exhausted sunflowers on the other. These flowers, heavy heads bowed, look to be weeping: over what do they mourn? The end of summer? Their imminent harvest? Death?

Caroline and Gene meet me in Précy-le-Sec for lunch. We meet up in a small park across from the church and take our place on the grass. Caroline pulls out of a bag of carrot sticks, a *quiche,* and a rich chocolate tart. Gene opens a bottle of Chablis that he purchased yesterday . . . in Chablis. They tell me about their touring of nearby villages and small sights they have seen. They have found a *chambre d'hôte* for us in Voutenay, the next town on the *Chemin*; it is an old house with a couple old-fashioned rooms, run by a sweet grandmotherly lady who is very happy to have a pilgrim priest as a guest for the night. Voutenay is another six kilometers further on, and the road will be mostly downhill from here into the Cure River valley. Though the wine and food have made me sleepy, I am not ready to quit for the day. While they drive off for more sightseeing, I take up the verge of the two-lane highway to Voutenay and get back to work.

The afternoon is warm but not hot, and there are more and more trees and shrubbery on either side of the road as it descends into the river valley. Once I get my walking rhythm back, my *après-repas* lethargy dissipates, and I move along at a very good clip, covering these six kilometers in just under an hour. As I approach my road's intersection with the main highway entering Voutenay from the north, Caroline comes walking around the corner to meet me. She is surprised that I am so close already; she was expecting to walk considerably further before encountering me. She leads me into town and down a small side street to a fine old house snuggled into a well-shaded garden.

I am presented to our hostess for the night, and she is indeed very much the image of a *grand-mère*: sweet and gracious and quite angelic in appearance, the kind of woman whose kitchen shelves are lined with home-made preserves, whose table always features a basket of varied fruit, and whose cheery cheeks glow. They show me to my quarters; my Gregory is patiently waiting for me there, leaning against the legs of an old-fashioned chair off to the side.

This has been a twenty-kilometer plus day; I am bushed but pleased with myself. My body is doing so well. It feels like a miracle. It feels like I have picked up my mat and am walking. Confidence and *bon courage* are filling me; I declare to Gene and Caroline that tomorrow, as I make my entry into the Vézelay of my dreams, I want to carry Gregory again. I want to walk into Vézelay with Gregory on my back. Gene thinks it is a good idea, since it is time to put my legs to a full test before they depart my pilgrim scene; but for me, it is more than an idea or a test: it is an expression of a sort of brotherhood I now share with this big galoot of a backpack. Walking into this holy city is something I very much want to do *with him*.

Tomorrow will be a big day for me, my Vézelay day. Just a week ago it seemed I would never find myself walking there, but just look, here I am now, less than twenty kilometers from its gates!

With morning's arrival, *Grand-mère* has set out a simple but altogether complete *petit-déjeuner* for us. We enjoy the fruits and yogurts and butter and jams and croissants and fresh coffee that have been spread out across her ample table. I make my final preparations of Gregory, packing my toilet-ries and clothing within, each item in its proper place. I haul him downstairs and thank *Grand-mère* for her hospitality. With Gregory snug on my back and Click and Clack in hand, I wave farewell to Gene and Caroline and walk down the driveway, out the gate, turn right, wander up the street, and over the Cure River; I am on my way to Vézelay!

Almost as soon as I am over the river, the vision of a large roadside crucifix arrests me. I have been passing these shrines now since I left Leuven and have not been making proper pilgrim use of them. They were set along the roads of Europe in former times not only as memorials and monuments, but also as reminders for passing pilgrims and wayfarers to not forget their prayers. I resolve that henceforward I shall take their call more seriously: I will pray at each one I come upon. But how shall I pray? The Lord's Prayer, for sure. *Our Father in heaven . . .* The Orthodox's Jesus Prayer as well: *Lord Jesus, have mercy on me, a sinner,* repeated three times at least. And for no particular reason except that it was taught to me as a child as an add-on to the Rosary's five decades, a grim prayer from another generation: *Oh my Jesus, forgive us our sins, save us from the fires of hell and lead all souls to heaven, especially those most in need of thy mercy.* I do the exercise for the first time here at this Voutenay cross, wanting it to be from here on an instinctive habit in my walking life. Then, in the ancient tradition of medieval pilgrims, I set a small stone on the cross's base to mark my passing, but even more, to affirm the enduring character of each and every prayer. Prayers, the stone says, don't disappear into the ether; once spoken, they have a life, an existential existence all their own. They rise to the heart of God and there take their place among the millions of other prayers being spoken, wept, screamed across the face of the earth this day.

From the cross, I take a left and follow a track through high, wet field grass along the riverbank. I am back on the GR 654, the red and white signage having reappeared now to guide my way, but my GPS does just as well. The route leaves the high grass and drops into a wooded area of oak trees and brambles closer to the river's edge. It becomes wilder and woollier, damp and slippery. A high escarpment of white stone rises now to my immediate right, some of it overhanging the path I now tread. The stone cliff above my head does not inspire confidence: chunks of the white stone have fallen to the path below. A sign appears warning me of *chutes de pierre*, falling rock; somehow it sounds less dangerous in French.

I survive my passage below the *chutes* with no brain damage and eventually come out of the woods in a little place called Blannay. I check both my GPS and keep an eye open for the GR flags to guide me through the village's streets, down to a bridge, over the River Cure again, and for a couple hundred meters, along a busy highway, then into the town of Givry. I climb steadily out of Givry, up and over some substantial hills, mostly forested, now following paved roads on the east side of the river, and thus, continue on towards Asquins, the portal to Vézelay proper. As the road rises, I am conscious of Gregory's heft pulling me down as I poke my way south. I come to a roadside cross and say the prayers I have committed myself to saying, leaving a small stone at its base.

Atop a crest in this road, I get my first view in the hazy distance of what must surely be Vézelay. I can just make out the outlines of the basilica with the rest of the village wrapped around its feet. The mountain it rides is far enough away that it appears blue; the fields and vineyards extending out from its skirts in every direction are emerald green. *There you are, dear lady, Vézelay! Finally, there you are!* I drop Gregory from my back, pull out my camera and snap a couple shots of the vista, though I know they will never do justice to the reality I see with my pilgrim eyes. It is a beautiful sight to those eyes, because I have spent a month hardly believing I would ever see it. This *feels* like a miracle and to my mind today, it *is* a miracle.

As I pick up Gregory, strap him back on and begin click-clacking my way down the road with Vézelay always before my eyes, a gospel hymn comes to my mind; well, not exactly the hymn in its entirety, but just the first line. No matter, I sing it aloud over and over again as I walk: *Oh, what a beautiful city! Oh, what a beautiful city. Oh, what a beautiful city. Twelve gates to the city: Hallelujah!* Bye and bye, the road delivers me into the heart of Asquins. It is just noon; the church bells of the Vézelay basilica call us below to pray the Angelus as they have done for centuries. I find a small café and walk in for a light lunch before making my grand climb up to Vézelay proper. I take a table to myself, setting Gregory on the chair next to me and Click and Clack under the table. This is a bar more than a restaurant, but the young man who tends to me assures me the food is worthy of my consumption. He recommends the day's special: *tomates farcis.* I do not have any idea what that might be, but take his recommendation and ask for a beer to go with it. He disappears into the kitchen only to reappear a moment later with the *de rigueur* basket of sliced *baguette* to accompany my feast. Then comes the cool beer. Then a plate heaped with a stew with plenty of tomatoes for sure, but also meat and spuds. I order a second beer to go with it. The *plat du jour* tastes just fine, and I wolf down the whole thing in a few minutes. I am sleepy and would like to end my day right here, but I have a mountain to climb, so I load Gregory onto my back and step outside to look for a special little church pilgrims are advised to visit before they go up to Vézelay. I am feeling a little goofy with my full stomach and double hit of beer so when I do not find the church, I just turn back up the road and head towards the Beautiful City.

Beautiful though Vézelay may be, I am nevertheless faced with a steep climb if I am going to get to its gates; what is advertised as a hill seems to me to be more of a mountain. I have a choice to make: follow the road as it winds around the hill, or take a goat trail more directly through the woods to the top. I choose the more gentle roadway and lean into the climb. The weight of Gregory on my back is something I am still getting used to, and as I trudge uphill, it is something to contend with. After only a short while, I am relying heavily on Click and Clack to support my weight as I climb. I find myself huffing and puffing now. When I come out of the shade into the direct light of the afternoon sun, I feel the heat of the afternoon and sweat profusely. Shade returns, and I cool slightly. Up I climb to Vézelay. Up I slowly climb to Vézelay.

After the better part of an hour, I lift my head to see the gate of the city, the *port nouveau.* I stop, drop Gregory, retrieve my camera, and take some shots of my entry into this French Jerusalem. I continue through the *port* and once within, the town seems deserted. I turn a corner in what I think must be the direction of the basilica and encounter a lone man coming my way. I ask him directions to the church, and he indicates I am going well: just keep following this street upward. *Aliya!* I make a final push up to the plaza that opens in front of the single-towered *façade* of the Basilique de Sainte-Madeleine. I cross the sun baked *place,* take a deep breath, then enter through a small door to the left. I am embraced by the refreshing cool of the great church. A masterfully carved stone tympanum rises above the central portal within. It dramatically depicts Jesus sending forth the twelve apostles on their missionary travels to the four corners of the world. My friend Jacques, the pilgrim's apostle, is among them. I pass under a smaller tympanum featuring the Ascension of Jesus, and once I step through the doorway, I am confronted by a forest of columns and high round arches, the stones alternating red and beige, beige and red. Though Romanesque, these columns and arches are more delicate and rise higher than in many other churches of its style. The light here is indirect and subtle, filtered and tranquil. The sanctuary and apse at the far end are very different from the nave: soaring and flamboyant in altogether Gothic style. I stand with Gregory on my back and Click and Clack at my sides and just take it in, or rather, just breathe it in.

It is more beautiful than I ever imagined; the cool and light and air that fill this place made of stone and glass wrap themselves around me and welcome me home. I gaze and behold and breathe. I am approached by a young Frenchman who asks from where I have come and to where am I going. He is incredulous that *un Américain* would be engaged in such a pilgrimage. Even more, I tell him, *un prêtre américain,* an American priest. Under these great arches, he takes my hand and shakes it and wishes me yet another *bon courage* for the journey ahead.

I begin a slow walk down the left ambulatory, taking in the fantastic capitals at the top of each column: some tell familiar stories from the scriptures while others feature images I do not recognize. I pass into the apse; the sanctuary is a fine example of post-Vatican II liturgical space: "noble simplicity" is how it is described by our liturgical experts. I come across a side chapel dedicated to Saint-Jacques, *le pèlerin*; an icon of James is located above a small altar in the center, to the right there is a contemporary statue of James, hand-carved in varnished wood. Before my pilgrim patron I light a candle, the fiery version of the rock placed at the feet of wayside crucifixes I have so recently taken up.

I continue my ambling until I find a stone staircase leading into the crypt below the central sanctuary. A low arched ceiling and only the smallest of windows opening into the church above deepen the crypt's womb-like feeling. In a large niche in the back wall, behind an iron grate, is the reliquary of Saint Mary Magdalene; this complex woman from the gospels is the reason this church exists. It was to her relics that pilgrims made their way here in droves in the Middle Ages; popularly seen as that most sinful woman who loved greatly, washed Jesus' feet with her hair, and so was forgiven much; she was strongly identified with by those pilgrims who felt themselves to be great sinners in search of new and better lives. That she was a central figure in Jesus' life is clear from the gospels themselves, but because she is presented so variously in the stories that feature her, getting a fix on who she really was in those same gospels is difficult. The mystery of her past and her relationship to Jesus has made her all the more attractive to those who came to this basilica to ask her prayerful assistance in their lives. I bow to her bones . . . well, really, to her great love . . . then turn to face the front altar of the crypt. There the consecrated host of Holy Communion is exposed at the center of a small gold monstrance. A few people are scattered about the pews, kneeling or sitting with hands open, deep in prayer, an aged monk with a long beard among them. I join them, setting Gregory and Click and Clack on the stool next to me. Again, as I did in Tonnerre, I settle into the place beyond the place: hardly thinking, breathing, beholding, being beheld. The place becomes both womb and tomb, beginning and end, alpha and omega. Word spoken and Word unspoken.

The sound of many voices singing in unison filters into the crypt from the basilica above, resonating amidst these low stone arches as if within the hollow space of a stringed instrument. It is a familiar melody, a hymn we know in English as *Now Thank We All Our God*, but the words I hear are German. As the tour group draws further into the basilica and closer to the sanctuary under which I sit, the sound of the voices, some harmonizing with the main chorus, grows richer and more vivid. The hymn swirls and dances about us and becomes one with our prayer.

I do not know how long I remain in Magdalene's place, but eventually, I get up and return through the foyer and back to the plaza in front of the basilica. I take my seat on the front steps of the church; I call Gene and Caroline to tell them that I have arrived safely. We agree to meet here for Vespers with the monks and sisters at 6:00 pm. I begin searching for the refuge where I have a reservation. I ask directions from a passerby and am sent a short way down the street to the left, and there it is, the Convent of the Franciscan Sisters; I am welcomed to the inner courtyard by one of the sisters, registered and shown a humble room that will be mine for the coming two nights.

After settling in, I wander back into the town, visiting the small shops that line my street; there are lots of artists and craftspeople selling their wares here. I buy a few postcards to send back to Leuven and then visit a religious goods shop near the basilica. Amidst the rosaries and holy cards and spiritual reading on offer, I spot a series of colorful images hand-painted, fresco-style, onto irregular chunks of medieval stone. There is a particular angel, subtly smiling in the medieval style that attracts my attention. He reminds me of the angel of my roadside daydream; "just keep looking at God", he told me, "without thinking of yourself". I want to give some kind of gift to Gene and Caroline to thank them for all they have done in the past two months to keep this pilgrim walking. This angel seems to be the right gift: an angel for my angels. I buy it with my VISA card and lug the weighty piece home, to be presented tomorrow night as we enjoy a final dinner together in the hotel where they are passing their days and nights in Vézelay.

I return to the basilica for Vespers and take my seat in the nave, very near the sanctuary. Gene and Caroline find me and after a quiet handshake and kiss, take seats to my left. Caroline whispers: "You have walked to Vézelay. Congratulations." I nod and smile in appreciation of the miracle of it, of where I am now, of how I have walked here.

The sisters and brothers of the Monastic Fraternity of Jerusalem, who now care for the basilica, file into the sanctuary and the delicate chanting of Vespers begins: *Dieu, viens à mon aide. Seigneur, à notre secours . . .* God, come to my assistance. Lord, make haste to help me.

The Mass follows, and in this place and at this moment, the extending of my hands to welcome the unleavened bread of the hungry and the cup of those who thirst, the self-giving love that is in and still beyond the bread and wine itself, this is a gesture more gracious and beautiful than any other I know.

As the liturgy ends, Gene and Caroline point out one monk whom they have already met, the sole Englishman in the Vézelay community, Father John Patrick; we walk around to the monks' convent and ask for him. He comes to the door, greets us warmly, and offers to stamp my *credencial* with the basilica seal. We genially chat for a while; he invites me to join the community as a concelebrant in tomorrow evening's liturgy. I would be honored, I respond.

Gene, Caroline, and I wander back into the town center, walking down a steep street towards their hotel, keeping an eye open for a restaurant where we can take our dinner together. We pick a place that had once been an old family home, exposed beams bearing country bric-a-brac cross from one side of the dining room to the other. An old fashioned bar dominates one side of the room. After dinner, we separate, they going down the street to their hotel, I up the street to my Franciscan refuge.

As I settle into my room for the night, I set aside my GPS; this gizmo has been a great boon to me for all these weeks, guiding me along, saving me from getting lost, helping me safely find shortcuts to save kilometers and hours. From here on, I shall go it alone. No GPS. Pilgrims have been walking these roads across France for over a thousand years without the aid of satellite navigation. I pull my GR 654 guide from Gregory's pouch as well. I will not be using it from here on either. I have a new set of maps prepared by the French Association of the Friends of Saint-Jacques that will guide me from here to Saint-Jean-Pied-de-Port. These maps are designed specifically for pilgrims walking from church to church, not trekkers walking from sight to sight. Instead of being packaged like a book, it offers a single sheet for each *étape* or stage. It also displays in a side column the names and phone numbers of refuges, hostels, and family homes that will take in pilgrims. Best of all, once a page is used, it can be tossed. It will get lighter and lighter as I go. I place all my trust in the new guide and bag both the GPS and the GR book for Caroline and Gene to bring back to Leuven.

There is one more problem that I must now face. From Vézelay, the pilgrim route has traditionally gone in two distinctly different directions before joining up again as one in the village of Gargilesse in the Berry region of France. The southern route passes through Nevers; the northern route runs through Bourges. Which one to take? The Bourges route is about forty kilometers shorter, and people are saying that Bourges is a city worth seeing. But the Nevers route, according to what I can see in the guide, offers more possibilities for refuge, especially in the first days. I feel stymied in making the decision; with time closing in on me, it is a toss-up, and I hate toss-up decision-making. I will talk it over more tomorrow with Gene and Caroline and see what we come up with. I put my maps and GPS away, say my prayers, and call it a day. Tomorrow will be completely a Gene and Caroline day: no walking, just sight-seeing and visiting before they return to Belgium and I continue down whichever route I might have by then chosen . . . *by myself.*

We meet for breakfast at a little *café* across the street from my refuge, then spend the better part of the day seeing the local sights. Once back in Vézelay, we want to investigate further the two route options so look for the pilgrim information office but find it closed. We stop in the tourist information office down the street as well, but the two young women at the desk are singularly uninformed about the matter. We are left to our own devices. We talk over the two options a bit, then I decide: I will take the longer route with the better housing options: Nevers it is!

We join the Jerusalem monks and nuns for 6:00 pm Vespers and Mass again, but this evening, I am dressed in alb and stole and participate from the choir stalls with the monks, doing my best to chant along with them, while Gene and Caroline participate from the first pew in the nave. At one of the most important moments in the liturgy, when the faithful come forward with hands extended to receive Communion, the consecrated bread and wine that we Catholics and many Christians welcome as the very Body and Blood of Christ, disaster strikes. The priest distributing the consecrated bread somehow notices something about the way Gene and Caroline are presenting themselves, just a bit differently from the typical Catholic, perhaps not holding their hands open in quite the same way as the others. He asks them quietly if they are Roman Catholics. When they respond that they are not, he dismisses them with a curt, "*Non.*"

I see Caroline and Gene return to their pew, then at the first discrete moment, I watch them leave the basilica. They often attend Mass in the Catholic parish in the Netherlands where her son and her grandchildren have been active members for years. The pastor there has always welcomed them to receive Communion with their family, and so they have been taught by that pastor that they should feel welcome in the church at this sacred moment. Here, in *this* church by *this* priest, they have just been taught that such is not the case. Once I catch up to them outside the basilica, I can tell Caroline has been weeping. Gene explains what happened, and my heart sinks like a rock. *I am so sorry.* Caroline can hardly speak, but manages to say at least, "It is not your fault". Vézelay, of all places, is not the place where any of us expected such a thing to happen. Whatever the theology or pastoral concerns that prompted this response from the priest, Caroline, in particular, experiences it as a blow filled with rejection from a church she sees herself in some way connected to through her extended family, and at the very least through her friendship with me.

Afterwards, we walk to the lower town and take a table in the hotel restaurant; an elegant dining room surrounds us with formally dressed waiters at the ready. Caroline is still distraught over what has happened in the basilica, and I listen to her as she pours out her feelings of being rejected and her resentment of being so excluded by my church. Again, I let her know how sorry I am that this has happened. I did not plan that the fresco angel I purchased for them would be a gesture of reconciliation, but this situation has made it so. I present my angel to Caroline and Gene and thank them for their many kindnesses and love. Angels, the both of them! They receive it warmly. Caroline tells me that as an only child, she has felt very much like I am the brother she never had. Her eyes glisten with tears as she shares this sentiment with me. I am moved, too. And with that, our own "last supper" is complete, our own communion consummated; Caroline's tears are those of an angel, as far as I am concerned.

We leave our table. Day is done. Tomorrow I return to life as a full-fledged pilgrim with no angelic safety net in the persons of Gene and Caroline to catch me if I tumble. Hopefully, I can keep my eyes fixed where they belong, without thinking of myself, and not fall . . . at least not too badly. Maybe, I pray, all this walking can heal not just us individual Christians, but our churches too.

With the new morning, I join Gene and Caroline in the parking lot near the basilica at 8:00 am to load Gregory into the Saab's trunk for the ride down the hill to the hotel. Before heading down, Caroline and I ask Gene for one last visit to the basilica; together, we quickly rush up the steps and inside. We slip over to the chapel of Saint-Jacques where Caroline lights a candle for me. I take a quick turn down the stairs into the crypt and pray before Mary Magdalene's bones: *May I love as you loved!*

Back in the nave, Caroline explains to me a couple of the scenes in the capitals of the church's columns, things she had learned from John Patrick, the English monk who had given them their tour before my arrival. Especially fascinating is a scene of two men at a mill, one pouring in the wheat, the other receiving the flour into his open hands. Her explanation: Jesus pours into the mill; Paul receives and shares it with the world. I tell Caroline that I hope my hands will remain open to receive all that comes my way during the days and weeks ahead along this Way.

We return to Gene awaiting us outside and ride down the hill for a buffet breakfast at their hotel. This being a buffet, I eat plenty now, but also, not so discretely, stock up on all I can fold into a paper napkin to keep as a snack for later in the day. I feel like a kid stealing cookies from the pantry. As a man on the verge of geezer-hood, it is rather delicious to feel that bit of kid-hood again. While we are munching on our croissants and dipping into our jams, Caroline says: "I was just thinking that the people with the greatest faults seem the easiest to love." I am not sure to whom she is referring. She must see my quizzical look, so adds: "I noticed in the basilica that the statue of Mary Magdalene had so many more candles burning in front of it than the other saints. It is as if we love more the saints who are most like us in our faults and failings." I take a moment from my munching to savor what Caroline has just said. It is a small but fundamental revelation, a message from one of my angels that opens my eyes and my heart just a little bit more along this Way. *The biggest sinners make the best saints: of course!*

Once chock-full of the delights of the French breakfast, we gather in the parking lot. I load Gregory on my back, square him and cinch him, take Click and Clack in hand, and together the three of us walk from the hotel down the highway to the head of the path to Nevers. Hanging from my neck by an elastic string, is not the GPS, but a clear plastic pouch with my new paper maps and guide within, today's *étape* open to view.

At the trail-head, we take some final snapshots, most with the town of Vézelay and its basilica rising in the background. Then we hug and kiss and say farewell, and I turn to the dirt path and begin walking by myself leaving Caroline and Gene behind, opening my hands to all that is to come.

10

Frères et Soeurs

The pilgrim route I follow post-Vézelay is well marked with small blue plastic plaques labeled with the traditional pilgrim shell and yellow arrows. Though written in French, the maps and directions in the guide hanging from my neck are easy to follow as well. I feel comfortable without the GPS, and in a way, more of a pilgrim *sans* the advanced technology than *avec*. The sun is shining this morning, making the dew-laden flora at either side of my path glimmer. I pass down through the village of Saint-Père, then find the route leading me into hill country, pushing me into extended climbs. After a day off, Gregory feels heavier than ever as I trod upward. Eventually, the morning sunshine disappears behind heavy clouds, and I am walking through dense forest and for the first time, I feel the chill of fall through my thin micro-fiber shirt.

Gene and Caroline call just to see how I am faring. Fine, I advise them. I am missing their company, but on the other hand, it is not a bad thing to be alone again. Solitude is integral to the pilgrim life: it gives me time to think, ponder, pray, fret, work through the fretting, just be. It also makes me appreciate more deeply the sparse moments of conviviality and friendship that come my way, when they come. They are all the more precious for their rarity. This is a great difference between the Spanish Camino and the French Chemin: In crossing Spain four years ago, I had some solitude in the morning walks, but plenty of fraternity in the afternoons. Here, now, I live mostly alone, morning, evening, night. Surprisingly perhaps, I like the French version better.

As I pass wayside crosses I fulfill my commitment: *Our Father . . . Lord Jesus, have mercy . . . Oh my Jesus, forgive us our sins . . .* From shrine to shrine and prayer to prayer I walk; I pass a night in the tiny village of Bazoches where, as evening comes on, I take a walk along the road leading into and out of the tiny village. The warmth of the afternoon has made room for evening freshness. I walk slowly along the old paved road; a breeze tousles my hair just slightly. The sky darkens. The first star appears. Then others. Then little by little, a whole heaven of stars are revealed. Far from any city, away even from the streetlights of Bazoches, the Milky Way becomes increasingly distinct and gorgeous. I know I am looking at the wispy edge of our galaxy, but I also know I am beholding what pilgrims have for ages beheld: their road south to Compostela, mapped for them in the stars above. This *Via Lactea* guides me too; it carries me not just to Compostela, but to wisdom, and to truth, and I hope somehow, into God.

With morning, the glory of last night's sky above is now the glory of field and forest here below. Breezes wisp across the fields, bending the grass and clover in unpredictable waves. Bourgogne is beautiful beyond words: green and grand. It extends in rolling hills out to the horizon, the squared and civilized fields stitched together by thick and wild hedgerows. This tapestry of flora, flooded with sunlight, bright and open, is interrupted here and there by stands of dense oak woods, intensely interior with roof of branch and leaf above and underfoot, crackling as I step on fallen acorns, most with their dandy berets having already fallen from their shiny brown pates. The open fields are such extroverts, every blade and drop of dew on show for all to see while the closed stands of oak are this earth's introverts, their secrets held deeply within. The fields sing, but the woods murmur. I am taken by both. This morning's earth and last night's star-strewn sky are for me here and now, *gratia plena*, an earth and sky that is just plain *full of grace*.

My map directs me towards a steep rise that looks as if it climbs forever. The road is dirt and stone, rutted by rains. I have been walking up and down these Burgundy knolls all morning, but this one is king of the hills. I take a rest before tackling it, sitting in a small patch of grass, beside the way with Gregory at my side, nibbling on a few raisins and nuts I have had in emergency storage since Vézelay. After ten minutes or so, I decide it is time to go after this newest challenge. So after restoring Gregory to my back, I take Click and Clack, shorten their length a centimeter or two for the steep climb ahead, and begin plodding upward. After a quarter-kilometer, I stop, lean against my poles, take a few deep breaths, then continue another quarter-kilometer. Then another. And so I climb. The view out and over the fields and woods I have walked since Bazoches is breathtaking. In the distance, some fifteen-plus kilometers away, I can still make out the rise of Vézelay and the Sainte-Madeleine Basilica against the skyline, lovely to the eye as ever.

Finally, I come out of the woods and find myself on the outskirts of a village named, appropriately enough, Le Chemin. I pass a few houses, round a corner, then hear someone calling to me: "*Monsieur, monsieur,* wouldn't you like a cup of tea?" I turn and find a man about my age standing in the gate of his garden, smiling and waving. I turn and happily agree to the tea. He welcomes me in, takes Gregory from my back and Click and Clack from my hands, setting them safely against the porch of the small house. He asks about me, and when I say I am an American, he switches into almost perfect American English, the hint of a Dutch accent giving away his own status as a foreigner in these parts. He is Adrianus, but goes by Art; he introduces me to his wife, Louisa. They invite me to sit at a garden table under an apple tree heavy with ripe fruit. The garden looks out over the fields and woods of Burgundy back towards Bazoches and Vézelay. Louisa brings me a glass of freshly brewed tea and some crackers and cheese, then with the duties of hospitality taken care of, joins Art and me at the table. As always, they ask where I began my pilgrimage, do I intend to go all the way to Compostela, am I married, and, of course, what do I do for a living? When I answer that I am single because I am a Catholic priest, they are intrigued: "A *Roman* Catholic priest?" *Yes, exactly.* They themselves have been raised in the Protestant tradition but have great interest in what the Catholic Church is doing or not doing in these complicated times.

I respond to their questions as best I am able, then Art asks me: "If you could meet with the new Pope and tell him honestly anything you'd like, if he were to invite you to freely advise him, what would you say?" After some thought, I respond: *I think that I would advise him, being both a new pope and an elderly pope, to use his papacy to listen. Speak or write when necessary, but as little as possible. No great speeches, no pronouncements, no encyclicals; instead be a grandfather who spends his days listening to his grandchildren, all of them, Catholic and otherwise. Let them crawl into your lap. Hold them to your breast. Feel the pulse of their hearts. Come to know the joys that brighten their eyes, the weight that bends them over, the freedoms they long for. Then near the end of your life, dear Holy Father, write one encyclical that expresses all that you have heard and seen and felt from your children around the world. That would be something.*

Art raises an eyebrow, nods, and says: "Yes, that would be something."

Louisa pulls two apples from the tree above our heads and offers them to me for the road. Art tells me something important: "You pilgrims have a special status in the lives of these people you are meeting along the way, these villagers whose hamlets you traverse. They are proud to have you passing through their places." Louisa adds, more practically: "These villagers live lonely lives with very few things to entertain them or offer them diversion from their hard work. There are so few people in their lives, so a pilgrim passing by brings them company for a moment or two and makes them happy. They give to you, yes; but don't forget, you give to them as well." I think I have sensed this truth, but never so explicitly as to find words for it myself; I am glad that they have done this for me. It is wisdom worth savoring. A small epiphany.

I have spent more than an hour in this garden with Art and Louisa. I am so happy to have had this time with them—so happy they invited me in. In just an hour, we have become more than good friends; as so often happens around pilgrim tables, we have become something more. Their caring mix of kindness and respect and wisdom make it clear that we are now *frères*, well, actually, *frère et soeur.*

Nevertheless, it is time to move on, and I will most likely never see these good people again in this life. I am getting used to this, but it is a strain on the spirit to *salut* new brothers and sisters in one moment and then in the next have to say *adieu.*

As I leave Art and Louisa's haven, it is considerably warmer than when I arrived. I am especially grateful now for the breezes that cool me and the oaks that occasionally shade me. At a few minutes before 2:00 pm, tired and hungry and hot, I walk into the town of Corbigny. There is a refuge here; I find the street but mistakenly enter the lobby of an old folks home. I realize immediately that these geezers standing about in pajamas and slippers cannot possibly be pilgrims. A nurse intercepts me and directs me further up the street, to the next building. A gate opens into a spacious yard, marked by a pair of cedar trees of enormous proportions. I amble up the drive to the front door of what clearly once was a school house. The door is closed and locked. A note posted in a window to the left of the door advises me that the refuge will not be open until 4:00 pm. That leaves me two hours to wait and no place to store Gregory and Click and Clack. I am famished so, with no other choice available, I continue back into the center of town to find a shop. I find first the church, so I go to step inside when I am hailed by a dwarf-size fellow sitting on a nearby stoop in the shade. He too has a backpack to one side and is snacking. I go to him.

"So you are a pilgrim too?" he asks. *Yes, I am a pilgrim.* "How far did you walk today?" *I began in Bazoches.* "That is not so far; I walked much further. I walk at least thirty kilometers every day." *That's good. I'm a little slow, I know.* "There's a refuge here, but it is closed until 4:00 pm. We have to wait. No priest here either." He rolls a cigarette for himself. His manner of emphasizing the fact that the refuge will not open until 4:00 pm seems to indicate he sees this as a serious personal insult. This little man annoys me with his strangely aggressive manner. I wonder if he is "all there." I tell him I'll see him later, then take a quick peek in the church, but hunger is getting the best of me, and I return outside and ask the mini-pilgrim about a grocery store. He directs me to the nearest *supermarché*, with the seemingly simple directions: "Left then right," which he repeats again and again. Even as I leave him sitting on his shady stoop and wander off, he yells after me: "Left then right!" I take the left then the right but get lost for a block or two all the same. I eventually see the ATAC Supermarché sign a couple more blocks to the left and head over; I leave Gregory and Click and Clack in a corner near the cash register and shop for my lunch: a green salad wrapped in plastic, bread, cheese, fruit juice, yogurt, sausage. I pay up, take possession of my pack and poles, and under the hot afternoon sun, amble back to the refuge garden.

Sitting on the grass in the shade of one of a grand cedar trees is the little guy. He greets me with the intrusive questions: "What did you buy? How much did you pay?" He leans over and rifles through my grocery sack, taking stock of each item within. I offer him some bread and cheese, but he declines my tepid effort at hospitality. "You do not speak French well. WHERE are you from?" *I'm American, but I work in Belgium.* "WHERE in Belgium?" *Leuven.* "Leuven? WHY are you in Leuven?" I tell him I am a Catholic priest and have been rector of the American seminary there. The pilgrim short-stack laughs heartily, pulls a wooden cross out from under his sweat-stained shirt and tells me he is a Trappist monk, also from Belgium. The joke is on me. He is one of my own, sort of, whether I like him or not. Now we are brothers. I can no longer dismiss him as just another Chemin oddball.

Frère Patrick tells me that he has already walked to Compostelle and is now on his way home. He has been on the road for the better part of six months. And with that, he announces he is going to sleep now and lies back on the grass, closing his eyes firmly. *Fine with me.* I finish my lunch and lay my head back against Gregory and relax in the quiet under the leafy limbs of this extraordinary cedar. I tell myself to be good to this annoying little Trappist. He must be full of stories, even if he is a bit eccentric.

A few minutes before 4:00, a lady carrying her own bag of groceries comes walking up the drive and greets us. She is our *hospitalière* for the evening and introduces herself as Hélène. *Frère* Patrick and I get up off the ground and follow her to the front door, which she unlocks, opens and ushers us through. She sets aside her groceries in a small kitchen, then invites us to take a seat while she registers us, asking, as always, to see our *credencials*. *Frère* Patrick goes first; for no obvious reason, he is argumentative, critical, and treats poor Hélène like a scullery maid. Hélène maintains her cool as he chides her for not being here earlier, for the way she has stamped his *credencial*, for not having tomorrow's breakfast at an earlier hour, for just about everything short of global warming. Finally, Hélène shows her exasperation, glancing towards me with one eyebrow raised in clear annoyance, then tells the monk to move on. The Trappist Typhoon surprisingly obeys, traipsing off to find the dormitory and take possession of his share of our common space for the night.

Hélène, as it turns out, lives several villages away and has herself walked the Spanish *Camino,* so she is no novice when it comes to the life of the pilgrim. More importantly, as a volunteer *hospitalière* for a week at a time, she sleeps here and will prepare breakfast for us. Best of all, Hélène is a very kind, understanding and altogether happy *hospitalière.* Hélène even checks the version of my pilgrim guide and advises me that there has been a change in the route out of Corbigny, a change made to avoid a busy and dangerous stretch of highway. She graciously draws out for me the new route following a rural road. Hopefully, *le petit Frère* Patrick is sleeping off his cantankerousness even as Hélène and I discuss the new route I shall follow in the morning.

Hélène points out a chapel along the corridor to the dormitory. The refuge is actually part of a convent of nuns; this is their chapel, but we pilgrims are welcome to make use of it. I poke my head in; it is a bit on the gloomy side but good enough for some quiet prayer.

I take a lower bunk in the small dormitory located to the back of the refuge, *Frère* Patrick napping at the opposite end of the room. I shower, launder, and set my wet clothing out to dry as always, then lie down for my own nap. There is one thing that Hélène has told me that gives me some cause for worry: the coming two days of walking will have absolutely no services along the way. The next significant town is Saint-Révérien, which also has a municipal refuge for pilgrims, but no *marché, super* or otherwise, no *boulangerie,* no *café.* Nor is there anything further on, not until I get to Prémery. I will have to go back to the ATAC here in town and purchase enough foodstuffs to last me until then. I'll try to be careful in my selections, but there is no way I will be able to avoid adding significant kilos to the burden on my back.

Once *Frère* Patrick is back on his feet, he proclaims to Hélène and me that he will cook up dinner for us, and he assures us it will be the world's-best-spaghetti, far better than anything on offer even in Rome itself. I offer to bring back a good bottle of wine from the store to compliment his perfect pasta. He now calls me *mon père* and after his rest seems, indeed, to be a significantly kinder person. He offers me a small pilgrim shell he has brought back from Spain as a gift as well as several "holy cards" of various pious saints I am not familiar with; his version of pilgrim evangelization, I presume. Though I do not suppose I could ever consider this peripatetic Trappist a candidate for close friendship, I am beginning to like him. There is a sweetness about him, and when he smiles, this pint-sized monk is actually rather endearing; if nothing else, you just have to admire a guy so physically challenged on his feet spending so much of his life traipsing back and forth across Europe for God.

I do my shopping, return laden with a fine bottle of red Bordeaux and at least two kilos of tuna, pork slices, granola bars, nuts, raisins, yogurt, and other assorted comestibles for the two days ahead. *Frère* Patrick is already at work in the kitchen with Hélène assisting, the two getting along quite well now that he is in charge. He must be a great trial to his abbot, which, perhaps, is why he is seemingly on the road more than he is in choir.

I take a little time in the chapel for Vespers, then join Hélène and *Frère* Patrick in the kitchen. His spaghetti is surprisingly good, covered in a garlic-laden red sauce and just as perfectly *al dente* as he claimed it would be. The wine we share among the three of us softens the trials of the trail and the annoyances that come with unexpected new friends. We all help clean up; *Frère* Patrick then reminds me that tomorrow is Sunday and suggests that I celebrate Mass for us in the morning before our departure. I agree, and we set a time before breakfast. He retires before 8:00 pm; I take to my bunk shortly after he does and wait for sweet sleep to come.

That sweet sleep does not come easily; I am awakened throughout the night by strange, eruptive sounds from *Frère* Patrick. I do not recognize them: they are not snores as snores are generally understood, nor are they flatulence; they come from his guts, lungs, throat and sinus system, but the sound is like nothing I've ever heard before: *kwaaaroom!* I am startled out of sleep almost on the hour by the eruptions, and I do not have my earplugs handy though I doubt they would help. *Kwaaaroom!* I toss, then turn, then toss anew with every eruption. *Oh, my God, Pat! Just shut up already.* Tomorrow ain't gonna be easy. *Kwaaaroom!*

Frère Patrick is up at 6:00 am, and I soon follow. In his skivvies he looks even lower to the ground than when fully clothed. In his waking persona, there are no further eruptions. He is busy as a bee pulling his things together and dressing himself in his specially cut blue jeans. I remind him of my promise to say Mass in the morning, but he seems to have forgotten all about it. "*La Messe?*" he repeats quizzically. It won't take long, I assure him. "*En anglais?*" Yes, English, of course; I can't do it in French. He leaves his stuff and troops out of the bedroom and into the chapel. I follow, set things up quickly, place a stole over my pilgrim duds, and begin our prayer: In the name of the Father . . . *Amen.* Grace and peace to you . . . *Et avec votre esprit.* Lord, have mercy . . . *Prends pitié de nous.*

The world's tiniest Trappist is seriously devout. He seems a different person in this chapel, his hands splayed open before him in prayer, eyes cast upward, responding in French to my English. The little liturgy we share, just the two of us, before breakfast, before the day's hike, makes me feel sorry for having been so hard on him yesterday. *Prends pitié de moi.* I guess when a man is as short as *Frère* Patrick, over a lifetime chips can develop on shoulders, even small shoulders, self-defense mechanisms take over, even unconsciously; a pint-sized chicken takes on the aspect of a banty-rooster. When all is said and done, and this communion I place in his hands now makes it clear, we are *frères.* He would drive me crazy if I had to live with him, even worse, share the same dorm with him for more than a night, but he is a rather extraordinary creation from the hand of God, even at that. This *petit pèlerin,* this *frère* is a *grâce* to me this Sunday morning.

We tidy up the chapel, then join Hélène in the kitchen for our *petit-déjeuner.* After eating our croissants, sliced baguettes with butter and jam, and sipped down our coffee and juice, *Frère* Patrick and I head back to the dormitory to collect our things and make ready for the road. He stops me in the corridor: "*Mon père:* do you have ten euros you can give me. I am just a poor monk, and I have nothing for my day's meal along the way." *Okay, okay, mon frère, you got it.* I dig into my wallet and spot him the ten. He offers me a bow and a *merci* and the extraordinary *Frère Patrick* is on his way out the door and down his road. Go in the peace of Christ, *mon frère. Nous rendons grâce à Dieu.* Thanks be to God!

Though I presume I will never see *mon frère* again, perhaps a bit grate-fully so, I no sooner have said farewell and given the standard double kiss to Hélène, walk back into the town center, and pass the church, than I hear the now familiar voice call cheerily to me: "*Mon père!* Left then right! Left then right!" He is sitting on the same stoop near the church door where I first found him yesterday. Being warmed by the morning sun, he is rolling a cigarette. I suspect my ten-spot has paid for this small earthly delight. I wave a pole in his direction in farewell, and walk off, left then right, as he has repeatedly ordered me, and promptly lose my way—again.

I backtrack to the main street out of town, re-find my Compostelle arrows and pick up the correct route. I have to depend on these arrows for some ten kilometers or so since I am following the revised route that is not in my guide. This is pilgriming without a net; attention is called for! Once out of town, I tread an ancient Roman road mostly westward, knowing that along this very route, on the very ground, under these very feet, thousands of pilgrims for more than a thousand years have trod towards Compostelle. I am part of something grand out here.

My eruption-interrupted sleep is taking its toll, as I feared. I slog along with just enough energy to continue, but not enough to enjoy. The day is a beaut, perfect for walking: cool, sunny, breezy; but it is lost on me this morning. At Chitry-les-Mines, I lose sight of my arrows and get lost in a tangle of small streets forcing me to track back to the last known arrow, not once but twice. I am frustrated and for the first time since Vézelay, I long for my GPS. I take a risk on a main road cutting through the edge of the village and sure enough, there ahead, is the long lost arrow of the Chemin. I cross over a canal with a small recreational lake to the left, then go around the lake, up a hill, past a number of elegant homes, and before long I am back among the angular puzzle piece fields of Burgundy.

In Guipy, I am pleased to discover that the small highway that leads me on is named Rue Saint-Jacques-de-Compostelle. I discover a small bar open on this Sunday morning along the highway. A green park set around an old chapel flanks the other side of the road. I roll into the bar feeling beat. I am stared at by the few patrons inside, some already deep into their day's drinking, judging by their glassy eyes. I hate this "bar stare"; it is the one and only thing about rural France that I find disagreeable. The bars here seem to be private places, the exclusive turf of those few who frequent them. I ask the bartender if I might have a coffee and a croissant. He nods ambiguously: "*Café, oui. Croissant, non.*" Okay . . . then a *café au lait, si vous plaît.* He nods to a small grocery area in the next room if I want something to eat. I take a look: the shelves feature mostly canned goods and candy. I take two Snickers bars and bring them to the back table where I have set Gregory and Click and Clack. The other customers look at me like I am really stupid for having Snickers in my hand. *Well, it is YOU who don't have any croissants!* I let my eyes rather snarl back at them. Man, I need more sleep.

One elderly lady, dressed in her Sunday best, seems to sense that this sweaty pilgrim is not doing so well on this sunny Sunday morning; she looks at me sweetly and says, "*Le Chemin est dur.*" Yes, it is, madame. *Yes, it is very hard sometimes.* I smile back grateful for the bit of respect and care she has shown me in this otherwise dark and unpleasant bar. I finish my coffee and wish her a *bonjour*, then take my things and cross the highway to the park and there I wolf down one of the Snickers bars in three bites. After the third bite, I hear the echo of Louisa's voice from yesterday: "These villagers live lonely lives with very few things to entertain them . . . so a pilgrim passing by brings them company for a moment or two and makes them happy. They give to you, yes; but don't forget, you give to them as well." *You did not give anything to these villagers,* my conscience accuses me. *Some pilgrim you are. Next time: do better.*

By early afternoon, I am climbing slowly into Saint-Révérien. I miss an arrow somewhere and go slightly off-track, picking up the hot paved road into the town instead of a cooler dirt track, but to no great loss. Traffic here is nil on this Sunday *après-midi.* I amble into a town center with nary a soul about and find the *mairie*, the town hall, closed up tighter than a drum for the weekend; next door is what used to be the village *école*; this school is where the refuge is supposed to be. I see a Compostelle plaque on the door. This is my home for the night. I try the door, and it opens. I drop my poles and Gregory to the ground and size up the place: a bunk bed, a table and two chairs, a kitchen sink and small refrigerator, and a shower. Perfect.

Perfect except for one detail: *Okay, where's the toilet?* I check about and find nothing, not even the proverbial porcelain hole in the ground once so typical of the French countryside. I take my phone and dial the number on the front door. I explain who I am and ask about the toilet; the man on the other end laughs at my predicament and explains, "To the left . . . to the left . . . outside!" I wander around to the left of the city hall, towards the church behind the hall, and see nothing. Then I spot them: lined up along what once was the *école's* playground is a series of well-used outhouses that must have served the school children of Saint-Révérien for God-only-knows how many generations. I open the old wood door to one and there it is: the proverbial porcelain hole in the ground. *Well, this will be fun at 6:00 am tomorrow morning!* I have a hearty laugh at the ridiculousness of my pilgrim life. Out here: laugh or die, pilgrim's choice.

I wander into the church and from displays and folios in the vestibule discover that this village, seemingly on the verge of a drawn-out death now, has a long and rather glorious history. A Roman town once thrived close to the present site. In the third century, Saint-Révérien himself arrived preaching Christianity but was promptly beheaded by the local Romans. That dastardly deed supposedly happened very close to where I presently stand. A Cluniac monastery once stood here, some of this church building being remnants of those Cistercian glory days. And of course, for the better part of a millennium, this town and its church have been receiving pilgrims on their way to Compostela. The *église* itself is most pleasing: it reminds me of the basilica in Vézelay, though on a much smaller scale. The capitals atop the church's interior columns are finely crafted; the Romanesque arches connecting them one to the other are graceful as they roundly span the space between the columns to the left and right. After browsing about the interior, I set myself down in one of the church's creaky pews, for the stillness of the place is a tonic to the constant movement of a morning-full of walking. A tourist comes in and begins clicking snapshots of the capitals and columns. My contemplative spell is broken, so I get up and return to my refuge and its bunk for my Sunday nap.

Upon rising, I take my journal and walk out the door and across the parking lot to the town's monument to the fallen of the world wars. It is not so different from the others I have passed in French villages everywhere: a plinth, scrolls with long lists of names engraved upon them, eloquent words of noble sacrifices not made in vain, a small square of grass surrounding it. There is also shade here, so I take my seat on the grass with my back against the base of the monument and begin writing of the morning's sluggish walk from Corbigny. I do not get very far when a little girl carrying a pink Barbie purse slung over her shoulder and leading a shaggy dog by a leather leash wanders past. She looks at me, smiles, walks on, then comes back. She is perhaps seven or eight years old. She comes to the small square of grass and sits down less than a meter from me. She lets go of the leash of the altogether docile dog, which sits down too, panting happily.

She examines me. When I realize she is waiting on me to take the next step in the interaction she has begun by sitting next to me on this cool grass, I look up and ask her the name of her dog. "Fresca," she reports matter-of-factually. I ask if he is a good dog, and she smiles and says, "*Très bon*". I ask after her own name. "Solange." I repeat it aloud after her and tell her it is a very pretty name. She smiles again, then hooks the leash to the dog and jerks him back into walking mode. After a quick pass around the surrounding parking lot, Solange and Fresca return and retake their positions for Part Two of our encounter. I ask her if she might spell her name out for me, since it is a one I have never heard before. She takes my pen and my journal and writes in block letters across the empty side column: S-O-L-A-N-G-E. She informs me that I do not speak well. I respond that I speak *anglais* very well and *espagnole* well enough, but, yes, *français est dure pour moi*, French is difficult for me. She laughs at my poor choice of words. I ask her to teach me some French words. The concept baffles her, so I draw a simple pig at the top of a journal page, the species made evident mostly by a curlicue on what otherwise looks like a balloon with legs and another balloon for a head. "*Cochon*," she responds matter-of-factually. I draw a butterfly. "*Papillon*," she tells me with a laugh, obviously finding the double wings I have sketched to be a quite silly representation of the reality. I try drawing an ant, but the image leaves her baffled once more. Oh well. We have both done our best, and I go back to writing while she empties acorns from her Barbie purse and begins counting them and separating them into bunches, those with berets and those without. Fresca pants. After a considerable silence as we tend to our distinct affairs, she asks me where my *mère* and *père* live. I tell her my *mère* and *père* are both *morts*. The news does not affect her one way or the other. Solange redirects her acorns from bunches into lines, a loose sort of military formation singularly appropriate under this memorial plinth, I suppose. I then ask her if she has brothers and sisters. "*Oui: trois frères, trois soeurs, trois chats, trois chiens*." I say, that's a lot of *trois*'s, and she laughs. Solange puts her acorns back in her purse one by one, then hooks

Fresca back onto his leash, says *au revoir*, and leaves me to my journal. What a beautiful little girl. She is just completely herself, and no fear of strangers has ever touched her. How extraordinary that one so young keeps alive the tradition of hospitality towards the pilgrim in this town, so long dedicated to the care of people like me. And the *manner* of her care, this is what is most extraordinary: just sitting, visiting, being quietly with, an agenda-free companionship. Solange is like a little sister to me today.

A very shiny Mercedes pulls into the parking lot between the monument and my front door. A large man with a strong German accent asks in French how I found entry to the *refuge*. When he hears me begin my answer, my own American accent just as evident to him as his German is to me, he switches to English. "Ho-ho, we are pilgrims too!" He points to a small pilgrim shell on a leather lace around his neck. He tells me that they stopped here yesterday but could find no way in. I respond that I had called ahead and made a reservation. For him and his wife, there was no crisis in yesterday's miss; they are walking with a helping car following them, driven by friends, much as Gene and Caroline did for me in the days leading to Vézelay. At their age, he assures me with his hearty laugh, they take every advantage they can to stay healthy on the road. He rolls with laughter again, then he wishes me well, and the Mercedes zooms off.

Later, as I work pork slices and cheese into a sandwich for my dinner, Solange returns, with Fresca of course, but also with a little sister whom she is intent on introducing to me: Natasha. As I munch on my sandwich, we sit on the stoop of the refuge. I watch quietly as she and Natasha play with a busty, blonde Barbie doll that has been delivered from her pink purse. What strikes me is that she is not just *playing* with her little sister; she is *caring* for her. I am moved: *sweet Solange: may you always be so good as you are this day!*

The *hospitalier* with whom I earlier spoke by phone pulls up in a small pickup, greets Solange and Natasha as if they were his grandchildren, perhaps they are, then taking a small cash-box in hand invites me inside the refuge to stamp my *credencial* and collect a few euros for the night's stay. He is as friendly as Solange, though probably seven times her age. He advises me to be wary tomorrow: there are no services and no food available until Prémery. I assure him that I have enough for the day's walk. He departs, kissing the girls on both cheeks as he goes; I then take advantage of the solitude to phone a *chambre d'hôte* in Prémery and make a reservation for bed, breakfast, and dinner, which I feel I owe myself after two days and nights of eating *baguette* sandwiches and granola bars.

As I go to bed, I consider *Frère* Patrick: did he make it all the way to Vézelay today as he had planned? I look forward to a sleep free of grand eruptions from this teapot of a Trappist, short and stout indeed. But with a day's distance, I find I actually *care* for him. I care that he arrive safely in Vézelay and that thereafter he travel well and that he have a good life in his Belgian monastery when, finally, his traveling days are done. *Protect him, Lord!*

11

Mon Père

I awake at 2:00 am for no good reason. Thereafter, I toss and turn, unable to reenter the land of nod, and listen to the nearby church bell ring off the hours with deepening despair at the sleep that I am losing; at the sixth hour, all is lost, and I get out of bed, put on my shorts and sandals, and make my way through the dark to the toilet outside. The stars are still visible, and that is solace to me: the universe in all its grandeur remains firmly intact above and below me. The stars, in their shiny multitude, feel like old friends cheering me on in spite of myself. I greet them: *Ah, there you are, my little étoiles!* Once back in my refuge, I pick at the remainders of my pork sandwich, slurp down two pots of cherry yogurt, drink a cup of instant coffee, say *Laudes*, pack up the last of my things, and walk out the door past the war memorial and down the street of this still somnolent village.

The morning is cool enough for me to see my breath as I walk. This is a first on this pilgrimage. I look at the face of my watch: September 10. *Summer is over for sure.* The fields and hills are quiet and tranquil as I amble through them. The dew clinging to every blade of grass, bramble branch, and silvery string of spider-web dazzles as the dawn light of the rising sun sweeps over the land, effortlessly pushing back the final vestiges of night. *The battle is won. Victory is assured. Darkness and her minions are defeated once again!* Looking very much like the angel hair we used long ago to decorate our Christmas trees, wisps of white fog hang low in the valleys, slowly rise, thin, then dissipate into thin air. Yes, autumn is coming, the soft streams of morning mist advise.

As I come over a rise, I see a figure on the road ahead. Drawing closer, it becomes clear that it is a young boy, pacing about and puffing steam from his mouth into the cold morning, slapping his hands against his arms to warm them. He wears a hooded sweatshirt, *capuche* up, and blends into the shade of roadside trees and the last of the morning fog. He could be a schoolboy monk. I wonder what I must look like to him: a clown perhaps, my floppy hat atop my head, overweight Gregory strapped to my back, bent over and moving slow as a snail, supporting myself and claiming ground with Click and Clack clicking and clacking on the pavement below me. At any rate, as I pass, our eyes meet, his are limpid and green and gleam like the morning dew, and he smiles at me as if he has long known me, so we greet each other with warm *bonjours*. I stop on the roadside, stand up straight, puff a small cloud into the morning chill from my own mouth, then ask him if he is on his way to school. He says, "*Oui,*" then smiles at me again. He is maybe eight or nine years old. I wish him well in his *études* and turn to go on my way, leaving behind this new friend. He calls after me: "*Au revoir, monsieur!*" I wave Click back to him in farewell, turn a corner, and he too becomes a memory.

I walk surprisingly well, considering the limited sleep I have had the past two nights. I have no great explanation, so it seems like I am being carried as much as I am carrying. My friends, the stars, whom I greeted early this morning when it was still night, though I cannot see them now, are carrying me this day, I am quite certain.

I take a break after about ten kilometers, sitting against a small embankment between road and field. It is warming up already, and it is not even 10:00 am. As best I can figure it, I have only about seven or eight more kilometers to Prémery. I get up and tackle them, but as they unfold, these kilometers prove to be slow and heavy. I continue on until I pick up the highway into town, which turns into a busy street. I keep my eye open for some sign of my *chambre d'hôte*, which is located somewhere along this very *rue*. Approaching the commercial center of Prémery, I catch sight of the sign I'm looking for, but the place indicated looks more like a restaurant than the kind of *chambre d'hôte* I've become used to along the way. I step in, and it is indeed a restaurant, a small place with no one in attendance. I call and move towards the kitchen and call again. Finally, a lady comes through the door from the kitchen, wiping her hands on her apron; she smiles and says I have arrived quite early, but no matter, the room is ready for me. She leads me out of the restaurant proper, through a small hallway, pointing out the loo on the way, and up a shaky set of stairs, to a small room painted from top to bottom in bright blue with white trim. A small picture of a blue sailboat on the blue sea hangs on one wall. *Ah! A room with a theme . . . just what I was hoping for!* She points out the shower next door, then cheerily advises me that the room is thirty-two euros, breakfast another six, and, if I want dinner tonight, add twelve more. This is adding up to a budget-busting night, and not in the nicest of places, but I agree to all charges and accept the invitation to supper: after all, I have been two days now subsisting on yogurt and homemade sandwiches.

At some point in the afternoon, I wonder if I took my daily medicine this morning. I have a batch of pills I take every morning and a couple more in the evening to keep my heart from going out of rhythm. Atrial fibrillation is my affliction, an annoying but mostly harmless condition I share with a couple of my brothers, something we inherited from our mother. I get up, check my pillbox for Monday, and see the whole collection waiting for me still. The dose is now hours, almost a half-day, overdue. I decide the best thing is to hold on until I can get back into my regular schedule with the hope that my heart's atrium will stay in sync in the meantime. It is a bit of a gamble, but the chances are good that all will be well. If I lose, and the fibrillation kicks in, then I will have to wait until the natural rhythm restores itself before doing much of anything physical, that could be one hour or twenty-four. This is the first time since beginning this pilgrimage that I have made this mistake. I take my lighter evening dose, set aside this morning's unused pills until tomorrow and hope for the best.

At 7:00 pm, I go downstairs for my dinner, but before being seated, I am presented to two men who have already begun their own suppers. They are both French-speaking Belgians and pilgrims. They arrived in town sometime during the afternoon. One is about my age, the other perhaps in his late-thirties. We shake hands and share our names, asking of course, where today's walk began for the other. The two of them hoofed over thirty kilometers today making my sub-twenty day seem measly and me a pilgrim piker. I am shown a separate table and take a seat by myself. A glass of red wine is brought to me. After our introductions, it feels a little odd to be seated here by myself and them there, just a meter or two away, but I don't want to impose myself on them. The elder of the two gentlemen, Daniel, must feel the same as I, because before I can even take the first sip of my wine, he asks if I don't want to join them at table. With relief, I agree and pick up my place setting and transfer to their table. We quickly move to animated pilgrim-talk: where we have been, what we have experienced, how our bodies are doing, what kind of equipment we are using. Daniel is animated and a born-extrovert, talking up a storm, while Jean-Pierre, the younger, seems painfully shy. They are both in great physical condition and are regularly doing thirty-plus days. My sense of inferiority is softened by the wine and the roast chicken and spuds that I am served from the kitchen, and of course, gratitude that I am walking at all, the *catastrophe* of Tonnerre being plenty fresh in my memory. The conversation fills the table with more than food; pilgrim fraternity is being shared here too, and that is all to the good. I've met so few in the weeks I've been walking: Herman in

Namur, Marie Claire and Mary Anne in Bragelogne-Beauvoir, *Frère* Patrick in Corbigny, now Daniel and Jean-Pierre; the company of those who *know* what this is like is precious for its rarity, and I don't want to miss out on the opportunity to just *be* with others of my pilgrim tribe.

Dessert comes: a creamy *flan* dripping with caramel sauce. As I take the first bite, I feel it: the familiar *thump-thump–pause for two counts–thumpity-thump-thumpity-thump–pause for two counts–thump* of atrial-fibrillation. I have just lost my gamble. I finish my dessert, excuse myself from the table and climb the stairs to my room, taking it slow so as not to dizzy myself by excessive exertion while this is going on. Once in my room all I can do is rest, sleep and hope all is back in order by tomorrow morning.

Upon awakening at 5:30 am, the ticker has not restored itself to orderliness. I get up and take the full morning dose of my meds immediately. I know without even thinking about it that I cannot walk today with my heart acting this way; the probability of spending another day in Prémery is hardly enchanting. At 7:00 am, I send a text message to Caroline explaining the problem. She texts back immediately that she will check with my doctor in Leuven as soon as possible to see what advice he might have. I go downstairs for breakfast and explain the problem to my host, adding that if it does not clear up, I will need to stay put another day. I am told, "*Pas de problem;* consider this place *chez vous.* If you are able to leave later, just hang the key next to the door on the way out."

I share breakfast with Daniel and Jean-Pierre, but they are quick to finish and return to the road. I return to my room feeling alone and lonely, a sense that is alleviated by a call from Caroline. The doc back home says I can walk as soon as the heart gets back in rhythm. I slowly pack up Gregory and have him ready to go. I stretch out on my bed and say my usual prayer to Saint-Jacques: *fix me!* Now I just wait.

After only half an hour, I feel my pulse: it seems okay. I wait a while longer, then stand. I wait a while longer, then walk down to the bathroom and back upstairs, the heart is beating just fine. This is great: it is not even 10:00 am. I put on my socks and boots, haul Gregory downstairs, hang up the restaurant key, close the door behind me, and leave Prémery after all.

As I walk, I can't help but notice something strange. It is a stiff climb out of Prémery, and a long climb too. I am walking just fine, and that is what is strange. Usually, after one of these runs of atrial fibrillation, no, let me change that adverb: *always* after one of these runs of atrial fibrillation, especially after one that has gone on overnight, I feel weary and exhausted once it is over. That poor little heart has had a rough go of it and usually needs its rest. But here I am, pulling myself and my fourteen kilos of Gregory up this hill, and I am hardly feeling it. To the contrary, I am feeling energetic, not even breathing hard, taking no rests, and I rather feel like I am flying up this road. What is the explanation? I have none. What is there to say but *Merci, Saint-Jacques!*

I cover the eighteen kilometers to Guérigny, the next overnight stop on my way, in what seems like no more than a breath. The last couple of kilometers lead me past a huge factory, probably a steelworks from the look of it, now completely silent. Warning signs tell me to keep out. Decrepit buildings on the other side of the highway, now empty, were once workers's housing, for sure. It is the most unattractive *entrée* into a French town that I have yet encountered. It reeks of an industrial revolution that has come and gone, leaving in its wake unemployment, depression, and probably an expiring community dangling, twisting in the wind.

Once past the factory and into the heart of the town, what I find is not what the factory predicted; Guérigny is a lively place with plenty of commerce, people on the streets, and school kids in uniforms with small backpacks dawdling their way home, some of them smoking to make themselves look cool in the authority-free interstice between the world of teachers and that of parents. At the edge of a shady park, I ask directions to my reserved hotel for the night from a small band of adolescent boys sharing a single cigarette, but the biggest of the lot, shrugs his shoulders, purses his lips and puffs a French teenager's version of "I dunno." Another tells me the main street is just through this park, past the church; it is probably somewhere there. I heed his directions but have to cut through a much larger gaggle of giggling girls dressed in plaid skirts, white shirts, and ties to match their skirts. Some are smoking. They are annoyed by this old man taking a short cut through the heart of their cigarette sorority. I arrive at the *rue haute*, the main street, of the town and find the hotel-restaurant where I have my reservation. I approach and greet the middle-age man folding up the sandwich board sign advertising the luncheon special. He sizes me up, recognizes me as tonight's pilgrim, and invites me into the bar. He signs me in, gives me a key, and though it is now after 2:00 pm and he is pushing his last lunch guest out the door, he asks if I have eaten. I tell him I have not and am hungry. He shows me to my room, then tells me to come back downstairs in a few minutes for the last of today's *plat du jour*. I do as he says, and after returning from the small but modern room given to me, I am seated, still damp with sweat, at my own little table. A smiling waitress commences the delivery of the successive courses of today's special to the pilgrim: bread, wine, salad, pork-chop with spuds and sauce, *crème caramel* for dessert. The staff of the place join the boss, the man who welcomed me, at another table for their own lunch. The six of them look very much like one happy family as they pass bread, pour wine, and tuck into their own pork-chops and spuds.

Later in the afternoon, I take my mobile phone and my journal and walk back to the church just a block across the main street. Boys, no longer in uniform, are playing rough soccer in the lot next to the church, the ball often enough slamming into the side of the stone building. I avoid their fierce volleys and step inside. It is a dark place: dank and moldy and un-inviting. I do my best to settle into some kind of stillness, but find myself anxious to move on, so I return outside and find a park bench in the shade of a plane tree and begin my usual scribbling about today's events and my thoughts upon them. While writing, I notice a car pull up almost in front of me. A man in a rumpled grey suit, pulls himself out, satchel in hand, crosses the street to the church, then disappears within. The priest? Perhaps there will be a Mass at 5:00 or 5:30? I close up my journal and amble back to the church, once again, dodging the soccer ball racing towards my head.

I find the man in grey in the sanctuary and ask if he is *le monsieur abbé*. He responds positively, whereupon I tell him that I am both pilgrim and priest. It is as if he has been expecting me for the longest time: he opens his arms to embrace me offering me profuse *bienvenues*. He animatedly asks if I wish to concelebrate the Mass with him and another priest who will be arriving shortly. I would ordinarily be impressed and touched by such a gesture of welcome, but in this case, there is one problem: I can smell alcohol on his breath as he embraces me. The poor fellow has the glassy eyes, fumbling manner, and just a hint of slur to his words that spells late afternoon inebriation. A few old ladies take their places in the front pews. The other priest, much older than either of us, enters the church and introduces himself to me; he clearly is not amused by his *confrère's* condition, but goes along with everything. The younger priest sets us to one side without alb or stole, and begins the liturgy. With expansive gestures and exaggerated eloquence, he introduces me grandly to the small congregation. His homily would have been fine had it not been for the alcoholic touch slightly un-tuning most of it. This is a good man slowly sliding downhill.

He calls the older priest and myself to the altar for the Eucharistic prayer, then, on the spot, invites me to say part of it . . . in French. I defer, but he insists, so I struggle my way through the words, carefully and slowly pronouncing them as best I am able. I am embarrassed by my effort, but all is well as far as the pastor is concerned. The liturgy is mercifully short, and as soon as all are dismissed in peace, he asks if he might place the parish seal in my *credencial*. We just need to drive back to his place where the ancient seal is kept. I presume that "his place" must be close by so do not worry too much about the dangers of being driven by someone clearly under the influence. Indeed, his place is not so far, the other end of the town's *rue haute*, but the drive, brief as it is, scares me almost to death. He weaves and crosses the center-line and briefly heads towards a parked car to the right. My fear is not only of his limited control of our vehicle, it is also something more primordial, or perhaps, *familial*. It brings back feelings from childhood of life with a good father also sliding downhill, slowly losing control, beginning to tumble, drinking, scaring us.

I don't like the fears of those childhood years anymore now than then, and they come back to me, just as real now, in this car, wandering just a hair over the yellow line then back again, then just a bit too close to the curb then back again. I do not do so well with alcoholism in others. I choke on it because, like a bad smell, it brings me right back to childhood hell. I loved my old man, still love him, but you know, when he drank, he was a different man. He became sad, then mad, then mean, then sometimes he *hit*. In riding in this car right now, I might as well be riding in our '55 Merc station-wagon, red and white and heavy as a tank, with Pop at the wheel and Mom on the right side of the bench with a kid between them and another in her arms, the rest, some nine more of us, taking up the mid-and back-benches, and the Old Man pissed and weaving and silent in his unknowable anger. How could we have known that he felt like a failure most of his life, that he could never measure up to his big brother, the Jesuit priest, that as a kid he laid awake at night in bed listening to *his* drunk old man beating up on his mother? How could he have known in advance that he didn't have the emotional quotient necessary to raise eleven kids? He had every right to be sore and mad, but a kid deserves a *stable* pop, a pop in control, a pop who is a rock. Ours wasn't. He drank, and he exploded, and once in a while he belted. So part of the tightness in my throat right now driving down this street with *mon père* is the knowledge that this same disease is always just a couple of cups of whatever from taking me over as it did him. That same miserable fault lives in my genes as much as it lived in my pop's, even as it now possesses this good old *père* of the church in Guérigny.

Anyway, I ride it out and shake it off as we arrive at the front door of his parish house, a mostly blank *façade* up a few steps from the street level. We enter a foyer with once grand rooms on either side, now dirty and decrepit, every horizontal surface covered in stacks of papers and books and garbage. Fruit rots on the kitchen table. This poor *père* is further down the hill than I thought. *Someone should intervene. Where is his bishop? He can still be saved! Someone, for God's sake, save him!*

The *père* finds his parish seal amidst the mountainous clutter and takes my *credencial* in hand, stamps it just a bit off-center, and offers to drive me back to my hotel. I decline the offer saying I prefer to walk since it is only a few blocks. He shows me to the door but then presses me again to allow him to deliver me to my place; he's on his way in that very direction after all, so

I back down from my fear and let him drive me. As before, we wander to the left and then the right, then swerve across the breadth of the *rue haute* to the front door of my place. I thank him for his kindness and promise to pray for him as I step out of his car, and he promises the same for me, and off the good *père* drives, praying for me as I pray for him. *Prends pitié de nous.*

I am not through with the wages of alcohol this day. I arrive at the restaurant just as the dinner service is beginning. I am invited by my host to take a seat, but it is clear he too has been liberally tipping a bottle. He is not as cheery as was the parish priest and certainly not as cheery as he was earlier this afternoon. As he presides over his tables, he is unhappy with everything and picks at his staff. There are just a few other guests in the restaurant also waiting for their first courses, nibbling on bread, sipping beer or wine. I do not understand what is said, but something one of the guests utters sends the host into a red-hot rage. He begins arguing with the young man in the booth, insulting him, calling him names I do not understand. The man being verbally abused takes refuge among the other three in his party, he retracts, and almost hides in his booth. Stony silence, except for the host's expletives, reign throughout the room. The staff stand perfectly still, their eyes cast down. I feel in full force exactly what I used to feel when my own pop would lose his temper at the dinner table, raging about the lack of salt in the saltshaker, throwing the thing across the room. The host comes to the workstation near me and begins violently chopping a *baguette* into slices; he really should not have a knife in his hand right now. The abused man and his party slide out of their booth, quickly moving toward the exit, then leave, the glass door slamming behind them. The host goes sullen and silent, his quick, choppy gestures revealing plenty of rage still boiling within. The staff slowly goes back to work. My main course is brought; I eat it quickly, pass on dessert, and get the hell out of there, just as when I was a kid, just *exactly* as when I was a kid: *escape* was my strategy for coping with this sort of boozy and bilious tension. Evidently, it still is.

Once safely ensconced in my room, I go silent. I lie on my bed, my head propped up by my pillow and think nothing, feel nothing, pray nothing. For a while. Then it comes back slowly: I am big now. I can see better from this height. Along with fear of my old man and his vice, wherever it shows up, in whomever it possesses within my sight, there is love. Strange that. I love my pop now and feel for him and am so sorry that he wasn't more happy or more free, or more . . . I don't know . . . more everything. From this height I look on these *pères* of my life then and now with whatever the French mean by *pitié*: compassion, I suppose. What else can I do as I lie here but hold these men in my hands and just hold them: *Saint-Jacques: you took care of my heart this morning; now take care of theirs.*

Lead them on . . .

Lead me on . . .

My praying thins into thinking. So this is what I think about alcohol: it blinds us to grace. As our minds and hearts go soft under its blanket of chemical warmth, our eyes see less and less of what is real, what is true, what is beautiful. It is a great trick: it makes us suppose we are feeling more even as we are becoming more and more blind to life and love . . . and God. Anyway, the two of them remind me of the hardness of life in small places, as Louisa told me; here I have met a real Country Priest, who, I believe, would join his literary brother in Bernanos' story, and from within his pain finally proclaim: *tout est grâce.*

I look at my guide: tomorrow will be a very short walk, I should be in Nevers well before lunch. There I will make a pilgrimage within a pilgrimage to visit a modern saint: Bernadette of Lourdes whose body rests among the Sisters of Charity there. To visit her in Nevers is one of the reasons I chose the southern route out of Vézelay exactly one week ago.

12

Bernadette

I enjoy a fine sleep, waking up at 6:00 am, quickly run through *Laudes*, pull myself and Gregory together, carry him and Click and Clack downstairs at 7:30 for breakfast in the restaurant. My host not only tends me with solemn courtesy, but far more importantly, he humbly apologizes for his regrettable outburst the night before. I don't get all that he is saying, but the look on his face of shame is so painful that I catch the *feeling* of his apology perfectly. I respond, *de rien*, though I am not sure it is the correct expression for "apology accepted", but it seems to work. In silence, he brings me my coffee and fresh sliced *baguettes*, fruit and yogurt, and orange juice.

I eat in silence out of respect for this man's remorse, then I'm on my way out of Guérigny by 8:00. It is a beautiful day for walking, and I am feeling great. I am treated to several passages through dark woods of oak and chestnut, now special places for me as their small world of diminished light and heightened sound grant me a sort of rest from the glare of the greater world beyond. I can breathe more deeply under their green canopies. I can slow down without actually slowing down as I pass along their paths. In these naves of green and brown and subtle echoes I am one with myself, my earth, my God.

Before long I am at the outskirts of Nevers, the largest city I have walked into since Reims. Homes and businesses and traffic soon abound. In the muddle of streets, my pilgrim arrows disappear from posts and pillars, my own map is ambiguous, and I am left untethered as I bumble along looking for the city center. I ask a lady on the street for directions and follow to the right as directed but end up in a characterless subdivision, clearly not heading to the center of anything. I backtrack and then pass some kind of pilgrimage site, the Compostelle shell emblazoned on its *façade*; the place is locked, but it is the clue indicating I am back on the Chemin. Having to stop at intersections and wait for the illuminated green stick man to appear before I can continue plunges me into modernity. I dodge to the left and dip down a side street to the Église du Saint-Étienne. I tuck into its dark interior, and once within this womb of stone, I find the very same peace I enjoyed in the oak and chestnut woods earlier this morning. I unhook Gregory and set him and his sidekicks, Click and Clack, on the floor next to a great round column. The cool of the place plays off my sweat, giving me a second or two of chill. These columns and the stone arches and round ceilings above and the light softened by high windows are indeed like a forest; here too one breathes, hears, pauses, is cooled. Some tourists approach to ask if I am a *pèlerin* and if I have walked here from Vézelay. I respond that I *am* a pilgrim, but that I have walked all the way from Belgium. They are delighted to meet an authentic *pèlerin* and ask to take snapshots of us together, me with Gregory on my back; I oblige them. Who would have guessed that I would become a tourist attraction, but here I am smiling for the cameras with my admirers, feeling a bit like Mickey Mouse at Disneyland.

I review the detailed map of the city included in my guide and set out for the convent of the Sisters of Charity. I traverse a grand park resonating with the sound of splashing fountains and the delighted squeals of children at play on squeaky swings. I am enjoying the panorama of humanity meandering along its paths: gangly teens pushing themselves on wide skateboards making it look like an act of tremendous rebellion, bent-over grandmas returning dutifully from their morning shopping, Moslem moms pushing prams, their faith revealed by heads covered with colorful scarves, an old priest, still dressed in black *soutane* as in former times, his hands folded behind him, rosary dangling, as he carries on his old life in this new century. At the far corner and across the street, I find the Espace Bernadette, the convent of the Sisters of Charity by another name, a name intended to beckon tourists and pilgrims to the famous visionary of Lourdes.

I enter the extensive grounds of the convent, a small museum to the left, outdoor chapels and grottos to the right, the convent, retreat house, and pilgrim center beyond. I find the main door, enter and present myself to the lady tending the front desk. My reservation for the night is in place, but I am too early to take the room. I drop off Gregory and Click and Clack with the receptionist then wander outside to visit the cathedral across the street, take lunch at a *döner kebab* place, kill some time, then return to the Espace Bernadette at the appointed hour where I am shown to a newly renovated room, clean as a whistle, with a window overlooking a pleasant courtyard. I settle in, then make my first visit to the tomb of Sainte-Bernadette.

Bernadette plays a role in the life and imagination of Catholics of my age as few other saints, reinforced by the Hollywood version of her life,

Song of Bernadette, which was required watching in every Catholic home, a rare example of "a *good* Hollywood movie," one that made us kids proud to be little Catholics, too. The story of this peasant girl's visions of the Virgin Mary at Lourdes, including a miraculous spring endowed with healing power, was told often and in grand detail to all of us who passed through America's parochial schools in the 1950s and 60s. Imitation Lourdes grottos of every conceivable size graced our yards, classrooms, and churches: Mary always dressed in white with blue cincture, hands folded, eyes beholding Bernadette and all of us children kneeling just below. Even our bedrooms boasted images of this Virgin often crafted in glow-in-the-dark plastic. A bottle of authentic Lourdes water was a *de rigueur* pharmaceutical in every good Catholic home; it was uncapped and sprinkled with great reserve and solemnity whenever someone in the household was seriously ill.

The young visionary grew up, became a Sister of Charity in Nevers, and after a not-very-long life, died in 1879. Her body was eventually exhumed not once, but twice, and found to be incorrupt; another one of those typical Catholic validations of God at work in our world; a non-corrupting body like hers *materially* demonstrates that God takes care of his special little ones, even in death, and can and does contravene his own rules, the ones he himself planted in nature, if he wants to. God is God after all. Not so hard to understand. This same incorrupt body is now encased in glass and is the centerpiece of a side-chapel of this convent where Bernadette lived out her brief years after the Lourdes apparitions.

It is this young woman of thirty-five years, dressed from head to toe in the traditional habit of her congregation, laid out as if asleep with a rosary strung among her fingers, whom I now visit. Her face and hands have been covered with a light mask of wax, making her body seem altogether lifelike. I take a place in one of the pews lined up before the reliquary. Others come, kneel or sit, take time to pray, step forward as close to Bernadette as they can. They gaze, some blow small kisses to her, then light candles in the foyer of the side-chapel or outside. It is as if they are moms and dads saying goodnight to their little one. I am moved by their gentle gestures as much, if not more, than I am moved by Bernadette herself. There is a sort of dialogue going on here between them and the saint, a family kind of communion made up of gestures, glances, sweet little kisses. I am pleased to be here in the midst of it, to be invited into this family of Bernadette and her many sisters and brothers.

I can understand why outsiders would see these kinds of gestures and the story of Bernadette itself as classic Catholic silliness. It is so foreign to many contemporary sensibilities, but just beneath the pious surface, there are truths to be mined. That someone like Jesus' mother, Mary, might make an appearance from "the other side" to a poor little girl much like herself on this side, just to reassure her that she is not alone in this world, that she belongs to a family as wide as the earth and as high as the sky; a family with members on both sides of the ultimate horizon of life is a lovely thing. We are not alone; that is just wonderful. But that is not all, there is more: the waters that flowed from beneath Mary's rosy feet in the Lourdes story is like fresh water bursting through the dam of hard earthly reality, or maybe, like tears flowing from God's own eyes, tears that can't be held back as he beholds us in our many troubles. So this is the subtle truth behind Bernadette's dead body: God cares and he sends his emissaries, like Mary, to bathe us, wash us, heal us of our many wounds. We are a family. This is what families do. Bernadette here, so quiet and still, is a little sister to me, too, so I blow her a kiss, light a candle, and wish her a good sleep with the angels and the saints.

Evening comes on. The sky is illuminated with touches of pink as the sun draws close to the horizon. Instead of going to my room, I walk to the small garden behind the convent that overlooks Nevers to the west. I want to watch the sun slip beyond the limits of this grand earth. An elderly couple are playing cards at a plastic table. As I pass, the gentleman greets me in heavily accented English: "Ho-ho! Pilgrim friend! Do you remember us? From Saint-Révérien? We met you there!" I do remember them now: the slick Mercedes that pulled up is still vivid to me. I shake the hands of Johann and Hildegard and am invited to join them at cards. I decline, saying I just want to watch the sun set. Ah, yes, they understand completely and leave me to my evening meditation. As the sun sets, and it grows dark, they gather up their cards, and as they head back to the convent, I join them now; as we dawdle in our return, we chat about our pilgrimages. They only have a couple weeks each year that they can dedicate to their effort, but each year they draw a little bit closer to Compostela. They love the walking and the time together as husband and wife. We part to go to our separate wings of the convent; "Happy walking tomorrow, Kevin!" Well, I guess that settles it: I shall walk tomorrow.

I awake not wanting to move. I remain in bed dozing and drowsing. Should I continue beyond Nevers today or remain here for a day of rest. I remember the Johann and Hildegard's parting wish last night, so I do get out of bed and begin preparing myself for the day. I decide that if I can find a place to stay tonight in the town of Saint-Parize-le-Châtel, about twenty kilometers from Nevers, I will walk; if I cannot arrange lodging, then I will stay put. I eat breakfast downstairs in the dining room by myself. On the way back to my room, I encounter my German friends and once again, the amiable Johann and Hildegaard wish me well. They look fresh and at ease as they prepare to return to yesterday's end-point to begin their day's walk. It seems like a "no-sweat" affair for them; I envy them their fitness and casual approach to their pilgrimage. Upon returning to my room, I make the reservation at the only possible lodging option listed in my guide for Saint-Parize-le-Châtel, another hotel/restaurant, so my walk is on. The guide seems ambiguous as to where the place is actually located, but I am assured by the person who answers the call that there is no problem and the reservation is set.

The Chemin out of Nevers passes not around the Cathedral, but *through* it, going in one door and out the other. Near the sanctuary, hung on a great column, is a crucifix from the thirteenth century. The Christ here is rare along the Chemin for he displays extraordinary serenity in his passion. Most along the Way display Christ in his agony, plenty of blood, a body that is wracked with pain, a face filled with hollow despair. But this one is a more rare type. The Christ here is at peace. His visage expresses a transformation from struggle to acceptance, from agony to tenderness, from hell to heaven. I wonder this morning, how did those twelfth and thirteenth century crafts-men do it? How did they capture that *interior peace* in the midst of this terrible and shameful death? Did they know it in their own hard lives? Do any of us know it anymore? Anyway, I love this Jesus, so kiss my fingertips and touch them to his pierced feet. *Give me just a tenth part of your peace.* Just as I do so, I hear someone approach me from behind, "*Monsieur Pèlerin!* You *are* a pilgrim, no?" Yes, I tell the gentleman; I am a pilgrim. He introduces himself as the parish priest and asks if I would like to have my *credencial* stamped with the seal of the cathedral. I welcome the offer, and as we walk to the sacristy, I tell him I am a priest as well. Once inside the back room, in the midst of the usual clutter of such places, censors hanging askew, albs and stoles tossed over the backs of chairs, candlesticks set aside for cleaning, he pulls from a drawer the precious *tampon* and solemnly stamps my document. He then advises me that the Chemin down to the bridge over the Loire and from there out of town is a little complicated, so he offers to guide me the first few blocks of my way. Down some steep streets we walk, then he points out to me the bridge I must cross a little further on, and wishes me, as he turns back to the cathedral, the pilgrim greeting I have grown to depend upon: "*Courage!*"

At about eight or nine kilometers out, I have to trek up a steep and lengthy run of country highway. The sun is shining, and the air is fresh, so the burden of the climb is not so daunting. I stop for a breath or two every few minutes. Approaching the crest, I turn back towards Nevers; from here I can see the city in the distance, the stone bulk of the cathedral and its upraised tower clear as a bell to the eye and even a few wisps of morning fog still laying low in the valleys. The morning sun is illuminating the church-scape for me, with its city spreading below, it as if its streets and homes were the folds of the cathedral's abundant skirts. In this light those old buttresses and arches and lacy tower seem to be most proud of themselves, sitting up, cocksure of their radiant beauty to my eyes so far away. At the sight of it, I repeat my wayside shrine prayers once again: *Our Father . . . Lord Jesus, have mercy . . . Oh my Jesus, forgive us our sins . . . especially those most in need of thy mercy.*

Once arriving at a small settlement of modern houses at the top of the hill, I am bushed, so sit myself down in the grassy shoulder of a local's driveway. I lay back in the grass. I know I allow my imagination full play in these matters; heavens, I even talk to my pack as if the thing were an overweight brother clinging to my back all these days, and as if it were a sainted pope to boot. I know I *pretend* a lot out here on this Way. I pretend to talk with and walk with and enjoy the company of persons I cannot see and who have been dead a very long time. I am quite sure agnostics and atheists and even a fair number of believers of a more contemporary ilk would *tut-tut* at all this spiritual play I engage in as I wander south towards Compostela. "You are just kidding yourself, humanizing these objects so as to create something where there is nothing. As you do with your backpack, so you do with your saints, with Bernadette, with James, with Jesus, most seriously of all, even your very God. Sorry Charlie: there's nothing there. Imaginary friends, all of them. Fantasy. Go read your Sartre. Your play is a joke on you. You will die as all men die, and you will be dead as all dead men are dead, and there will be nothing, *nada, rien,* zip of you left, not even a spark, not even a quark, just fertilizer for whatever organic matter survives beyond you. You poor boy: grow up."

I understand the point. It makes material sense to me. I have to chew on it again from time to time, but in the end, I look up at this blue sky above me, or look out at the distant cathedral of Nevers across the emerald fields I have just spent the last two hours ambling through, or I look into the night sky to behold the *Via Lactea,* the Milky Way, sweeping across it, or I feel a breeze cool the sweat on my back, or I enjoy the memory of a kind smile from a little girl named Solange, or see serenity in the face of one just crucified, and *I know peace* within for a moment, and so *I just don't believe* the contention that it is all just a big, stupid, dumb accident of a universe that we find ourselves within. My overactive Catholic imagination gets me closer to the truth. Myths and miracles and seeing in my mind's eye all manner of things unseen are more real and more true and certainly more beautiful than dumb chance. And which is more inexplicable: something from nothing and chaos racing to order for no good reason, or that all things have been fired into being by the wink of a God delighting in creating all of it with you and me as part of it? I choose the wink. It is so much more satisfying. It is a lot more fun. It is so much more lovely. I would not trade my saints and spirits and triune God for dreary old *nada*-ness any day. My imagination at play with Bernadette and Gregory and James and Jesus and God makes the universe sparkle. And one more thing as I idle my way through issues of spiritual truth or the lack thereof: my belief that my own *personal being*, which I have a profound sense of right now, is something much grander than compost gives me a joy under this big blue canopy of a sky that is too rich to *pretend* it doesn't exist. So I stand, wink to Gregory, yank the great old pope up onto my back one more time, and head down my merry way towards the relics of my sainted pal, *Jacobus Magnus*.

I make my way into Saint-Parize-le-Châtel and easily find my way to the front door of the Hôtel du Commerce. I am lucky to have a room, for the place is hopping with motorcyclists and their crews from a major European racetrack between here and Nevers, Magny-Cours. I am shown to my quarters, a dumpy place not anywhere worth, in my opinion, the 60€ that I am paying. At least the shower has warm water, and the toilet down the hall is reasonably clean; best of all, there is a balcony with the afternoon sun warming it: perfect for drying the day's laundry. I take dinner in the hotel restaurant: roast pork, cauliflower, a glass of red wine, and a dessert I have grown overly fond of: an *isle flottant*, a glass of creamy custard with a lovely dollop of meringue floating atop.

As I float off into sleep, one image bridges consciousness and dream: the pierced feet of Jesus from the Cathedral of Nevers. I kiss them again; day is done.

13

The Stars of Auvergne

At breakfast, I ask the fellow serving my croissant, orange juice, and coffee if there is a more direct way to Saint-Pierre-le-Moûtier than the one shown in my guide. He takes a look at my map and shows me a country road that has little traffic and should be just fine for a walker like me. It will save me at least four kilometers this morning. With Saint-Pierre now much closer, I can easily adjust my goal for the day to the town of Le Veurdre, where, the guide informs me, a family welcomes pilgrims. I make a quick phone call to the place and am assured they have room for me. I thank the waiter for sharing his local expertise, drink down the last of my coffee, and begin the day's walk along a one-lane paved road that is all mine for the next two hours. The morning air has autumn coolness about it, but it is refreshing and not enough to raise even a single goose-bump. My feet and legs are in good form. My back hardly notices the weight of Gregory. Click and Clack robustly keep time.

After a couple of hours, my heavenly little road intersects with a much busier highway, trucks whizzing by in both directions. I take the left-hand shoulder and walk for the better part of another hour into Saint-Pierre. Besides trucks and cars, motorcycles built like jets that have escaped from the tracks of Magny-Cours roar past me like swarms of yellow-jackets and then, having found their petroleum honey-pot, pile up around the pumps of the ATAC fuel station on the outskirts of Saint-Pierre. Their leathered drivers doff their helmets, stretch their legs, and dangerously smoke cigarettes near the pumps. What a contrast I am to them in look and lifestyle! The thrill of speed is the name of their game, so they are slick and streamlined, and everything they see is a blur. My life is almost as slow as life can get; I am hunched and misshapen by my backpack, and I have only my feet to get me down the road, but at least I can see the world I walk through in fine detail.

An acorn can amaze me, the sight of it sets off a riff of wonderment that passes from seed to branch to leaf to trunk to roots to earth to God. I do not envy the speed-demons their way; I love my walker's life for what it allows me to see and savor along the Way.

I continue on into the center of Saint-Pierre, a lively little place with a fine Romanesque church at its heart. The church's treasure, at least for me, is on its exterior: a lovely statue of Saint-Jacques gazes down on the passing pedestrian from a niche on the corner. He is so homely and humble, worn down by the years and the elements, yet he does not abandon his post over this small portion of the Chemin. *Walk with me, old Jacques. Just walk with me. Don't let me walk too fast. Keep my eyes open along this Way.* I doff my cap to the old saint, turn back to the street, and head out of town.

Within a couple of hours, I approach a damper and greener climate bordering a substantial river. Upon coming up to a bridge, a sign informs me that I am leaving the Bourgogne and about to enter the Auvergne; just across the bridge is my home for the night: La Veurdre. I cross over and into a town deep in its midday slumber. Not a soul stirs. I find no sign to indicate in which direction I might find the Rue de Vignoble and my pilgrim hosts. A car drives slowly by, then parks on the street near me. A middle-age woman steps out, on her way to the local beauty shop to my right. I approach and ask directions; she is altogether polite and points me up the road, asking if I am staying with la *famille Foucaud.* I respond positively, and she assures me I will be well cared for. I head towards the outskirts of the village, take a left at the Rue de Vignoble and find a steel gate with the pilgrim's *coquille* attached to it. I am home.

Even as I step forward to ring the bell, the gate begins to roll open automatically, and I am greeted by *Madame* Foucaud in the central yard of what once must have been a grand farm. The old farmhouse is obviously well renovated, and the outbuildings have been mostly turned into a modern office and clinic for the *madame's* physical therapy practice. This is not a *chambre d'hôte,* Catherine Foucaud explains; she and her husband are veterans of the Chemin themselves and so have transformed a separate farm building just beyond their own house into a pilgrim refuge. It is not a business for them but a service to fellow pilgrims. I am guided to the refuge; it is a beautiful little place with a living room, cooking area, a bedroom with sliding door out to a green lawn, and a spotless bath and shower. This is a whole apartment done up with style and class, and it is all mine; no other pilgrims are expected this evening. She invites me to join her and her husband, Paul, for supper, and I gladly accept.

Once settled, I review my maps and lists of accommodations for the next few days. Over the coming stretch, there are two choices for accommodations: one only ten kilometers from Le Veurdre and the other just over twenty. I choose the twenty-klick option, Valigny, and phone ahead to make a reservation at the town's only *logement*. The lady who answers curtly gives me the answer I don't want to hear: her place tomorrow will be completely *complète*; it is a Saturday after all, she tells me, but she would have room for me on Sunday. A new plan comes to mind: take tomorrow as a day of rest, enjoying the comfort and ease of my refuge here in La Veurdre for a second day, then walk on to Valigny on Sunday. I will ask Catherine if I might stay on; if not, I'll have to put in only a ten kilometer day tomorrow, hardly worth the sweat and cleanup required.

At 7:00 pm I wander over to the main house. I am welcomed to a patio that serves as the transition from the Foucaud's elegantly traditional farmhouse interior to the expansive lawn and garden beyond. The table is set, wine is poured, the baguette is sliced and passed, a garden salad is shared out, a chicken casserole is served, and finally a dessert of custard and caramel tops off the evening meal. All the while, Paul, Catherine, and I share stories about where we have come from and how we find ourselves here, now. The red wine loosens my French tongue and once again, I am surprised to realize, when it is over, how easily I have communicated with so little grammar and vocabulary at my disposal. Before the evening is complete, I have inquired about staying on an extra day, and the Foucaud's are happy to allow me run of their place for a day more. Tomorrow will be my first day-off since Vézelay; after eight days on the road, I believe I merit a rest; God got his after only six.

Night falls. There are no streetlights nearby. From my room, I step outside. My eyes become accustomed to the dark. I look up. *Mon Dieu! Les étoiles!* The stars that I so love are on full display! The *Via Lactea* stretches from one horizon to the other, winding and weaving and cloudy with stellar light. It is so brilliantly close that I feel I can reach out and take hold of it, pull myself up onto it, walk it, dance my way along its sparkling cobbles all the way to Compostela. And so why not? I do clamber up and do a jig atop that starry way, sweeping across the edge of the galaxy to the Holy City. Along the way, I spot the Big Dipper just over my shoulder and locate then the North Star, Polaris, the pole around which all else spins, the great symbol of the one thing that is firm, dependable, unchanging, ever true.

Good evening, Polaris.

"Good evening to you, Pilgrim."

And from your great height how do you see things on our earth so far below?

"Your earth and its species and especially your own race are all lovely."

But what of our wars and famines and addictions and poverties and abuse of one another? Are they so lovely?

"No, they are not so lovely, you are right, little Pilgrim, but from this distance, we stars see them as they are, in the midst of so much more. From here, they are part of something much greater, something that is beautiful, and the unbeautiful things cannot overwhelm the greater beauty of which they are a part."

Our race seems especially unbeautiful to me sometimes.

"That is a failure of your vision. You are too close. Come and see what I see."

Come to you there?

"Yes, come to me here."

How?

"Just come."

May I fly to you?

"Fly you may."

So I shall fly.

"Welcome to the Little Dipper, little Pilgrim. Take my hand and look to where I point with the other."

Yes. Fine. I'll happily take your hand, though I didn't previously know stars had hands.

"We have hands when you need us to have hands . . . and eyes too . . . and hearts as well . . . and voices."

Voices?

"Yes, we sing. We are stellar performers. Our harmonies are splendid, our melodies sublime. You must open your ears more profoundly and listen to us more often."

Yes, indeed, I must, and my eyes too, I suspect.

"Yes, do so now. Behold, little Pilgrim, your earth from above: it is a marvel of blue and white and green and brown. A perfect round of dirt and cloud and sea and flesh. It cries out peace. It is a gift. It is precious. Even its many ills cannot disfigure its face. And beyond it, a sea of night, but in that sea, cast from one end to another, we stars in our trillions, ordered into galaxies that are pinwheels on the handlebars of God's celestial bicycle, we spin and whirl and whir as he rides like a kid down the street of time, laughing all the way, free. Is this not beautiful too?"

Yes, it is beautiful, too.

"And do you see any ugliness, any ungodliness, in this?"

No. None. Except that it cannot last forever. Someday it must end.

"What must end? What is this *it* that must someday end? Beauty? Loveliness? Song? Dance? Godliness? You mistake matter for grace. I'm showing you grace, you are seeing only matter. Look there: the *Via Lactea* that you were just now dancing along. How do you see it?"

It is beautiful beyond words. It stretches out from one end of the night sky to the other, a highway made of a billion stars. It is gloriously beautiful for now, but what I meant by "ending" is that one day or another, the stars will burn out, the galaxy will collapse into a black hole, eventually, the whole universe itself will either expand into nothingness or collapse into nothingness.

"What do you know of stars? I tell you, and I speak as a star myself, I am Polaris, after all; I tell you that you are wrong, because you do not see the truth of the earth, the truth of stars, the truth within the universe. What I see is generosity, a hand strewing stars, setting them spinning, copiously spilling them out by the billions, planting them with life, loving them. It is the strewing, the gifting, the spilling, the love that is true and beautiful and does not end. As for the stars: so for your earth and your race. Do you not also sing? Are not harmonies part of your best prayers? Do you not also sacrifice yourselves for your children? Do you not wander and wonder, little Pilgrim? This is what is real and what is true and what endures. It is Beauty. It is Truth. It is Grace. All things come to it. Every wound is healed within it. Every death is a birth in it. Eventually, the many become *one* in it. That is what I see from up here. That is what I know. That is why I see you and your race and your earth as *lovely*. You and all that you are part of is *lovely*, born of *love* and growing into *love*. Do you see it? Do you hear us sing now?"

Yes, I think so. I will try to listen better. I will try to see better. I will try to walk better.

"Be on your Way, then."

Good night, bright Polaris.

"Good night, little Pilgrim."

I awake at first light. From my bed, I can see the warm rose color of the new day breaking over the silhouette of a distant tree line. I enjoy the view through my sliding glass door all the more knowing that I don't have to get up, get ready, do anything today but take in whatever the Creator gives me to take in. I do get out of bed, pull on my pants and a shirt, and in my bare feet, step outside to get the full view of the dawn. The grass is damp with dew and cool underfoot; it sends little electric shocks through my soles and up my legs. I am not cold. The sky grows lighter, the pink and peach and orange of the rising sun becoming more pronounced as it gets closer to mounting the horizon. The fiery edge of the sun finally appears, then more of the great orb rises with surprising lift. The light of the sun crawls across the landscape towards me, illuminating the emerald fields as it steadily draws forward. Finally, it strikes my toes and creeps up my legs and over my chest and into my eyes, which I must close to the brightness. It warms me, and I can see the light even through my eyelids, red and veiny, and I might as well be within another world, a red planet of some kind. I turn away and open my eyes and scan the real world of green and blue and rose.

Above me, a new spectacle is unfolding: a series of cirrus clouds form themselves into a perfect *coquille de Saint-Jacques*, the cockleshell that is the universal emblem of the pilgrims of Compostela. The clouds fan out from a condensed base near the eastern horizon and cross half the sky, still illuminated with rose and coppery light from the rising sun yet with hints of the white that they will become in just a few moments more. The *coquille* in the sky grows larger and thins as the clouds spread further apart, but the shell holds its shape long enough for me to break away from beholding it, to gingerly step back across the lawn, jump back into my bedroom, grab my camera from Gregory's side pocket, and return to the lawn to snap a few photos of it. Proof. This marvel of the morning sky is not just my imagination! This cockleshell of cloud is as real as anything I have ever seen, and I have now the pictures to prove it. It is surely a sign: *Saint-Jacques, you've got me covered. Big Jim, you have my back.*

If I had walked this morning, I probably would have missed this. I am happy with my decision to take a day of repose. The remainder of the day passes slowly but tranquilly. I listen to Byzantine liturgical music, wander into town for lunch. The afternoon sun grows warm, so I return to my refuge and idle away the afternoon, letting my feet, legs and back enjoy their day of rest. I rejoin the Foucaud's for a simple evening meal, then return to my refuge. Tomorrow is Sunday; I will find Mass at the parish church of Lurcy-Lévis at 11:00, Paul and Catherine have assured me.

The first day of the week brings a new concern: my pilgrim guide has printed at the top of today's pages a warning that the Chemin through the Auvergne is not always well posted. I am warned to walk with caution and to depend primarily on the written descriptions of the twists and turns of the Way since the now familiar yellow arrows attached to trees and posts may disappear from view for substantial stretches. *Oh, great.* My problem with the written descriptions is that they are written *en Français*; most of the time I can easily figure out my *gauches* and *droits*, but there are also more detailed descriptions of essential landmarks that are sometimes beyond my limited linguistic abilities. I will have to be extra attentive to my guide and map today and in the days to come. I hate the thought of getting lost, but millions of pilgrims have walked these same roads over the centuries, and few had the maps and guides I have hanging around my neck. If they could do it, I can do it. *Just begin.*

This same map indicates that my route is no longer heading mostly south, but in a westerly direction, a trajectory that will eventually align me for my march through Limousin and Aquitaine and on to the western Pyrenees and the village of Saint-Jean-Pied-de-Port, the last stop before entering Spain. It is another indication to me that this pilgrimage, despite its incremental daily advances, is actually progressing rather significantly. As best I can figure, I am about at the halfway-point of the French segment of the pilgrimage. I am getting somewhere: it has taken six weeks of walking to get here and will take about six more to get to the Spanish border, then four weeks beyond that to arrive at Compostela, if I should ever get that far.

The Auvergne is blanketed by a heavy fog this morning, and there is a real chill in the air. I follow dirt and grass paths this morning. It feels good to have unpaved earth under my feet again. I feel closer to the earth, somehow more wild, more primordial. The fog lifts slowly leaving behind a glistening earth: each blade of grass, the limbs of the hedgerows' brambles, the barbed-wire fences, and most especially, the spider-webs spun between any and all of the above, are soaked with drippy dew, and the light of the morning sun makes blades, barbs, and branches dazzle with a billion jewels, or better, a billion daytime stars. The lacy intricacy of the spider webs, in particular, awes me. How do those small creatures do this? Each web is a miracle and maybe, in some spidery way, a galaxy unto itself.

Further on, my dirt road leads me directly to the edge of a rushing creek. It is too wide to jump, and I can see no stepping-stones. It must be a meter in depth at the center. I read my guide carefully. It says there is a bridge, but I see no bridge. I lean over the water as far as I safely am able and peer upstream and downstream and still see no bridge. I walk back up the road several meters to see if I might have missed a turn-off in one direction or another. I find none. I go back to the edge of the creek and contemplate the possibility of wading it. I dip my fingers in the water as a test, and it is very cold. *What, in God's name, are they thinking we are supposed to do here?* I haven't seen a Compostelle arrow in an hour, so it is possible I am lost. I begin to panic and get nervous. I backtrack up the road again a few meters, keeping my eye open for anything that might be a track or a trail to the left or the right. On the way back to the creek feeling sure that the only way forward is going to be a wet one, I spot a slight indentation in the nettles and brambles to my left. I roll down my sleeves for protection and push the bushes aside as much as I am able, keeping the flesh of my hands pulled inside my cuffs and Click and Clack tucked inside my armpits. Indeed, there is the slightest of tracks through here. The branches scratch and claw at me as I push my way through. I watch out not to slip on the increasingly muddy terrain. I get stung by the nettles despite my best efforts. After three or four meters, I break into a small clearing: there is the creek, and my good God, there is the bridge. *I am saved!* The bridge is not much, but it is enough to travel dry-shod to the other side. I feel sheepish that the guide was right, and I just didn't see it. *Open those eyes, Pilgrim!* With my now open eyes, I take a look at my hands; I notice at least two places where the barbs on the brambles I have just passed through have drawn blood. The ruby-redness has a beauty all its own. It is already coagulating; I shall heal.

I arrive in Lurcy-Lévis with fifteen minutes to spare before Sunday Mass. The church bells are already furiously calling the faithful to the liturgy. I am not yet within eye-shot of the church, but as I work my way through the village streets, an elderly gentleman steps out of his home just as I pass and wishes me a *bon dimanche*. I ask him in which direction I might find the church; he smiles broadly and tells me that is exactly where he is headed, and he will gladly guide me along. We walk a block together, then turn a corner, and there, just ahead, is our church.

I take a seat next to a large column, leaning Gregory and Click and Clack against the stone, then settle onto my own small stool. My interest is piqued by the various persons preparing the sanctuary for the liturgy. A portly young woman carries the missal from the sacristy and places it on the priest's presidential chair. A couple of children have vested themselves in white robes with red rope cinctures around their waists; they prod and push one another with laughs as they retrieve portable candles, still unlit, from beside the altar, to carry in the procession to come. A young lady bearing the characteristics of Down Syndrome carries two large baskets from the sacristy to a table set obtrusively in the central aisle, obviously to be used for the offertory collection; more importantly, she smiles and waves at everyone she sees along her way up and down the aisle. A fellow in his seventies, skinny as a rail, sporting a bushy mustache, and wearing a powder-blue leisure suit from another era, stands at a podium near the old pulpit and exercises his vocal chords. An aged priest arrives from somewhere else, lumbers through the nave, and after a few handshakes and waves to his parishioners, slips into the sacristy to prepare himself for what is probably his third or fourth Mass of the weekend. Others, regular folks, some quite aged, others young, a couple of families with kids, take their places too. There is light-heartedness in the air, a sense of expectation, a gladness in being among old and good friends again.

The French people who still come to Mass generally dress up for the occasion: old ladies wear pearl necklaces, the gentlemen wear suit-coats and ties, the young at least wear polished leather shoes rather than their Nikes or Adidas. This is beautiful in a simple sort of way; care is being taken, relationships are being reinvigorated after a week away, the balm of Sunday softens the edges of a week's worth of troubles. I love being here, looking at all this. This pre-ritual ritual has a certain haphazard character about it even as it seems to be following certain well known, but invisible directives. It is like a folk-dance. That word *folk* is the key: it is not under the direction of the pastor; he is part of it, but he doesn't preside over it; it actually belongs to the *folks* who are its actors and dancers, just as this old church, which they and their ancestors have cared for all these centuries, belongs to them more than it belongs to him. In a few moments, he will claim his presidential chair, and everything will change: the *folks* will take to their pews, the small choir will snap to a sort of attention, the organist will hit her first blowy chords, and we'll all stand and be in the thick of the great prayer, following the rubrics, letting the words and gestures and the symbols layered over mountains of symbols, pray for us and in us. But before the *pray*, these few moments of *play* are jewels and stars for me. I lean against Gregory for just a moment, then stand as the man in the leisure suit invites us to sing some old hymn I do not recognize; the procession commences down the center aisle: girl and boy servers, cross-bearer, lector carrying high the Scriptures, pastor. *Lovely*.

The Gospel reading is that of the prodigal son, his forgiving father, and the self-pitying "good" brother. The priest reads his homily rather than proclaims it, but I don't care, at his age he is doing his best, and what I can make of the message is worth listening to: Our true vocation in life is not to be the bad boy, *but the bad boy who comes home.* Thus we give our Fathering God the opportunity to exercise his love, his mercy. I find myself with small tears as the priest goes on. To be the good son, made so by our own efforts, denies God this same opportunity, denies him his Godhood towards us, for God's Godness is his mercy. *Yup.* This is a priest who *gets* Jesus, and I learn from him.

Following communion and a blessing, the procession re-forms in reverse, and we sing the pastor and his ministers back down the central aisle, and then the *folk* break into handshakes and greetings and chatter galore. My guide to the church takes my hand and leads me to others who then engage me in the usual questions and answers about who I am and where I have come from and why am I going to Compostelle. They assure me that I am blessing them even as I know they are the ones blessing me. It is all perfectly jolly and folksy and holy. I know them as *my* folk even as they now know me as *their* pilgrim. The folk drift off one by one or family by family, and I am left with Gregory and Click and Clack but for only a moment. The priest ambles forth from the sacristy, so I introduce myself both as pilgrim and brother priest. I thank him for his homily on the sons, and he thanks me; he asks why I did not join him in concelebrating the liturgy, and I am embarrassed to have no good answer, except that I just got busy watching his people. He nods as if he understands, but I don't think he gets what I am trying to say; I suppose I have not chosen the correct words. He walks me out to the *place* around the church, offers me a *bon courage* then disappears in his Peugeot, off to celebrate yet another Mass somewhere down his Way.

I take a seat on a small wall under an immature tree, pull out my lunch from Gregory's top hatch, and watch the townspeople and tourists in the expensive restaurants across the street consume their *toast champignons* and *quiches*, washed down with draughts from tall glasses of amber beer. A nun dressed in a grey habit approaches and sits beside me. She tells me she is a hermit and instructs me with a light laugh that we are doing the same thing, just in different ways. I chuckle in agreement, and we sit there like brother and sister, both, hopefully, bad enough to give God a chance to be God for us, each in our own way.

I am heading out of Lurcy by 12:30, and the day has become surprisingly warm; what happened to September's autumn cool? The twelve kilometers to Valigny are slow, and my step lacks the bounce of this morning's walk. I follow a paved road in this second leg of the day's journey, which also makes the route less fun than the dirt paths of the morning. Most distressing is the predicted lack of route markers through the Auvergne. They have not completely disappeared, but they are fewer and further between, and I am coming upon crossroads and Ys now that are not labeled at all. I have to rely fully on my written guide and maps to make my choices as to which road to take. So far so good, but that is because I am being especially careful as I go along; I feel uneasy without those physical guideposts painted on posts and pillars to guide me as I walk. I remember the cockleshell in the morning sky over Le Veurdre: *Big Jim, you have me covered.*

I spend an uneventful night in a rustic restaurant-hotel in Valigny, then after a rain-soaked morning on the road, arrive at Charenton-du-Cher where I have a reservation at a private home of *M. & Mme.* Mativon. I walk through the great gate at 9 rue du Château de la Grave, into the yard, up to the door, and ring the bell of the great house. The door is opened wide by an elderly lady who, upon seeing me on her doorstep, opens the door even wider to let me pass with an expansive *bienvenue* as I pass.

Madame Mativon and her husband are in the middle of their lunch, so she first shows me to my upstairs room, then invites me to join her and her husband for lunch. I drop Gregory and my sticks and follow the *madame* back downstairs and into the cluttered but altogether homey kitchen for a plate of green beans, fried potatoes and a pork chop.

The years have been harder on *Monsieur* Mativon than on his bouncy wife; he eats slowly, falls asleep at the table, and generally seems unwell. She carries the conversation forward, asking me the usual pilgrim questions. She surprises me in one thing: rather than ask me what I do for a living, she tells me that I must be a priest. I say yes and ask her how she knows. "I don't know; you just *seem* like a priest." I am rather amazed at her intuition and have a good laugh with her over it. After lunch, *Madame* Mativon shows me around the house; it is actually quite a bit more than just a house: it is a *manoir* reflecting in every piece of wainscoting and hanging chandelier great gobs of former glory. No more: the wainscoting has been heavily over-painted, and the chandeliers are dusty and missing the occasional crystal droplet. An expansive lawn and garden extend out from a glassed-in sun porch. Photographs of what it once looked like hang in a hallway accompanied by colorful family trees going back well into the 1700's: a magnificent place built for nobility. *Madame* Mativon informs me that it has been in her husband's family for six generations. It will pass to their daughter who lives elsewhere. It will probably be sold after the two of them have died and gone to God. A noble family facing its demise is the story told by this old *manoir*. Yet, the Mativon's are sinking money into the property; an attached barn is being converted into some kind of apartment complex. I don't get the impression that the work on the barn will stave off the slide of the whole into further deterioration, but it is something, better than doing nothing in the face of the inexorable sweep of time shooshing us and our grand things into the existential dustbin.

After my tour, I return to my attic room where there is no heat, and the damp infiltrates everything. I wash myself, then my clothes, and hang my socks and pants and underwear from the ancient beams holding the roof in place above my head. I have little hope that any of it will be dry by morning.

I lie down for a while and enjoy just listening to the patter of the rain on the roof and the occasional rumble of thunder beyond. Shortly, I hear voices in the hallway, one light and lilting, the other fairly booming; they are speaking German. They sound remarkably familiar. Could it be? I get off the bed, slip on my sandals and peek out into the passage. Standing there, big as life, are the senior pilgrims I first met in Saint-Reverien, then again in Nevers: Johann and Hildegard. I call to them, they turn to me, their faces lighting up as they recognize me: "Ho-ho, pilgrim friend!" We shake hands heartily and begin sharing our pilgrim adventures since our last visit in Nevers. This, actually, is their second evening with the Mativons. They show me their room: utterly the opposite of my own. They scored spacious and elegant digs reflecting the former elegance of the *manoir*. Johann invites me to join him downstairs in the sunroom for a good old-fashioned sing-along. Of course, I'll join him. While Hildegard and *Madame* Mativon tend to dinner in the kitchen, *Monsieur* Mativon, Johann, and I take our places in ancient stuffed chairs just as the late afternoon sun breaks through the day's heavy clouds and fills our sunroom with the golden light of early evening. Johann has his guitar in one hand and a satchel filled with lyric sheets in the other. Everything is in German. "We now will sing pilgrim songs from the homeland," he declares. He begins strumming and singing in a resonant voice that was made for this: *Schön ist die Welt, drum, Brüder, lasst reisen wohl in die weite Welt, wohl in die Weite Welt . . .*

Johann offers me this translation:

"Fine is the world, so brothers, let us travel all through this wide, wide, world, all through this wide, wide world."

Johann's folk song makes me proud, proud to be a pilgrim who goes where e'er he pleases, as long as he doesn't stray too far from his paper guide!

He chooses another, picking up his simple strumming anew, he sings: *Muß i denn, muß i denn, zum stadtele hinaus, stadtele hinaus, und du, mein schat, bleibst hier?* I know this melody from an old Elvis Presley recording, the only lyric I remember being something like, " . . . because I don't have a wooden heart." I do my best to sing along with the German lyrics. The aging *monsieur* is leaning back in his chair, eyes closed, smiling slightly, as if in the midst of some musical ecstasy. Johann once again translates the pilgrim love song for my benefit: "I must go, I must go, I must leave this town, but you, my dear, must stay here. And when I'm back, and when I'm back, on your doorstep I shall appear." I wonder if old *Monsieur* Mativon is dreaming of past wanderings, long-gone pleasures, a youth when love would have made him profess sentiments like, " . . . but when I'm back, on your doorstep I shall appear."

After a few more bouncy songs, we are called to the table, so the guitar and lyric sheets are left behind as we casually move to the once elegant dining room, a grand fireplace, mantle and mirror dominating one wall, large windows open to the front courtyard on the other. The food served is delicious, but our multi-lingual conversation, so warm and facile and so much a part of life in today's Europe, is the true delight of the evening. Johann and Hildegard fairly bubble with stories and anecdotes and lessons from the Way. *Madame* Mativon holds her own in the conversation department, while *Monsieur* Mativon slowly and deliberately takes in his dinner with a simple smile on his face. Before we leave the dining room, *Madame* Mativon brings to us her *Livre d'Or*, the requisite guestbook, which she insists we must inscribe with our names and messages. I write in English: *May he who said 'Those who welcome you, welcome me,' bless you for your kindness to this pilgrim and all pilgrims who find a roof, a table, and warm friendship in this old house. Grace to you and peace,* Monsieur et Madame *Mativon!*

As I prepare for bed, I check my clothing and my boots: they are still wet and surely will not be dry by morning. If it is still raining in the morning, I will have to put them on damp so as to keep at least one pair of dry clothes ready for tomorrow afternoon. As I tuck myself in, I can see the sky beyond my window light up with lightning. Thunder continues to rumble in the distance. Tomorrow could be difficult.

14

Father and Son

By the time I awake, the rain has stopped. I am grateful. I put on dry
underwear and socks, but my pants and outer shirt remain clammy and
send a chill through my body that seems to cry out, *Just quit already!* I say
my morning prayers then head downstairs for breakfast. Our hosts are still
in bed, but everything has been left out for us: coffee is ready to be brewed,
just flip the switch, orange juice and yogurt are in the fridge, cake and bread
are set at the center of the kitchen table; it is "help yourself" all the way.
After breakfast, I return upstairs, boot up, and carry my pack and poles to
the foyer. Hildegard and Johann come from the kitchen to cheer me on;
Madame Mativon descends the oak staircase to wish me well, too. Kisses
and handshakes are shared, and then I am on my way.

I find myself under a dark grey, but for the moment dry, sky. I pick up
the highway out of town to the west, but upon reaching the Berry Canal, I
diverge from both the GR 654 indicators and my pilgrim map so as to follow
a clean trail on the canal's left bank. This canal route will save me a couple
kilometers today, and for the moment, it makes for fine off-pavement walking. My good fortune does not last long; within a couple kilometers, the path
thickens with increasingly tall grass slowing me down, and that grass is still
very wet from last night's rain. I try to lift my steps to avoid soaking my boots
more than I have to, but with fourteen kilos on my back, the effort becomes
too much to maintain. Soon enough, the leather of my boots is dark with
the damp. Eventually, the moisture seeps even deeper, and my socks begin to
absorb it. I fret over the increased possibility of blisters, but as I walk on, the
feet seem fine, so I focus my attention more on the slowly flowing canal to
my right, wide and languid and opaque with dirt and late-summer slime. It is
not much to look at, but it attracts birds, and their songs fill the morning air.
The foliage that lines its banks takes on a dark green cast under the thick, dull

sky. With Click and Clack in hand, I pick and poke my way, keeping my balance on the uneven vegetation. It is hard work; I am sure that whatever gain in kilometers I may be winning here, the additional energy I am expending walking through this stuff will more than make up for it.

Eventually, as I enter the urban area of Saint-Amand-Montrand, the trail becomes a beautiful pedestrian and bike path with park benches lining it; the red and white stripes of the GR reappear. Old men throw breadcrumbs to ducks paddling in circles waiting for their treats. Old women pass by carrying groceries in canvas shopping bags. I keep an eye peeled for GR signs directing me into the heart of the city and the church of Saint-Amand. After I pass a couple of bridges over the canal carrying substantial traffic, I begin to get nervous; I have not seen a GR stripe for a while. I have gone too far. I take the next bridge across the canal and enter the city center then begin asking directions to the church. I am directed back to the east several blocks. I eventually spot the church spire, and it is easy then to get myself to the front doors of the church. It is a heavy Romanesque building: on the outside something like an overweight mama, and on the inside, all dark and round and filled with the subtle smells of Catholic cult: incense and wax and stony must.

To the left of the sanctuary, an informal and comfortable chapel for quiet prayer has been set up. I set Gregory on a chair and seat myself on the next one over. I am alone. I rest here. Though my eyes are closed, my ears hear every creak and crack and footstep on stone echoing about the old place. I can almost hear the voices of those long-forgotten craftsmen who carved these stones. Are those the Latin words of a hundred thousand baptisms still echoing off of pillar and arch? And the private prayers of generations of ancestors, pleading God and favored saints for this blessing or that mercy: am I hearing them too in this great silence? I slip into the *grace zone* I have come to know so well out here on this road. It is a still place. It is full. I add my prayer to those of so many others through the centuries and whisper: *Don't let me even want to quit.*

I get up, take up Gregory and Click and Clack and step through the great wooden doors to the world outside, still dominated by the low, heavy clouds that have been the trademark of this summer and fall. I feel ready for a coffee, so take only a few steps before I am back within the alternative universe of a smoky bar. The old men with glassy eyes sipping their brandies and the burly younger men quaffing their beers give me the look I have come to know so well. "Who are you, and what are you doing in here?" I don't care anymore about these stares but take heart instead in the warm greeting of the lady tending the bar. We begin the pilgrim question and answer routine as she smoothly operates her big Italian *espresso* machine and pulls out a fine *cappuccino* to warm me from the inside out.

Reinforced, I return to the slippery cobbles of Saint-Amand and follow the GR flags out of town; I have almost eighteen kilometers yet to walk today. A couple hours later, as I pass over the Cher River again to enter Orval, the first direct sunlight in two days appears through a break in the clouds. It warms me, and after only a block or two of walking, I must stop to take off my Gore-Tex jacket and stuff it into Gregory's side pocket. The light is delicious, and I feel free and easy as can be as I climb out of the village. The cloud cover is actually breaking up quickly, separating into fluffy white marshmallows against the blue sky.

For the remainder of the afternoon, I walk in alternating bands of shade and sunshine. As I arrive in Loye-sur-Arnon, I find handmade signs directing me to the private pilgrim refuge where I have made a reservation for the night. To my surprise, the place is almost two kilometers outside of town and well off the pilgrim route. These last kilometers are tough ones. Thirty kilometers yesterday and almost as many today is a lot for me, and these final two pass by ever so slowly. I lumber along the paved road, turn a corner, lumber some more, then turn up a dirt road to a farmhouse set on a rise and framed by fir trees.

I approach, and even before I arrive at the house, a man comes out to greet me. He is in his mid-sixties, dressed in gardening duds. He waves me up to where he stands and introduces himself as Paul. "You are Kevin? We have been waiting for you. It is late to be still walking." I explain that I have come almost thirty kilometers today, and a good number of them through high and wet grass. He nods in understanding and shows me into a workshop, a segment of which has been turned into a kitchen. Another small area is the shower and toilet. The bedrooms, he points to a steep stairway, are above. He leads me up, but Gregory still on my back forces me to follow carefully and slowly. The attic is ample and well furnished. I have my pick of the two rooms, but Paul tells me the bed is better in the far room, so I choose that one. I leave Gregory leaning against the bed, and Paul and I return below, where his wife, Anne, is waiting to meet me. They are among the few Frenchmen I have met along this Way who have presented themselves using their first names, an informality that appeals to this American and makes me feel especially at home with them. Anne shows me that the kitchen is stocked with beer, canned food, and pasta so pilgrims can prepare their own supper. I take a beer, kick off my boots, and sit out in the yard for a moment of refreshment before returning to my usual afternoon responsibilities. My feet love the freedom they now enjoy. I look them over, and they are fine. No blisters. No hot spots. Good, firm calluses right where I need them. It amazes me that they work so well, these feet of mine, step after step, kilometer after kilometer. Tendons and toes, heals and arches: they all work so wonderfully together in their un-hailed labor of moving me forward. They are the real heroes of this pilgrimage, I affirm as I wiggle my toes in the late-afternoon breeze.

As it turns out, I will not be alone this evening. At about 4:00 pm as I am resting on my bed, eyes closed, thinking little of anything, I hear the door below open. Paul guides new pilgrims into the refuge. I hear two new voices speaking English, but accented: probably Dutch. Heavy steps sound as the three of them climb the stairwell. I get up to welcome my new pilgrim roommates. One is a tall fellow in his forties, angular and thin, the other is young, late teens or early twenties, long blond hair trailing out from under his backward baseball cap, the end of his nose sunburned bright red. They are father and son: Sietse and Evert. They have been on the Chemin together since Vézelay. They are indeed Dutch and hail from an island of the coast of the Netherlands called Texel. They have been walking 40-plus kilometer days, following the GR 654. The two of them look altogether bushed as they drop their packs, kick off their boots and socks, and begin settling into the room next to my own. They have an easy manner with one another and immediately welcome me into their back and forth repartee. I express admiration at their aggressive walking schedule; they respond that they only have two weeks for this adventure together and want to get as far down the road as they can. I share that I'm using the *Amis de Saint-Jacques* guide rather than the GR 654, and saving a considerable number of kilometers over the GR route; Sietse and Evert are very interested since it is the first they have heard that there is any alternative to the zig-zaggy, see every sight, approach of the GR. They ask to review my guide and maps, and I happily hand them over and explain how to use them. As it turns out, Paul and Anne are members of the *Amis* group in the area and have copies of the guide available for sale, so Sietse and Evert buy one for themselves, young Evert taking charge of its care and management. His French is worse than mine, so I explain some of the basics: *gauche* is left, *droit* is right, *ferme* is a farm or farmhouse.

Sietse asks what I am doing for dinner since it is a two-kilometer walk back to town. I tell him I was planning to eat something from the kitchen below, spaghetti or something. He calls to Evert and asks him to go check out the kitchen, then as an aside, tells me that Evert is an expert in spaghetti and that he works in a restaurant in Texel. Anne and Paul's son, François, has fresh tomatoes for sale from his garden, so these will be added to the sauce.

As my new friends shower and launder, I find a chair in the garden and take time to write in my journal, say the evening psalms, and look out over the fields and distant hills as the sun draws low, making shadows long while illuminating the rest with increasingly golden light. Eventually, I can hear Evert in the kitchen, knocking around pots and pans, so I go in to see if he needs help. *"Nee."* He is just fine and wants no assistance, except to set up a table and chairs outside; we will watch the sun go down as we eat, he tells me. I do as he asks, and before long the three of us are seated at our makeshift dining table, enjoying Evert's spaghetti, not exactly up to Trappist standards, but good enough, the fresh tomatoes he's thrown into the red sauce making up in rich flavor any lack elsewhere.

Over dinner, Sietse tells me that while his wife and second son are home, this is a special time on the Chemin for him and Evert to be together as father and son. Quality time. Bonding. Getting to know each other *as adults*. This is the name of the game for him. I tell the two of them that I admire them for their courage in doing something like this. Evert cannot figure that out: *courage?* I try to explain that it would be easier for the two of them to just go their own ways, to leave their father-son relationship as it always has been, that this project they are doing together seems to be to be one that carries risk: they could end up hating each other under the pressure of walking almost forty kilometers a day, or coming to know each other better than they want to, discover dark sides of one another that could hurt them. I find myself speaking more about my own father and this son than these two; it really is I who would have found it very risky to have done something like this with my old man, *too risky* to even consider. Better to leave sleeping dogs and all that. I am saddened that I never knew both the risk and the gain that these two are enjoying now, that my pa will always be a mystery, or better, a *complex* to me, more than a known and loved human being, a *person*. They assure me they are both doing fine with one another . . . so far.

As the sun sinks quickly below the horizon, the three of us clear our table and put our garden chairs back where we found them. The sky is clear of all clouds, a great omen for tomorrow. Sietse and I wash dishes, while Evert goes upstairs to call his girlfriend back in Texel. I take a few moments outside by myself before heading upstairs; the first star of the night has made herself visible to my naked eye. Soon enough she will be accompanied by sisters and brothers in their billions.

We are all very tired after hefty walking days, so it is not long before lights go out and all of us are tucked into our sleeping bags. I end the day in their language: *Goede nacht, mijn vrienden; good night, my friends.* *"Goede nacht, Kevin,"* they respond.

Well, actually, I do not have a *goede nacht* after all. I toss and turn and lie awake through most of the night. This is as inexplicable as it is irritating: I just walked thirty kilometers; I should be very tired. I have no great worries rolling around in my mind other than just getting further down the road. I do know now that I'm going to have to be extra careful today to manage my moods; sleepless nights usually make me grumpy and impatient with anything that isn't the way I think it should be. I finally give up and get up. After packing and booting up, I head to breakfast in Anne and Paul's farmhouse dining room.

While waiting for my coffee, Anne brings me a couple albums filled with snapshots of those pilgrims who have come before us. Since they began welcoming pilgrims, they have conscientiously taken photographs of them and collected them in these albums year by year. It is surprisingly pleasant to page through the collections; this rogues' gallery, page after page, reveals an extraordinary diversity of people walking this Chemin: old ones, young ones, bearded ones, clean-shaven ones, pudgy, skinny, smiling, serious. There is much that is common to them all; they all are wearing boots or hiking sandals, they have trekking pants or shorts with lots of pockets like my own, caps with wide brims abound. But there is something more here: there is a sort of golden thread tying us together into a band of brothers and sisters, a certain *look* that is not just a matter of a smile, a particular posture or a ruffled forehead common to all. It is something else, perhaps something like whatever it was that gave my vocation away to *Madame* Mativon: we all look satisfied, fulfilled, pleased, well, just happy *on the inside*. Because we are doing something important, something inexplicable, something kind of mystical, and doing it together, all of us are bound together by a bond that no one else can every fully understand: in our common aches and joys, exhaustion and exhilaration, despair and hope, we are in this common mission somehow happy.

Soon enough Paul and Anne, François, Evert and Sietse have all joined me around the table, the morning conversation a mix of French and English with a little bit of Dutch on the side. The major concern of Paul and Anne is that our picture be taken for their album; we will be the newest inductees into their growing gallery of pilgrim guests. After the last *croissant* has been consumed, we meet in the garden, our packs and sticks stacked to one side. The three of us are lined up while Paul stands back with what now seems like a dinosaur of a camera, chunky with buttons for rolling film from one side of its guts to the other. Evert and I both offer Paul our smaller cameras so that we can have pictures too, albeit digital ones. He kindly snaps away, hands back our cameras, and with that little pilgrim rite completed, Evert, Sietse, and I begin making our goodbyes to this fine family of three who have been so kind to us. I'd like to have had more time with them. I would like to know them better. There is real sadness in our parting. Alas, it is not for pilgrims to hang around, so our friendships are always quite provisional. And so it is here: the three of us load up our packs simultaneously and without ever having discussed it, head out of the farmyard together as a sort of little family of our own: father, son, and me.

We follow the directions Paul has given us for a shortcut back to Loye-sur-Arnon that leads us through a stand of pine trees, the smell of which on this early morning remind me of Spokane. I enjoy the sense of connection these trees give me between my old world back home, the world in which I grew up, great pines shading our family's yard with their needly boughs, and this other world in France that I now inhabit so much later in my life. It is all one, despite the thousands of kilometers and forty-odd years that separate here and now from then and there. Smelling these pitch-laden pine trees, I could be ten again, chasing after my brothers, riding imaginary horses, playing like television cowboys; or I could be more than five times those ten years, ambling along this pilgrim path that goes back in time more than a thousand years. It is the same me. That little cowboy has grown up into a pilgrim, but I am still he, and he is still in me.

The three of us are mostly silent as we walk along; each of us intuitively knowing that there is something sacred about these first moments of morn-ing walk. The smell of pine in the air, the cawing of a couple crows in the near distance, the sweet tweet of sparrow just to our left, the first dew-free flutter of a butterfly crossing our path: these things call for attention, and for me at least, to attend to them is to attend to their creator, that is, to attend to *grâce*. So I, too, am plenty happy right now, from the inside out.

It is not long before Evert and Sietse pull ahead of me, and from my position a few meters behind them, I can still hear them laconically chatting or teasing one another in Dutch. I take pleasure in seeing them ahead of me thus: father and son, side by side, day by day, liking each other's company.

At other times, young Evert pulls ahead, leaving Sietse and I, the old farts, to ourselves. He is practicing at being lead dog for awhile, leading us, expecting us to follow him, practicing manhood. At these times, it is Sietse and I who laconically talk about this or that: the fruit that can be pulled from these trees close to the road, apples and pears, mostly, but sometimes blackberries, too. "You know, Kevin, you could walk most of the day living on this free fruit, never having to buy anything else. It is just here for the taking. Nature provides." Sietse is right, yet I have been walking through this autumn fruit basket without plucking much of anything. It has been there, near at hand, perfectly good food, and I have just plodded on past, not tak-ing. What is true for apples and pears and blackberries, I suppose, if I exam-ine my heart a bit, is true for God: he too is here in abundance and too many of these days I walk past without paying attention, taking, savoring. *Okay, God, I'll try to do better.* I take one of several apples Sietse has pulled from a tree whose branches are hanging over a barbed wire fence and avoiding a wormhole, take a big juicy autumn bite of nature's gift to passing pilgrims.

At still other times, Sietse moves ahead or falls behind, and it is Evert and I walking together. He tells me about the fancy restaurant where he works as a waiter. Their island has become a tourist destination for other Dutchmen, its fine beaches drawing in increasingly large crowds of visitors. He likes meeting the restaurant's guests and serving them, and he is learning to cook, which is fun for him, and of course, the money in his pocket is great too. He has a girlfriend, whom he is missing a lot, but he is also happy to be here with his dad for a while.

Evert and I come upon Sietse lying comfortably in a grassy field to the side of the road, his hat shielding his face from the sun. We jump the ditch and join him, dropping our packs and laying ourselves down in the tall grass. I cover my face as well. A fair breeze occasionally whispers over us, making the grass wave just slightly, but cooling our sweat all the same. Fifteen minutes pass; I feel ready to go, but they are still recumbent. I take a swig of water, then lie back down, my head resting on Gregory's haunches. After another fifteen or so, Sietse rises, Evert and I follow, and together again, the three of us continue down the road.

Sietse wants to know more about my previous pilgrimage, the one across Spain. After a few preliminaries, he asks me a particularly tough question: "Kevin, how did your other pilgrimage change you?" Maybe he wants to know what he might expect from his own weeks out here. I begin with some easy things: *I came to love and respect the earth more; its beauty and tenderness really got to me after so many days of walking across her. I learned what it was to live with others with almost no fear among us, a fluid but real community formed among us pilgrims as we walked along; and the best thing was that this freedom from fear made it easy for us to extend ourselves, to be generous, to care for one another in exceedingly tender ways. By the same token, it revealed to me how fear-ridden our society really is and that this fear is one of the primary causes of our present social and spiritual dislocation.*

Sietse wants to know more: "And what about your religion, being a priest, did the pilgrimage change that too?" Yes, it changed that too. I pause to think about this a bit, then speak careful to say something important correctly: *I think it made my relationship to Jesus more fundamental to me, and that relationship became much more like that of a companion with Jesus, rather than just as a distant believer in him thousands of years later. I feel now more like we walk together, that we are brothers, that we are fellow pilgrims on this way through life. He is my teacher, my mentor, my great friend. He shows me the way without leaving my side. Sometimes we walk, sometimes we rest, sometimes we give each other room to be alone for a while, sometimes we are silent with one another, sometimes we talk late into the night with the left-overs of bread and wine between us.* Sietse listens attentively and understands; after all he was raised in the Dutch Reformed tradition of Christianity, so this kind of talk is not so surprising to him. The questions and answers end for the moment, and we walk on in silence.

Evert begins to slow down. Even worse, as the day grows warmer, he is beginning to limp. Sietse and I catch up to him as he leans against a stone wall bounding the yard of an old farmhouse. "I think I have a blister." He pulls of his boot and sock and sure enough, on the base of his foot is the watery pouch. While standing on one foot, he drops his pack, leans down to pull out of one of its pockets a nail clipper. I interject that this is not a good way to proceed, but it is too late, and with a quick snip, he opens the bubble on his foot, and he is squeezing the fluid from the blister. His dad retrieves a silicon pad from his pack to glue over the wound. Evert risks an infection treating his blister this way, but he moved too fast for me to advise him otherwise. He rolls his sock back up over his foot, pulls on his boot, and limping still, accompanies us further down this day's Chemin.

At close to 3:00 pm, we complete our twenty-five kilometer journey into Châteaumeillant. As always, our map delivers us to the main church of the town. Sietse and Evert follow me into the church. We drop our packs and set them aside and begin to wander about the mostly Romanesque building, taking in its arches and columns and images of saints from times gone by. We reunite after a short while; I ask my companions if they would like my twenty-five cent lecture on church architecture. They both enthusiastically say yes, so I begin explaining the old Latin root words, nave, apse and transept, then some of the details of this church's Romanesque style, the heavy columns, the small windows, the rounded arches, then finally, compare it to what we do not see here, Gothic verticality and flamboyance. They have never previously heard any of this and are fascinated. They take another look around the church with their eyes a little more open to its character and history, then we reload our packs and return to the street. We walk through the town and out again in search of tonight's refuge. It is located just beyond the town limits, near a small lake and resort; it consists of several rooms in the basement of a civic activities center. It is modern, light and cool but without the warmth of a home. Evert's blister makes the two of them decide to stay the night here with me and not continue any further. I am glad for the company. We have to be let in by a town employee who arrives in a small pickup, opens the doors for us, shows us the baths and toilets, and leaves us to ourselves. A pilgrim on bicycle also shows up and takes a room. He also is from the Netherlands and introduces himself as Toon. He is well into his sixties but has the physique of a man half his age. Sietse and Evert share a room, while Toon and I each take one for ourselves.

After washing, we hang our laundry on the metal fire escape to dry, then recline on the green lawn to enjoy the late afternoon sun. As it draws lower to the horizon, Sietse suggests that we had better get into town to find something to eat for the evening. Toon has his own store of food and wishes to eat alone, so the three of us walk back into town, but find all the available restaurants closed. A single bar is open, so we enter, but it has no food on offer. The bartender directs us further back into town, but again, we find nothing. A single butchery is open, but barely: it is already 5:00 pm, closing time, and the sausages and cuts of meats are being put away by the lady within. Sietse tries the door, and it opens. He asks if it is too late to buy something, explaining that we are pilgrims, and everything else seems to be closed. She is happy to serve us; there is plenty of sausage, of course, but also, she has an unsold pizza she can offer us. We pay up, take the pizza in hand, then return up the street to the bar, adding a bottle of red wine to our store, and head back to the refuge.

We take our loot into the small kitchen upstairs, where Toon is already ensconced, eating his own dinner. We share out the wine among the four of us, then the pizza is warmed in the microwave and sliced among the three of us. Toon begins to talk of himself and his pilgrimage on two wheels. His bike is not a speed-demon, and his age is a factor so he rides slowly, but still and all, makes far better time than we foot-bound pilgrims. I ask how many flat tires he has had to repair since leaving his home in the Netherlands: "None," he proudly reports. He is a nice enough fellow, but he seems to belong somehow to a different pilgrim world than we walkers. He speaks of kilometers in their hundreds, while we can only boast of our twenties or thirties. His daily issues concern mechanical things like chains and gears and brake cables, while we are preoccupied with bootlaces, dirt or pavement, and the care of blisters. His pilgrimage takes place a half-meter off the ground with lots of whirring technology separating him from the earth below, while we are attached rather directly to the earth through our tired feet. It's not a big difference, after all he's a pilgrim too, but he's a pilgrim in a different way, a different speed, a different key, and we feel it. We clean up the kitchen and head to our rooms. Evert, Sietse, and I gather in their room to talk over tomorrow; we'll walk together again, but while I plan to end the day in La Châtre, they are hoping to go further, and that will probably be the end of our shared pilgrimage.

Yet again, I do not sleep well. After I turn off the lights and crawl into my sack, I slip into a *demi-monde* somewhere between full wakefulness and dreamy unconsciousness. I am trapped inside my maps and cannot get out.

I am not asleep; I am not awake. I am surrounded on all sides, above and below, by the swirling topographical elevation lines, the cold geographical feature markers, and small black names that I spend so much of my walking day tending to so as not to get lost. On the road, they are safely contained on the throwaway pages that I wear around my neck, but here, at night, they wrap themselves around me and jump out at me and threaten me. I pull myself out of this half-dream, turn on the light, check my watch: 12:30 am. I have been lying here for more than two hours. I take a drink of water, eat a granola bar retrieved from Gregory's top pocket, listen to a few old songs by Joan Baez, then turn off the lights and go back to bed. I feel more restful now and disappear into the world of full-fledged dreams, the echo of Joan singing, "*Gracias a la vida que me ha dado tanto . . .*", Thanks be to life, for having given me so much.

I wake up late. It is already 8:00 am when the sunshine streaming through my window breaks through the threshold between sleeping and waking. I get up and hear Evert and Sietse pulling themselves together next door. I make use of the bathroom down the hall, wave good morning to my pilgrim pals as I pass their open door, and begin packing up for the day's march to La Châtre. I stretch my tendons then join Evert and Sietse upstairs in the kitchen for breakfast. Toon is already there, sipping his tea and nibbling on toast. We pull together our own makeshift breakfast, and Toon contributes to our humble fare by offering us bread for toasting. We eat quickly, clean up the kitchen, and head back to straighten up our rooms, collect our packs, and get the day underway.

As soon as we are ready to walk, Evert takes off ahead of Sietse and me; without even a look back, he strikes out on his own, following the guide they bought yesterday, leaving Sietse and I to follow mine. We follow behind, but the distance between son and father grows. Sietse is quiet as we walk, and I cannot help but notice the odor of something slightly spoiled in the air between us. It is not long before Sietse explains: after breakfast, the two of them were in their room together, ready to leave, when Sietse asked Evert to fold the blankets on his bed and return them to the small closet in the corner of the room. Evert did not see the point of this and said so. Sietse told him more forcefully that it was a sign of respect and gratitude for those who provided housing for us. Evert did as he was told but went sullen. Then he took off. Sietse explains a bit more: Evert is not as mature as his age might suggest; sometimes he behaves more like a sixteen-year-old than an adult of twenty-four years. Sietse thinks it's best just to let him walk on; he needs the time and space to work through this bump in their road together. It will pass, he tells me, but he also adds that this is the first time Evert has acted this way since they began walking, and I can tell this behavior isn't fitting his paternal plan for their time together. As Evert disappears beyond the next curve in the road, the feeling of something bigger than just a morning spat grows.

It is not easy being a father. It is not easy being a son. I remember Sunday's Gospel reading and the fine little homily that followed and take a chance at offering Sietse a bit of biblical wisdom. I ask if he knows Jesus' story of the good father and the two sons, one "prodigal", the other a "good boy". He says he remembers the story from Sunday school as a kid. I remind him of one of the story's messages, different from that of the pastor in Lurcy-Lévis, but to the point here and now: The father freely let the prodigal son leave with half his fortune; he truly lets go of him even knowing that nothing good will come of this. It is, however, this very son who eventually returns, not just chastened by his experience living on the dark side of everything, but loving his father in a new and deeper way than ever before. Meanwhile, the "good son," the one who never did anything wrong, is in the end profoundly resentful and disrespectful to both brother and father. Letting sons go is one of the hardest but most important works of a good father. Sietse likes the story and goes quiet as he mulls it over, no Evert in sight.

After two hours of walking, Sietse and I decide to take a break in a pleasant looking grove that becomes visible as we round a curve in the road. As we approach, we find Evert spread out in the grass, his head resting on his pack, enjoying the shade of the plane trees. He lifts his head, smiles at us both, and welcomes us to his little paradise. We drop our own packs and join him prostrate in the lovely soft grass. "There are some grapes over there if you want them," he points. He is not mad anymore. We are back to being a pilgrim threesome again. Sietse gets up to investigate the vines hanging over a rock wall just across a small road from us. He brings back to us several bunches of fruit, and we begin pulling the grapes from their twiggy vines and popping them into our mouths. Their hide is tough, but they are juicy and sweet with just a hint of fermented zing in them. The small pits are bitter in my mouth if I inadvertently crack one before separating it from the pulp and spitting it out; I suppose that is what Evert and Sietse have just done: they've spit out a small bitter seed from an otherwise pretty fine relationship. I like Evert and Sietse a lot. After a few minutes of quiet, I break the restful spell and exclaim: *You know, I'm just about as happy right now as a man can be; I have sweet fruit to eat, plenty of shade on a sunny day covering me, soft grass under my back, and two good friends at my side. What more could I want in this life?* Sietse and Evert both laugh. Sietse says, "I agree." And Evert says, "I agree."

In the quiet that follows, the only sounds are of small birds in the trees and the breeze softly rustling the grass below and the leaves above. *Gracias a la vida . . . que me ha dado tanto . . .* The song I went to sleep by slowly seeps to the forefront of my consciousness. "Thanks be to life . . . that has given me so much." *I agree.*

The three of us eventually rouse ourselves from our roadside roost, and continue on towards La Châtre, the two of them on lead while I bring up the tail. Again, I enjoy watching them walk together, but now even more than yesterday since their bond is all the more important, having been given a gentle testing this morning.

Time passes on the road, and positions change once again. Evert is ahead, and Sietse and I walk together. We turn a corner into a small village and are confronted with a substantial wall surrounding the village cemetery. The ornate tombs with their individual chapels of glass and wrought iron rise above the wall and proclaim to us both the stark reality of death. No matter how elegant the stone above, the reality beneath is, still and all, one of stench and demise. I feel Sietse's question coming even as he opens his mouth to ask it: "Kevin, do you think there is life after death?" Once again, I take time to form a simple answer: *I do.*

I then take even more time to form a more full thought on the subject. *I believe in God, and I don't believe that God could just let a person he has created and loved disappear into nothingness.*

Pause.

There is a part of me that sometimes does not believe so much, the "evidence first" part of me. The absoluteness of death is real. Flesh doesn't last forever. Everything goes. How can you argue with that? Look at those tombs: the people under them are really dead. But there is another part of me, a more important part of me, and I hope, a truer part of me that knows that we are more than flesh.

Pause.

The loveliness in us, the goodness in us, is just too real to simply disappear, to be gone forever, to be dead dead.

I feel tempted to say something more, but feel if I say any more, this will become a sermon rather than a conversation. Sietse ponders for a bit, nods, then adds that he has long thought that we come back as different people, better people, in further lives. I add with a laugh: *For me, one life is probably enough.*

We say no more about the grave topic as we follow behind Evert, but I continue to think about it in the silence of our walking together.

Death.

I roll the word around in my mind for a while.

Death.

Death.

Death.

It *is* such a mystery. It is one thing to simply look at the tombstone of someone I've never known or loved and logically think: *gone for good.* It is another to shake with grief as we behold the body of a wife or brother or dearest friend. Grief founded in love of another, it seems to me, prompts us, maybe even impels us, to belief. So much of grief is simply asking the aching question: *How can it be?* This life, this love, this beautiful person: how is it that all of this could simply slip away or be crushed into nothingness? Our very being cries out against what our eyes affirm in the dead body of our beloved. Our cry against death seems to be hardwired into us as human beings. As it is the source of our grief, so it is also the source of our belief. The impossibility of this *person* being here one moment, then absolutely gone the next is just too crazy, too disjunctive to our sense of love's endurance, too *unbelievable*, that we are pushed by death to believe, to believe that there must be *more.* So it is that I believe in the *More.* So it is that I believe in *Life.* So it is in the end that I believe in *God.*

With just a little over two kilometers to go, we decide to stop in Lacs for lunch. This will be our final meal together before we go our separate ways. We step into a country restaurant and are welcomed to take a table by the young man pulling a couple of beers from the tap at the bar. His English is almost perfect and has almost no discernible accent. We decide to make this our big meal for the day and order the daily special, three full courses with wine and all the bread we can eat. The young man who was tending bar now takes our order and picking up on Evert and Sietse's accent, asks if they are from the Netherlands. When they respond positively, he tells us he too is Dutch, having followed his French wife here, only to divorce later. He remained, bought this place, and has been here ever since. He invites us into the joke of it all by adding: "Well, that's life, no?" Our meals come in waves, and we finish up stuffed from the food and woozy from the wine. We pay our bill, throw on our packs, make our farewells to the Dutch divorcee, and head down the road to La Châtre.

The last two-plus kilometers should be a snap, but we are heavy with lunch and so move more slowly than usual. Evert leads the way, makes a couple errors reading the guide, and so detours us through La Châtre, before we climb through the streets of the hilly town to find ourselves finally at the church in the town center. We enter, look around a bit, then return to the street where I must now say farewell to my pilgrim friends after two days of amiable friendship. As this morning with Paul and Ann, it is not so easy. I try to make it as quick and painless as possible as we stand around in front of the church: *Well, Sietse and Evert, I've really enjoyed walking with you, and I thank you for your friendship. Maybe we'll meet again down the road, but if not, God bless.* Sietse says much the same thing back to me. Evert is quiet. We shake hands in a manly fashion, then after a moment's hesitation, we give each other bear hugs made altogether clumsy by our obtrusive backpacks. Evert's hug is a second or two longer than Sietse's. This kid likes me. *Goede reis,* happy travels, I wish them in Dutch, then in French: *Courage!* They wave a last time as they amble down the street and around the corner and soon enough, out of town.

15

Don't Quit

The emptiness that comes from separating from good friends along the Chemin wallops me like a punch in the gut. I am alone again on this long road south, and I don't like the feeling at all right this moment. I look for signs to the youth hostel where I hope to spend the night but do not find a single indicator. The hollow feeling within me only grows darker. I ask directions from two elderly ladies standing at a corner holding themselves up with canes. They are gowned in simple cotton dresses with well-worn sweaters covering their rounded shoulders. Their canes are simply rough sticks that they have recruited into their service, sawn to size, limbs chopped off, one end polished by the sweaty palm that grasps it firmly for support. One of the ladies points me down the street to a house situated beneath a cliff; that, she says, is the Auberge de Jeunesse. Now the bad news: She informs that the *auberge* will not be open until 5:00 pm; I can ring the bell, but it will surely be of no use. I sneak a quick look at my watch: 2:00 pm. *Oh great.* I walk to the house, ring the bell, and find that the old lady's pessimism is justified; no one answers. She has followed me to the door and engages me once again. She reveals to me that her granddaughter serves as a stewardess on an Air France 747 and speaks six languages, including *anglais*. She is proud of this fact and shifts her cane to her other hand as she simultaneously shifts her body weight to the opposite hip. Getting back to my own situation, she cheerily informs me that just beyond the *auberge*, there is a bridge over the river, the other side of which will offer to me a grassy field. It is a cool place where I might spend my afternoon. She is delighted to be of such great help to me and widens her wizened face into a broad smile that makes me feel better about the long hours ahead with nothing to do. She then slowly turns and canes her way back to the corner over which she and her friend reign.

I wander down the street as directed, cross the bridge, and find the left bank to be covered in deep green grass and shaded by the outstretched boughs of grand trees planted here perhaps a century ago. Avoiding the worst of the goose dung that is spread over the place, I drop Gregory to the ground, pull out of his pouches my iPod and journal, then turn him sideways to make of him a proper backrest. I tug off my boots and settle in for my long afternoon of waiting for a roof over my head. There is no point in going back into town since everything will be closed until 5:00 or so anyway; these French towns take their afternoon *repos* most seriously.

I close my eyes and enjoy the cool of the shade and the soft sound of the water rolling by in the small river separating me from the village. I review my maps for the next couple of days and phone ahead to make reservations for the coming two nights, the second of which is Gargilesse, the end of the Nevers route I've been on since leaving Vézelay. From Gargilesse on, there is just one Chemin south, and I hope that it will double the number of pilgrims I meet. I have been spoiled by friendship these past two days, and I want more. I doze in an effort to let the ache in my gut heal.

At 5:00 pm on the button, I am standing at the door of the *auberge* ringing the bell to no avail. Just as the first little wave of distress begins to form, a young lady jauntily comes down the street towards me, flashes me a smile, and as she arrives at the door, pulls keys from her purse and unlocks the door. She welcomes me in, invites me to leave Gregory to one side as she hands me papers to fill out and takes my donation in euros for the night. She grabs a key, flies through the dining area to show me the microwave and TV, then pulls a collection of bed sheets, blankets and towels from a closet, and invites me to follow her upstairs. Each room has two bunk-beds, but she tells me I am probably going to be alone tonight. She points out the bath and toilet down the hall, then tells me I'm on my own from here on; in the morning just leave the key behind, please.

I wash, launder, and hang my dripping clothes on any available nail or hook for drying, then head into town to shop for tomorrow's breakfast and lunch and find tonight's dinner. I consume the better part of a pizza in a small restaurant and quaff two beers while doing so. The beer leaves me feeling just the slightest bit goofy and settles down the existential loneliness I have been feeling without Evert and Sietse to accompany me. As I wander towards the *auberge* and a good night's sleep, I pass through a small park overlooking the lower part of the town where my *auberge* is located, a stone retaining wall holding the upper level of the park in place. The retaining wall boasts a view across rooftops and out over the darkening fields beyond the town and to the hills beyond, now purple, almost black, as the low light of dusk dims to night. I take up a position on the stone wall to enjoy the dark grandeur of the vista spreading out before me. From this perch, my legs dangling in thin air, I feel like I am sitting on the edge of the earth, not looking out into an abyss, but beholding the fullness of the earth and beyond.

I presently come to realize that I am not alone on this promontory: a single teen wrapped in a hoodie with cowl pulled up over the back of his head sits on the wall further on, looking out, oblivious to my presence, enveloped in a world of his own. I wonder what he is thinking about: Death and life? God and beauty? Sadness and joy? Fathers and sons? He reminds me of the hooded boy I met in the fog not so many mornings ago. Here he is again, now grown into teenage-hood. Maybe this hooded figure there and here is like the stone and wrought iron crucifixes along my way; he is Jesus, alive, meeting me here and there, guiding me from one place to another, keeping an eye on me, protecting me from the abyss. Just maybe.

As I feared, at 6:00 in the morning, the laundry hanging about the room is still plenty damp. It is the first thing I check, even before heading to the loo. The hard reality of clammy underwear discourages me beyond reason and drops me back into the hole I felt yesterday when Evert and Sietse moved on. I have no friends at hand to pull me out of this psychic dump, so I go about my morning affairs with no sense that there is some great purpose in all this. I almost wish I had a good reason to quit, but I have none. My feet and knees and tendons are all just fine, not even a blister gives me cause for catching a train home. Again last night, I awoke mid-stream and could not get back to sleep for quite some time. There has been a restlessness afoot within me these past days, something I have not been able to see clearly or name; perhaps the wet socks and underwear are the humble revelators of my present dis-ease: zeal, zeal for the mission, is leaking out of me. Another part of me, probably the greater part of me, does not want to quit and understands that what I am presently about is something monumental in my life. *Jesus, James, Gregory, Click and Clack: don't even let me want to quit.* I repack Gregory, the damp clothing either tucked in side pockets where it won't get anything else wet or dangling to dry from Gregory's outer skin, held in place by safety pins. The wool socks and blue microfiber underpants dangling from Gregory look like medals hanging from the chest of some insane general. They will wag nicely as I walk, I am sure. I eat a peach, some nuts, and a third of the altogether uninteresting ham and Emmental cheese sandwich I bought last night.

I step outside, lock the door, and leave the key in the mailbox as directed. At 7:00 I am aware of how dark it still is out here on the street; there is just a hint of morning light on the eastern horizon; summer is really over. Time is moving on, the earth is tilting its northern pole ever-so-slowly away from our lovely yellow sun. Up the steep hill back into the park I climb, then through the center of town, stopping in the church for just a moment to repeat my new prayer: *Lord God Almighty: don't let me even want to quit.* Then I am on my way for the day.

As I am working my way through the busy and confusing streets and avenues leading out of La Châtre, a gaggle of schoolgirls spot me lumbering down the sidewalk. They run over to me and are all twitter and giggle. They ask me what I am doing and where I am from and to where am I going. I tell them I am a pilgrim, that I have walked from Belgium, that I am walking to Spain, and that I am an American. They are delighted to meet such an odd person doing such an odd thing; the obvious leader among the girls knows a few words of English and tries them out on me with strong French inflections: "Good morNING, MisTER." *Good morning to you. How are you?* "I am veRY well, *merci*, oh, thank you!" The other girls are absorbed in the simple conversation and applaud their friend for her efforts. I say, *Au revoir!* And they answer as a group, still atwitter: "*Au revoir, monsieur*". The leader who spoke to me in English adds: "*Courage, monsieur*". And I make her words into another prayer: *Yes, courage, Lord. Give me plenty of that courage.*

Once out of the confines of La Châtre, as if to further test me, today's Chemin offers me a plentiful dose of hill-climbing. The fields through which I pass are less green than those that have been my companions for so long; there is much more brown, and everything feels drier than ever before. I do not have a great store of energy today, so I make myself content to ramble up the road at a laconic pace. I do not really care if I am slow today; I have no records to break, no appointments to keep, just get over the next hill, and the next, and the next.

The sun warms me as it rises higher in the sky, and as it does, I begin the process of healing the morning's doldrums. Yes, the fields are more brown than before, but look at them more closely and what do I see: amidst the clods of red dirt formed into long, rough furrows are small blades of next year's wheat already showing themselves. The delicate, chlorophyll-laden blades are all the more beautiful for their present fragility. What a wonder that they should grow so! It cannot be easy for a seed so small to make it in this tough world: to avoid the hungry birds above, to be buried for so long, to wait for rain, to sink the most tender of roots into the roughest of soils, to dare pop their little green heads above the surface, none of this can be easy. But then to finally see the light, to stretch upward under the warm September afternoon sun, to become big and tall and strong, and then eventually to produce more seed, seed as remarkable as itself, and to do it all so profligately: in their hundreds and thousands they produce the next generation, and all this so that I might eat a delightful *baguette* tonight! Indeed, what a wonder among a world full of wonders! Even the barren field has its delights. Even this long road on its more dismal days, is filled with revelation. *God of tender wheat, don't let me even want to quit!*

My nineteen-kilometer morning ends in Neuvy-Saint-Sépulchre. As I leave the dirt road and step up to the concrete sidewalk of the street that brings me into the heart of the town, I notice a strange sound coming from below. There's "clack" all right, but "click" is sounding more like "pong." I look down and am devastated to see that the steel head and plastic basket are missing from my old pal, Click. Concrete is connecting directly to aluminum pole with each tap. How could I not have noticed this major equipment malfunction sooner? I take a look at the end of the pole: it is already filling up with dirt and debris. I feel like I am at the deathbed of a friend. *Alas, poor Click, I knew you well. You, along with your partner, Clack, have been with me since I first set foot on the Camino four years ago, got me up and down the hills and valleys of Spain for more than 780 kilometers, waited patiently in the closet for four years until this new journey began, then faithfully served me all these days through muck and mire and mud, through city and village, across woods and fields, up and down, preserving me from even a single serious fall. Your slight and slim aluminum body won't hold up long without your tough little titanium head to take the daily beating I give you. Can you make it a few more days, my little friend?*

I pong and clack my way into the heart of Neuvy, its massive basilica to my left dominating the scene. I wander about the town center looking at streets signs and trying to find my way to the address given in the guide. I cannot figure it out. I get that desperate feeling again: *I am tired of this! What am I doing out here?* I wander to the basilica. I find the doors open, so I enter the building, built sometime in the twelfth century. A massive rotunda dominates the edifice, great columns supporting it from below. The church was build by some lord or duke having just returned from pilgrimage to the Holy Land. The fellow brought back with him a few relics from Jerusalem's Church of the Holy Sepulcher, naming his own building after that of Jerusalem.

Among the treasures held within the round arches that surround me are the blood Jesus shed from the cross, a fragment of Jesus' tomb, and a copy of one of the nails used by the Roman soldiers to crucify Christ. To the modern believer, these relics, and so many like them throughout Western Europe, are of very questionable pedigree; European crusaders were notoriously gullible purchasers of such things from the clever locals; nevertheless, like the bones of Saint James in Compostela, they became the center of spiritual life for towns and villages like this one. Great festivals developed around them, pilgrims flocked to pray before them, and often enough, miracles were claimed to have been accomplished through them.

Relics such as these kept the medieval Christian feeling close to Christ and the saints in a very physical and sensual way. The devotion of generations of Christians who made use of them to feel more temporally and physically connected to the divine, makes them, in my opinion, worthy of respect and care even by us more modern and critical Christians.

Near the reliquary of the blood of Jesus, Saint Ignatius' prayer is inscribed, my favorite line being: "Blood of Christ, inebriate me!" I like the complete disregard for propriety held in that line. *So deeply may I imbibe this drink that it makes of me a foolish drunk . . . a foolish drunk for Christ!* This is not a prayer for the prim and proper Sunday churchgoer; it is for the risk-takers, the wild ones, those prone to abandon, the clowns of God and his fools for faith. I am, at least at home, perhaps too prim and proper myself and not foolish enough when it comes to God. Out here on this Via, there is more room to get drunk on grace and go a little bit crazy with God. I rather like the buzz that comes with it.

I find my refuge down the street and around a corner; it is a fine place, and so I settle in. This has not been an altogether easy day, but the pleasant atmosphere of my refuge and the fact that I now have a place to rest takes the edge off my troubles. Just beyond the house, the street opens into a green park surrounding a small lake. Dogs are being walked, children play within eyesight of their mothers, teens hang out, snuggling and smooching, presuming themselves to be invisible to the rest of humanity. I take a walk along the grassy bank of the lake, towards a restaurant at the far end, then turn back as the sun slowly slips low in the sky, and the shade on my path suddenly takes on a slight September chill. I am missing Sietse and Evert more than I would have expected. In my loneliness on this Chemin, I remind myself yet again: *Don't even think about quitting!*

I leave Neuvy by way of a path through the park just beyond the refuge. The sky is dark and threatening at 7:00 am as I click and poke my way along the lake's bank. Before I have passed the turnoff to the restaurant at the far end of the lake, it is raining lightly. Beyond the park and its shady trees I am once again among open fields. The rain thickens. I am tempted to feel sorry for myself, as if I have a right to bright and clear days every day, but today I push back against the temptation to go into *poor me* mode and instead, choose to do this wet walking for others: for Gene and Caroline back in Leuven, for my brothers and sisters, my nephews and nieces. It works for a while, and so I push on not minding the damp, head down against the rain . . . for a while.

I cover the nine kilometers to the village of Cluis in about two hours but am daunted by the steep climb up into the town center. The rainwater rolling down the pavement in ripples and waves soaks my boots. I consider calling it a day right here but decide to take a warm coffee and a *croissant* in whatever bar I might find open before making any decisions. I pass by the village church, try the door, find it locked, so continue another block into the village center. I arbitrarily choose one among several open bars and step inside. As always there are a couple of old fellows already working on the day's inebriation, but a friendly lady about my age waits the bar, and she warmly waves me to a table, commenting on the rain which has soaked me to the core. I want to answer something like, "good weather for a duck," but don't have a clue how to say it or make it sound like a joke in French. I ask for a *café au lait* and a *croissant* but am told I have to purchase the *croissant* next door at the *boulangerie*. I step outside again, pop into the *boulangerie*, but instead of a *croissant*, I am attracted by beautiful raisin rolls displayed in a tidy row and buy one of those instead.

Just as I cross back to my bar, I am thoroughly startled to hear my name loudly called: KEVIN! I turn but do not see who has yelled. I scan the street, then spot two figures draped from head to toe in heavy plastic ponchos crossing the small *place* between this street and the church. They wave to me, turn and come my way. As they draw closer, I make out the faces deep inside the hoods: Sietse and Evert! This is extraordinary: my return from the *boulangerie* and their departure from their refuge a minute or two either way and our paths would not have crossed! We shake hands and clap each other on the shoulders, and I invite them into my bar. They themselves are just now getting started on their day's walk so hesitate a moment, then realize that pilgrim friendship means they *have* to stay; they easily give in, step inside, shake the rain off their ponchos and place their orders for coffees. At our table, they tell me they spent the night here in Cluis. We all thought we would never see each other again, yet here we are! We decide to go on to Gargilesse together. How could we not?

Our coffees are consumed, our packs are reloaded onto our backs, and the three of us head into the inclement day warmed more by our surprising pilgrim reunion than by the coffee. As in days gone by, we trade positions: Sietse and Evert ahead, me behind. Evert ahead, Sietse and I tailing. All three of us side by side. Each of us on our own. The rain only stiffens; the pavement beneath us sloughs the rain to either shoulder in rolling sheets that just keep coming and coming. My boots hold out the worst of it for another hour or so, then the right gives up altogether, and the water rushes in, making a sloshing mush of my wool socks and microfiber liners. The left boot keeps up the good fight for another hour, but then also succumbs to the onslaught, joining its brother in surrender to the elements. Even with all this rain and boots full of it and my clothing soaked, I do not wish, even secretly, to quit now. My friends make me brave; they are the answer to my prayer. They restore my zeal for the Way.

We troop, finally, into Gargilesse, the long-awaited village along the Creuse River that marks the reunion of the northern and southern pilgrim routes from Vézelay. It is nestled among verdant hills dropping down into a deep river valley. Its houses are made of stone, smoke rising from some of the chimneys on this damp day. We hold up at the entrance to a restaurant-bar, Hôtel des Artistes, which also advertises rooms to let. Sietse and Evert want to stay here, but I have made a reservation already at another *chambre d'hôte* somewhere else in town. I inquire at the bar about my place and discover it is up a steep hill from here, perhaps a kilometer or so. Sietse and Evert are not inclined to follow me. I tell them that I do not want to stiff the host, so I should at least phone him to tell him I am not coming. I dig out my phone from Gregory's side-pocket and make the call. I explain our situation. The gentleman who answers wants us all to come; he has a room that can handle the three of us at a reasonable price, and he will drive down to pick us up. We decide to accept his offer and wait under a tree for his arrival.

A red Renault rolls down the hill and pulls up to us. A tall man gets out, shakes our hands, introduces himself as Francis, and asks where we are from. His own accent gives him away, and in just a moment or two, he and Sietse and Evert are jabbering in Dutch. We drive up the hill to a beautiful old house set among chestnut and oak trees: Le Haute Verger. We are welcomed inside and led up a tight staircase to a large room with two beds, a cheap fold-up bed set up at the foot of the other two. I ask if the radiator has heat, and our host tells us it is too early in the season to turn on the heat. The place is chilly and damp, and getting damper the longer we and our soaked clothing remain within. I pull off my boots and pour a soupy brown liquid out of each one into the sink. I ring out my socks, and the same brown liquid spills into the basin. We take turns in the shower; at least it has hot water, and this helps warm my bones. We are all thinking the same thing: we would have been much better off in the place down the hill. I have led them into this, and so I weakly apologize, but Sietse say it's no big deal. I find our Dutch host and ask about some place warm to dry our clothing and boots. He says we can use the furnace room in the basement. So there is heat? No, he answers, just the warmth of the hot water burner, but it should be enough to dry things out before morning. I do not like the sound of that "should".

I report the news to my companions, and we begin hauling our wet clothing, socks and boots to the basement furnace room and stringing them up on the household's laundry lines. The boots sit atop the boiler itself. It will be close whether this stuff will be ready to wear by 7:00 am tomorrow, but we have no alternative. Sietse announces that he wants to walk back into town to visit the plethora of art studios in the village as well as the church. The rain has stopped, so Evert and I join him, and together, we walk down the hill and into town; stopping in the studios, looking over the artwork mostly in unimpressed silence, as we mosey along. There are two other sites worth visiting in Gargilesse: the twelfth century Romanesque church and the home of the novelist, George Sand. Now George is not a man; as was the custom in the late nineteenth century, women writers took male pen names to better sell their works in highly sexist times. I do not know her writings, but we take a tour of her house, free to us as pilgrims. The house contains a wide-ranging collection of Sand bric-a-brac, interesting to browse through, but we are done with the whole place in about fifteen minutes.

Next stop: the local *église*. We climb up a steep street to the church entrance and make our way into one of the Chemin's more beautiful village churches. Of course, it is yet another Romanesque structure: the great columns, thick walls, fine sculptured cornices, and rounded everything, now so familiar and homey to me, but what is extraordinary about this particular church are the delicate frescoes in the lower level. Still close to Byzantine in style, they are rich in detail and theology: one wall features a sublime Christ Crucified, the ceiling of a crypt chapel is covered in biblical imagery with a central oval displaying the Risen Christ. I gaze and gawk and snap some pictures until I am scolded by another visitor who points to a small sign with a camera circled and crossed in thick red.

Sietse and Evert wander by, heads tilted back at the frescoes above us; they ask me for an explanation of what they are seeing, so I do my best to point out some of the significance of the imagery: the Crucified Christ on one side, the victim of human viciousness in all its awfulness, yet peaceful and forgiving of what has been done to him. The Risen Christ almost opposite, proclaiming the victory of the God of Love over death and all vileness, a tender victory shared with us. Flesh and blood, light and life, God not far off, not isolated in his heaven, but here walking with us, eating with us, dying with us, catching us when we die and lifting us up to himself, rising above death and beyond evil once and for all. I am moved in the telling, and it all makes great sense to me. I love this story both in word and icon. It is *his* story. It is *my* story. It is *our* story.

We all gaze some more, then quietly file up the ancient stone staircase and out into the open air still heavy with the damp of this most rainy of days. We wander back towards the main street of the village, find an open bar and share a round of beers, then mosey back to the restaurant where we first stopped earlier in the day and take a table for dinner. The bartender, as is now so common in these villages, is not French, but a Flemish Belgian, who with his wife has settled here, taken on this business and is making a go of it, though it cannot be easy. I ask him if he finds the locals warm and welcoming to newcomers such as himself. He responds that for the most part yes, but occasionally some prejudice is expressed in small ways. "The thing is, without people like us investing in these little villages, there'd be nothing here. This place had been closed up for a couple of years before we bought it and reopened it. Both they and we know that."

Steak and *frites* and more beer fill us; it is already 9:00 pm, almost bedtime. The three of us climb the kilometer of black pavement in the dark back to our place for the night, Evert leading the way, his small LED headlamp guiding us upward. I am chilled by the time we arrive at our room, as are the others. We take turns brushing our teeth, then with hardly a word, slip under our wool blankets and end another day, together again.

16

One Way to Spain

The new day begins at a casual pace. We stir at 7:30 am, slowly get our morning ablutions taken care of, then head down the old staircase to the basement to collect our possessions from their overnight dungeon. The clothing is mostly dry with the exception of my wool socks, which will have to hang off the back of Gregory with hopes of air-drying as I walk. The boots are damp, but serviceable. Gregory the Great is leaking water out of the foam pads that wrap themselves around my waist. They have acted like massive sponges and won't be dry anytime soon. Luckily, the bag itself is dry, so I haul the old pontiff and my clothing up to our room and begin packing anew for the day ahead.

Francis and his wife have set out an ample breakfast for us; he remains to chat while she disappears into the kitchen. He is an artist and many of the paintings and drawings decorating the house are from his hand. This village of artists seemed a fine place to retire, so they bought the house and the extensive land surrounding it some years ago, and it's been home ever since. Offering a few rooms for paying guests helps cover the bills.

By 9:30 am we are ready to go and make our farewells to Francis and cheerily head up his drive then down the steep kilometer to Gargilesse proper. The trees drip with dew. Fog is general over the land, making our voices echo as we talk. Water leaks from the foam of my belt, soaking the lower reaches of my Gore-Tex jacket. At least this morning it is not raining. We amble through the village, the smell of chimney smoke softening the feel of it, the mists diffusing the view of everything we see.

For the first time since Vézelay, there is only one pilgrim route south; those of us who split north or south in Vézelay are reunited from this village on. I would have expected a doubling of pilgrims along our route, but for the time being, it is just the three of us as we pass through country that is marked by oaky valleys with rushing streams veining through their hearts; the occasional village is laid out to follow rough terrain, and so everything is catawampus: streets and alleys, and *places* are never at right angles. This is a more feral France than I have seen previously.

We are also treated to a steady climb most of the day, for we are heading into the western flanks of France's Massif Central, a region of mountains and plateaus occupying a sizable portion of France's south-central interior. Well, it is a steady climb in the sense that generally we are going up, but that "going up" includes plenty of more particular "ups and downs;" in fact, some of these "ups and downs" are *very up* and *very down*. Sietse is having pains in his lower legs, which especially bother him when he is walking downhill, so he turns and walks backwards for relief. We chat face to face as he does so, his lanky body taking the reversal in stride; I give him occasional cautions if there is an obstacle ahead. Evert leads us, walking strong, even sometimes breaking into a youthful jog up a hill, not exactly a gazelle, but boundy enough. He no longer allows himself to get so far ahead that we are much beyond his sight; I guess it is his way of showing that he both leads us and cares about us. Even with his youthful energy in plentiful supply, he is showing signs of pilgrim fatigue; when we stop for a rest, he speaks more and more of his longing to return to life on his Dutch island.

We walk in comfortable silence for much of the morning. There is so much to hear, so much to listen to in this wild and woolly world through which we now amble. Creeks run fast with yesterday's rain, their tumbling song echoing in the canyons they themselves formed over unknown geological ages. Diminutive tweety-birds flit from limb to branch in the oak canopies above our heads. Breezes blow through those great trees and make them creak in low tones even as their rustled leaves whisper in a kind of harmony.

This morning's twenty quiet kilometers lead us to Crozant, a lovely village that rises above the Creuse River. A castle mostly in ruins dominates entry into the town. Sheep and goats graze on the hillsides, sometimes attended by a shepherd herding them one way or another. Near the castle stands a restaurant and hotel complex. I have made no reservations for the night so, after managing yesterday's choice rather badly, I gladly leave the task of choosing in the hands of Sietse and Evert. The restaurant is open for business, but the waitress tells us there are no rooms available for the night. She advises us that in the town center we will find a place that takes in pilgrims, the name of it having something to do with *soleil*, the sun, I explain to Evert. We have to climb a steep hill to arrive at the main body of Crozant; Evert and Sietse race each other to the top, while I take my time on the climb; I finally crest the hill and catch up to Evert and Sietse waiting for me seated comfortably on the steps of the village church. After I take a minute or two to catch my breath, we amble together through town looking for a hotel with "*soleil*" in its name. Artist studios abound as in Gargilesse, as do references to George Sand, and even more, to her friend, Claude Monet. He, too, spent time here, and it is easy to see why: the place is a visual delight on this September afternoon, an impressionist's paradise. I ask a passerby for directions to L' Hôtel Soleil. She smiles, since I don't have the name quite right and corrects me, "L' Éclat de Soleil. Just turn the corner and walk half a block, and you will find it on the right." Sure enough: we turn the corner and walk just a few paces, and there it is. Tables with plastic red chairs are set up outside, most filled with tourists quaffing beers and nibbling on *quiches* or *croques*. A blue plaque with the yellow pilgrim *coquille* is posted near the door. We enter the bar, ask for rooms, and are cheerily offered the "pilgrim rate" by the lady tending bar.

Up a narrow staircase we climb, our packs still on our backs, and into two bright rooms we are shown. I get a room to myself, while Evert and Sietse share. We drop our loads, then while Sietse begins unpacking, Evert and I decide to go back downstairs for a beer and lunch. We find a free table and put in our orders, refreshing ourselves under the boughs of a leafy plane tree. Sietse eventually joins us, and it becomes clear some important decisions are being discussed between the two of them. Evert is tired of the pilgrimage and is more anxious than I was aware to get back to Texel. He wants to make tomorrow his final day on the road. From La Souterenne, the next town with public transportation, he will catch the bus that will begin his journey home. Sietse would rather he continue on, but Evert can make his own decisions. The question for Sietse is whether to return with Evert or continue walking for another week or so. They discuss their options for a bit, then move on to other conversation, leaving the issue unresolved for the moment. Before breaking up, we decide that since this will almost certainly be Evert's last night on the road, we will splurge for a last supper together in one of the local restaurants.

After lunch, I clear off the small table in my room and set up my simple wares for saying Mass: bread, wine, scriptures. This Sunday, the scriptures are all about slavery and particularly slavery to money: it is either God or money that we honor but can't be both. Greed kills us individually and threatens the future of our race. God is the exact opposite of greed. God's way of love, the self-sacrificing type manifested in the death of Jesus, is *my* only hope and *our* only hope. As I sit here at this small table, wine and bread at hand, that hope is made substantial in this bread and wine, which I take in hand and pray: *Blessed are you, Lord God of all Creation. Through your goodness we have this bread to offer, fruit of the earth and work of human hands. Let it become for us . . .*

After my little liturgy, I pick up my journal and pen, and head back into town in search of a place to write up the previous two days of events and thoughts along the way. Yesterday, in Gargilesse, I missed writing in the journal, something rare for me, so have now to catch up before I forget the details. I sit on the church steps for a while, but they are hard and cold, so I move towards the hill that I earlier climbed. I find a park dotted with benches. I take up an empty one and look out over a splendid view of the castle across the valley and deep below, the rushing rivers that meet here. This fluvial junction was strategically and commercially important in medieval times, hence the sturdy castle to protect it. The low afternoon sun is sinking but still high enough to illuminate with its golden light the green hills now flecked with the yellow and red of early autumn, the flowing water below, and the creamy stone of the castle beyond. Goats roam the castle walls and below along the hills. They also wander into my little park, one coming to me, perhaps looking for a treat of some kind, and sniffs at me. I sniff back but do not like the woolly and wild smell of the animal. It defecates near my foot then moves on.

I behold, write some, behold more. It is perfect. I find Evert hovering near me. I invite him to sit down on the bench; not wanting to interrupt me, he hesitates, but when assured he is no interruption, he joins me, and the two of us talk. He tells me he has really liked being with me and getting to know me. I do not seem like an old man, he tells me. I thank him for the compliment and then tell him I think he, too, is a fine young fellow. *You are smart and kind and you care about your father a lot. That is so good. I will miss you after tomorrow.* I hope this time on the pilgrim road with his dad will become a watershed moment in his life, something that he will later recognize has changed him forever. He asks for my email address, and so I write it down on a corner of the back page of my journal, tear it off, and hand it to him. *I hope you'll write.* "I will," he assures me.

Now it is cold enough to make me shiver, so together, Evert and I walk back to the hotel, where we meet Sietse and the three of us go in search of our Last Supper.

We make our way to a very nice hotel down the street that is reputed to have the best restaurant in town. We are conspicuously not dressed like the other guests with their ties and pearls. The tables are covered in cloth, and the napkins are linen. I feel a bit out of place, but none of the other guests seem bothered by our pilgrim vesture. We order the set meal: three fine courses with wine. Our conversation turns almost immediately to the question left hanging since lunch; Sietse reports that he has spoken by phone with his wife about whether he should return to Texel with Evert or not. She has not been a great fan of this adventure, it seems, but she is open to Sietse being gone even longer. His younger son, however, is really missing his dad and desperately wants him to come home as soon as possible. After reporting this, Sietse then turns to me and asks: "What is the pilgrim spirit, Kevin? Do I have it? My wife asked me why I wanted to keep walking, and I had no answer for her." I hesitate to respond, gathering my thoughts for a few moments as we all pick at our dinners. *To feel the pull, the draw, the interior attraction, and to want to follow it, even if it has no name still, that is the "pilgrim spirit". The "why" only becomes clear as time passes, only long after the walking is over. If your family is okay with you following that pull a while longer, I think you should follow it.*

He says that if he continues beyond La Souterraine tomorrow, he wants to walk alone, no offense to me, he just wants to walk alone. I tell him I think that is a very good sign that he really is a pilgrim, and I certainly take no offense; walking alone is an important experience. The solitude of the pilgrim road is where I do my best thinking, my best praying, where I am most a pilgrim. Evert expresses frustration with all this "pilgrim talk"; he just wants to go home. Sietse tells me how much he appreciates my advice and my friendship. "I feel like we got to know the real Kevin, not just the 'priest,' though maybe for you the two are the same."

The new day brings new troubles. Evert is sick. As we awake and set about our morning tasks, Sietse tells me that Evert has had an upset stomach through the night, did not sleep well, and is feeling very weak this morning. We meet downstairs in the restaurant for breakfast. Evert barely eats. I suggest that it may not be the best idea for him to attempt walking the twenty-five kilometers to La Souterraine after all. Perhaps there is a bus from here to there that he can catch. Evert says an emphatic "yes" to the suggestion. Sietse checks with the lady in charge of the restaurant this morning and is told there is no bus service between Crozant and La Souterraine; the only option is taxi service. They ask the lady to call the local taxi driver, and the deal is done. I will be on my own again today while Sietse and Evert wrap up their pilgrimage together. It is still an open question whether Sietse will accompany Evert back to the Netherlands or not; I suppose it will depend on how the young man is feeling at day's end.

I retrieve Gregory and what is left of Click and all of Clack, and return downstairs to say goodbye for the second time to these two great friends and thereafter, to begin my own day's walk. We snap a picture of ourselves in front of *L' Éclat de Soleil*, shake hands, embrace one another, say thanks for everything, then I pull Gregory up to my back, take poor Click and Clack in hand, and poke and clack my way down the street, out of town, then following a dirt road, descend into a deep valley, heavy with damp, a canopy of green leaf obscuring most of the grey sky above, a roaring river churning through its depths. I can smell the dirt and wet of the earth. Even as I miss the company of Sietse and Evert, I also love the solitude of the moment. I am alone again. There is a lusciousness about having no one but myself, my pack and poles, my silent God, near. A dam stretches across the river, but the water flows over it with abandon; a fine old stone house across the river is beautifully framed by tree branches, so I stop to take a picture or two.

I rise slowly out of the deep valley, but once back on pavement, the climb upward continues relentlessly; I continue walking the shoulder of the paved highway that will lead eventually to La Souterraine. From behind me, a taxi roars past honking its horn, Evert and Sietse are in the backseat, waving wildly. I wave back with Click and Clack and am quite sure this is really the last I will ever see of these pilgrim pals. *Au revoir! Tot ziens!* Good-bye, father and son!

The kilometers into La Souterraine pass slowly. I have made no advance reservations for a bed tonight, but La Souterraine should be a big enough town that finding a place will not be so very difficult. As I enter the town, perhaps big enough to qualify as a city, I keep my eye open for a *chambre d'hôte,* hotel, or if really lucky, even a pilgrim refuge. The streets wind and curve as they lead me to the center and the church, which I find closed for major repairs. A signboard near the church indicates that there is a tourist information office in the Place du Gare. I size up the streets as displayed in the map and head then towards what I presume is the train station. I find neither train station nor information office. I feel almost dizzy with small streets going every which way, no right angle or straight line to be found among them. The street I have chosen closes in on me, becoming so short on breadth that a car would have to pass through it with the utmost caution. I am lost. I pass by a small house with an open window; an old lady leans against the sill taking in whatever action might be poised to occur on her street. We greet each other. She asks if I am a pilgrim. I say yes, I am, but I am not finding the Place du Gare. She laughs and says I am going completely in the wrong direction. I ask if there is a hotel nearby. "No," she tells me, "but just up the street and around the corner, on the Rue Serpente there is a big house that will take you in; the very nice English-speaking couple who live there take in pilgrims." I cannot believe my good fortune, so thank the old lady as profusely as I am able in French, then trod up the street and around the corner.

The house is there, indeed; a grand affair with a simple sign hanging in the window, in English and French, advertising itself as Maison Numéro Neuf and indicating that pilgrims are welcome for a cheap fifteen euros. I ring the bell once, wait, no answer, ring a second time, wait, then, just as I

am about to impatiently ring a third time, the door opens, and an Englishman welcomes me in. Duncan introduces himself to me with a grand smile.
He and his wife can put me up for the night, no problem at all.

The place is actually a full-scale *chambre d'hôte*, but they have room
enough for pilgrims, too, who get the "low-rent district" up on the third floor,
still only minimally restored. Duncan introduces me to his wife, Lisa, who
has just come downstairs with mop and bucket in hand. Duncan lifts Gregory
from the foyer floor, though I protest that I have carried him across half of
Belgium and even more of France and that I can manage him a few more
flights of stairs, but Duncan dismisses my words and serves me as if I were a
prime minister and he a butler. Up to the third floor we go, and I am shown
the available rooms. I pick the one with a single bed, overlooking the *Rue
Serpente*. After cleaning up and doing my laundry, I return to the streets of La
Souterraine wanting to pay my usual visit to the church, buy a new notebook
to serve as the third volume of my journal, number two being now almost full,
and check out the medieval city gate dedicated to Saint John.

Metal scaffolding, all tubes and knobby knuckles, angularly wraps itself around the church's twelfth century stonework. I try the various doors
of the church but am left to admire its heavy rectangular steeple and round
roman portals strictly from without. This church has been a pilgrim stop for
some eight centuries, and I am sad that I cannot also pass through its ancient
stone portal. I walk on to the Port-Saint-Jean, a rectangular city gate from the
thirteenth century. It is a massive piece of work and would intimidate even
the most fierce of brigands. From the top of a defensive gate like this one, it
is easy to imagine the citizens of La Souterraine pouring boiling oil over the
heads of their attacking neighbors. Defense: the handmaid of greed, that is
the name of the game in this world and ever so has it been. Walls and gates
and fortifications are what we are best at building as human beings. The club
of Cain migrates inevitably to the Big Boy bomb of Truman. How did we get
this way? It is so strange that the way of fear is the course we chose somewhere
way back in time, and all these millennia later, here we are, shaky and angry
atop fear's grand battlement. This wall built on fear of others is precisely what
Christians have called "original sin" for the last twenty centuries or so. Alas,
we have failed miserably to overcome its attractions. Perhaps that is the point:
our better selves just can't free us from our lesser selves. We Christians and the
rest of our human race continue to pour boiling oil on the other to protect our
stuff from them. The pilgrim's view of the world and his neighbors from the
low and slow perspective of the Way gets us closer to another way. Out here
we mostly walk along our way without defense, without greed, without anyone to fear. We have so little, that losing any of it doesn't really matter much.
Perhaps, this is why Jesus spent so much of his adult life walking back and

forth between Galilee and Jerusalem; this was where he honed his freedom from fear and his liberty from greed.

At dinner, Duncan says that tomorrow will be a good day for walking, but the rains will return on Wednesday and Thursday, just as I climb to the highest point of the French Chemin, Monts d' Ambazac, and back down again. I am feeling generally quite fatigued this evening, my legs are antsy, and the soles of my feet hurt. I can feel the need for a day-off growing. For now, sleep must do as my medicine. Tomorrow I will walk with the sun. After that, we shall see, especially if the weather turns grim again.

I awake early, well before my plastic watch begins its incessant chirping, rest in bed a while, then get up and begin pulling my things together. I had good dreams last night, though I cannot remember much except a feeling of residual well-being. My legs and feet are fine this morning, and last night's weariness has passed. There is no rush today, because I have to wait until 9:30 am for the nearby sporting goods store to open, so I can buy new trekking poles. I dawdle in my room until 9:30 then walk down to the sporting goods store to search for the new Click and Clack.

I enter, look about, but do not spot what I am looking for. I ask for help from the single attendant who is inexplicably grumpy; he simply points in the general direction of a far wall, so I wander over and find just one set of walking poles. They have no spring-loaded shock absorbers in the handles like Click and Clack; shiny black plastic replaces the comfortable cork of the originals, and worst of all, they are red and not metallic blue like my old friends, Click and Clack. *These will never do.* But Click is seriously wounded and cannot continue. I have little choice. I take the impostors to the cashier and plop down my euros, which the grump takes without a word, handing me back my change. As I turn towards the glass doors, I realize that, contrary to Duncan's assurances, it is now pouring outside. Braving the rain, I walk back to the Maison Numéro Neuf, my new poles in hand, to pick up Gregory, thank Duncan and Lisa, and get this day started.

Duncan tells me that though there is a municipal refuge in Bénévent-l'Abbaye, he has heard it is pretty grimy; he gives me the business card of a *chambre d'hôte* that also caters to pilgrims there. I get my phone, call to make a reservation, and am told that there is room for me tonight, and if I would I like dinner, that will be available as well. I wish Duncan and Lisa well with their business and thank them for their kindness to pilgrims like me. I hand the original Click and Clack to Duncan, who accepts them with the promise to give them to whatever pilgrim might come along in need of one good and one not-so-good hiking pole. *Adieu, mes amis.* It is time to walk. *Good-bye, Duncan and Lisa. Thanks so much. You are good people. I will remember you.* And I am out the door.

17

Holding Up the Church

I walk through the winding streets of La Souterenne to the town center, find the post office, and mail my old journal back to Belgium. I am soon out of town and once again among green fields. The rain has stopped, and the sun is shining through clouds that are breaking up quickly. I am feeling good. I am alone again in the quiet of the Limousin countryside, and this quiet envelopes me in its peace.

I am now clearly making my way up the northwest corner of France's Massif Central, one of the most rigorous climbs of the whole Chemin. I have been worrying a bit about what is ahead, but all I can to do is take it one step at a time. For now, the route rises generally and consistently but is not overly difficult. My new sticks are working well enough, though I do not like the feel of the plastic handles, which makes my palms feel sticky. Do I dare dub them Click and Clack, like their forbearers? Why not? I raise them up into the air, holding them high. *I hereby dub ye: le nouveau Click et Clack; may we pilgrim well together . . . all the way to Compostela! Amen.* I then drop them so they land on my shoulders, royal-style, first Click, then Clack. Dubbing done; now back to work.

I watch grand cumulus clouds sail slowly across the sky; their dark underbellies threatening more rain, but their sheer size combined with their ability to glide so effortlessly from one horizon to the other gives them a magical aspect. It is as if five or ten of Michelangelo's domes have been set free of their earthly riggings and allowed to rise into the sky, and there catch a breeze, making of them a flotilla of cupolas gliding away towards some other world. I continue down the road, sun warming me for a few minutes, then the shade of a cumulus cupola cooling me, then sun again. There are occasional gusts of cold-edged wind buffeting me, too, reminding me that I am now well into autumn.

I grow hungry and look forward to stopping in the village of Chambo-rand for whatever the local restaurant might have on offer as its *plat du jour*. I enter the village but find no restaurant; I drop Gregory and pull out of his top pocket a can of tuna kept in emergency reserve, a small sandwich bag of almonds, and a puny French granola bar. This is no *plat du jour*, for sure, but it will be enough to keep me going to Bénévent-l'Abbaye. Having finished my tuna and almonds, I lay down in the grass and watch more clouds roll by; they no longer resemble the elegant stone birettas of Roman basilicas, but have wisped out into the feathery wings of angels. A high-flying pas-senger jet crosses the sky, scratching the heaven's blue skin, leaving behind a thin white contrail as evidence of its passing. I close my eyes and through my lids can see sunlight passing red and warm.

Once the energy of the tuna has kicked in, I head down the road with new bounce in my step, Click and Clack II keeping time, Gregory riding high. It rained here earlier, so the pavement is still shiny black under the midday sun, and the fields to left and right positively gleam. The green of these fields is not just one green, but many, variegated, multi-hued, and so multiply textured that I would like to extend my hand out and run my palm across it all, feeling the particular character of each distinct field, petting the purring earth in response to its kindness to me this day.

I climb the rest of the afternoon. In particular, the last kilometers into Bénévent-l'Abbaye are a real pull. As I enter the town, I begin my search for the *chambre d'hôte* where I have my reservation. This is not a big town, but the streets go every which way. I look in vain for the address given to me, then call my hosts again. I describe my position on the town's main street, and the lady on the other end of the line tells me to just turn this way, then that, and I will be there. I try following the directions but end up back on the main street so call again. The second time around I pay better attention and indeed, within just a block or two, I find the front door of the place, just as a raindrop lands on the end of my nose, the first of the day. It is followed by several more, and then more still, but I am saved from the imminent downpour when the door opens to my knock, and Clare invites me indoors with a wide smile and a warm British-accented "Welcome!"

Clare tells me that she had planned to put me up in their *gite* a few blocks away, but since the rooms of their *chambre d'hôte* are unreserved for the night, it will be easier for me and for them to just have me remain here, in one of their nicer rooms, but still at the pilgrim price already agreed upon. I am shown to my room, a comfy place painted in light pumpkin with a large window opening to the street below. Clare knocks and asks if I would like to have her do a load of laundry for me. I enthusiastically respond that I would love to throw everything into her big machine; what a luxury: to have every piece of clothing I own be clean at the same time, a fresh start! I pull everything from Gregory's core, keeping aside just enough to remain reasonably modest over the next hour or two, and stuff the mass of micro-fiber everything into a plastic shopping bag to hand back to Clare.

After showering, I discover my first blister of the entire pilgrimage at the end of my second toe. Strangely, I did not feel it during the day's walk, and it does not seem serious in any way. For the first time since leaving Leuven, I take out my needle and thread, open a small bottle of Betadine antiseptic, and treat the blister in the way I learned from fellow pilgrims in Spain four years ago: I pierce the head of the blister with the sewing needle and run the thread through, leaving enough thread hanging loose on either side to tie the ends together, forming a fine little wick that will drain the fluid within without much risk of infection. The red Betadine fluid is sloppy to use and easily stains anything it might touch, so I carefully undertake this minor surgery away from my host's bedding and carpeting. My fingertips finish the job rusty red with the sticky stuff, but I am happy to have the blister on its road to healing.

The man of the house, Chris, returns from work, and we are introduced to one another by Clare. They invite me to join them at the kitchen table for a cup of tea. They want to know the usual details of my pilgrimage: Where did I begin? How long have I been on the road? How is it that an American is doing such a pilgrimage? I respond to each of their questions, and with the last, tell them that I am a Catholic priest, having just finished eight years of service at our American seminary in Belgium. Chris responds: "A priest? But you are so normal!" *I hope so,* I answer a bit taken aback. It is a strange expectation to me: that priests should be abnormal. Why is it that normalcy is presumed to be exceptional in our case? I suppose it is our own fault: we set up these expectations ourselves through a long history of pomposity, stuffiness, putting on airs of superiority when dealing with others. It is a defensive wall little different in purpose than the Port-de-Saint-Jean and its battlements. That miserable original sin again at work! The model of Jesus and the Twelve as they wandered from village to village in Galilee and Judea provides a counter-model for us clergy. The story of Jesus allows us to see that he and his companions were low-to-the-ground walkers, pilgrims re-ally, and yes, really quite normal. That normality set him apart from the Jerusalem bigwigs. So if on the road and in my life I am normal like Jesus, I am pleased. May I "walk even as he walked,"[1] to quote a favorite line from the later Christian scriptures.

1. 1 John 2:6

For their part, Chris and Clare see the care of pilgrims as an unexpected blessing, a sort of spiritual spin-off of opening a bed and breakfast in France. It was only after they settled in Bénévent-l'Abbaye and began renovating this house as both their new home and a business, that they realized they were right smack dab on the major pilgrim route across France to Compostela. They are committed Protestant Christians, and the care of pilgrims fits well with their faith. It has given them a way to minister out of their faith right from their own home. And so here they are, sitting at their very own table with a weary Catholic priest as their pilgrim guest. Clare tells me, "We always hoped someday we'd have a Catholic priest come by, and now here you are!" I am honored.

Their teenage son, William, comes home from school, drops his small backpack in the kitchen, politely shakes my hand, says hello, and sets about completing his homework.

Before supper, I take a walk through the streets of Bénévent-l'Abbaye and wend my way over to the great church at the far end of town, once the chapel of an eleventh century abbey, most of which is now lost. I enter through the massive portal, an even more massive tower rising above it. I sit for a while in a wooden pew, thank God for the day's safe travels and Chris and Clare's hospitality, then get up and wander about. The capitals atop all the columns are highly decorative: intricately carved images of griffins and monsters, even palm trees adorn some of them. One figure captures my attention: it is of a small man with hands upraised, seemingly supporting the very roof of the church from his perch high above me. I admire his age-old resilience, his never-failing strength, and most of all his fidelity to this odd vocation: what a job to have and to do it for so many centuries! What if he took even one break? Would the whole church come tumbling down? *Ha! Stay right where you are, little man . . . at least until I am out the door!* Later, I find a small printed guide to all the images in the church and read of my man up there; in fact, he is not holding up the church as I had imagined, he is praying with his hands held up and open in the ancient *orans* position. He must be a priest, then. He is I. Or better, he is what I *should* be: holding up the church in steady prayer. Would that it were so; out here on this road, day after day, I do pray, but much of the time my mind is just on idle, taking in this, taking in that, not really thinking much at all. Certainly not praying, at least in an explicit way. Though, in a less explicit way, I also know that my idle mind is not necessarily the devil's workshop; God works there, too, and hopefully, even more so. The fact is that sometimes those rambling non-thoughts lead into something deep and consoling. I think my idle pilgrim mind is God's workshop; it is where prayer gestates. And the walking, just the walking, in and of itself, by itself, is plenty holy. No thought required.

Such is the pilgrim prayer. If the walking itself is not prayer, then this is a massive waste of time. But it is not a waste of time, big or little; I know that this is an adventure of spirit and heart, a blessing, a way to a simpler, more gracious, holier life, and that means it *is* prayer, whether or not gold-edged books are opened, hymns sung, lips wagged, profound thoughts thunk. So, like the little stone-carved man above me, I lift up my hands in my own pilgrim way, and maybe in some small manner, this walking is holding up the church roof too. Is it too grand or too presumptuous the occasional thought I have enjoyed that we pilgrims, girding the world with our ambling, are actually keeping the whole fractured thing from fragmenting into a thousand agony-ridden pieces?

Clare has prepared a fine French-style meal, and the accompanying wine warms me and makes me chat on about the little stone man I met in the old church today. Chris tells me that the weather report for tomorrow is all rain, but the next day, Thursday, should be fine. As evening draws on, I feel the weight of the day's fairly relentless climb so ask if they would mind if I stay an extra night, depending on how I feel in the morning. I explain that my body may be telling me it is time for a day-off. There are no other reservations for the next few days, so the room is mine if I want it, they assure me. I am about three days out from Limoges, the next big city on the route. With a day-off now, I would land there on Saturday, perfect for finding a church with a Mass on Saturday night or Sunday morning. I am missing the Eucharist and feel hunger for it, not the Eucharist itself, but the Eucharist celebrated with a wide and vast congregation, singing and kneeling and processing and its many voices praying in one voice: *Notre Pére . . .*

I awake at about 4:00 am feeling sheer tiredness in my legs and soreness even in my feet. My body is crying out for a break, and the morning's weather confirms my inclination to just stay put today. Recovery is the name of today's game. My mind needs rest too; it is full to the brim of pavement stretching ahead and upward, squiggly lines on maps, kilometer calculations, and small yellow arrows tacked to posts directing me this way or that. It is such a condensed world that fills my brain right now; the more I walk without a break, the smaller the world inside my head becomes until I can hardly think anymore. I fall back asleep but wake up to a new day burdened by heavy clouds and a sharp edge of coldness that makes me shiver as I pull back my blankets and put my bare feet on the floor. Before I even arrive at Clare and Chris's breakfast table, I have chosen to stay home for the day.

So today I am to rest, renew, take stock. This is my self-given challenge. After breakfast, Chris sets me up at a computer in a small office off the main hallway, and I spend more than an hour answering e-mails from friends and strangers who are following my daily blog entries as I walk.

Their messages are filled with encouragement and let me know that I am not alone in this pilgrim Way. Many say they feel like they are walking along with me through the text-messaged words I send back to Gene and Caroline in Leuven every afternoon, and which they then post to my blog. This is a ministry; my occasional doubts about whether this pilgrimage is worth all the sweat are answered by their supportive and loving emails to me. I respond to each one and thank them for their kindness in accompanying me along the way. Sitting at this computer for this hour or more is an exercise of the heart. It reconnects me to the communion of saints, this living cloud of witnesses that is holding my roof up, cheering me on, and carrying me forward along this old and holy Chemin. I could not keep going without them, this I remember today, and it strengthens me to know I am not alone and have never been alone.

I return to my room, pull my fleece from out of Gregory's wide-open gob, and go out to the street. I continue on to the church and enter again through its open doors. At first, I just sit myself down in one of its wooden pews and rest here, idle within God's workshop. I ponder little, consider almost nothing, let my mind wander as it may, gaze for a while, close my eyes for a while too, breathe. I can feel my heart here. Life! Life, in all its subtlety and beauty and mystery, is such a surprise. One moment there is no me, then in a split-second my Pa's wiggly little spermatozoon breaks through the outer lining of my Ma's somewhat bigger ovum and bang, next thing you know, *I am*. I did nothing to deserve this; how could I, since I did not exist prior to that little bang not so different in its metaphysics from the Big Bang that got the universe off to such a blazing beginning.

I am. This astounds me and has always astounded me whenever I have stopped long enough to let its reality overtake me. I remember walking home from St. Charles elementary school, maybe about fourth grade or perhaps fifth, on an autumn day, by myself, dawdling as I went, for I was a great dawdler when walking home from school, and taking the left hand turn onto Cora Street, lined for two blocks with maple trees, beautiful in the summer when the arms of those trees reached across the street itself to hold leafy green hands, forming an emerald tunnel above Cora; but in the autumn, the trees were just as beautiful in their arthritic barrenness. And below, at my feet, mounds of brown and golden leaves just waiting to be kicked up by my dawdling feet. The musty smell of those leaves as they slow-tracked themselves to dust-hood was wonderful, and the sun was shining, though it was cold enough to wear a jacket over my white shirt and blue uniform sweater, and as I kicked at those leaves making them fly, it hit me: *I am. I am real and I am here and I am aware of myself and I am alive. Kevin. Ambrose. Codd: I am!* Surprised by me, that is what it was, and pretty much ever since then I have loved being, just being. Moment following moment, adventure upon adventure, leaf landing atop leaf: life! It is all gift. It is all just one great grand gift. *Grâce!*

I feel a shiver come over me sitting so still here in this dark and cold church, so I rise, wander over to an information table and pick up a large tablet that explains each of the church's stone capitals one by one. I follow the guide, and looking back and forth between the tablet's description and the designated capital, work my way from column to column, and eventually back to my lifting and praying little man that so took me yesterday. We greet one another again as old friends do. All in all, I am simply amazed at how the medieval mind that built this church was so extraordinarily symbolic. Signs and numbers and tales of wonders communicated truth much more than hard, cold facts. That mind was at home with mysteries and multiple meanings and a web of relationships that went far beyond the physical. I like that mind and know that this pilgrimage has made my own more like it. I am pleased about that. Those medievals were not so dumb as we moderns sometimes so haughtily presume. Their way in the world may well have been substantially healthier than ours; they had more room for dreams, more respect for the power of symbols and rituals, more trust in God's hold on their lives.

I remember something from yesterday's walk that I had almost forgotten: a rainbow in an almost completely cloudless sky. I was walking along a small rural road, farms and fields all about me, when I spotted in the far distance to my right a heavy cloud with the bottom falling out in vague diagonal sheets, rain for sure, slowly moving my direction, but above me and to my right and mostly to my left, blue sky dominated. The combination of sunlight and rain over that western horizon produced a full rainbow, rich in color and perfect in its round arch, its two extremities disappearing into the green earth below. I remember wondering if rounded bows such as this might not have been the inspiration for Romanesque architects of centuries past? Did they pose themselves the challenge of creating rainbows out of stone? If so, what a grand challenge to take on in the brief span of a human life!

I return home to join Chris, Clare, and William in the living room where a robust fire has been built in the hearth. While William reads, tucked into the folds of an overstuffed chair, we adults chat about the life of a pilgrim, which is so attractive to them. They are happy to be able to share in this mission of prayer and ancient service to humanity by at least welcoming us into their home. I tell them, that without hosts like themselves, we pilgrims would have a much harder time of it, if we could do it at all. People like Clare and Chris and William belong to the family of little men and women holding us up as we go. We retreat to the kitchen where dinner is served, then after warm good-evenings, I retire to my room. Tomorrow will be a long day of trekking, but this day free of walking has done, I already know, all I needed it to do. I am free now to continue up and over the Massif Central. As I drift into sleep, rain falls outside, its soft patter on roof and gutter softening the way into this night's dreams, whatever they may be.

Clare has breakfast waiting for me while Chris moves about getting ready for a day of work, and young William gathers school things into a small backpack for his own day's work. Even a cursory peek out the windows of the house reveals a dark morning. Fog lays heavy over everything beyond the panes of glass. I just do not want to leave the warm nest they have provided for me the last day and a half, but I do what I must do and get up, gather up my belongings, re-stuff Gregory, and haul my load awkwardly downstairs to the street level *foyer* where my great Meindle boots await me. I lace them up, shake Chris's hand, give Clare a little embrace, take Click and Clack in hand, and as they wave to me, I set off.

It is cold, really cold, for the first time this year. An edgy wind is blowing up the street straight into my face. Micro-droplets of mist cut into my face and hands. Clouds hang so low that they envelope me and the buildings to my right and left in their gauzy folds. The scene is from a Dickens's novel, for heaven's sake. Bleak. I hesitate, look back, wave a final farewell to Chris and Clare with Clack, then face directly into the wind and mist and fog, and start walking.

I am out of Bénévent in no time and follow the left-hand verge of a small highway, shiny black with the night's rains. A pick-up passes, honks at me, then pulls over to the right. I catch up to it to see if there is a problem. It is Chris in the cab. He is on his way to work but is just checking to see how I'm doing. I tell him I am fine, and he again wishes me well, then engages his transmission and trucks off down the highway, disappearing into the haze in short order.

Surprisingly, even with the inclement weather, I am doing more than fine this morning; my legs have lost the heaviness of the previous days, my back is straight again, I've got rhythm as I bounce down this highway in time with Click and Clack's regular taps atop the black macadam. I avoid as much as I am able the dirt tracks that are recommended to me by my guide, because I know that after last night's rainfall, they will be more mud than road. I climb steadily. Field and forest pass. I am conquering these hills with gusto. The road twists and turns. Fog softens the edges and lines of posts and wire making one field blend into the other. I climb steadily. My energy is just great. I haven't walked this fast and this steadily for a very long time. I time myself: six kilometers an hour! I am fast approaching the high point along the Limousin's segment of the Chemin, almost seven hundred meters above sea level, according to my map. The misty countryside tells the same tale: substantial fir trees on either side of the road now tower over me, their crowns disappearing into the day's fog. It is also plenty cold; my internal furnace, stoked by my walking, keeps my core warm beneath my fleece and Gore-Tex, but my unprotected hands and fingers grow frigid. I don't mind the chilled digits and nose: I am about to conquer the mighty Massif Central!

As I draw into Saint-Goussaud, I am wrapped in more than just fog; this is a major cloud that I have ascended into. The town itself is altogether still, and no one but me stirs through its midday streets. I hear nothing. Not even the cocks crow. I have just summited one of the *monts* of the Monts d'Ambazac and should be able to see forever, but the weather has played a great trick on me: with this fog I can hardly see my hand!

I turn a corner and to the left, on the road leading out of the village, is a restaurant, the windows well illuminated from within. I amble up to the front door and find it unlocked. There is a small bar to the right with a young man pouring a golden beer for a couple of local boys dressed in plaid wool shirts and baseball caps. Except for the French that lilts from their lips, they could be loggers from North Idaho. I drop Gregory and set my poles alongside him, and ask about lunch. I am told I will have to wait fifteen minutes while the cook makes his final preparations for the meal. I am invited to order a drink, so I ask for a *café au lait* but get an *espresso* instead. I accept it gratefully, then take a seat at a small table near Gregory. I sip my coffee slowly, wanting to make it last until my lunch is ready. It warms me for the most part, but my fingers remain stiff and bone cold. I stretch and wiggle them to get them back to normal, then wrap them around the warm porcelain coffee cup. Finally, the cook behind the bartender gives a high sign, and I am told I may now move into the dining room. I begin to collect my things, but am advised they will be just fine where they are. I smile and thank the young barkeep for his kindness and then pick a table in the spacious dining room with a view outside towards the ghostly shapes of trees beyond the plate-glass window. I order the *plat du jour*, a ten-euro offering: a chunk of grilled beefsteak accompanied by *pommes frites*. Perfect for a day like today. I eat it too quickly, and I have finished before I have had time to appreciate it. I order dessert to extend my stay at the table: cream-filled *profiteroles*, which I savor slowly so as to delay my return to the outdoors. I have knocked off an hour of my day in this place now, and with all this inactivity, my damp clothes have become clammy, and my body gives up resisting; there's just not enough fire in my furnace to ward off the shivers. I pay my bill, collect Gregory and Click and Clack, and walk back into the

noiseless cloud that envelopes Saint-Goussaud. Before setting off, I take one
more look at all that presently envelopes me. From up here, I could hold up
the roof of the world, I am sure.

Just as I spent the morning climbing, as soon as I leave Saint-Goussaud, the descent commences. My route takes me off the paved road and
onto muddy goat-trails that wind through woods of fir, then of chestnut
and other leafy trees and bushes. I pick my way along, avoiding gnarly roots
and slick stones, everything but me covered in fuzzy green moss. The hiking
warms me up again, and I am happy as I move on towards Châtelus-le-
Marcheix, my goal for the day. I seem to have made peace with the damp
that has so otherwise plagued me during this summer of rain. I am enjoying
this day's walk as I have enjoyed few others. I have been strong all day and
made great time, and the woods through which I pass are as peaceful as
woods can be. No big bad wolves to be wary of here.

I roll into Châtelus, which, my guide assures, has a municipal refuge
waiting for me. I find the post office, but no church. I keep an eye open
for the refuge, but find nothing. A small shiver of despair and fear runs
up my back. I see a lady leave the post office so I call to her from my side
of the street asking about the purported refuge. "*Pas de problem!*" she assures me. She crosses the street and shows me to the door of a small apartment building, the street level unit being reserved for pilgrims. The door
is unlocked, and she shows me in, only to be confronted by a more elderly
woman already within, stuffing great wads of crumpled newspaper into her
hiking boots. *Bonjours* are cheerily exchanged, and the perky and petite
boot-stuffer introduces herself to me as Jacqueline. Her own backpack and
walking sticks have found a place on the floor of the apartment's kitchen;
she is still dressed in her pilgrim duds and is as damp as I, so she must have
arrived just moments before me; strange we didn't meet along the way.

After we shake hands, and I have introduced myself with the usual
pilgrim facts of my life, she begins to cheerily explain to me the importance
of crumpled newspaper in the care and feeding of wet boots. This is nothing new to me, and I've utilized the practice myself on numerous occasions
during my pilgrimage, but Jacqueline adds a new wrinkle: once used thusly,
these sheets of newsprint remain valuable resources for the careful pilgrim,
for even after usage, they can be uncrumpled, dried and carried in one's
pack for the next day's use as well. Now this seems really rather ridiculous
to me for what is the point of carrying the weight of all this paper if one
can easily find more paper at almost every stop along the way, for if there is
one thing France has no obvious shortage of it is newspapers. Jacqueline's
enthusiasm for making the most out of her newsprint is so infectious that

I cheerily feign full acceptance of the practice for myself, though it is one I will not make use of tomorrow morning.

This is what I learn of Jacqueline's story: This short and compact lady, somewhere in her sixties, is no slouch when it comes to walking. She spends a fair amount of her present life trekking about Europe. She is an experienced pilgrim, having previously walked from La Puy, another great French jump-off point to Compostela, to Santiago. She has done numerous hikes in England, which she likes very much for the wonderful paths that crisscross that island. In the past year, she tells me, she has hiked over a thousand kilometers. The present effort began for her in Vézelay, and she tells me I am the first pilgrim she has met since her departure from the city. She is very weary of the rain, the cold, and the aloneness of this journey, so she plans to call it quits after tomorrow's long walk to Saint-Léonard-de-Noblat. Her physical and spiritual fatigue is not so evident to me; perhaps, in finding finally a fellow pilgrim with whom to share life for a while, she has also found her natural chipperness restored for the moment.

After we take our turns making use of the shower and washing our clothes, she invites me to join her for a walk up to the village church, which, most unusually, is located not in the center of town but on its outskirts. Together we amble up the street, climb a slight hill, and find ourselves at yet another Romanesque monument to God, this one surrounded by hundreds of immense grave-stones, many of them quite recent additions to the church yard. A square tower covers the main entry, which is deeply set within the ground level of the tower. We pull at the tall, slender wooden doors only to find them firmly locked, so we are left to taking a good look at the exterior alone. There are some fine little carvings hiding under the eaves, easily overlooked if one were in a hurry. Neither Jacqueline nor I have anything in our lives worth hurrying about at present, so we take our time with the curious characters that seem to be observing us from under the gutters as much as we observe them from below. Like gargoyles, I can only suppose, these mostly ugly faces were meant to drive away any evil spirits that might be prowling about, but to us modern-minded folks, they are mostly just funny faces, their noses bulbous, their brows heavy, and their frowns snarling at Jacqueline and me, clowns carved in stone.

We then wander among the graves, especially spending a few moments with those of young men who perished in the wars of the last century. Many have photographs attached to their tombstones. They observe us from below even as we observe them from above. With their uniforms so perfectly trimmed, their faces so resolute, holding no visible fear of what was soon to befall them, their caps proudly set, they speak to us of naïveté, bravery yet untested, and most of all, they speak to us the unanswerable question:

"Why? Why did you do this to us? Why did we have to die *like this?*" I wonder how many tears their mothers and sisters shed over the ruin of flesh that was returned to them? What kind of ache tore at the guts of their fathers and brothers, an ache they could hardly let out or they too would die of grief as they shoveled dirt into these graves? The grey skies begin to well, and small drops dampen our hair; I imagine that the sky above now sheds the tears those fathers and brothers could not allow themselves to shed. Faces: The old ones laugh at our human stupidity and try to scare away our evil from above. These newer ones from below, in their innocence, convict our modern times of the same old sins that have always plagued humanity, but are now magnified a million times by AK-47s, sarin gas, land mines, and worst of all, H-bombs.

Jacqueline suggests we get back to our refuge before the rain becomes worse. She has her cell-phone in hand, trying to catch enough of a signal to send a text message to advise her family of her plan for terminating the pilgrimage. She says she has just enough bars on this rise to get the message out, but in town, which is in a sort of digital hole, there is nothing. I was not as clever as my pilgrim friend, for I did not bring my own phone with me so will have to hike back up here if I am to send out my daily report back to Caroline and Gene in Leuven.

As we walk back to the village center, we pass an old man working in his garden. Jacqueline stops to chat, and he warms to the conversation with us pilgrims. I do my best to follow their French and do understand a fair amount of it. She asks why the church is situated outside the town. He shrugs his shoulders: "That's the way it has always been." He seems to remember hearing that once there was an abbey there too, so that must be it; monks would not want to live in town. Jacqueline asks why the town then would not have had its own church. He shrugs his shoulders, purses his lips and puffs: "Who knows? Maybe we are not such holy people here?" And we all have a good laugh.

I eat my dinner alone in the dining room of the only *chambre d'hôte* in town. When I return to my own place, Jacqueline is already tucked in for the night and presumably asleep. Without turning on lights, I quietly undress and call it a day as well.

The new day is born of late-September chill, though there is no wind and no rain. I follow the road out of Chatelus, mostly downhill, Jacqueline somewhere well ahead of me. My legs remain strong, my energy high, and I am clocking six kilometers per hour as I surge through the Limousin. If I pause or rest for too long, the heavy September weather stages a *coup* against my body, and the shivers take over, so I keep moving as my only way to fight back. At ten kilometers I do take a brief *repos* on the stoop of the locked church of Les Billanges, then stop for lunch in Le Châtenet-en-Dognon. I pull into a restaurant and find Jacqueline just finishing a coffee. She chats with me for a bit as I place my order. Before my lunch comes, she is up and on her way with a cheery salute. Jacqueline clearly waits for no man. The lady tending the bar wads up newspaper and stuffs them between several logs in the massive hearth opposite the bar and gets a warming fire going. "For you," she says. "You look cold." I wonder if the crumpled newspaper was a gift from Jacqueline who will not be needing it any longer.

As I pick at my *tartine* and sip at my beer, a straight shot of sunshine pours through the front window of my little restaurant, brightening my table and making my glass of amber beer glisten. The weather is changing, and it could be a warm afternoon after all. I follow the D19 highway, a fairly straight shot towards Saint-Léonard-de-Noblat, and in my walking I remain strong. Along the way, I meet up with Jacqueline one more time; she is seated by the side of the road nibbling on a snack. I sit down near her and pull from Gregory's top pouch a granola bar. She expresses her relief that these will be her final kilometers on the Chemin. She is ready to return to Paris, until the next time, of course. She politely but firmly makes it clear to me that she wishes to walk into Saint-Léonard alone; that is just fine with me, so I get up, roll Gregory onto my back, pick up Click and Clack, and leave her to her snack.

As I approach Saint-Léonard, the afternoon has actually become warm, and I am sweating as I traverse the uphill side streets into the heart of the city. I find the church of Saint-Léonard and enter into its immense coolness. It is a marvel of confusion: various architectural styles and many architectural eras are tacked onto one another in a most haphazard fashion. It is a weird place but beautiful in its weirdness.

With Gregory still on my back and sweat making my shirt cling to my skin, I begin my solitary procession from the stern of the nave towards its dark prow. My eye catches a crucified Christ, carved from wood in an early medieval style, hanging from a column to the right of the sanctuary. It is unpainted and slightly disfigured on one side by rot, but what a lovely Christ, even from this distance. I draw closer and stand, my eyes almost level with his pierced feet. His face is serene. His eyes seem open and closed at the same time. The sequence of life, death, yet more life, all seem to be present at one and the same moment. What I behold here is a transition from one manner of being to another and still another in a single image, a single face, and all this captured by the artist's fine hand. Most of all, this Christ's outstretched arms seem to embrace me and all I am doing out here. I step forward and kiss his feet. I find myself crying, really crying, for the first time in a thousand kilometers. I cannot resist being taken in by him. I cannot elude his gaze. I cannot shun breathing his breath. I cannot escape the reality of his death. I cannot avoid falling into his heart. And so I cry.

My eyes dry as I visit the tomb of the town's patron, Saint-Léonard, then return outdoors and begin searching the streets for the Tourist Information Office so that I might register as a pilgrim and receive the key to the municipal refuge. I wander about a bit, ask a passing lady for directions, and am pointed back beyond the cathedral. This is a lot of additional wandering about for someone who has already trekked thirty kilometers today, but I find the office and enter. The young lady at the desk looks up at me and says in perfect English, "So you must be Kevin." I respond affirmatively and with astonishment: *Yes, I am Kevin, but how did you know?* "Your friend, Jacqueline, has already been here. She told me you would be coming. She already has the key to the refuge." She then draws out directions to the place, actually just a few doors down from the church. She stamps my *credencial*, and I return to the streets of Saint-Léonard, find the address given to me, then after passing through a large courtyard shared with several public offices, enter my home for the night.

As expected, Jacqueline is already well installed in the unusually large refuge. We each have separate bedrooms but share the bathroom, shower and a large kitchen and dining area. She greets me and asks me what took me so long. I tell here I have been visiting the church. Since it is her final night on the Chemin, I invite her out for a simple dinner. After cleaning up and settling in, we go looking for a place but find nothing very reasonable. We settle on a take-out pizzeria and buy a bottle of cheap wine and two pizzas, which we haul back to our digs for dinner at home. Conversation over dinner is a bit of a trial for both of us; she fairly chirps when she speaks, which makes her French difficult for me to understand at times, but she is patient with me, and we get along well, the simple wine warming the friendship between us. She is really a sweetheart and like all my pilgrim friends I gain and lose, I will miss her.

As we nibble on our pizza slices, Jacqueline takes the opportunity to give me some advice about my boots. She has noted that they are too wet. "You know, those boots should be doing a better job of keeping your feet dry; wet feet, you know, are the primary cause of blisters and fungus. You are asking for trouble if you continue to walk in those boots. They are exhausted. They are spent. If I were you, I would buy myself a new pair as soon as possible. I'm already on my third pair this year." Well, I am not so sure I can just abandon these Meindl boys after all our kilometers together. They are like friends to me now, but I am no expert when it comes to boot technology, so maybe she has a point. I just don't know and make no decisions in the matter.

After dinner, she prepares her belongings for the train ride back to Paris, while I read up on the town patron, Saint-Léonard. A nobleman in the court of Clovis, he converted to Christianity along with his king at the end of the fifth century. He requested from Clovis the privilege of liberating whatever prisoners he might find worthy of freedom at any time he deemed fit, and the right was granted him. He later became a monk and hermit, settling here in the Limousin, where he eventually founded the abbey around which this town grew. Legend says that prisoners who called upon the monk's intercession would have their chains miraculously broken, which the grateful ex-prisoners would then carry to the sainted Léonard as testimony to his mercy. It is a lovely story, for freedom is so much more than just another word for nothing left to lose, with apologies to Janice Joplin; Léonard reminds us that freedom is an expression of mercy and the letting go of past wrongs, and so it means new life to the forgiven. It is a kind of resurrection and in this, freedom is a great spring of hope for us all-too-enchained human beings. May many such chains be so broken, especially in our own time. That is my prayer tonight.

Tomorrow, God willing, I will walk as a free man into Limoges, one of the French Chemin's noble cities.

Morning light makes its way to my closed eyes signaling that sleep now comes to an end. The smell of the coffee Jacqueline has already perked wafts my way, drawing me out of my sack into our little kitchen to sip of its aromatic blackness. Jacqueline is chattering away as she sweeps and reorders the various kitchen utensils left about by our occupation of the refuge the past half-day. She is obviously happy as a lark knowing that she is leaving this Chemin later in the morning, trading in her boots and poles and pack for the steel wheels of a train that at precisely 10:00 am will whisk her away to Limoges, then from Limoges, another to Paris and home. As for me, boots, poles, and pack yet beckon, and so after finishing a small cup of her coffee, I busy myself with my morning routines. She has wrapped last night's leftover pizza into rolls, so as not to take up unnecessary space in my pack, she explains, and covered them in foil for me to take along as lunch. A few minutes before 8:00 am, I double-kiss Jacqueline on her cheeks—*oh, I have become so French*—and ask her to pray for me, to which she happily agrees. I'm not sure why I so spontaneously ask her for prayers since it is not something I very regularly do out here, but her companionship these past few days has seemed more to me than just company; she has seemed like a little sister in faith walking with me, cheering me on, instructing me in wadding newspaper correctly and in her small way also holding up the roof of the world in her walking.

18

All You Saints of God

Saint-Léonard-de-Noblat is shrouded this morning in a drippy fog that makes the sound of my poles on stone echo even more than they usually do. The route out of Saint-Léonard is marked by a steep descent, crosses an old bridge that to my unprofessional eye may be the work of those empire-building Romans, then after another kilometer, turns left and up, ascending steeply for another four or five kilometers. I am climbing well, though without yesterday's verve. The fog chills me, so I have to keep moving to stave off the shivers. I eventually climb out of the valley cloud and know the warmth of the morning sun upon my face. I turn to look back and see below me a cottony cloud filling the valley out of which I have walked this past hour and a half; Saint-Léonard-de-Noblat is completely hidden from my view from up here, except for the great stone steeple of the *église*, which punctures from below the white blanket covering the rest of the valley. It fairly boasts that not even the clouds can conceal its grand height; even more nobly the steeple proudly points to all that is above, all that is beyond.

I pass more than a few roadside crosses, most constructed of wrought iron rather than the carved granite of previous days. I stop and place a stone on the base of one that is an easy reach with no thistles about to dissuade me. I like putting the stones on these crosses; it makes me feel a communion with the other pilgrims who have passed before me who have done the same. Our small cairns remind us that though we mostly travel one by one, we nevertheless form a fraternity of like-footed pilgrims out on this Chemin.

At about ten kilometers into the morning's walk, I come to the village of Aureil. I climb up into its heart and find the church doors open. It hosts relics of two saints, Gaucher and Faucher, the former having been only eighteen when he founded the nearby abbey in the eleventh century, the chapel of which, a poster explains, remains standing and which I will pass shortly along my pilgrim Way. Faucher seems to have been one of Gaucher's monks.

Near the entrance to the church is a table holding a *livre d'or,* or guest book. I take a peek. The most recent two entries are in English, inscribed by a husband and wife from California, earlier in the day. The husband is a newly ordained deacon of the Catholic Church, and he prays to Gaucher and Faucher for his wife, that she might adapt to and accept their new life as ministers in the church. Her inscription follows and is much longer. She prays intensely for her husband in his new ministry as a deacon, for their children, for the leaders of the church, and for its pastors, priests and deacons. I am especially grateful for her prayers for me as a priest and pastor, and so feel moved to go to the front of the church and spend a little time with the bones of Gaucher and Faucher; I ask the saints to give this deacon and his wife a kindly smile from above. I return to the *livre d'or* and add my own intention: *Gaucher and Faucher: walk with me for a while today as I continue down the pilgrim road to Compostelle.*

I return to the warm sunshine bathing Aureil at the moment, drop Gregory and set myself up on a stone wall; it is time for my morning snack and the pizza rolls prepared by Jacqueline are calling to me. There is no one about. The solitude that Gaucher sought here remains, at least for the moment. It is altogether sweet under this sun to eat cold, rolled pizza and have Gaucher and Faucher, as well as the deacon and his wife, as new companions on this day's journey.

I still have more than a few kilometers to Limoges, so I roll Gregory the Great onto my back and slide my arms through his straps and get a whiff of his less-than-subtle body odor. He needs a good scrubbing. *Maybe, Gregory, in Limoges I can give you a well-deserved bath.*

I follow the ancient pilgrim route along a bramble-ridden path to Bost-las-Mongeas only a half-kilometer further on. The old abbey chapel is indeed still here, but it is now private property and is attached to a farmer's barn. The Romanesque windows and portal are still visible from the outside, but entry is prohibited. Yapping and growling dogs fend off any attempt to see more of the old place, so I move on.

The kilometers pass as the day warms; I am tired as I arrive in Feytiat, a bedroom suburb of Limoges. From here on, the route is dominated by the noise of speeding traffic on a major highway just to my left. The developing city is unpretty and busy. My guide now abandons me and advises me to follow instead bronze *coquilles* placed in the sidewalks; they will guide me into the center of Limoges. Finding the bronze pilgrim shells and interpreting their directives proves to be a significant difficulty from the start. I cross a major intersection back and forth twice trying to track them, then finally take a best guess and head off in a wrong direction altogether; the bronze shells disappear, and I realize I must be walking badly, as my French hosts would put it. I return yet again to the initial *coquilled* intersection and start over. This time, I walk a circle around the intersecting streets and finally, to my joy, find the next link in the *coquille* chain, and the next, and so I am on my way into Limoges.

I have made a reservation at Limoges' Grande Séminaire, formerly the local church's training ground for priests-to-be, but now, lacking priests-to-be, it is some kind of multi-purpose center that also welcomes pilgrims like myself. The coquilles have put me on the right street, the Rue Eugène Varlin, but the Grande Séminaire itself seems most elusive. I walk block after block keeping an eye open for some such place until finally, I spot a massive building ahead and wonder if that could be my home for the night. I approach, looking for a sign but see nothing at the first entry in the high wall surrounding it. I push a bit further on and find a second gate, look inside, and see signs indicating that diocesan offices are within. I amble up the driveway to a grand building with a grand entrance and a grand white statue of Mary holding the child Jesus set on a grand plinth, all assuring me that I have grandly arrived at what was once the Grande Séminaire of Limoges. I approach the front doors but cannot enter; the place is closed for the lunch hour. I must dawdle about for another six minutes, so I find a bench, set Gregory to one side, pull out the remainder of my pizza, and take my Jacqueline-prepared lunch right here.

An old man comes from within the building and begins slowly pacing around the circular drive and garden in front of the building; his hands remain behind his back as he looks off into another world. I see a rosary dangling from his fingers as he strolls past me. After a round or two, his gaze returns to this earth, he looks at me, then ambles over to my bench and seats himself to my left. He asks if I am a pilgrim. When he learns I am an American, he switches from French to simple English, then when he learns I speak Spanish, he takes up that language as the easiest of the three for the both of us. He tells me he is a priest, and I tell him I am the same. He responds: "You are young!" I do not feel so young right now, but in comparison to his 86 years, I guess I am. We chat for a while, then, *le curé* struggles back to his feet and leads me inside the *foyer* of the old seminary to meet the secretary. The young lady signs me in, takes my euros for the night's stay, stamps my *credencial* with the diocesan seal, and shows me to a small room featuring a sink, a bed, and a small window that looks out to the old city of Limoges with its various church steeples all pointing above and beyond as did that of Saint-Léonard-de-Noblat.

I have been thinking about my boots since Jacqueline advised me to ditch them in favor of new, waterproof ones. She was just sure that I had worn my old faithfuls out by now. If I am going to follow her advice with hopes of avoiding further days of wet feet, then Limoges is the place to buy them. This is a real city with real stores. I send a text message to Gene and Caroline asking what they think. Thus begins a flurry of text messages and phone calls between us; Gene thinks I'm nuts for even thinking about new boots mid-pilgrimage: this is what knocks people off the Camino. He tells me, "New boots are the worst thing you can do to your feet! All boots leak in downpours; go buy wax and silicon spray and give them a good freshening up; get a pair of gaiters to keep the water from trickling down into the boot tops, and that should be good enough!" I back away from Jacqueline's position under the clarity of Gene's always pragmatic advice. Gene even looks up on the Internet a nearby sporting goods store. Thus I head to the town center. I cross the river over an old bridge and amble uphill towards the cathedral and the Église Saint-Pierre, but bypass both with the hope of getting to the shops before closing hour. I find the brightly lit sports store recommended by Gene and Caroline and find the boot wax and gaiters, as well as a polar-fleece cap for the colder days that are surely coming, and some thin silk gloves for my hands. At a specialty shop, I find a pair of lightweight long-johns and snap them up. I pick up a few groceries for tomorrow's walk.

By the time I return to the street, it has begun to rain, making me grateful for my new boot supplies and giving me a good excuse to stop in at a Quick, a European interpretation of McDonald's, for a burger, fries, and 7-Up. While sitting in a booth next to a large glass window between me and the shiny-slick street beyond, I make a decision: Tomorrow, Sunday, will be a day of rest. I will stay here another night.

I finish my quick and not so pleasant meal and head for the closest church, the Église Saint-Michel. I enter and discover an almost square interior with plenty of Gothic ornamentation, a low ceiling arching from pillar to pillar like that of a crypt, and great spreads of stained-glass all about. Up front, the relics of Limoges' founding bishops are prominently displayed: Saint-Martial, followed by Saint-Loup and Saint-Valérie. The heavy overcast outside makes the windows glow low, the church interior being suffused with a subtle and soft quality. After some time, I pass through the stone vestibule and back into the streets of Limoges, where a Gypsy woman awaits me with a paper soda cup from Quick. I leave one euro with her and wander home to an early bedtime.

Just as soon as my head drops to my pillow, my heart begins misfiring: boom—flutter—boom-boom-boom-boom—flutter—boom, and off it goes for probably the rest of the night. I have taken my a-fib medicine faithfully, so there is no reason for this, but there is nothing to be done, so I go to sleep on my right side to diminish the feel of the irregular pumping. *Stupid heart: behave!*

I awake at 8:00 am to find the heart still acting up but go about my morning business anyway. It will pass soon enough, I am sure. I eat breakfast, waterproof and wax my boots, and sure enough, by the time I have finished buffing the boot leather, my ticker is ticking correctly. I put on my sandals, grab my camera, and head back into Limoges to get a better feel of the city on this Sunday morning, and if I can, catch Mass in one of the churches downtown, guessing that 10:00 am would be the right hour for Mass. I cross the old pedestrian bridge back into the city center and climb up to the cathedral. There is almost no one about. I am surprised to find the doors to the church locked tight on this Sunday morning. An old man is sweeping a sidewalk nearby, so I ask if there is Mass here, this morning. He responds simply, "yesterday" and returns to his sweeping. This is very strange indeed: a cathedral with no Sunday morning liturgy! What kind of place has "the eldest daughter of the church," as France has long been known, become? I wander then up to the Église Saint-Pierre and find its doors closed and locked as well. I am now doubly irritated with France and its headlong rush into secularization, which feels to me right now like a betrayal of ancestors and a flash-in-the-pan affair with flimsy, ephemeral nothingness. I grumble my way past half-timbered houses and up to the last of the city-center's great churches, the one I sat in last night: Saint-Michel-des-Lions. I find the doors not only open, but the sound of ebullient singing gushing out of them. I am filled with surprise and shame as I pass through the great doors and step into a nave filled to the gunnels with people: black people, white people, old people, young people, singing, singing, singing some up-beat French hymn of praise! Indian women are dressed in sweeping saris, Nigerian men are draped in gold and green, aging French *dames* have necks wrapped in fashionable pearls and their husbands, handsome ties; Gypsy mothers in dark dresses hang near the doors, leaving their Quick cups behind as they join in the prayer. Young parents abound and even more, the children they hold. *Saints: all of them!* Up front, the priest hovers above a family with a baby dressed in white, baptism soon to follow. He is a masterful leader of the liturgy; he doesn't dominate but guides the energy of the community forward, like a sailor managing the sails of his ship to best catch the wind and move the whole *barque* forward. He balances solemnity and intimacy perfectly. I am caught up in the joy of it and am welcomed into a pew by an old woman who has little space to share. We smile at each other, and she goes back to singing the hymn of the moment. Lay persons proclaim the scriptures, then the priest gives a dynamic homily that keeps coming back to Naomi, the little girl about to be baptized. The baptism is observed by the whole body with rapt attention, then the rites of the Eucharist push forward until they culminate in a wave of believers moving forward in communion for communion. Final prayers and a blessing and then a procession and hymn carry the priest, Naomi and her family down the center of the nave and towards an open space near the back of the church. There, flutes of champagne and small snacks are passed around by the family of little Naomi. I take a glass and snack on a rolled up slice of some kind of delicate meat, then spot the priest and introduce myself to him as a pilgrim to *Compostelle* and fellow priest. He cheerily shakes my hand, wishes me well on my *mission*, and then is pulled aside by a parishioner anxious to talk with him. Ah, my *mission*! That is a very good way to look at this journey; it *is* a mission, a strange one, perhaps, but a mission nevertheless.

I am delighted by the vibrant prayer within this lovely and oh so very Catholic–in the "universal" sense of the name–family. I am also ashamed at my earlier thoughts dismissing the complex Catholicity of my host country. France and her living saints of so many colors, little Naomi, just the newest among them, just evangelized me!

Once back in my room and considering tomorrow's 27.5 kilometers hike to a place called Flavignac, I find no intermediary refuge along the way; I have little choice but to walk the whole stretch. I will make up for it by dividing the next long *étape* into two shorter ones. Tomorrow will not be so easy. I must resist discouragement. Just as I am making these plans, a text message comes in from Gene and Caroline. It is touching and caring but sets off in me a reaction of self-defensiveness: the bout with atrial fibrillation has them concerned; they think I am pushing too hard, not enjoying myself, not meeting people along the way. They tell me I should slow it down and smell the roses as I go. *What do they think I have been doing here today? I AM taking a day off! I've met people today: a Gypsy with a Quick cup, an old lady who invited me into her pew, a fine pastor! If I had an option to walk less than twenty-seven-point-five stupid kilometers tomorrow, do you think I wouldn't take it? I do get to know people on the road, when there are people to meet. Sietse and Evert and Jacqueline can testify to that. This is not the Spanish Camino where a hundred thousand pilgrims can be found, for heaven's sake. I am alone out here!*

I take a deep breath and with it comes understanding: Gene and Caroline are right, of course; I am pushing myself down this road more than letting the road carry me. There is a difference. I fight too much with the normal obstacles I face: the rain and mud and tired muscles. I do need to smell the roses more as I go and let things unfold as they will, as God wills. This is a mission, yes, but it is also a prayer. I have met other pilgrims who seem to be a lot more carefree and happy than I am in the pilgrim Way. I will try to do better. I write a message back thanking them for their advice and I dare say, their care for me, then get myself ready for bed.

I take a last look through my small window at the Limoges skyline at night. The towers of the churches of Saint-Michel and Saint-Pierre are elegantly illuminated. It is a beautiful sight from here. The rain makes it all glisten. My heart is steady tonight. Gaucher and Faucher, Marcial and Loup and Valérie, and all you saints of God: *pray for us weary pilgrims as we pass along your Way!*

I awake at 6:30 to my alarm, but I have been sleeping atop my left arm, and it is completely useless. I cannot move it in the slightest so cannot turn off the incessant chirping of my watch. I get out of bed, my left arm still hanging dead, but begin to feel the tingle of life returning to it, and walk directly to the window to check on the sky. There are clouds about but not too heavy, and so I am pleased. Today, the first day of October, marks the beginning of my fourth month of life as a pilgrim, if I count the month in Waterloo. *That long, really? Man, oh, man!*

Even as I return from the toilet down the hall, the sound of rain pounding on the roof and running like little rivers through the gutters just beyond my window drains any optimism I had for the coming day. I look through the window, and I am amazed at how the scene has changed from just a few minutes ago: the city of Limoges, still in the dark, is coming to life streaked with white headlights and red taillights magnified innumerably by the millions of raindrops now washing across the city. It is beautiful from this perch, but to spend the day walking in this stuff is a prospect that sucks the courage out of me. I eat my little breakfast in my room: leftover *quiche* and two remaining pots of warm yogurt. I pull my possessions together, pack them into Gregory, pick up my sticks, and with hood up, head into this first day of October. The secretary at the door of the Grande Séminaire wishes me *au revoir* and waves as I pass through the wide doors of the old place; I wave back, feigning courage and determination as best I am able. God has pity on me this day, for almost as soon as I am in the street beyond the seminary courtyard, the rain lets up, and I can see the morning sky clearing. My courage returns. *Flavignac: here I come!*

Working my way through the streets of Limoges so as to get back on the official pilgrim route, I am having trouble. Too many streets here have nothing on the corners to indicate their names. Before long, I am lost, look-ing haplessly from my map to the streets about me and back to the map. I wander on slowly, hoping to see some concordance between my guide and the reality of pavement and curbs and storefronts all about me. I grow increasingly frustrated as I waste half-an-hour bumbling about. Finally, I catch a break: there is a street sign: I am, miracle of miracles, right where I am supposed to be. Then I spot a Compostelle arrow glued to a pole, and I am really sure now that I am finally on the Chemin.

In another fifteen minutes or so, I am making my way up an avenue with another merging into it from the right. Along that other street, I spot a young woman, her back loaded with a pack and trekking poles busily supporting her as she clips along. We recognize each other as pilgrims at almost the same moment, and both of us wave our poles in greeting. She carefully crosses over to my side of the street, and I greet her: *Une pélerine!* She responds cheerily, "*Oui,*" and we introduce ourselves to one another. Welcome to my world, *Monique!* She is from Quebec and has been walking from Vézelay with the hope of making it at least to Périgeuex before having to return to her homeland. She is somewhere in her early-thirties, I would guess. Her English is about as limited as my French, but we seem to be communicating reasonably well, in spite of the limitations. I ask her if she minds walking together for a while and that I fully understand if she prefers to guard her pilgrim privacy. She is happy either way: "*seul ou ensemble*" she tells me.

As it turns out, Monique has been having trouble navigating through the outskirts of Limoges too. We are using the same guides, but the distance between arrows on the street has been flummoxing us both. As we join up here at the junction of our two avenues and begin walking together, we are already looking for the next arrow but not finding it. We put our heads together and at times, walk both sides of the now-suburban streets looking for our next arrow. Often enough we walk in silence, some distance apart, protecting one another's pilgrim space. The quiet is of a different quality from that when one is walking altogether alone; the silence is now something shared and a choice, rather than simply imposed by the hard reality of aloneness. It becomes something like a tether between us, of which both of us are responsible for holding an end, and because of the silence, we must care for together, we are responsible to one another; this silence is like a gift now because of its shared character.

My day-off in Limoges has not had much effect on my legs and back. My legs feel as if they are each ten pounds heavier than usual. Gregory feels more *magnus* than ever; could the few things I bought in Limoges have added *this* much extra weight to his heft? Monique is no speed-demon either; we are walking at almost exactly the same pace. Fields and farms pass as we amble together under the day's low skies.

As we pass through the village of Aixe-sur-Vienne, we are again being rained upon, so we stop for coffee and croissants in a small restaurant. By the time we have finished, sunshine is streaming through the window, and we step into a different world than the one we left only a few minutes ago.

They sky is quickly clearing, amazingly so, and for the rest of the day's walk, we remain not only dry but wonderfully warmed by this early-October sun.

The roads through the Haute-Vienne countryside lead us through shimmering green fields until they finally guide us into Flavignac, a small town boasting not much more than a tiny lake, and for us pilgrims, a municipal refuge. We troop down to the city hall to pick up the key from the town officials and have our *credenciales* duly stamped, then return to the apartment set aside for us. It is a cracker-box, but clean and tidy and as soon as we drop our packs, pick our bunks, and decide who gets first dubs on the shower, it feels like home.

The village church is just across the street, so while Monique is showering, I amble over and walk through the open doors into the nave of the old place. This church is occupied: a circle of elderly men and women are gathered in a side chapel that has been glassed in and given the gift of electric heat. There is a table at the center of the circle with a bouquet of fresh flowers carefully set upon it. They read from their Bibles, sing a fine old French hymn, then after a time of quiet, someone leads a prayer and blessing. I enjoy watching them through the glass, more even than taking in the modest details of the church itself. The stones are the house, but these old timers are the church itself. They are lovely to regard because they too are saints, and saints are always so dear to behold. I leave them to their prayer and return to the refuge for my own shower. Once I'm washed and my laundry hung to dry, Monique invites me to the local bar for a beer, an invitation I am more than happy to accept; this has been a twenty-seven kilometer day, so a little dose of hops, yeast and froth is certainly called for. The bar is a fairly miserable place; it is dark and smells of stale cigarettes. A mother does her best to tend the bar and her kids at the same time. She pours our beers, gives us a bowl of peanuts at my request, and we take our purchases out to the patio facing the main street of the village. There Monique and I deepen our pilgrim bonds as we do our best to chat about who we are and what in God's name we are doing out here. Monique returns within and comes back with two more beers and together with our peanuts, we fill ourselves to the point that a later dinner does not seem to be necessary. We finally go off in different directions, Monique to buy bread for tomorrow and I back to the refuge to draw in my laundry before the few drops of rain now splattering about us become another downpour.

The beer has made me drowsy, so I lie down on my bunk and close my eyes and drift along somewhere between here and dream. I hear Monique come in, and after putting aside her purchases, she too takes a rest. Later, she reads, and I listen to music. A few hours pass, and I ask if she is interested in returning to the bar for a light dinner. She declines, preferring to mix up some instant soup and enjoy the fresh baguette she just purchased. She invites me to join her, so I take a seat at her table. We have become fine mates in this single day on the road, and we are a good fit, two pilgrim peas in a pod. Breaking bread and slurping hot chicken-noodle soup together is a grace note that warmly ends a long day. After washing up the few dishes and preparing our packs for the morning, we take a walk to the small lake just a short distance from our refuge, then it is time for bed. We part ways and head for the hills, as my old man used to say at bedtime.

In the morning, Monique and I have coffee and share the remnants of last night's bread and cheese. We are both on our way by 8:00 am. The pavement outside our refuge is wet from a rain during the night, but the morning sky is clearing, and it looks to be a dry and cheery day ahead. We walk the day without having to dig out our rain gear even once, though we eventually hit sections of the route that are all mud or tall, wet grass. The leather of my boots turns black with the damp but holds off the worst of it, so I am pleased.

Along the way, an old man comes down the road toward us, walking crookedly with a cane to support himself. Even from a distance, he shoots us a huge grin, and as we draw closer, he clearly wants to chat. He is dressed in the clothes of elderly French men: heavy pants tucked into rubber wellies, suspenders holding them up from his shoulders, a shirt stained with break-fast, a vest, a tie, a worn jacket over it all. His face is deeply rutted from years of working under the sun, but the wrinkles make the twinkle in his green eyes all the more pronounced. Monique takes the lead with our new friend. She explains that we are *pèlerins*. He bows to us and puts his hand over his heart to indicate he honors and loves us. He asks about me since I have been mostly silent until now, and so I tell him I am an American. His grin grows even grander and takes my hand to shake it heartily. He tells us he is 86 years old, and he walks this road every day. He understands perfectly what we are doing out here and wants us to know that his road is ours for the day. His smile never dims in the least. After we repeatedly say *bonne journée* to one another, we salute and continue on our ways. I comment to Monique that I feel like I just met God the Father, to which she quietly laughs in accord.

Monique and I find ourselves lost in the woods not long before we should be arriving in Châlus. We both check our maps but cannot figure out where we have gone wrong. Despite being rather seriously turned around, we successfully bumble our way back onto the proper route and follow a paved road the final bit into the town. This is where I intend to spend the night; Monique plans to go on another fifteen kilometers or so. As we enter the town, we come to a busy highway that passes through the place. We wait for the light to turn green and cross over the four lanes to the far corner dominated by a large hotel-restaurant named, "Richard, le Cœur du Lion"; a sign announces that it has rooms available. We pass it by and follow our guides instead towards the church at the center of the village. This requires walking up a fairly steep street towards a castle, then turning to the left and descending once again towards the square where the church sits. It is a 19th or 20th century edifice lacking charm and weight; my first thought is of something out of the imagination of Walt Disney. Here Monique and I make our farewell. She tells me that it has been a pleasure to walk with me the past two days, and I tell her I feel the same about having walked with her. We give each other an awkward backpacker's hug, make our final *au revoirs*, and off we go in different directions: Monique carrying on south towards Compostelle and I to secure a room for the night with Richard the Lion Heart.

The room I am offered is adequate though the noise of the traffic on the highway below is irksome; more serious is the angle of the window: it is unlikely I will get any direct sunlight this afternoon for drying my laundry. My clothes will likely be damp in the morning, as were those I laundered yesterday. *If anyone should think this a vacation, just try wearing wet briefs for two days in a row!*

I take lunch in the restaurant downstairs: a leg of duck and fried spuds are the *plat du jour* accompanied by a small carafe of red wine. It all makes me sleepy, so I return to my room for a nap, followed by a planning session for the coming two days. By phone I line up a hotel for tomorrow and a *chamber d'hôte* for the following night. I wander up the street to the town's only attraction: the castle where the indomitable Eleanor of Aquitaine's son, Richard the Lion Heart, took the arrow in his chest that ended his young life. What can be seen from the street is all turret and tower, parts of it nicely restored, it seems, but the site is closed to visitors today, so I continue back into the center of Châlus. I find the plain vanilla church open and though it is singularly unimpressive as a building, I find in an obscure corner of the church a stone carving featuring a lovely Gabriel and an equally wonderful Mary. Both have wide eyes set into tender faces. They delight me. The Annunciation is such a great moment in the Gospel of Luke; Gabriel handles the responsibility of upending Mary's life with such delicacy and care for her. This icon in stone captures that delicacy as well as Mary's innocence in responding with her famous *fiat*, "yes." I regret that I do not have my camera with me now to take a snapshot of the image. Maybe I can catch them tomorrow on my way out of town. This Mary and this Gabriel are the only memorable thing I have found in Châlus so far.

As the sun sets and the dusky darkness of early evening settles into my room, I am discouraged again by the weather report for tomorrow: it is all rain and thunder and lightning bolts. I miss the company of Monique. Damp laundry hangs about. Massive trucks roar by just beyond the far wall. Hotel rooms are always the most dismal place to spend a pilgrim night; in this one, I feel more alone than usual. I crawl into bed and remember the old man who reminded me of God the Father and smile at the memory of his smile. I remember the wide, kind eyes of Gabriel and Mary. I remember my prayer in Limoges and repeat it as I fall to sleep: *All you saints of God, pray for us!*

19

Coquille Saint-Jacques

Another night. Another morning. I take one rainy day to walk to La Coquille, then another to Thiviers.

Along the path to Thiviers, my guide informs me in the briefest terms that I should keep my eye open for an "ancient rock of prayer". I have no idea what exactly this sight might be, but I do keep my eye peeled for it, and sure enough, a rough sign or two indicate that I am approaching something ancient and important. There it is: in a field, just on the other side of several strings of barbed wire. It is a humble enough stone: about the size of a dinner table and even has something of the shape of a table . . . or an altar. There is no informative sign indicating its age or use. I am not that far from the prehistoric paintings of the Lascaux Cavern, so I suppose it may be a relic from pre-Christian times, perhaps a place of ritual sacrifice. I don't really know and have no way of finding out, at least not out here, not today. *Well, blessings on whomever once prayed here; blessings on those who at least knew they were not their own creators and masters of their own destiny, who sensed something bigger and better than themselves in this life.*

Sometime later, I have left the dirt paths and am ambling down a small paved road, chestnut forests to either side, the leafy branches reaching up and over the roadway forming a green and brown canopy above me. I am feeling good. Nothing hurts. My feet are a little wet inside my boots from the October damp but not bad. I am thinking of nothing. I am just walking. My mind is a happy blank. It is dark along this road, dark like a church. The light of day filters green through the chestnut canopy above. All is soft. Then in a blaze that lasts only a moment, *I WALK INTO GOD!* I walk right smack dab *INTO GOD!* God envelops me. He wraps himself around me. *These trees, this damp, this dark, this road, these feet, these legs, this earth, this universe: we are all in Him and of Him and enveloped by Him.* Oh, my God! *I just walked right smack dab into YOU!*

I cannot hold on to the sense for much more than a second or two, but the residue of its searing revelation endures as I continue through my chestnut forest. For a moment, I have no doubts; God is so true and so good and this reality, this goodness, this love, is so *real*. No doubt, no darkness, no evil, no war, no fracture of the human race in any of its many fractures can diminish the power of the holy and one and altogether infinite kiss I have just been given. This is what I have been walking for and waiting for all these pilgrim miles; I am electrified by the light of it!

I walk into Thiviers just before noon and pull my way up a fairly steep street towards the church, but the additional pull of gravity as I climb is nothing compared to the lightness I still feel in my body from my little theophany in the chestnut woods. With a God-induced serenity I have felt too little along the Way, I find my refuge for tonight along this same street; I knock, and the door is opened by Jeanine. She invites me in and introduces me to her husband, Joos. They are Dutch, natives of Tilburg, a university town located right on the Belgian border. They are very happy to have a pilgrim from Leuven staying the night with them. Their *chambre d'hôte* has room for tourists, but they specialize in caring for pilgrims like me who wander into town. The place is full of Compostela trinkets. *Coquilles* are everywhere. Images of Jacobus himself abound. Coffee-table books featuring grand photos of the Santiago cathedral are stacked on, what else, coffee tables . . . and end tables and bookshelves. They assure me that I won't have any trouble walking through northern Spain in November; they've heard the cold is not so unbearable then. They encourage me to simply go and go and go . . . all the way to Santiago. They have never been pilgrims themselves, but they are great aficionados nevertheless. The house is old but in good condition. Jeanine is already at work preparing a Dutch take on a Spanish pilgrim dinner for me and a few other guests who are scheduled to arrive a bit later.

After my shower and laundry, I wander back into the town center to take a closer look at the church and then dip into an Internet shop to answer emails. It takes me an hour and a half to get through the long string of correspondence, including a brief note to my bishop back in Spokane. Within minutes of hitting the send button on that one, my mobile phone starts ringing. It is the very bishop I have just emailed. We chat amiably for a while; I assure him I am doing fine and experiencing something special out here on the road. He says something like "We're looking forward to your getting home and back to ministry," and without much thought, I add, *Thanks, Bishop; but this IS ministry for me for now.* As I walk back to Jeanine and Joos's, I am frustrated by this: so many people presume I am on some kind of weird vacation out here. This is *work*, sometimes, hard work. This is *ministry*, because it is the proclamation of the Gospel on foot. This is church on the down-low. I am doing what Jesus and his apostles did most of their lives. I am praying on foot for the bishop and my family and my friends and our sad, old, tired, beautiful world. If my God-moment earlier today teaches anything, it is that this is where I am meant to be. This is what I am called to do. This is my *vocation*! I am walking into God out here, for God's sake!

I am decidedly not on *vacation* here.

I enjoy supper with Joos and Jeanine and their other guests for the night, then retire early. I dig out my small travel breviary as I have done on so many early mornings and late evenings along this pilgrim Way. I prop my pillow against the wall behind the head of the bed and recline. The psalms are often touching for me and reading them quietly helps me keep my focus on what is important about my pilgrim ups and downs. "May these mountains bring forth peace for the people and these hills, justice."[1] That is a pretty good prayer for a pilgrim climbing hills and gazing at some pretty beautiful mountains in the distance. These ancient songs of grief and praise with God always as the intended recipient capture in one way or another just about everything there is to say to God: God: you are great! God: where are you? God: give me a break! Blessed be God! Always in the end: *Blessed be God*.

My head hits the pillow, and I entrust all my dreams to the One I met on the road this day. *Blessed be God forever.*

At 7:30 am, it is pouring rain in Thiviers. By the time I step out the door of Joos and Jeanine's place, the rain has stopped, and I remain dry as I walk out of town and begin following today's dirt paths towards Compostelle. As the day develops, it is unseasonably warm and two layers of shirts are one too many, so I strip off my outer one and tie it around my waist. I walk well today; the dirt roads are a pleasure. I meet no one.

As I trod through an oaky woods, an odd question occurs to me, sort of a riddle in search of an answer: *what is the heaviest thing I carry on my way?* The answer comes to me out of the blue: *Dad!* I have a great laugh over it, because it is so perfectly surprising and perfectly true. I have to admit yet again on this long walk south the old man weighs heavy on my shoulders. Now long dead, I believe in some way I have made my peace with him, but the malformation that is the result of growing up in fear never completely heals, and so, I do still carry him, and his weight is not negligible. I present the evidence to my interior court: as I found out again back in Guérigny, I still hate conflict, argument, and sudden eruptions of anger. I instinctively look for escape routes from any room where there is yelling about. Isn't it funny

---

1. Psalm 72

how we can't escape our parents even when they have escaped us? I love the holy joke in it. And this is my conclusion: I actually don't mind carrying this weight; carrying Dad down this road all these days is my gift to the old man and a way to let both him and me know that, in the end, I love him.

I trundle my way down a country lane with a large pasture to the left, marked off by strings of barbed wire running from worn post to worn post. On the distant side of the pasture is an ass that, as I pass by, looks up, pricks up her big ears, then comes lollygagging across the field, clearly desirous of a visit with this stranger. Her head sort of lolls from side to side, and her eyes seem alive with expectation as she draws closer. I am tickled by the amiability of the animal, which upon finally reaching the fence separating us, looks directly at me, then wiggles her ears about thus signaling readiness for a chat.

Well, Miss Ass, I hope you are having a fine day today.

"I am. The grass is rich, and the autumn is mild, and I have a visitor to talk with."

And do you receive many visitors along this road?

"Not so many. A pilgrim or two like yourself."

And do you chat with them as you do with me?

"With those who know how to visit with animals; some of your kind are useless as conversationalists, as you may know."

Yes, I have known a few like that. For my part, I like talking with the animals I meet along the way. There is wisdom in your ways; you eat, you sleep, you are curious, and you never take yourselves as seriously as most of us do. And as far as I know, no mule has ever murdered another mule out of anger or vengeance. You don't threaten the world or instill fear in your children.

"Yes, we have all that in our favor. We can be a little mule-headed, but we are generally pretty happy most of the time with things as they are.

Did you know that the occasional mule walks to Compostela as do I? Would you like to be a pilgrim mule?

"I don't know. I've never mulled that over. I suppose it would be a happy thing to do. Would it be hard for a mule like me?"

I don't think so. I think it is harder for humans like me.

"So it is hard for you?

Some days it is hard.

"Then why do you do it?"

Just because.

"That's not a fair answer. 'Just because' doesn't answer the question, even an ass like me knows that."

I'm sorry. You are right, Miss Ass. But it is hard to put into words or glances or ear wiggles why I am doing this. A priest I met a few days ago called it a mission *and that is true. It is a* mission *I am on. I believe it makes me more real and you more real and my family more real and the world more real. At least that is my hope. That is why I do it.*

"Mules don't have missions, I guess. We either work or we don't work. We either walk or we don't walk. I suppose that is what separates us and why I'm on this side of the fence, kept, and you are on that side, following a way."

I suppose you are right. I am happy to be on this side of the fence.

"And I'm happy on my side, too. We mules are pretty easy to please."

We human beings are not. We tend towards restlessness. We like having missions. We find it hard to live without great goals.

"Well, my friend, walk well. I hope you complete your mission. Greet the Apostle for me when you arrive."

I will. I promise. Au revoir, mon amie.

"Au revoir."

I walk into Sorges at 12:30 and follow the yellow arrows to the village's old church and its municipal refuge next door. A note on the door makes it clear that it will not be open for occupancy until 4:00 pm, so I have more than three hours to while away before I can settle in. I wander about a bit and discover that this part of the Dordogne is truffle country, the earthy delicacy rooted out of the ground by pigs. There is a museum to the local industry here, but the doors are locked, so I wander some more and find a pizzeria that is open. Perhaps they have on offer a truffle pizza? Not a chance! Following consumption of my ordinary pepperoni version, I walk to the small *place* before an oddly constructed church. The church's exterior *façade* features two portals of differing sizes and design huddled below a triangular crown. The structure feels squat and out of balance. Near the entry is a twelfth century baptismal font carved from white stone featuring four pilgrim conches emblazoned on the exterior of its bowl, reminding all who enter that this old place has been a pilgrim stop for centuries. I am only the latest of many thousands across the ages to take refuge under its stone arches. I am made to feel at home by the stone font. This is my place. It was built for me and my ilk.

After browsing about the church, I take a seat in an old wooden pew, set Gregory to my left and lay Click and Clack down to his left. I rifle through his top pocket and pull out my journal and take time to write a bit about this mostly uneventful and quiet day. An elderly lady dressed in a worn cotton dress and an even more worn black sweater enters, lumbers past me without paying me any mind, and makes straight for the first pew directly in front of the altar. There she kneels and leans heavily on the supportive board in front of her. She turns into a heap of praying old woman, still as stone, except for the sound of holy muttering occasionally drifting back towards me. I close my own eyes and join her in her devotions from a distance. Suddenly, I am jerked awake as a phone begins to bawl, raising a god-awful racket inside the hard rock walls of the church. The old lady rises, lifts her sweater in search of a pocket, fumbles about, then retrieves her squawking machine, clicks it open, then yells at it something I cannot understand but which I imagine to be "Leave me alone for God's sake! I'm praying here!" Her spiritual composure now completely discombobulated, she rises, lumbers back down the central aisle towards me, and this time, catches my eye, shrugs her shoulders, purses her lips, poofs, then offers to me a wide grin as if I'm in on the joke of it all. I cannot help but smile back, the eyes of both of us twinkling at the uneasy juxtaposition of modernity and antiquity, ring-tones and rosaries, yakking and praying, all mixed up together. In other words: *life*.

I return to the refuge just before opening hour and as I arrive, so also does a tall and slender woman carrying a couple bags of groceries. She sets them down, pulls out a key and opens the door, picks up her groceries, then looking at me for the first time, waves me in. Michaelene is a fit and trim 50's something, maybe even early 60's, and is doing a two-week stint as *hospitalière* of the Sorges refuge. She knows plenty about our pilgrim life; she herself walked to Compostela from her home a few years back and now commits herself to the care of pilgrims like me. Though she lives only twenty kilometers from Sorges, she spends the nights here and often prepares supper for the pilgrims, if there are any. For the moment, she boils water then offers me a cup of warm tea and an apple. She tells me that Monique was here last night, and that she told her to expect me today. Other than Monique yesterday and me today, Michaelene has had no other guests during her stint here so far. This seems to be a pretty strong indication that the flow of pilgrims south is thinning as autumn grows deeper. I discuss it with Michaelene, and we decide together that the Vézelay starters are now running out of their two or three week time allotments for walking and are heading home rather than continuing. I feel a little pang of sadness as I realize I will have even fewer pilgrim companions on the road ahead, at least as far as the Spanish border, which Michaelene estimates, is about 400 more kilometers. Doing the math rather quickly, I estimate I have walked some 1100 kilometers since leaving Leuven.

Michaelene is a delightful companion. She is completely committed to my well being and offers to prepare supper for us both. I admit that I had a rather substantial and filling pizza earlier in the afternoon, but she dismisses my concern, assuring me that dinner will be light and healthy, and gets busy preparing a few pots and pans for the meal.

Michaelene's supper is as light as advertised: a simple soup and a few slices of a baguette accompanied by a little red wine. It is fine. She knows from Monique that I am a priest and seems genuinely pleased to be taking care of me without making any big deal out of my vocation in life. That I am a pilgrim is what most matters to her. After eating, she reads a while even as I prepare my things for tomorrow's walk. Then we both retire for the night.

At 6:30 am, Michaelene is already getting the coffee ready and preparing a few things for breakfast. I peak out my dorm window and see nothing but fog; I can barely make out the church just across the way. Today's destination: Périgueux, a fairly major city on the pilgrim route.

Following breakfast, Michaelene offers to accompany me out of town so I don't lose my way; getting back on the pilgrim path is a bit complicated, she tells me. I accept her proposal without hesitation not only for the security it will provide against a false start to the day's walk, but also because I hate to lose her good company and cheer on this dark morning. As we step outside, we are draped in a damp cloud that makes me stop, drop Gregory to the ground and pull out my rain-jacket before continuing. I also pull the flashlight from the side pouch and place the strap around the crown of my head and flip it on. I want to be seen by oncoming traffic. It feels silly to be so illuminated, but it is better than being wiped out by a Volvo semi-trailer hauling truffles to Paris. We arrive at my jumping-off point; Michaelene gives me a light embrace and turns back towards the refuge. I am on a path lined by trees on either side. The mist is so thick that it is dripping from the branches above me as if it were full-fledged rain. The sound of the drip-drop-drip-drip in the morning silence is beautiful and adds a contrapuntal rhythm to the click-clack-click-click of my sticks and the padding of my boots on the soft earth below.

I am soon into high grass, and my boots are getting soaked as the stuff whips at them. I ditch the official route and detour to a paved road that takes me the twelve miles into Cornille. The fog and mist accompany me the whole way. I have trouble seeing through my glasses; the moisture collects on the lenses then forms into little rivulets that wiggle downward making all that I see rather phantasmagoric. I am weary in my walking this morning. Even more troubling is a tendon on the bottom of my right foot. I have had a very mild case of plantar fasciitis for a couple of years; it comes and goes but never gets too very bad, but today I am feeling it heat up inside my boot. I will need to do more stretching this afternoon and in the coming days.

Beyond Cornille, the fog finally lifts, though the skies remain low and grey. As I walk, I pass a ranch, hundreds of geese overpopulate a large field, moving as one, a cackling carpet of grey. I cry to them: *Flee for your lives, you geese! Make a break for it now or you'll be seeing your livers served up atop little pieces of toast on Christmas tables all over France!* Alas, not a one takes my warning seriously, so I see nothing but *foie gras* in their future.

COQUILLE SAINT-JACQUES 223

Like all the bigger towns and cities along the pilgrim Way, the appearance of busy streets, traffic lights, and flashy storefronts is a bit of a shock after days wandering through France's rural quarters. Périgueux is no exception. Its bigness holds promise of resupplying my small reserve of food stocks and maybe even finding some stronger clothing for the colder pre-winter weather that cannot be far away. The busyness all about is intimidating. The bigness makes me feel small and something of a goofball with my pack and sticks and lumbering manner.

I find my way to the city refuge and settle in. I walk into the center of town to see for myself what is advertised in my guide as the exceptional Saint-Front cathedral. It is no longer so early in the day, so I rush as much as I can rush to get through its doors before they are shut tight for the night. I wander through the streets of Périgueux until I find the church and even from the outside I am dazzled. This escapee from Byzantium boasts a breasty multiplicity of stone domes rising above the chest of the church as if giving suckle to the low sky above. One after another these teats in stone tempt God above to come down and nurse on this earth's milk. "Come be one with us, oh you big God! Get a taste of our life's delights and terrors! Don't stay up there; come on down, *God on High*! Drink with us! Nuzzle with us! Eat with us! Talk with us! Die with us! Take us into yourself even as we take you into ourselves!"

The doors are still open to the cathedral's interior, and I am enthralled as soon as I step over the threshold from city to church. The interior of the domes don't tease or tempt, they cover and mother and hold and enfold. They dissolve anger and settle the dust of worn old resentments. They calm nerves and soothe souls. The darkness within is not absolute; it is touched by enough light from outside to make it holy instead of hellish. Great Roman arches hold the whole thing up like the muscular arms of some patient giant who never moves. The altar and sanctuary are contemporary and somehow fit well within the whole. The altar is square, carvings on the base of wine and wheat recall the altogether earthy roots of the mysteries that are celebrated upon it. This table at the center of this universe declares in its eloquent silence that, indeed, God *does* come down and eat and drink of our joys and terrors, *is* one with us, doesn't remain up there, cozy and aloof in his godhood, but risks it all, dives headfirst from the clouds and crashes through our earth's dark clouds, is born, lives, loves, suffers, dies . . . *avec nous*. I walk through this great story told with no words, a story here whispered in stone, subtly toned by streams of light passing through dark space, mothered by domes from the inside out, all of it subverting our self-pity that largely believes we suffer alone.

After perhaps an hour inside the cathedral, I am politely requested to leave. I ask the usher about Mass, and he tells me to go to the church of

Saint-Martin; there I will find the liturgy beginning at 6:30 pm. I have some time on my hands so do my big-city shopping while I have a chance. I find a funky little sports shop specializing in snowboards that advertises sweat-wicking underwear in its show window, so I go in to ask about a long-sleeve undershirt. The young dreadlocked kid at the cash register has just what I am looking for, he brightly says, and shows me one or two possibilities. I choose one to try on, so he guides me to a dressing room where I strip down to my waist to give it a go. It is tough to get on; the problem is I have worked up a sweat walking through the streets of Périgueux, and the material is sticking to me like duct tape. I finally get it over my head and stretched down to my waist and, outside of the sticking problem, it feels good. I take it off again with as much difficulty as I had getting it on and buy the thing. The amiable hippie gives me a ten percent discount because, he says, it is the last one in the shop, and they are happy to have it gone, but I wonder if he isn't just being kind to an aging pilgrim. As I leave the store, I take a glance back; *snowboards in southern France? How can that be? Wait a second: I must be getting close to the Pyrenees.*

I walk to the Saint-Martin church for Mass and find the church to be a bit on the dingy side compared to the Saint-Front cathedral. Nevertheless, it is filling up with people of all kinds and sorts, and that makes the place come alive in a way very different from my experience in the wide, empty, dark spaces of the cathedral. These human beings all have within their hearts this inexplicable desire to find communion in this life, somewhere, anywhere in this life: communion with one another, communion with their own selves, communion even with their creating God.

Here at Saint-Martin's they are doing something I've never seen before: the bread has been broken, the Lamb of God litany sung, and now the altar servers have just walked to the back of the church, to the very last pew in the church, and are inviting the folks seated there to come forward first to receive communion. *And the last shall be first.* It is taught without a word being spoken. *Amen.*

And so I buy my dinner in a bakery: a big slice of *quiche* accompanied by a bottle of fruit juice. I find a bench in a nearby park and watch people of all ages come and go: kids running like crazy, mothers pushing prams, old folks walking slowly arm in arm. A bunch of well-pierced teens dressed in "Gothic" style clothing with painted hair hang close and happily ignore me as I munch down my eggy *quiche* and sip at my juice. The communion *in there* spreads out here, too. We are all in this mystery-laden universe together, whether we know it or not.

I go home, stretch my tendons, listen to the iPod for a while, hope for a good sleep, and call it a day.

20

Yes and No

The seventh of October, the first of day of a new week, has dawned grey and low and hazy. It is not the weather I would wish for, but I am used to these conditions now; I am feeling good about the coming day's trek, which will be a fairly long one with twenty-six kilometers to knock off before I find myself in Saint-Astier.

The first forty-five minutes or so on the Chemin only get me through Périgueux. I take the city blocks and cross-streets as they come, one after the other, until I am finally amongst field and forest again. The mists of the morning thicken even as the sun rises higher; that sun, a dim white light in the sky, is not bright enough even to make me avert my eyes from its perfectly round form. My glasses are fogging, and then the fog turns to beads, then to drizzles snaking their way downward across the lenses. I stop and take out my rain jacket to protect myself from the damp that is penetrating my shirts and making me feel clammy as I walk. I cover Gregory too with his green canvas.

After almost two hours of walking, I come to the village of Chancelade and find here an Augustinian monastery dating back to the twelfth century. It is still a working house of prayer, and at least a few monks yet inhabit its ancient cells. I would like to take a peak inside, but the great doors to the chapel are locked tight, and there is no sign indicating a Sunday morning Mass available for outsiders like me. A car drives into the gravel lot; a middle-aged man gets out and checks the doors himself, shrugs, then drives off. Another vehicle harboring an elderly woman and her husband, dressed for Sunday, pulls in. They too are disappointed to find the doors solidly locked but get back in their Peugeot to wait. I take a seat on a stone bench and dig out the last of yesterday evening's sandwich from Gregory's top pocket. In the monastery gardens just beyond the parking area, I glimpse a young person dressed in red rain gear wandering among the trees. I wonder if the figure in the mist might be a pilgrim. She approaches, her backpack and wooden walking stick making it clear she is indeed of my wandering tribe. She drops her pack and sits down next to me on the stone bench. We begin talking about our journeys and ourselves. Patricia is Dutch but presently lives in France with her husband. She began her own pilgrimage from their home, walking first to nearby Vézelay, then picking up there the GR 654. She intends to walk at least to Saint-Jean-Pied-de-Port. She prefers the GR to the more direct route I am following precisely because it is less direct and leads her into more interesting territory, the exact reasons why I have eschewed the route as much as possible. She enjoys the woods and doesn't mind the zigs and zags that so annoyed me prior to Vézelay. Patricia, like me, is disappointed that there seems to be no entry into the monastery today, but it is not as if both of us have not already seen the interiors of a lot of these kinds of places. She mentions in passing that today is her birthday, completing thirty years of life. I ask if she plans to spend the night in Saint-Astier, and if so, perhaps I could treat her to a birthday dinner and a glass of wine to mark the occasion. She says she will be staying in Saint-Astier, and mentions the same *chamber d'hôte* that I have reserved, but probably wouldn't be interested in an evening out. In passing, she also mentions that I am the first pilgrim she has met on the Way. Patricia stands, pulls her pack back on and wishes me a good day.

There is still no sign of life in the monastery chapel, though other Mass-seekers have arrived and are looking frustrated with the state of affairs. I myself give up hope on the brothers within, so throw Gregory onto my back, pick up my sticks, and approach a steep trail that takes me up and out of Chancelade.

An hour and a half later, I pass Patricia, who has her poncho spread out beneath her in a grassy field as she nibbles on snacks. We greet one another as old friends, but I keep on walking so that she might continue enjoying her birthday solitude.

At the village of Gravelle, the road finally levels as it picks up the l'Isle River. I am grateful for the change in terrain, but I also notice more the increasing ache coming from the bottom of my right foot that began yesterday. Walking on this flat road makes the pain more noticeable. I can step on it well enough, but it is there, making itself felt and making me a little bit scared about where this could eventually lead. It is beginning to feel like there is a lump under my heel and the arch of my foot, but as long as I can walk, I walk.

The late morning becomes exceedingly foggy, and I have to put on my headlamp for safety as I follow the bank of the highway into Saint-Astier. It has become a singularly unattractive day, and I am feeling my spirits flag. Maybe my foot problem is telling me to take a day off. I hadn't planned on doing so here, but if I can't knock this plantar thing back a bit tonight with massage, stretching, and a big dose of ibuprofen, then maybe a day of rest is what my body is calling for.

I walk and walk, and Saint-Astier never seems to come close. I feel like a suitor being politely stiffed by the object of my affections. The fog hangs low and makes distance seem distant indeed. The first street light and a few odd houses appear through the mist. Now that I am actually in the town, it still takes a good while to walk my way into the center and find my *chamber d'hôte* for the night. As it turns out, it is an old house to which I have to climb down from street level by way of several steps. No one immediately answers my knock. I drop Gregory and sit on the lowest step for a moment, and begin figuring what to do next. Suddenly, I am greeted from the street above as the lady of the house arrives from the grocer. She lets me in, drops off her goods, and shows me to my quarters. My room features a great double window opening out to the l'Isle river that flows wide and swift behind the house. Upon opening the window, the rush of the river flowing over great stones and an old concrete dam make a lovely sound that fills the room. No iPod needed today; I have one of earth's most sonorous songs to fill my soul in this old room. The hymn of the river is accompanied by the smell of its wetness and a vision of variegated green thriving on the riverbanks. Swans are my only companions as I take all this in from my perch above the river. I take my shower, put on dry clothes, launder the damp ones in the sink, then lay myself down for a nap in which the fluvial music carries me into pilgrim dreamland. Roads and steeples and rivers offer themselves to my subconscious, as the bits and pieces of a half-dream that does not quite congeal into a full story.

I awake to find a slim note slipped under my door. It is from Patricia. She writes that she has arrived too, is in the next room, and would like very much to have a birthday dinner with me after all. I am happy for her change of heart on the matter. Her door is closed, so she may be napping as well; I don't knock, but slip the note back under her door with a simple OK! added to her words.

Later, we meet in the hall between our rooms and head out for our supper. On the way out, I ask our landlady if it might be possible to stay a second day so that my sore foot might mend. She advises me that no other guests are expected, so the room is mine for the additional day if I wish. I think I do wish it, but I will decide definitively in the morning. Patricia and I wander through the streets of Saint-Astier, and finally settle into a pleasant pizzeria; we have walked into a world filled to the brim with the aromas of baking bread and frying meat and cheap wine. We take a table, place our order, and when the wine comes, I toast Patricia on her birthday and thank her for allowing me to share this little *fête* with her.

Our pilgrim talk begins. We tell each other our stories from life and from the Chemin. She has been married since a very young woman; her husband is presently attending a conference on Hindu meditation at a Hare Krishna seminary in Belgium, a place that I know; I tell her I have a good friend, one of the monks, living there. For my part, I offer the broad outlines of my life and that I have walked from Belgium.

Patricia asks me if I have had any special experiences along the Way, like mystical experiences, so I share the story of my tears before the crucified Christ in the church of Saint-Léonard. She is delighted to tell me of her own tears in the same church. "Imagine, both of us cried in the same place!" For her, the moment came as she stood before a statue of Mary. Suddenly, she knew Mary, not as a saint, not as the formal Mother of God, but as her *sister*: a sister with whom she has been walking side by side, hand in hand, as sisters do, along this whole *Chemin*, a sister she has known all her life even when she didn't know she knew her. In that moment of *knowing*, she cried at the ancient friendship just revealed to her. Patricia is not a Catholic; in fact, she was raised a Protestant, she tells me, and since her early teenage years hasn't been involved in churchgoing at all. Patricia shares that her present pilgrimage has given her a new appreciation for the power of these churches that we pass through in all these villages and cities along this Chemin: so many people for so many years have prayed in them, they have a life in them that endures for us latter-day visitors. She tells me that as a personal response to experiences such as her encounter with the image of Mary in Saint-Léonard, she now begins her pilgrim day every day by taking quiet time in the village church before taking off on her walk, to "go inside" herself there.

Patricia's mobile phone begins to buzz. She looks at the screen and asks permission to take the call, it being her actual sister on the line. She switches into Dutch as she begins speaking into her small phone. I understand enough to hear her tell her sister: "Yes, I am having a good birthday. I am with another pilgrim tonight in a pizzeria having dinner; he is an old American priest. Yes, he is a very nice man . . . " *Old?* I smile, which Patricia notices; she smiles back with the realization that I understand her Dutch.

Once my dinner companion has wrapped up her visit with her sister, she returns to me. Patricia asks if I am happy being a pilgrim. I hesitate in my response. *Yes and no.* I pause to find worthy words, then explain. *"No" in that I find myself weary often enough; weary of the laundry, the packing up, the weight of Gregory on my back going uphill, tying up boots and untying boots, polyester clothing. "No" for the rain of these past months, which has grown so tiresome day after day, along with the consequent mud, and now it is cold, too. And "no" for the clothes not being dry by the next morning, and having to put on wet underwear, and the tug of a tendon that threatens to blow up on me.*

But also "yes" in the beautiful things of nature that I am privileged to regard close up and with care because I am moving so slowly. I love the solitude, and I love the occasional fellow traveler that I meet, like yourself. I like the opportunity to "go inside" as you describe it. I find solace in the moments of inspiration and revelation, and I love writing about it in my journal. I like knowing that I will know more and understand more about what is happening to me later on, long after the walking is done. "Yes" for the gratitude I feel that so many friends are following me from their homes and praying for me as I go forward. And "yes" for the sense I have that there is a "big picture" beyond me and that I am part of that big picture. "Yes" because it all is a great privilege; this I know, and this I really love about being a pilgrim.

As I end my answer, I realize that Patricia is a better pilgrim than I. She walks more gracefully and struggles less than I and therefore grows less weary than I. She, and the Chemin to Compostelle, are just a more natural fit than am I with the road we share. I don't know why I struggle out here, with the elements, with my body, with my temptations to despair, but there it is, and I am doing my best with what I've got.

It is getting close to bedtime, so I pick up the tab and together, Patricia and this "old priest" walk back to our refuge along the Chemin. If I stay in Saint-Astier tomorrow, which I am now fairly sure I will, I will lose yet another dear pilgrim pal and this one after less than a day together.

Once back in my room, I turn off the light and open the window. I want to both hear the river and behold it for a while. Even through the dark of night, a slight luminescence is visible where the water is being roiled by stones and chunks of broken concrete. This thin, almost invisible, vision of the river is all the more beautiful for its very thinness. This is the thing: the river's dim visibility makes what little is visible all the more precious, and the sound of it all the more dramatic. It is alive whether seen or unseen. Like the stars above the clouds which cover this patch of earth tonight, it does not disappear because I don't see it or don't think about it, or don't care about it; in this, it is so very much like friendship, like love, well, like God.

The universe and all it contains does not disappear because I sleep.

God does not disappear because I do not know him.

I do not disappear though I die.

I toss and turn. I am too warm under this comforter, and the room has become very humid with all my damp clothing hanging about. Midnight comes and goes. Then one, then two. I toss and turn yet more, but eventually slip into a dream forgotten as quickly as it unfolds.

Even as I rise at 6:30 am and walk to the loo and back, I know my foot is asking for a day of rest. The fasciitis is far from relieved. I go back to bed and doze until 7:30 or so. I finally get up, dress, and go downstairs for breakfast. Patricia is at the table having just begun her *petit dejeuner*. I inform her that I am going to take it easy; no walking for me today. Patricia agrees it is the best thing. She and I linger over our croissants and coffee, then about 9:00 am, she decides to begin the day's journey. She throws on her poncho, then her pack, and we step outside into another misty and rather cold morning. She intends to stop at the church for her morning meditation, then head on to Mussidan. We embrace clumsily, and we say we really enjoyed each other's company yesterday, and she thanks me for sharing her birthday with her. Then Patricia climbs the concrete stairs to the street, turns, and disappears into the pilgrim Way.

I return to my room more hermit today than pilgrim. I open the window to the l'Isle river, say my morning prayers and simply dawdle there letting the rush of the waters below pray for me. Even after my prayers, I harbor anxiety about my foot. I turn over in my mind a couple of worst-case scenarios: a painful walk all the way to Saint-Jean-Pied-de-Port, or worse still, a complete breakdown somewhere before the Spanish frontier. I know I had better take advantage of some part of this morning to stretch my tendons, and especially those extending across the bottom of my right foot. I take up a position on the cold floor, lie flat, then cross one leg over the other, then reverse the stretch, then repeat. I sit up and pull the toes of my right foot forward and hold them thus for a while. I do the other foot as a precaution, then repeat and repeat and repeat the course. I wax my boots, eat lunch, stretch and exercise again, pray, gaze out my grand window upon a grand river, and so goes my morning, my afternoon, my hermit evening.

I return to conscious life at 6:15 am, stretch while still in bed, then take a look out my black window to see if the night sky is giving away any portents about what I might expect from the coming day's weather. I see little through the glass, so open the panes to the cool of the outdoors and the always lovely song of the river below. Now I see it: a star, then two, then three, shyly making themselves known to me below. The clouds are breaking up, and so I trust a good day for walking is ahead.

Even better news this morning is that my plantar fasciitis seems to have pretty much disappeared, and I trust I have beaten this beast. I'm going to be fine.

21

For C. J.

Following breakfast, I round up my gear, pay my bill, and step outside. I am met with grey mist. So the morning stars have tricked me. The fragile front they earlier revealed has been closed by a superior force: the heavy damp of this Dordogne October. I click-clack my way out of town less than pleased, but at least very pleased that my foot is feeling fine. My worst-case scenarios won't be coming true any time soon.

My road tags along the l'Isle River and so remains fairly level with few climbs or descents to slow me down. The road crosses the river several times, and I enjoy these moments of walking above the turbulent waters, their roll under my feet lifting me just enough from the pavement to carry me on. At one point, the route leaves the D3 pavement that I have been following for days, offering the promise of a substantial shortcut. I take it but am bitterly disappointed to find myself deep in mud that sucks me down, followed by tall, wet grass that grabs at my ankles, holding me back and making me curse and swear and despair. At least the new wax I rubbed into the leather of my Meindls is working, and my feet stay dry within.

The dull pain from below has returned; my healing is not so complete as I had earlier imagined. I continue on some ten or twelve kilometers to Douzilac. There I meet an older woman on the road, tall rubber boots on her feet, rubber gloves protecting her hands, and a cotton apron across her front and tied behind her back. She has just dumped a bag full of garbage into a village bin across the muddy street. Before reentering her fenced yard, she engages me with a warm smile and asks me where I began my pilgrimage. At first I answer *en Saint-Astier*, but then realize she is asking about the *very beginning* of my pilgrimage, so I correct myself and inform her of my first steps *en Belgique*. She smiles wide in approval and amazement, then wishes me a very heartfelt *"Bon courage!"* Her smile lifts my flagging spirits and self-preoccupation at least for a few moments. I find my way to the town center and take a rest in the local *église*. Ironically, my pause in church seems to have aggravated matters; as I return to my feet and carry on down the road, the tendon flares and is no longer just a dull ache, but a veritable pain, sharp and edgy and almost enough to make me cry. *This is not how I want to end my life as a pilgrim!*

From Douzilac, the road climbs steeply, finally leveling off atop a wooded plateau. It is pretty up here, and I try to let the green and brown of the place fill me with wonder, but my efforts are half-hearted under the burden of a troubled foot. I stop alongside the road, lay down Gregory and dig into my medical kit. I pop a couple of ibuprofen tablets with hopes of moderating the pain some, and indeed, as I walk on, it does seem to help considerably. The road now descends, leading me back to the river and the village of Saint-Louis-en-l'Isle. The ibu's don't hold. My final four kilometers through the mists to Mussidan are full of ache and despair. *Saint-Jacques: aidez-moi!*

I pass through a deep grove of chestnut trees; I hear a sort of hymn of nature I have never encountered before: I hear *autumn*. A single acorn high above gives way in free-fall towards the earth. It strikes another acorn, which strikes another, and pretty soon, a whole battery of acorns cascading, striking, banging, bouncing, ever more and more, and with the great moisture about, the sounds resonate into a most fulsome rush of altogether random and nutty percussion, and then it slows and subsides and silence reigns. I feel like *Saint-Jacques* just sang to me. No words, just a brief refrain of care from above. I will try to remember this sound and hope I might hear it again before I pass from this world.

I walk into Mussidan and find it, at least so far, a rather unattractive town. I pass by the church, probably a nineteenth century construction, and enter to make my thanksgiving for having traveled safely today. A lone man is within, kneeling, curled over his fists, deep into some great sorrow. I pass by, trying not to disturb him, and find a place for Gregory and me to sit, lean, support one another. Click and Clack are set to one side. Before me is a baptismal font, a small garden of river stones neatly installed around its base. Each stone has a name painted on it. A small sign informs me that each name belongs to a child baptized here during the past year. It is a beautiful thing. I will try to remember this too. Even with these stones and those tumbling acorns to brighten my mood this day, I feel I am sinking. God knows that burdened man behind me has a load of troubles far deeper than mine, but mine seem burdensome enough. The old temptation to despair of the Way, to abandon this mission, reasserts itself. *Crap.*

By the time I get up to leave, the sorrowing man has already disappeared back into the mist-draped city. I find the public refuge the town makes available to pilgrims not far from the church. I locate the key and enter. Well, I enter one door that opens into the kitchen and bath. A sign within tells me that to enter the sleeping quarters, I must go back outside, pass through a separate door, and climb a staircase to my bedroom for the night. I take Gregory upstairs with me but leave Click and Clack below. This is a simple place, a little dingy, and there is no heat. I know my clothes will not dry by morning. My foot hurts. I am alone here. Really alone. The wave of pilgrim despair grows deeper as I settle into my bedroom. I feel abandoned, useless, pointless. Why keep going? This is meaningless. *NO! Remember the acorns, you fool! Remember walking into God, you idiot! Remember Patricia and Michaeline and the Trappist Tramp! This is something GOOD you are doing here! This is OF GOD, you whiny wimp of a pilgrim!* Okay. I will try again to not give up. I will not despair of the Way. I've walked almost a thousand kilometers, maybe more already; I can't give up those walked kilometers because of a foul mood.

There is a great oak tree just beyond my window; in the unrelieved mists of this day it looks mysterious, and I hope that it will drop a single acorn, leading to a cascade of acorns rattling happily to the ground. I want to hear autumn one more time. I want the oak to speak to me and tell me to keep going. I want to be assured that what I am doing is a good thing. No acorn falls. Silence reigns. *What the hell. I'll just go take my nap and try to sleep off this pissiness.*

Once settled in upstairs the phone rings on the stand next to my bed. I answer and find Gene and Caroline calling from Barcelona where they are vacationing. The conversation carries the tone of gloom that has been hanging over me much of the day. We discuss my foot issues and ways to further care for it. Gene recommends lots of stretching. I pose to them the issue of, foot allowing, whether I should just stop in Saint-Jean-Pied-de-Port and call the pilgrimage complete, or plan on continuing through Spain, retracing my pilgrim route from four years ago. Caroline encourages me to not make any decisions just yet. There is still plenty of time. A cheerier day will greet me tomorrow or the next day or even the next. I'll know when I know, she assures me. They are sympathetic to the weariness of the Chemin. I'm not crazy or lazy, they tell me. They wish me a good night and a better tomorrow and end with a touching "we love you" that in itself softens the hard edges of this grey day. I turn off the light and lay my head down on my pillow, and look forward to awaking to a new, better day.

I do not sleep. I toss and turn until 2:00 am. I get up, use the bathroom, dig out my iPod, plug the wired buds into my ears and listen to Fernando Ortega's lovely *Grace and Peace*. It soothes me and in the dark, it feels as if Paul and Jesus and the Father and the Saints are singing these words to me, especially to me, in my pilgrim predicament: *Grace and peace to you, our brother . . .* I have long used those same words to end my own letters, and now they come back to me, *for me.* The hymn ends, and I pull the buds from my ears and hope for sleep in the silence. It eludes me for another hour, but somewhere further into the night, the dreams come, but they are weird and unconnected and unsatisfying.

I awake at 6:30 am. With only a little more than three hours of sleep, I get up to look outside; through the dark I see rain dripping from the eaves. Harrumphing at the sight and with the hope of getting another hour of sleep, I return to bed, but once again, I remain quite awake. I am in no hurry to get going; perhaps the rain will ease as daylight comes. After an hour of dozing, I definitively get out of bed and begin my morning routines. I concentrate special attention on stretching the tendons in the bottom of my foot. I carry my things downstairs for my simple breakfast. I put the coffee on and dig out my day-old *pain aux raisin* and *croissant.* I sip my warm coffee until it is down to the black sediments, rinse the cup, take out the garbage, and walk into the rainy morning. Passing the great oak to my left, I greet it with a less than hearty *bonjour,* and with head down against the rain, follow the Chemin south.

As the kilometers pass, the blanket of cloud above slowly tears and splits into cotton ball clouds, giving me occasional stretches of warm sunshine interspersed with longer stretches of grey and cold. I relish the breaks and am happy that they are growing longer and warmer as I proceed. At about noon, I take a rest in the church-yard of the hamlet of Fraisse and eat an apple and a few nuts. I examine the sky, and though it is yet dominated by the week's clouds, the bits and pieces of blue sky above restore a sense that there is a bigger, warmer, brighter reality beyond the grim and grey that tends to dominate my attention. "Come on. Cheer up, little pilgrim," the blue above whispers.

As I walk today, the plantar fasciitis is always present, but dully, and for the most part, I walk with reasonable ease. Every once in a while, it sends a sharper ache through my foot, but I override the zing of it. But then a particularly angry shot of lightning heads north to my brain, and I have to stop for a moment. I swear at my pilgrim patron: *Saint-Jacques: why are you letting this happen to me? If you want me to come, then for God's sake, aidez-moi! Walk with me here!* As soon as the words slide aloud from my mouth, my pilgrim imagination conjures up the little man, grizzled, bearded, and robed in his brown wool rags, floppy hat with the cockleshell sewn into the raised brim. And he *does walk with me,* step by step, not talking, just walking. It is as vivid a daydream as I have ever had, and it consoles me. My doldrums break up like the clouds above, and cracks of sunshine and blue sky grant me a helpful dose of hope. Jacques and I walk this way for a long time, through the woods of oak and pine and along the paved roads toward La Cabanne.

With Jacques beside me, I come to a crossroad and find there a real man, old and wrinkled like Jacques, but wearing farmer clothes and tall rubber boots against the day's mud, collecting his post. He has a great twinkle in his eye and nods to me in silent greeting. Using my pole as an arrow, I wordlessly ask him if I am to go left or right. His hand points to the right, then with a laugh ambles over to me for a conversation. He shakes my hand and asks the usual questions of passing pilgrims. He is impressed that I am an American walking through this backwater of France. He is even more impressed, taking on a serious look out of respect, that I have walked all the way from *Belgique*. He then says the words that make my day, or better, make my week, the words Saint-Jacques would say if he were in a talking mood: "*Vous êtes très courageux.*" "You are very courageous," he tells me. *Well, yes, I am!* The old man salutes me as I carry on: "*Bon courage, monsieur!*"

Five minutes further on, I hear my name called from behind me. It is a woman's voice. This is extraordinary; am I imagining it? "Kevin! Kevin! Are you Kevin?" I turn to see who is calling. A woman on a sturdy bike is pedaling up to me. She is smiling widely. I don't have any idea what this is about. As she puts a foot down to stabilize her bicycle loaded with packs, she asks me again: "Are you Kevin from Spokane?" *Yes. But how do you know me?* The middle-aged lady, all trim and athletic, explains: "Michaelene in Sorges told me about you when I read your message in the *livre d'or*. My son went to school in Spokane for a year! I've been looking for you for days. I thought I'd never catch up to you, but here you are! This is a miracle!"

Her name is Hildegard from somewhere near Frankfurt. She tells me that this is the second segment of a three-year pilgrimage; last year she bicycled from Frankfurt to Vézelay. This year she is cycling from Vézelay to Saint-Jean-Pied-de-Port. Next year, she tells me she will *walk* the Spanish segment of the pilgrim Way. She explains that she has learned finally that she is missing out on much of the pilgrim experience because of her speed and dependence on her two-wheeled machine to get her down the road. I agree; walking is not so easy, but the experience is deeper and richer: slow food for the soul. We talk a little about my hometown, its downtown waterfall, its wonderful walking trail that goes for miles clear into Idaho, its Jesuit university, Gonzaga, where her son and I both studied, and before fifteen minutes of such chatter have passed, we have become the dearest of friends standing out here in the middle of an obscure French road all by ourselves. What now bonds us is not Spokane, but this Via and our vocation as pilgrims. Hildegard wishes me well, rebalances herself on her heavy-laden bicycle, and leaves me behind. *Man, that was one of the briefest pilgrim friendship yet! Courage, Hildegard!*

After more kilometers through forests of oak, I pick up the D20 highway and follow the pavement into the hamlet of La Cabane where I have a reservation for the night at a private home. At a turn in the road, I catch sight of a pilgrim conch on the gate of a farmhouse to the left of the highway and make my way to the fenced garden. This is my place for the night. A very large and shaggy dog ambles up to the gate and woof-woofs happily at me. The dog is followed by a smiling and waving lady who jaunts across the yard to let me in. She lifts the latch on the gate, swings it wide, and greets me with a grand *bienvenue*. She introduces herself to me as *Madame* Noëlle, untypically inviting me to use her first name, and then presenting the great dog of the house to me as Romeo. I ask if there is not also a Juliette, and Noëlle laughs loudly, catching the Shakespearean joke with delight.

Noëlle leads me to her home, a single-story, low-slung ranch house with the roof extending out over a busy patio running the length of the place. She introduces me to two friends who are visiting her for a few days, Nicole and Martine. She apologizes that her husband is not here to also welcome me; he is in the hospital for the moment, but I don't quite understand why. They all graciously welcome me and invite me to ditch my muddy boots on the porch. I feel utterly embraced by these ladies who are all smiles and laughs as we get to know one another. The house within features dark, hand-hewn beams, everything wood and brick, with the ashy smell of cold fireplace subtly wafting throughout. I'm shown to my room, do my laundry in the bathroom sink, then as I hang up the clothing on the laundry lines behind the barn, I notice that the clouds have definitively dissipated, and the afternoon is clear and sunny. I join Noëlle near the front porch, and we look out to the sky to the north from where I have just walked; a heavy front of clouds hangs low over the distant forested hills. A rainbow has formed. A roll of thunder unfolds then dissipates. I am glad to have left that cloud behind and stand now in this sunshine. All I need now is a dove carrying a palm frond to declare definitive peace between the weather and me. Noëlle stands in just fine for Noah. She asks me if walking alone is not too hard. I hesitate. *It is hard, but I am doing it.*

Noëlle gets busy on dinner while I settle in a lawn chair to soak up the last of the day's sunshine and the light breezes that caress my cheeks. Dinner is served at a large table, and over *confit du canard*, sautéed vegetables, sliced spuds cooked in dark duck juice, long loaves of *baguettes*, and ample glasses of Bordeaux, the four of us have a grand old time, story-telling and laughing and coming to know each other ever better. Full and giddy with life, friendship and not a little wine, I finally excuse myself from the table and head to my room for what I hope will be a much needed good night's sleep. As I end my prayers for the day, I feel that I am finally out from under my grey pilgrim cloud and am grateful to Noëlle, Hildegaard, the old man collecting his mail, and Saint-Jacques, who walked with me today when I needed him most.

With morning, the feast from last night continues over a not so petit *petit dejeuner*. Nicole, Martine, Noëlle, and I relish our sense of being sisters and a brother, of being at home with one another, and I put off as much as I am able any thought of departure, but the moment to retrieve my Meindle boots from the front porch and work my feet back into them comes. I don't want to leave this dream refuge. I give each of the ladies a double kiss on the cheeks, then load Gregory's straps over my shoulders, and buckle another in front. I give Romeo an ear-rub, then take Click and Clack in hand and with the eastern sky pink with dawn, I walk out the gate, cross the D20 highway and take a back road southward.

As I mosey through fields and pass among farmhouses, the sky above me is a miracle of spotless blue. The sun climbs steadily and warms me deliciously. I must stop, drop Gregory for a moment and remove my jacket. The fog and cold and mist and rain and mud have passed. To my right I notice a vineyard, the grape-laden vines strung to their posts and wires with care and precision. Harvest cannot be far off. This is the first such vineyard since my Bourgogne days, months ago. Then the grapes were small, hard and green; now they are full and rich and packed purple with juice. Oh, how far I have traveled as measured by the vine! Time passes. The seasons follow one another. All things living grow, give up their fruit, die, and are reborn in the succeeding generation. I feel as if these present vines are friends from my past, once young, now grown old. They welcome me back into their lives, and I welcome them back into my own. *Everything growing from the earth: bless the Lord!*[1]

Soon enough, the terrain changes, and I find myself in the midst of fields and pastures dedicated to cows and bulls and gamboling calves. As I turn a corner and follow a single ribbon of cow-dunged pavement, I am stopped in my tracks by a herd being moved down the road to another, fresher pasture. A farmer and his wife prod, guide, and push the cattle forward. I admire their skill in getting this mooing mass of beef down the road. They are pros. They succeed with little fuss, and before long, the woman returns to her other labors while the old guy buttons his herd into its pasture, securing the gate and returning back up this road towards me. As he draws closer, I see from his face that he must be well into his sixties. He

---

1. Daniel 3:76

looks worn and tired. He greets me with the simple words: "*À Compostelle?*" *Oui*, I tell him and then respond to the usual questions for the pilgrim from afar. Eventually, the farmer asks me what I do for a living, besides walking, of course. I tell him I am a priest, and in response, he shakes his head in sad disgust, not at me, but at the situation of the church right here. "We have almost no priests anymore," he tells me. "The few we have are not for us in these small towns. Our churches are closed. We have nowhere near to go on Sunday morning any longer. Mass is only found in the big cities nowadays. The times are changing, and we are left behind. It is the same with our villages and our farms. My own children do not want this work, this life, this farm. They all want to live in Paris," he adds with obvious disdain for Paris. "Who will do this work after me? Who will produce the milk for our grandchildren *after me*? Milk will become the new petroleum," he goes on with a sour smile, "its price will only go up and up and up because there will be less and less and less." He sighs again, looks up at me, straight into my eyes, and lets me see into his: "*Bon courage, monsieur.*" And I respond: *Et bon courage à vous, monsieur.*

The change in weather is not the only prayer answered this morning. My plantar fasciitis is behaving. I can feel it, but it is not paining me nor slowing me down. Today's walk will only amount to about fifteen kilometers, so I have high hopes that healing has happened, maybe not completely but enough to get me on to where I must go. I thank Saint-Jacques for his intervention on my behalf, and practically run up the hills and down the other sides of this rolling countryside. After a steep and long climb, I gain the top of a substantial hill that displays below a panorama of a great plain. The fields and the vineyards and the Dordogne River snaking among them below and even the birds winging by at eye level are lovely in their expansiveness, glimmering under the October sun, proclaiming in the way of nature the grandness of their creator. I find myself in a kind of heaven up here. A quiet ecstasy takes hold. The vision from this height engenders joy. Just joy. Unadulterated joy. Unadulterated knowing. Unadulterated God. I raise Click and Clack, and even with Gregory on my back, we spin and dance a little jig together. Yes, from this joy, this knowing, this God who grasps me now, everything else follows, creation, birth, life, love, *courage*, mission, grace, death, falling into God's hands forever . . . It all makes sense. The unified theory of everything. I drop my sticks and Gregory and fall in the tall grass, arms and legs spread as if to make a snow angel and here I rest. *Merci!*

Okay, I've had my mountaintop moment for the day, but it is time to get back to the world below; Sainte-Foy-la-Grande with its streets and houses and shops and people awaits me. The climb down into the city is a steep and rather dangerous one. It is little more than a goat-path pocked with stones and made slippery by wet grass and mud. I slowly and cautiously pick my way down, the work made more difficult, of course, by the weight on my back, but my sticks keep me balanced and upright all the way down.

Saint-Foy is grand enough to qualify as a pretty good-sized city with a bustling commercial center cut through by the even more grand Dordogne River. My route brings me first to the river, the right bank of which offers a fine path with the occasional bench for the young to nuzzle and the old to rest. I have a reservation in a parish house, now converted to pilgrim use. I find the front door, but it is locked tight with no key in sight. I drop Gregory on the front stoop and search out my mobile phone to call the lady, Madame Colette, with whom I spoke yesterday to make my arrangements. She assures me she will be there in just a few minutes, but even as I end the call, another lady drives by, sees me, pulls over, and gets out to assist me. She hastily introduces herself as Françoise, also a member of the team that has established this refuge. She has a key, directs me in, and begins showing me around, pointing out in particular, the *livre d'or*, which she insists, I *must* sign before I depart in the morning. The kitchen is on the main floor; the bedrooms and bath are up a steep wooden staircase. I drag Gregory and Click and Clack up the stairs and find two great rooms, each with four beds. The choice of eight beds leaves me stymied for a moment, then I make a completely arbitrary choice in the room to the left, Françoise following me in and opening the shades to let in the light of the early afternoon. This is one of those simple kindnesses that could so easily be overlooked, but I do not overlook it. It touches me and makes me feel God as much as the grand view from the height above the Dordogne. Françoise explains to me that this is a new venture; she and her friends, being pilgrims themselves, felt a need to have a refuge here in Sainte-Foy-la-Grande, so they worked with the local priest and went to see the local bishop in Périgueux who graciously gave them permission to use this house as a pilgrim refuge. The pastor now lives elsewhere in town. It has only been open a few months, and the numbers of pilgrims passing the night here are not yet high; they are good enough. The numbers aren't important: we care for one pilgrim at a time, Françoise tells me. Her pilgrim pals, Colette and Reina, show up briefly to cheerily welcome me. How am I doing? They ask. *Bon. Très bon.* I reply. *I will go on.*

Saint-Jean-Pied-de-Port, where I began four years back and where I must at least finish this year, feels so close now I can almost see it through this open window.

I awake an hour before my alarm. It is 6:00 am and still dark. I get out of bed and open the shade to peer out over the Dordogne and towards the city center. Fog reigns. I can barely see the streetlights across the wide river. My spirits, so high last night, plunge for a moment, but I rescue them from free-fall by telling myself fog offers no great obstacle and at least it is not raining. On the mantel of the cold and empty fireplace is a plastic bottle shaped like Our Lady of Lourdes. Inside is water, the healing waters of Bernadette's home town in the French Pyrenees not so far from here. I could use a dose of Mary's healing touch, so I take off the boot and sock of my right foot and sprinkle it liberally with the Lourdes water and pray a Hail Mary as I do so. I am afraid for this foot. Though I had a good day yesterday, this morning, even before pulling on a boot, it is already aching.

I am out the door and heading across the wide bridge over the Dordogne River at 8:00 am. I walk enveloped in fog. As I cross into the center of Sainte-Foy, I enter the Department of Gironde, leaving behind the Dordogne, which has hosted me for so long. For some reason, those who rule over this department, in their peculiar wisdom, have decided that their government should be the only agency putting up arrows and directional signs, even for pilgrims on foot. I have been warned that the little yellow arrows I have been following since Vézelay and which correspond exactly to my paper guide and maps, will disappear now that I have crossed into the Gironde; from here on, they have been replaced by the governmental versions, which do not necessarily correspond to the guide prepared by the *Amis de Saint-Jacques de Compostelle*. So beside the morning's soupy fog, I now have this bureaucratic silliness to be concerned with. I work my way through the streets of Sainte-Foy-la-Grande and pick up the busy highway D672. I must walk very carefully here for the speeding traffic is fairly constant, and I am mostly hidden from view by the mists surrounding me. I choose to follow my *Amis* guide rather than the departmental arrows, which makes interpreting the various rights and lefts and straight-aheads a double chore.

The highway takes a left turn at Saint-Andrés, and there I leave it to climb a steep dirt track into vineyard country. From here on, the day's walk is full of ups and downs as the route angles its way among the squared off plats of vines. I draw up and over a substantial rise and from a distance hear the sounds of engines and gears and spinning machinery. The road takes a gentle turn to the right, and I spy the source of the commotion: harvest. A tall blue machine rides up and over the vines like a long-legged creature. It has fingers that spin and shake the grapes from the vines and somehow collects them within its raised belly. When full, it takes its load to a waiting truck and dumps it within, then returns to the next row of vines.

The technology at work here distracts me for a few moments from my greater concern this morning: My foot is still aching. I can walk, but I am feeling every step. My dousing of that inflamed tissue with Lourdes water is not having the desired effect, though the problem is still a long-shot from being a "pilgrim-stopper". I back up the Lourdes water by singing to myself the refrain from Ortega's *Grace and Peace*. Over and over the simple mantra repeats itself: *Grace and peace, grace and peace, grace and peace to you from God our Father in the Lord Jesus Christ* . . .

I take a break in the hamlet of Caplong, finding refuge in a small stone edifice at the entry to the cemetery and churchyard. As I munch on an apple, my phone beeps, and so I dig it out of Gregory's top pouch. I read there a text message from Caroline reporting that something terrible has happened to Gene's grandson back in the US; C. J., a twenty-year-old, is suffering from schizophrenia and had a major break last night, leading to hospitalization. They ask me to pray for the boy. I quickly text back, that I surely will, all the rest of the day, and tomorrow too. Mental illness is such a burden, one that I can hardly understand. I know melancholy well enough and have a few times in life slipped into depression, but they have never lasted long. A major illness like this is different; it is one that must be borne for a lifetime, controllable only with daily medication. This is something I cannot even imagine. I am lucky. It could so easily be otherwise. What would life be without the experience of joy to balance its burdens? I can imagine many things, but this is rather beyond my powers. All the more reason to walk for those who suffer in this way today. C. J.'s illness is so much more serious than my achy foot; *if a miracle of healing is in order here, then let his take precedence over mine!*

A long final pull uphill is required before I complete today's nineteen-kilometer walk and enter the small town of Pellegrue. I try to make each step of the way a prayer for C. J. Click taps, "Bless!" Clack taps, "C. J!" Click taps, "Heal!" Clack taps, "C. J!" And so it goes down the road.

I was informed yesterday when I made my reservation for the town's refuge that I would find the key at the bar at the town square. I find a bar and enter but am told by the aging waitress that I'm in the wrong place: "Go around the corner to the *other* bar, and you will find your key." I follow her directions, and sure enough, there is the *other* bar, and I approach the bartender who happily offers me the key and wishes me a pleasant stay in Pellegrue. I'm not sure how to find the refuge, so a young man nursing a beer and a cigarette at the far end of the bar offers to guide me. He speaks English rather well and engages me as we walk across the street to the town's visitor's center. The refuge is accessed through a doorway just behind the center. The young fellow tells me to call on him if I have any other needs and leaves me as I slowly climb the steep stairs to my room for the night. It is a pleasant place, though fairly small. It offers to the pilgrim a small kitchenette, a couple of bunk beds, a decent bathroom, and a small table. I drop my sticks and pack and return then to the bar for lunch. The bartender welcomes me back, and I put in my order for a cheese sandwich and a forty-centiliter mug of lager.

After lunch, I follow the side street past my refuge up to the town church set on the highest point of the village. From the outside, it is a strange affair: the portal is clearly Romanesque, but the upper level rising above a Gothic window has been cut off in a horizontal line from left to right, and added to the whole, a very weird tower with a bull-nose for its head, looking more like an Islamic minaret than anything native to French Catholicism. Within, it is a different story. The interior is lovely with its Roman roundness. I take a seat in a wooden pew near the tabernacle with the intention of further fulfilling my promise to pray for young C. J. Before I focus on that intention, I notice that the windows on the right side of the church have been filled with the modern stain-glass of the Loire studios of Chartres. This is the same chunky, angular, faceted glass that filled my childhood parish church back in Spokane with color and imagery. This is the glass that formed much of my religious imagination as a child, and I am glad to be near it again at this moment; its presence here makes me feel at home, so far from home. A lady is busy cleaning the floors and arranging flowers around the altar. I can pick up their aroma even from here. I promised Caroline and Gene to light a candle for C. J., but I see none about. I ask the lady if there are not some available; she tells me that they make too much smoke and dirty the walls, so they have been prohibited. This is probably the only church in all of France that is protected by such a concern. The candle for C. J. will have to wait for another day along the pilgrim Way.

I like watching the woman about her work. She is busy but in a tranquil way. She knows what she is doing and does it well. It is impressive in its smallness. It is an act of love and an act of faith, and maybe in some way too, an act of hope: hope that by keeping these old buildings clean and beautiful and *ready*, people might one day return to them for solace and thanksgiving and remembering. In this place of hope, I pray for C. J.'s mind, and I pray for my foot.

When I end this day and crawl into bed, my heart begins to flutter. I turn over to my right side to feel less the irregularities of my atrial fibrillation. Now I add a prayer to my list: let this bumpy heart calm down before I awake; I want all the energy my body can afford for tomorrow's twenty-five kilometer march into La Reole.

I awake on this Saturday morning with my heart stable and my foot feeling pretty good. As the sun rises, the sky is clear and there is no fog; it is going to be beautiful day. I pass the church, head out of town, and make my way towards La Reole. My foot feels okay, though not great. The route takes a steep run uphill. As I climb, the ache at the bottom of my foot increases, and I begin to favor it, making me limp slightly. With yet more walking, it is getting worse. The limp grows more pronounced. I am only about three kilometers out, and I feel increasing panic as the fascia seems to become ever more inflamed. My route diverges from the paved road, the arrows directing me now along ill-defined trails through vineyards. I am glad for the softer ground under my boots since it seems to ease the growing ache from below. Soon enough, I am lost and wandering about looking for the next arrow and trying to figure out how the directions in my guide correspond to the terrain I find myself in. My frustration level increases as I take guesses as to where I should proceed. One wrong guess, and I will be in big trouble out here. The tall grass that has overcome the trail is wet and whips at my ankles. The extra lifting of my legs to escape the grass's grasp seems to be aggravating my sore foot. This is a bad combination I've got going on here: pain and disorientation at the same time.

Eventually, I am relieved to discover anew the governmental pilgrim arrows directing me forward. The disorientation issue now resolved; the pain remains a primary concern. I limp down the road and arrive in the village of Saint-Ferme. I have walked only five of my projected twenty-five kilometers, but it has taken me over two hours to do so. I am failing. The limp is now so pronounced that I can hardly balance myself. I am almost hopping on my left foot as if it were a pogo stick, balanced to the left and right by Click and Clack, while I put as little pressure as possible on the aching right foot. How to describe this? It is as if I have a broomstick stuck in the bottom of my boot from front to back, or perhaps a dull knife, and with each application of pressure, the foreign object below burns its presence into my foot and leg.

The only thing grand about Saint-Ferme is the massive abbey that dominates the village. It is long ago abandoned as an abbey, though the church remains as a place of prayer and worship. On a better day I would delight in wandering about the place, but today I mostly pass it by as I head for a park bench in the small *place* in front of the church. I drop Gregory on the bench and set Click and Clack in the bend of the seat, then sit down myself and hurriedly take off my boot and sock to take a look at the problem below. There is some redness, and it is very sensitive to the touch. *I don't know how I can go on.* That is my first thought, but not yet *I cannot go on,* and a long ways still from *this pilgrimage is over.* I swallow back the desperation that is growing in my gullet. I take a deep breath and tell myself: *first things first; this is a pilgrimage after all.* I put my sock and boot back on and limp up to the church and enter into its voluminous darkness, formed by great stone walls and a broad roof above, broken only by small Roman windows letting light slip in as angular slices cutting through the space like knives. I find a tray of vigil candles and light one for C. J. and another for me, then sit for awhile in the silence, trying not to feel, trying not to think, for fear of where those feelings and thoughts might lead.

I hobble out into the bright October sunlight and retake my place near Gregory. I reach into his pouch and pull out my phone. I don't know what to do next, so I'll text Gene and Caroline. *Foot is very bad. Can hardly walk. Call.* It seems like the message takes a long time to go, so I take a look at the signal bars on the phone's screen and see barely one. *Oh great.* At least there is enough signal to get the text message sent, but to talk? I notice a *boulangerie* across the street so limp down to see if there might be an attractive snack there to give me solace. A man dusty with flour is at the counter, so I buy a *pain du raisin* from him and take it back to my bench in the *place*. The phone rings, and it is Gene: "What's going on?" he asks. I begin to tell him, but before I get very far into the story I lose the signal, and we are cut off. I limp about to see if I can find a better signal. It rings again, and I get a clearer connection, so I begin again. He suggests I rest a while and apply some Flexium, the potent analgesic cream he lent me when my knee gave out back in July. I finally say the words I have been fighting against speaking or even thinking; they tumble out without me wanting them to come out: *Gene, I don't think I can walk any further.* I despair at their escape.

Always the problem solver and supremely pragmatic Gene begins listing options for me: rest a while and see if it's better in an hour or two, if not, see the local doctor; if worse comes to worse, catch a bus to the next town with services. *Okay. Let me check with the baker and see what's available. I'll call you back when I know something.* I hang up and slowly make my way to the bakery. The baker's news is not good: There is no bus service here. There are no taxis here. There is a doctor here, but it is Saturday, and she most probably is not around. *Then just how do I get out of here if I can't walk out of here?* He shrugs his shoulders and gives me the classic French puff through his pursed lips. *Great.*

Well, it is not all bad: the closest town with bus service might be Monsegur, another five kilometers down the road. There is a taxi there, he assures me. He then digs out his phone book and begins the incredibly labored process of running his finger down long columns of names and numbers looking for the taxi company; when one column runs out, he proceeds to the next, then turns the page and repeats the slow search. I am increasingly frustrated and desperate. Finally, he finds a number and writes it on a scrap of paper for me. I return outside to make the call. Just then a car carrying a young couple drives into the *place*. They get out of the vehicle and are speaking English with an Irish lilt; they walk up to the church for a look-see. When they return, I approach them and explain my predicament and ask

FOR C. J.   245

about a ride out of here. They would be happy to help me but are in a rush to the airport in Bordeaux for their flight back to Dublin. But, they assure me, they have friends who are on their way here and aren't in a rush, so he'll just call them and see if they can come and pick me up. The gentleman makes the call and then reports to me that within forty-five minutes his friends will be here, and they will be more than happy to take care of me. *I am saved.* They take off in a rush, and I call Gene to tell him my escape from La Ferme is now assured. Then I sit and eat my *pain du raisin* and wait. And wait. And wait. An hour and a half pass, and no friends arrive.

I call the taxi number given me by the baker but get no answer. I return to the baker. He tells me there is also a taxi in La Reole. As before, he labors over the phone book listings, but eventually finds a number and writes it on the same scrap of paper as before. I return outside and find a place near Gregory with a couple bars on my phone and make the call. I'm in luck: the call is picked up. The taxi driver tells me he is in Bordeaux right now with a passenger and wouldn't be able to pick me up until late tonight. I ask if there is another taxi service in either Monsegur or La Reole; he laughs and tells me he is the only taxi in *both* Monsegur and La Reole.

I return yet again to the baker and report my completely desolate news. I now know with full surety that I cannot walk the five kilometers to Monsegur, much less the twenty to La Reole. The pain in my foot is growing more sharp with every hour that passes. Even without Gregory on my back, I am having great difficulty just managing the short distance from my park bench in the *place* to the *boulangerie* and back again. Before the baker can shrug his shoulders, purse his lips, and get his puff out, his wife appears carrying a small white poodle in her arms. She smiles at me, evidently notices my distress, and asks her husband what is wrong. He explains briefly, then she gives me a broad smile and orders her spouse in no uncertain terms to give me a ride to La Reole; she'll tend to the bakery while he's away. He accepts her order with cheery resignation, then directs me to get my equipment while he brings his bread delivery truck around to the front.

This is all moving so quickly. A couple hours ago, I was a pilgrim on the road to La Reole, and now, suddenly, I am lame and being carried in a bread truck across this rolling road to La Reole, vineyards on every side and as far as the eye can see in every direction. *I should be walking through this, for God's sake!* The baker is amiable enough as we bump along down the small road, but doesn't have much to say, nor do I. He asks me where I want to be dropped off: in the town center or at the train station. I decide to go to the train station to check out the schedule in case I choose to go on to Bordeaux for assistance. The baker pulls into the parking lot in front of the small train station. We get out, I collect my things from the back of his truck, pushing aside the day's few remaining *baguettes* to get at them, then offer him twenty euros for the ride. He grins and puts up his hand in a "stop" gesture, and says something like, "what are friends for?" I wave as he drives away, then try to enter the station, but find the doors locked. I follow others around the side of the building to the tracks and there check the schedules.

This is what I discover: tomorrow, Sunday, there is only the rare train to Bordeaux, no more than a couple throughout the whole day. Today, Saturday, there is at least one every hour. The next one arrives in ten minutes. If I catch it, I'll be in Bordeaux within an hour and a half. There I will have options and time to consider. La Reole on a weekend offers me nothing. I make my decision: I try to buy a ticket from a machine, but can't make the apparatus accept my VISA card; a young man standing nearby tells me not to worry since I can buy the thing on the train itself. I then call the family with whom I have my reservation for the night and tell their answering machine that I won't be coming. Almost as soon as I hang up, the train to Bordeaux comes lumbering into the station to collect me and Gregory and Click and Clack and haul us all back into civilization.

I climb up into the train and limp my way to an empty seat, sit down, set Gregory in my lap as if he were my son, and Click and Clack to the side. As the train pulls out of the La Reole station, I have one final thought: *I guess my prayer that precedence for healing go to C. J. was heard.* Just one miracle on offer today. Mine gives way to his. I go numb.

The train ride to Bordeaux takes just an hour. Our final glide into the modern *gare* is the end of my life as a pilgrim, I am almost certain. To the sound of massive brakes whooshing and steel wheels whining to a stop, I spiral into a kind of half-death.

I let the other passengers off first, then with Gregory on my back and Click and Clack in my hands, I limp down the aisle to the door. I step onto the stone platform, putting my left foot down first, then wince as I put weight on the right. I slowly work my way out of the *gare* to the great *place* that buffers the station from the city. I take a look around and see an Etap Hotel straight ahead. There are seedier places about, but I am tired of the hard life and want to indulge myself in something more modern and clean. I waddle over slowly and enter the lobby to ask for a room. They charge me forty-six euros for the night; not much more than my usual *chamber d'hôte* out on the road. I take possession of a small room that will be just fine for a night or two; I unload Gregory and begin setting myself up: toothpaste and brush, pills, shampoo, clean clothes, all in their place. Then I text Gene and Caroline to let them know where I am. Almost immediately, Gene calls back and begins a lengthy discussion with me about options and possibilities. I tell them I am sad but doing okay. Gene suggests that I get in to see a physical therapist that specializes in this sort of thing and tells me he will begin searching the Internet for someone here in Bordeaux. He also offers to get in touch with my brother, Bill, back in Spokane and try to set up a phone call between us. Bill is a physical therapist and knows plenty about this sort of injury, so I agree that that would be great.

I pass the remainder of the day and the evening quietly settling into my new reality. My mission, my dream really, has most probably come undone. I write a discouraging update in my journal, say my prayers, listen to *The Lark Rising* by Ralph Vaughn Williams and fall asleep.

I awake to Sunday, the first day of the week, new life and all that. I *have* to get to Mass this morning, no matter my miserable foot. I need others today. I need communion with them today. I cannot just give up and die like a dog here in this boxy hotel room. I limp out of the glass and plastic lobby and slowly work my way through the sycamore-lined streets and avenues of Bordeaux to the church of Sainte-Croix. The doors are open wide to receive me, broken, humbled, and dying inside, so I enter and take my place in a pew midway through the nave. An elderly priest comes out of the sacristy and begins passing among the benches warmly greeting the worshipers, shaking the men's hands and occasionally giving an elderly woman a delicate double kiss that is the trademark sign of affection and respect of the French. He then comes to me and takes my hand in welcome. His hand feels wonderful in my hand. Flesh in flesh, humanity touching humanity. A kind of healing passes from his palm to my own. I tell him I am a pilgrim to Compostelle, and a priest. His face registers a moment of surprise, but within a half-second, he is taking me by the hand and inviting me into the sacristy so that I might join him in celebrating the liturgy; then he stops for a moment and asks if I have an official paper documenting my status as a priest. I say that I do, but it is back at the hotel. He then tells me it is not important, and we continue a step or two, "But you are a *Catholic* priest, yes?" Yes. "A *Roman* Catholic priest, yes?" *Yes, I am a Roman Catholic priest.*" He chuckles and says, "Well, you never know these days."

Another, even older priest, joins us in the back room and prepares to celebrate with us. And so the three of us process into the sanctuary of the church and begin the ancient prayer that is prayed in all languages, but is above all languages, or so it especially seems to me right now. A group of teens preparing to make a pilgrimage to Rome proclaim the scripture readings of the day. After the Lamb of God is sung, the *père* offers me a segment of the consecrated host he has just broken in quarters, and I hold the bread, broken and shared, in the palm of my hand before consuming it. I now know this bread in its brokenness. I know it well. I see it with the old eyes of someone also broken. I love it. For me, right now, this fractured fragment of *pain* is all that is deep and true and good. I know this Jesus. I raise the small piece of bread and consume it. *I am hungry; you feed me.* This is as intimate as I get with God. The pastor hands me a gold ciborium filled to the brim with a hundred small hosts; I take it and stand beside him as the folks come forward from the nave to receive. At some point, I find myself misspeaking the simple affirmation of faith that is spoken to each communicant; unthinkingly I am saying *Cœur du Christ*, instead of *Corps du Christ*: "Heart of Christ" rather than "Body of Christ". I catch myself in the small error, but do not mind, for in some way, it seems as true as the prescribed words.

As I leave Sainte-Croix, I am feeling the pain in my foot more than earlier, so I slowly make my way back through the Sunday-quiet streets to my room for a rest. As this day after the disaster in Saint-Ferme unfolds, I attend to the feelings swirling within. They are a mix of despair and hope, bravado and discouragement. They do not yet have much firmness. Their present inchoateness bothers me, but I know I have to be patient as we figure this thing out. One part of me resists mightily the notion of ending my pilgrimage now. *I can beat this thing. I can endure the pain for a while. I overcame just as much four years ago when I was walking across Spain. My previous injuries healed allowing me to continue; why not this one? With Saint-Jacques on my side, I can continue on, at least as far as Saint-Jean-Pied-de-Port, which is only another two hundred kilometers or so from La Reole.* On the other hand, I am losing steam. I am slowing down. Even if I were to find "acute care" for this thing, how long would it take before I could get back on the road: another month? And where would I spend that month? Here in Bordeaux? In this hotel room? I could quit now and come back in April of next year before I go back to the States and finish, so its not necessarily over forever and ever amen. *I don't know. I just don't know yet.* This not knowing is like the fog of the Dordogne: it leaves me taking a step at a time, not seeing beyond the moment, calling me to be patient for its dissipation. I buy a cheap lunch from a streetside kebab stand, then head back to the Etap.

I phone my Galician friend, Toni, with whom I walked into Santiago four years ago, to tell him of my situation, to tell him of my confusion, to tell him that I might need a place to stay in Spain if I cannot go on. He assures me that he will welcome me to Santiago de Compostela and offers me his apartment in Ourense as long as I need it. I guess now I am waiting for the call from my brother, Bill, to see if he thinks there is reasonable hope of healing the foot in a timely manner.

Once back in my hotel, I receive the prearranged phone call from my brother. I take the call at the public phone in the hotel lobby. Though we chat for a long time about possible treatments for the plantar fasciitis, there is a fairly clear bottom line to our conversation: Bill tells me that this problem is very difficult to treat, and it can easily be mistreated. It generally does not heal quickly and can even become chronic if the abuse of the foot continues. *What are the chances of a quick turn-around on this, one that would allow me to continue walking?* Not impossible, but very low. This is bad news and moves me forward towards a decision about the future of my pilgrim life. Bill is caring and supportive and puts the best spin on bringing the pilgrimage to an end: "You've walked plenty already. You've done what you could. If you have to stop now, you can still be proud of what you've done." I pass the gist of the conversation on to Gene and Caroline in a final phone call of the day, already well past 9:00 pm. They sadly concur that perhaps it is time to give up walking further.

I turn off the television and the lights for sleep, and realize that I am feeling still the numbness that first took possession of me as I rode the train from La Reole to this place. It is not an agreeable state, this numbness, but I cannot shake it off, so I go to sleep and pray for relief.

Day three in Bordeaux, and I've got to get out of here. I need to begin making some plans. I walk across the *place* to the *gare* and look over the schedules to see what is going into Spain and when. The bus to Santiago de Compostela leaves at 12:30 am tomorrow, arriving in Compostela sometime after 3:00 pm the following day. The train, on the other hand, will get me only as far as Irun, just across the border; from there I would have to arrange other transportation on to Compostela. I choose the slow way, the one with an escape hatch in case I change my mind, and buy a refundable train ticket to Irun for tomorrow. There, I've made a decision, though it is not irrevocable. Returning to the pilgrim route is now far less likely, almost impossible, but not quite.

Not quite, for just a few minutes later, back in my hotel room, I receive one more call from Gene: would I like him to make an appointment for me at the big sports clinic here? I finally say it: *No, Gene, I'm done. I'm going on to Spain tomorrow. I've had enough.*

My walking is officially over; the words have been building for some time, and now they have been spoken. I have spoken them dejectedly, sadly, numbly, but decisively, and they cannot be taken back. Gene accepts my decision and agrees that it is probably the wisest course of action. He and Caroline remind me that the pilgrimage is not over; it is just moving to a conveyance other than my feet. "No sadness!" I am told. I send a text message to Toni in Ourense telling him I expect to arrive in Compostela on Saturday.

I take a couple of ibuprofen tablets, rest on my bed for a while, and then consider this strange thought: tomorrow night I will sleep in Spain.

22

By Hook or By Crook

It is the sixteenth of October, three and a half months since I walked out the door of The American College and down Leuven's Naamsestraat with Gregory the Great, the first Click and Clack, friends surrounding me and cheering me on. And this morning, I limp out the door of the Etap Hotel in Bordeaux, lumber across the street to the station a cripple, and alone as alone can be, except for Gregory and the new Click and Clack, catch my train to Irun, leaving behind not just France, which has been my pilgrim home for so long, but my pilgrimage itself . . . well, at least the walking segment of the pilgrimage. I cannot process this reality, so I just do what I must do as if I were in some grim dream. I mount my train, store Gregory and Click and Clack above my head, the pilgrim shell that accompanied me across Spain four years ago, and this year across half of Belgium and most of France, dangling from Gregory's chest and hanging now over the edge of the rack above my head, swinging back and forth as a reminder of who I was until now. The train passes along beautiful beaches and wealthy resort towns, but I want none of them. I feel instead like praying for one of those angels of the Old Testament to come, pull me up by the hair, carry me above all this, and drop me back in Saint-Ferme, so that I might continue my pilgrim walk, as it should be walked.

We slowly chug into Irun after dropping most of our passengers off on the French side of the frontier. This town looks ugly to me. I get off the train and go to the ticket window to make inquiries. I try to speak in Spanish, but it comes out of my mouth as a mish-mash of French and Spanish. Wait a minute: I *know* Spanish! But no matter how hard I try to speak it clearly, my *yo estoy*'s come out as *je suis*'s, and my *pero*'s continue to sally forth as *mais*'s. It is altogether disorienting, and the lady at the window is slightly annoyed with me. I make it as simple as possible and just ask for a ticket to San

Sebastián. I pay my euros and take my train ticket and go back to the plat-form to await the great rolling machine that will deliver me to the big city.

I find myself weirdly not myself. I feel completely *alien* here in this station. I am an alien in that I am not where I belong. I am an alien in that I am not who I am. I am tumbling inside and out in a demimonde of existen-tial alienation. *So this is what that is!* I want to puke. I want to scream like that poor man on the bridge in the famous painting by Munch: shrieking at everything and nothing and everything. Dizzy with defeat, I board my train, look blankly out the window as it rumbles round to San Sebastián, no more than twenty kilometers down the track.

I disembark almost as quickly as I embarked: To Gregory and Click and Clack I say, *Welcome to Spain, boys.* I am momentarily confused by the signs above the platforms announcing this place as Donostia. It dawns on me that this must be the Basque name of the city. I walk out of the station and into beautiful Donastia, San Sebastián, whatever its name. It is a city in which I have no idea where to go. I follow other travelers across a wide bridge with the hope of finding a room for the night. As I hobble down the sidewalk, a young woman on a bicycle passes me, turns as she does so, and calls back to me, "*¡Buen camino!*" the universal greeting among pilgrims in Spain. It cheers me and pulls me out of my existential funk just a little. It unfreezes me just a little. I feel just a little less numb knowing that one person in this big city knows who I really am.

I spot a *pensión* sign a couple blocks away and make my way to the front door, ring, and a woman's voice invites me upstairs to the first floor. The *señora* of the place is waiting for me with door wide open as I climb the steep stairwell. The first thing she asks me is if I am with someone. I tell her no, that I am alone. She grimaces and reveals the bad news that the only room she has open tonight is a double, and it goes for fifty euros. Her hus-band enters the room, and they both ask if I would be interested in another place they own down the street, near the cathedral, where there is indeed a single room for just thirty euros. That would be just fine, I tell them. They ask me about my pilgrimage, and when I give them a few of the details of my life these last months, they are touched by my story and so happy that I have come to them for lodging. The *señor* grabs his coat and leads me back through the streets of San Sebastián to a far less dignified building with a couple small rooms above busy storefronts on the street level. I am led upstairs, given a key, and shown my room. The *señor* lets me know that a surfer occupies the other room but has been a good tenant for the past week and won't be any problem for me. His gear is spread around the common area between our rooms. I give over the thirty euros I owe and then am left alone to settle in. *A surfer? Where am I?*

I drop Gregory and Click and Clack in a corner, lock the door behind me and step outside for lunch. I walk a block or two down a busy street and find a sidewalk restaurant advertising a ten-euro daily special. I take a seat in the sunshine and put in my order for the special, basically fish and chips, and a beer. I ask my waiter the way to the San Sebastián beach, and he points me back down the street I have just come: "*derrecho*" he says, "straight ahead." After I have finished my meal, I limp down the street towards the city beach. It is not long before I come into a large *plaza*. A lovely panorama greets me: a sun drenched crescent beach stretching a kilometer or two with the bay beyond blue under the afternoon sky. People mill about, happy and bright. I amble through the *plaza* and descend down a concrete staircase to the sandy beach below. I take off my sandals and socks and head towards the water. The thick sand feels great on my achy foot. It is like a summer day here: warm and sun splashed and people playfully swimming in the blue bay. I walk in the gentle mingling of sand and water at the knife-edge of the Atlantic, letting the wavelets wash over my feet and ankles. This is my therapy. I walk the beach from one end of its crescent to the other, then back again. It is therapy not only for my foot, but for my soul as well. I am not going to scream after all. I settle into this lovely scene, into Spain, into a new and different form of pilgrimage. I walk and let the waters of the Atlantic and the sun above and the passing couples who smile at me warm me.

As the sun draws low to the west, I climb up out of the water and sand, restoring my socks and sandals to my feet, then walk slowly back towards the cathedral. My foot still hurts but not as much as before. I am grateful.

The doors of the high and lacy Gothic Catedral del Buen Pastor are wide open, so I enter to look around. Evening Mass will begin at 7:30, a sign informs me. It is now just 6:00. I wander about, take a seat, pray a while, then return to the broad plaza in front of the church, where I take out my journal and pen and begin writing of this day.

This place is Europe at its best: mothers push prams, children toss big blue balls against the side of the church and race to catch them on the rebound, teenage boys and girls snuggle and cuddle and walk by with their arms wrapped around each other in the first stages of lust and love, old men with berets shadowing their heavy brows sit on benches, smoke, and discuss whatever, old women dressed in black walk together slowly, husbandless, being company to one another. A gaggle of boys has lost a soccer ball behind the grate of the church; one of the ten-year-olds climbs up and over the two-meter grill, down the other side, and throws the ball out to freedom; the others cheer. A gentle breeze cools us all as it makes the trees adorning the *plaza* rustle. In the background, I hear not only Spanish, but Euskera, the language of the Basques. All the talk of so many is blended together by this *plaza* into a lovely murmur that harmonizes perfectly with the rustling of the leaves of the nearby trees. A five-year-old girl dressed in a school uniform has been eyeing me as I sit on the stone wall surrounding the upper level of the *plaza*. She leaves her father and mother a few meters away and skips her way over to me. She sits next to me and asks after my name. *Me llamo Kevin.* I call myself Kevin; and how do you call yourself? "*Me llamo Paloma.*" She continues to bounce and stand and sit and hang over the edge of the low wall we are sharing. Paloma wants to know what I am writing in my notebook. I tell her that I am writing about her. She is thrilled by this and asks to see. I show her my small and indecipherable script; she shrugs at the incomprehensibility of it all and laughs and tells me that she already writes in school and can spell many words the other children cannot. I ask her to spell some words for me; she takes my pen and writes "*Paloma*". *It is a beautiful name, and I'm glad you can already spell it.* Her little brother of two or three toddles over, and she introduces Eduardo to me. He shakes my hand, then is picked up by his sister and held in a close embrace, out of which he wiggles free and toddles off after a pigeon. I cast an eye over to the parents of these children; though they are watching, they are smiling and happy to have their little ones entertained by this stranger. This lack of fear is a beautiful thing. There exists in my country no such thing as this *plaza*, at least as far as I know; our downtowns are mostly empty, our churches are surrounded by parking lots, our malls breed anonymity rather than humanity, our cities nurture fear rather than freedom. I feel sad for my own people that we no longer know the simple joy of spending the cool of the evening, outside, around the church, at talk and walk and play. Like the sea and sand and sun earlier, I feel it softening me, bringing me back to meaning, back to life, back to who I am.

I close up my journal and walk back into the cathedral for Mass; the old prayer of remembrance and thanksgiving is about to begin. Within these rites, I remember my days of walking and give thanks in the breaking of bread and the sharing of the cup for so many: for *Pére* Bernard, *Pére* Paul and the Three Searchers of Thorembais, Solange, Evert and Sietse, Monique, Michaelene and Patricia, Paloma and Eduardo, and I remember and give thanks finally for the girl on the bicycle who began the process of unfreezing me as she called back to me, one pilgrim to another: "*¡Buen camino!*" *Buen camino,* indeed.

After a fine sleep, I wake, shower, and find a coffee and sweet roll in a small bar near the cathedral, then return to my room to collect my things. I lug Gregory several blocks to the bus station and catch the 10:30 am bus to Bilbao, then another to Santander. I take a room in the first *pensión* I encounter after leaving the bus station. It is a pleasant place, but the walls are very thin, and I can hear everything that goes on in the rooms next to me. Water pipes pass through the walls so there is fairly constant gurgling.

In the evening, I go out looking for a nice fish supper, but after much walking around this somewhat decaying business district near the bus station, find nothing very attractive, so settle on a grim take-out pizza place. The food offered is of minimal quality and though it fills me, it does not satisfy. I take the leftovers home.

I have not felt like a pilgrim today. With all this bus riding, I begin sinking back into the numbness I have been working so hard to leave behind. My foot is throbbing tonight. I undress, crawl into bed, read my evening psalms, and fall asleep.

My first job after waking, showering and finding a coffee bar for breakfast, is to buy a ticket for the eight hour bus ride tomorrow all the way to Santiago de Compostela. Tomorrow, by hook or by crook, I will finish this pilgrimage. Not the way I wanted, but *a way*.

I while away the day then in the evening, I visit the Santander cathedral for 6:30 pm Mass, arriving just as the priest is entering the sanctuary. Today, he announces, is the feast of the evangelist, Luke. The Gospel reading for the occasion is that of Jesus sending forth his disciples two-by-two. He asks those disciples to travel light, to accept what is put before them gratefully, and to proclaim the simple message in deed as much as in word that the Kingdom is now among them.[1] I realize that this is the very same Gospel passage proclaimed by *Père* Bernard way back in Godinne! My, what a wonderful story to bracket this whole adventure! I hope so much that since my first hearing of the story along the banks of the Meuse, during the past seventy–something days, such is what I have somehow done: *walked as they walked*. Walked as *he* walked. *I so hope!*

As Mass ends, I limp over to the sacristy, introduce myself to the priest as a pilgrim and ask for the cathedral seal in my *credencial*. He puts me in the hands of an elderly nun who is obviously in charge of sacristy management. She takes my document and disappears through a dark passage for several minutes and then reappears through the same passage with the latest seal inked within. She smiles as she hands it back to me and says, "*Buen camino, señor*".

As I leave the cathedral, I wonder what it will be like tomorrow to return to the city of James, Jacobus, Jacob, Jacques, Santiago, Iago. I hope it will be like returning home, returning to an old friend.

I am feeling very tired. I return to my room near the bus station, eat cold left-over pizza from last night as tonight's dinner, write a while in my

1. Luke 9:1–6

journal and send out a text message to Caroline to be posted in my blog. Then I crawl between my sheets, fluff my pillows, pray the evening's psalms, and decide to end this day by listening once more to Fernando Ortega's *Grace and Peace*, the hymn that has become my best musical friend during this pilgrimage. I take my iPod in hand, roll my thumb around its circular tuner until the screen highlights the hymn, place the buds in my ears, then push the central button to play. Several laconic piano chords open the piece that I now know so well, and my eyes begin to well. I sniffle. Then the contemplative repetition of the greeting of Saint Paul to the Thessalonians begins: "Grace and peace . . . Grace and peace to you in God, our Father . . . " And I am now weeping. "Grace and peace to you in God, our Father . . . and the Lord, Jesus Christ . . . and the Lord Jesus Christ . . . " More than weeping now, I am sobbing and almost wailing, and I cannot control it; I cannot stop it. The salty tears and the sobs upon sobs pour out from deep inside of me, finally escaping from their cold, black cave, crashing and banging about violently on their way out, and it goes on and on and on. I am afraid all this howling that is pouring out of me will attract attention beyond these thin walls, so I cover my mouth with a pillow to muffle the sound of this unexpected release from my soul. The hymn continues in my ears: "Grace and peace, grace and peace to you in God, our Father . . . " And still I heave and cannot stop it. I try to catch my breath, to control myself, but I cannot secure anew my sobriety. The numbness, the frozenness, the disappointment, the anger, the end of a dream, the end of the road, the *death* of these last days, all of it comes pouring out of the depths of my guts, until my grief runs out of itself, and I am left mewling and whimpering and wiping my eyes of tears and the edges of my mouth of saliva, and I slowly settle down into a state of exhaustion in which I think nothing, feel everything, and drift down into whatever God is.

I am awake at 5:45 this Saturday morning, the twentieth day of October, and ready to finally get to Santiago de Compostela. My bus leaves at 7:45 so I have plenty of time to repack Gregory the Great one last time, now with Click and Clack strapped securely by Velcro to his flanks. I pack my sandals inside Gregory and wear my boots to reduce his heft. I eat the last slice of cold pizza, now two-days old, and lumber back to the Santander bus station. I buy a bottle of water and a few small snacks of nuts and raisins for the long ride, clamber up into the coach as soon as its doors are opened by the chauffeur, and take my reserved seat tucking Gregory with Click and Clack tied to his flanks into the rack above my head.

The long road to Compostela travels through some spectacular country, offering vistas of the sea and passing over extraordinarily high bridges spanning gorges that leave me feeling as if our bus and I are traveling through mid-air. The hours pass and eventually signs appear announcing the approach of Santiago de Compostela. I am almost there. The bus snakes its way through the outskirts of the city and finally rumbles into the station a half-hour later than scheduled. As the diesel engine shuts down, I collect Gregory, lug him and Click and Clack down the aisle, and walk him down the steps towards the platform. I look up before I myself have even hit solid ground, and there, just ahead, is Toni dressed in a businessman's coat and tie, smiling broadly, and calling to me: "¡Hola, Kevin!" He lifts Gregory from the final step of the bus, and asks if this is the famous Gregorio he has read about in my blog postings. I tell him it certainly is, then he sets Gregory to the side, opens wide his arms, and welcomes me back to Santiago de Compostela with an *abrazo* that is firm and solid and lasts and lasts. I feel dampness form in my eyes, but maintain control of my emotions much better than last night. This embrace of welcome is precisely and exactly what this old pilgrim needs as he walks into the city of James the Apostle. It is as if James himself were welcoming me home.

Toni tucks Gregory into the trunk of his waiting car, then asks if I am hungry and suggests that after a meal along the Camino route into the city, we walk the last few kilometers together to the cathedral, as we did four years before. We choose a restaurant and both order the daily special, a fried pork chop with *papas fritas* and a small salad on the side. We chat softly over our meals for this seems like a sacred moment, to be eating together again in Santiago. Toni is now in his early thirties and has a good job as manager of a semi-governmental institute. He and I met along the Spanish Camino as I was making my way towards Santiago de Compostela for the first time; we became fast friends as we walked together back then. I feel so happy to be with him again. It feels so good no longer to be alone.

Toni suggests that we drive back towards the city, leave his car at about two kilometers from the center, and walk those last pilgrim *camino* kilometers together, to end this pilgrimage together, as we did before. He notices my limp and asks about my foot, and I tell him it will be good enough. I would walk these two kilometers even with just one foot. We begin our mini-pilgrimage down a busy street leading us towards the city. I hobble along while Toni adjusts his pace to my own.

We cross some busy streets then pass through the Puerta del Camino and enter into the medieval district of the city. A few more blocks over streets paved with large, worn stones, and we pass the cathedral's north side, the portals of its transept opening to our left. Toni and I then make our way into the Plaza de Obradoiro, the broad square that extends out from the main face of the cathedral. The afternoon sunshine is still burnishing the baroque *façade*, at the top of which, in a supremely high niche, the stone image of Santiago looks down upon all his pilgrims below. Toni and I stride over to the o Kilometer stone in the center of the Plaza de Obradoiro that marks the end point of the pilgrim Via from all corners of the European continent. To stand over it, then bend down to touch it now is not like the first time four years ago; it is not as thrilling, but it is peaceful and humbling and satisfying.

Toni leads me up the staircase, through the great portals of the cathedral, and into the narthex where we take a moment to gaze up to the Puerta de Gloria, the twelfth-century Romanesque entry into the cathedral, the one that first greeted pilgrims before the present baroque *façade* was tacked on centuries later. I don't pause to gawk long; I have something else to do before becoming a tourist here. I walk through the nave towards the main altar, then fall in line to the right of the altar so that I might climb a small and steep stairway cut into the great gilt stone and wood reredos where the central statue of Santiago reigns over his cathedral, directly above his bones held below. I follow behind a few devoted visitors while Toni follows me. Then it is my turn to step up onto the platform, directly behind the bust of *mi hermano Santiago, mon frère Jacques,* my brother James. I look out over his right shoulder beyond the sanctuary and through the nave and out to the Plaza de Obradoiro, then to the north and on to San Sebastián, and Bordeaux, and Saint-Ferme, and Pellegrue, and Limoges, and Nevers, and Reims, and Rocroi, and Namur, and Leuven, and the little American College on its Naamsestraat where I began all this. Then I stretch my arms over Santiago's shoulders and give him the great *abrazo* of love and respect and most of all, gratitude, that all his pilgrims offer at the end of their long walks. *I am here, brother, after all, by hook or by crook. I thank you, for calling me through dreams and by stars and in wild imaginings and leading me along your Way.*

After some while, I let go of Santiago's shoulders and step down the stairwell on the opposite side, then follow it around into the crypt below the high altar where the relics of James are kept in a silver casket. I take my place on a kneeler and make here my prayers. At first, I find no words. Then something comes to me: I have also carried a small wooden box with locks of hair cut from my mother and father at the moment of their deaths; I take it in hand from deep in my pocket and I pray for them too down here. I ask them to forgive me my failings as a son, and I tell them I love them. I pray for my sisters and brothers back home, for our seminarians in Leuven, for Caroline and Gene, for young C. J., for Toni, and one by one, the persons who have populated my life over these months. And, finally, I pray for myself: that by the time I die and my life here is complete, I will be left with only one thing: thanksgiving for every second of my life and the knowledge that it has all been a grand gift. Let my last words be those of Bernanos' priest: *Tout est grâce.*

I climb up out of the crypt and wait for Toni to follow. He asks if I don't want more time down there; I have no idea how much time I just spent in the crypt. *Yes, I need more time, but it is enough for now.* It is getting late, and I need to find a place to spend the night. Toni recommends a pilgrim place, the Hotel LaSalle, operated by the order of priests that educated him as a boy. We walk several blocks to its front door and enter and ask the receptionist for a room for a few days. She obliges us and gives me a key. My quarters are small but clean and include a shower and toilet; it is plenty enough for me now.

Before leaving for the night, Toni gives me another long *abrazo* and wishes me a good night promising to return tomorrow in time for the pilgrim Mass in the cathedral at noon. I crawl into my bed and fall into a deep dream where Spanish is mixed with French and images of the Way flit through my subconscious like playing cards being tossed one by one across the face of the earth.

I am awake at 8:00, wash myself, then unpack my soiled clothing from Gregory's interior and wash them in the small bathroom sink. I hang everything up to drip dry, pilgrim style, then walk into town to retrieve my *Compostela*, the official document proffered by the Archdiocese of Santiago to pilgrims who have completed at least one hundred kilometers of the Camino. It is only a piece of paper, but it is precious to most pilgrims insofar as it is an acknowledgment of something great that has just happened in their lives. Four years before, I had to wait in a long line to receive my *Compostela*, but this time, I walk right up the old stairwell and into the pilgrim office of the archdiocese. I proudly present my *credencial*, with its first stamp from the Archdiocese of Mechelen-Brussels and many, many more from the villages, cities, and cathedrals I have passed through over the past three and a half months. A young lady receives the *credencial* with a smile, opens its accordion pages, looks over the impressive collection of stamps on one side, then turns it over and examines the reverse side with its equally impressive imprints. She frowns, turns it over and back again, then asks me if I did not walk the final hundred kilometers into Santiago itself. *No, I was not able to do that since I had to end my walking due to an injury to my foot, but I walked over 1,200 kilometers through Belgium and France.* She then delivers the blow: "But you cannot receive the *Compostela* if you have not actually walked the *final* one-hundred kilometers into Compostela." *But I walked 1,200 kilometers in Belgium and France; there is the proof!* "Lo siento, señor, I am sorry, the rules of the Archdiocese are very strict on this." I say to her: *It is not the last one hundred kilometers that makes a pilgrimage a pilgrimage,* señora. She smiles wanly then offers to stamp my *credencial* with the official archdiocesan seal, but the *Compostela*, she insists, she cannot give me.

I stare her down. She silently and almost ashamedly digs out her precious stamp to give my *credencial* its final seal. *This is a sin against the Holy Spirit, the holy spirit of pilgrimage: to box the pilgrim reality into just one hundred silly kilometers!* I am disgusted.

A young pilgrim at the next window, sweaty, bearded and still bearing his pack on his back, looks over to me and speaks the truth: "Don't worry; you don't need their piece of paper to be a pilgrim. God knows how much you walked. God knows you are a pilgrim. *Dios te conoce.*" I collect my *credencial* from the girl and thank the young pilgrim who spoke the truth to me, and leave the office. I wander the streets around the cathedral still feeling sour disappointment at what has just happened to me, but savoring the words of the young man: *Dios me conoce.* God knows who I am, and that is enough.

In time for the noon Pilgrim Mass, I return to the Plaza de Obradoiro, enter the cathedral through its main portal, pass under the Puerta de Gloria, and make my way through the nave of the church, now filling up quickly with pilgrims and tour groups. I walk into the sacristy and present myself to the sacristans as a pilgrim-priest. I am told to return at ten minutes before noon. I have about fifteen minutes to wait, so return to the church nave and take up a position among the increasing number of pilgrims filling the pews and aisles of the great building. I enjoy watching them all. Many, like the young man in the archdiocesan office, are new arrivals, still sweat-laden and burdened with their backpacks; others are day-old arrivals, now washed clean, and looking fresh but still with their pilgrim shells hanging from their necks. They greet and embrace as they meet up after separations on the road. Some take positions of prayer, kneeling with heads bowed, others gawk at the details of the Romanesque church. There is liquid movement within the whole, like that of the sea, waves and swirls and intermingling of one group with that of another. I look up to Santiago, perched high above the main altar and greet him as informally as I can: *Hey, bro.*

I enter the sacristy and vest myself in an alb and stole as a concelebrant of the imminent liturgy. I sign my name and diocese into a large book spread open on the vast table in the center of the room. There are a number of Spanish priests already vested as well as a few pilgrim priests from various lands like myself. The Spanish priests keep to themselves, while an Italian takes up a conversation with me as we stand about. He asks where I am from, and I tell him from the State of Washington. "Ah, Seattle!" *Well, not exactly Seattle, but not so far either.* I discover another English-speaking priest in our midst when he is asked by the sacristan to read one of the Mass intentions in English. I introduce myself to him. He is Robert from somewhere in England. And now it is time to process into the sanctuary, for the opening hymn has begun. I find myself at the head of the double line of priests, just behind the deacons. This means, that after reverencing the altar I am seated in a choir stall at the very back of the sanctuary, far from the altar but close to the reredos and the image of Santiago that I embraced yesterday. I find my attention wandering from the liturgical rituals up front and fixing, instead, on Santiago, just above and to my left. I am still feeling the after-effects of the young lady's denial of my Compostela in the archdiocesan pilgrim office, so I take up the matter with the apostle. *Well, Iago, here I am, in your church, above your bones, yet without pilgrim credentials. I hope you don't mind. It wasn't a perfect pilgrimage, for sure, but I did my best. I walked. I hope I have walked as you wanted me to walk.* Santiago remains silent, but I don't care. His silence is eloquent, more eloquent to me at least than the homily being delivered up front. From within that silence, at least this is what I imagine now, he sees me and knows me as one of his own.

I am the last priest to receive communion from the altar. I take a broken piece of consecrated bread in hand and lift it to my mouth and consume it. Then I take the ancient cup and likewise raise it to my lips and take a deep draught from its round bowl, finishing the last of the consecrated wine within. I am fed and my thirst sated. I return to my seat in the far court of the sanctuary and watch the pilgrims file forward also to receive what I have just received. There, in those open faces, in those hands extended, there, in those booted feet and sweat-stained arm-pits, there, in those legs, in all those beating hearts, in all this obvious yearning, there too is the Body and Blood of our God.

Know them, Lord.

Feed them, Lord.

Lead them, Lord.

As the principle liturgy comes to its conclusion, the great silver *botafumeiro* is lowered, lit, and incense placed in its massive mouth by a crew of select men dressed in brown cassocks. This massive incense-burner is then swung from one side of the church's transept to the other, gaining increasing height above the heads of the pilgrims with each pass. It trails a white cloud of smoke and fills the church with the aroma of myrrh. The three magi of Saint Luke's Christmas story carried myrrh to the child Jesus. I wonder how the three searchers of Thorembais are faring in their journey to find meaning in this universe. May the smallest whiff of this myrrh-laden smoke make its way back to them. May they find some bit of the true God in their quest. I would like for them to some day to find their way here, to this table, to this cup, to this bread blessed and broken, but I leave that in the hands of God with the kind assistance of his missionary in Thorembais, *Père* Paul.

We priests return to the sacristy as we came in and remove our liturgical robes to reveal, mostly, the clothing of pilgrims beneath. I experience
a sudden impulse to approach the English priest, Robert; I do so without
forethought or planning. *Robert, do you have a minute or two? I'd like to go
to confession.* It just seems like the right place and the right time and the
right person, someone who speaks my language. He agrees immediately,
puts his hand on my shoulder and guides me into a medieval courtyard just
off the sacristy. We lean side by side against a low stone wall connecting the
stone pillars of the colonnade surrounding the grassy central court. I begin:
*I am sorry and ask forgiveness for my impatience along my pilgrim Way, for
the pride I have felt in walking better than others, for the jealousy I have felt
towards those who walked better than I. I am so sorry for all my whining and
complaining and wanting to quit instead of just relishing every moment along
my Way. Most of all, I ache for not seeing God more, for not praying more,
for not living the Gospel better along the Way. I hope, I hope, I so very hope
I haven't been a failure as a pilgrim . . .* I begin to cry. I get a bit more out:
I hope I've been a good man as I have walked along . . . I cannot continue
speaking, the weeping overtakes any further words I intend to say. All of this
has been poured into Robert's hands. I sob and cannot stop. He waits. When
I am finally able to wipe the last tears from my cheeks, he speaks a few kind
words, then blesses me, and we return to the sacristy. I apologize for falling
apart, to which he responds: "It is fine. We are brothers, are we not?" Robert
and I part with an embrace, and I walk back through the emptying cathedral
and down into the Plaza de Obradoiro to wait for Toni.

I place myself as conspicuously as possible near the center of the *plaza*
and keep an eye peeled for my friend. While standing there, something important dawns on me: if the *catastrophe* of Sainte-Ferme had not befallen
me, if that mini-death had not stopped me in my tracks, I would not have
wept this sea of tears with Robert and those of Santander. Failure has been
the prerequisite for this salty reconciliation with myself, perhaps the truest
end to any true pilgrimage.

Toni finally strolls into the Plaza de Obradoiro, spots me, waves, walks
over to the center of the *plaza* and greets me. After lunch, he suggests an
easy walk through the city, and in particular, a *paseo* through a lovely garden
area that looks back towards the medieval city and the cathedral. We follow
a path along a creek that breaks into a small grassy park, where we lay down
under the sun to give my increasingly achy foot a rest and to enjoy the clear
sky, the white clouds sailing across the blue sea above. The red leaves of
small maple trees planted nearby add a dash of brilliant color to the scene.
Here we chat laconically about our lives. Toni fills me in on his work and
how he and his fiancé, Belén, are looking for an old house somewhere near

Ourense to purchase, fix up, and make ready for their family. I feel extraordinarily happy with this friend by my side, under this wide, azure *bóveda*. Toni is, I believe, now my best friend in the world. He speaks softly, sings gently, shares his soul generously, embraces easily. He is one of the finest human beings I have ever come to know.

At the end of this day, we go our separate ways, and I walk back to my hotel. Tomorrow, it dawns on me, is Sunday again, the First Day of the Week, the Day of the Lord, the Eighth Day of Creation, the Day beyond all Days. I shall live.

This Sunday morning dawns bathed in sunlight and all the warmth a late-October day can muster. I go to Mass again at the cathedral, then meet up with Toni for another lazy day together. As night comes on, I decide that I am now almost too full of Compostela. Tomorrow, I will go to Finisterre by bus and end this pilgrimage at the End of the Earth. It is time to put a period to this story. Finisterre, medieval tradition has it, is this last piece of Iberian land before the sea spreads out to its infinite horizon. Finisterre will be that period.

I have one other small mission to accomplish before I leave Compostela. I must hand over to Santiago a small packet of handwritten prayers and intentions that I have carried with me all these months; each was written by a seminarian or friend or acquaintance back in Leuven who asked me to carry them to the Apostle Santiago. They have been folded up tightly within my red, high-tech, waterproof wallet, either hanging around my neck or stuffed deeply within Gregory the Great's most secure pouch.

The next morning, I return early to the cathedral, take a place in the forward section of the nave reserved for prayer, a place where I can get a good direct line of sight with the statue of the Pilgrim Santiago above the main altar. From below, I offer the paper intentions to him. Then I carry them up to Santiago himself and as I give him one final *abrazo* I make sure the papers are touched upon his wide shoulder. Finally, I carry the small parcel of prayers below and begin looking for a place to leave the intentions behind. I wander around the ambulatory behind the main altar looking for a discrete location and almost settle on a small chink in the stonework near the Holy Door of the cathedral, but bypass it and go a little further on. And then I see it: directly behind the main altar, as close to the tomb of Santiago as one can get at this level, there is a polished marble railing topped with a high glass window, presumably put there to keep the tight precincts directly behind the altar free of wandering pilgrims and tourists like myself. But just above the stone railing, there is a small hole in the glass, almost unnoticeable. It is just the right size for a hand to pass through. *There. There it is!* My fist is grasping the notes and I try fitting it through the hole in the glass; it just barely goes through. If I set them on the inside of this railing, close to the window frame, they might remain here for days without being discovered and swept away by some dedicated janitor. I raise them to my lips and give these bits of paper I have carried so far a small kiss, then pass them through the glass with my hand, release them gently, and let them settle on the stone ledge, almost invisible to anyone passing through the ambulatory. I pull my hand back through the glass, ask Santiago to take in hand these prayers and take care of those who wrote them. I then wander around the remainder of the ambulatory to the nave and finally, out into the streets of Compostela.

From there, I walk to the bus station for the ride to the End of the Earth. I expect the coach ride to last about an hour, but it is slow going as the bus transits along many winding, two-lane roads and slows down even more through one fishing village after another. It is a perfect October day, and the sea beyond the coastline is as brightly blue as the sky above. The bays we travel around are dotted with colorful fishing boats that bob at their buoys, waiting patiently for their next run out to sea.

Two and a half hours later, we finally pull into the open-air bus port near the village center, I sally forth into the town knowing nothing about where to go or how to get there. The fishing harbor loaded with boats is just down a slight hill. To the right is a small street with a pilgrim refuge; a sign posted on the door makes it clear only walkers and cyclists are welcome. All I know about this place really is that the *faro*, the lighthouse, is where most pilgrims end their journey. As I walk the street along the port, I see no *faro*. I walk to a large pier jutting into the bay and from there notice some sort of small castle on a rise just opposite me on the far side of the bay. I walk around and up to the place. The Castillo de San Carlos is not the *faro*, but a fishing museum; I am met at the door by an enthusiastic fellow who offers to give me the grand tour for one euro. I inquire about the *faro*, and he gives me the directions I need. It is now almost 3:00 pm, and my bus will depart the village for Compostela at 7:00 this evening, so I opt to hoof it to the *faro* to be sure I will be back in time for the bus.

I find my way out of the village and begin my climb up the paved road that shall carry me to the *faro*. The sun continues to shine, though it is now noticeably lower in the sky; a few fluffy clouds add contrast in white to its deep blue. The ache in my foot almost disappears. I pull off my rain-jacket and open wide my shirt for it is deliciously warm and a gentle breeze cools my sweat. I rise, walking by myself, occasionally passing another pilgrim or tourist, with cheery *buen camino*'s exchanged among us. For the first time in days, maybe even weeks, I feel real joy as I walk, as if I were born to this. These are my final three pilgrim kilometers of almost one-thousand-five-hundred such kilometers, and they are everything a pilgrim could hope for in a day's journey! The blue sea to my left, the surface slightly unsettled by unseen breezes, the clear sky and golden October sun above, the brown and green hills to my right, all become one with me and I with them. We are indivisible and inseparable. All creation now proclaims the glory of her Creator, and I now, feet and heart, body and spirit, person and being, scoundrel and saint, wordlessly proclaim with her this one life, this one love, that in this moment is all in all. The words of one of this morning's psalms return to fill me:

My heart is ready, O God, my heart is ready.

I will sing, I will sing your praise.[2]

I round a curve in the road to find a bronze sculpture of an old pilgrim like myself, probably Santiago, straining upward in climbing this hill; I can see in his face that he shares the same joy I know right now. It *is* Santiago. He *is* walking with me. *Still* walking with me.

I can see the lighthouse now. I am close. As I approach, I am greeted first by a tall granite crucifix standing high above the stones of this *cabo* and the surface of the deep blue sea beyond. I divert from the pavement and clamber up to the cross where I firmly place a stone on its base to mark my passing and look up to the feet and legs and body and bowed head of this *Cristo*, looking back down upon me, and say one more time my litany of childhood prayers. *Our Father . . . Hail Mary . . . Glory be . . . O my Jesus . . .* I wrap my arms around the stone cross holding the Christ and hold it and hold it and hold it for as long as I can.

I head back to the road and soon enough come to its own "o Kilometer" sign post. I approach the *faro* itself, but enter only as far as I am allowed without having to pay a fee. No museums or tours for me now, something bigger is happening here. I walk around the left side of the lighthouse and find another granite crucifix, squat and as low to the ground as the other was high. I scramble over to it, but stop short because two teen girls are investigating it right now. I wait. From here I am only a few meters from the end of the *cabo*, the rocky cape extending out into the Atlantic. I behold glistening sea to my left, to my right, and straight-ahead. A couple of steel radio towers just a short ways from here are proudly flying the flags of pilgrim shirts, briefs, bras, boots, tennis shoes, all worn out, dirty, and left behind at this end point of their many journeys. I turn back to the granite cross: along its thick horizontal arms pilgrims have used fist-sized stones to hold down small pieces of paper with prayers and intentions written on them. The two girls have been lifting some of them and reading them aloud. They are as varied as the human beings who left them behind. "Bless me on

2. Psalm 57

my way home." "Thank you for a safe pilgrimage." "O dear Christ, heal my brother of cancer." "Lord, I am sorry for my sins." "Help me believe." They are the remnants of conversions completed, or better, begun.

The girls drift away, so I approach. I don't read the notes as they did; it seems rather like listening in on an intimate conversation of which I am not a part. But I do feel a need to leave something of myself behind here too, *but what?* I stupidly have neither paper nor pen with me. I still need my shirt and jacket, for soon enough the sun will go down, and it will grow cold. I can't go home without pants or sandals! I think of the handkerchief in my back pocket, it has wiped a lot of sweat from my brow over these months. It is one I inherited from my father upon his death and in one corner there is embroidered a very fancy "B" for Bob. Bob, Robert, Dad, the Old Man, Pop. He had his faults, but he loved us as best he could. I love him, too. I remember along the way once answering my own riddle: *What is the heaviest thing I am carrying?* And without thinking I answered, *My dad!* And it was true then and has been true until now. So here I lay down that load, that small burden, that which he did not do so well, to let it be blown into the sea once and for all, and to give thanks for that which he did right, for his love, incomplete or complete as it may have been on any one day, to let the light of this day, the grace of this liminal place, the firm embrace of this end of the world and this beginning of heaven, to let it all bless him and me and all of us. I take the handkerchief embroidered with the "B" of Bob and soaked with the sweat of his son, open it wide, let it flap in the breeze for a moment like a flag of victory and surrender at the same time, refold it as it has been folded a million times over the past fifteen years or more, kiss it, then place the handkerchief on the right arm of this cross and set a stone upon it to keep it from flying away too soon. *Be free!*

And then, one final time, I have a good pilgrim cry.

I find a quiet place amidst the rocks, and there I let the breeze and the sun and the sea and the saints and the crosses and the memories and the friends and the pilgrims and the stars, the billions of stars of the Via itself, calm me and console me and dry my tears and carry me out to that hazy horizon where one finally slips beyond the impossibly thin line between sea and sky, beyond *Finis Terrae,* beyond even the stars, and into that otherworld where all our *ways* finally fold into *THE WAY.*

Afterword

A fter I walked away from the *faro* at Cabo Fisterra, I spent some weeks in Spain, then some months in the Philippines, and finally wended my way home to Washington State and took up again ministry as a parish pastor, first spending two years in Othello, an agricultural and largely Mexican-American town located in the central part of the state, then as pastor of the Saint Thomas More Catholic Student Center at Washington State University in Pullman. In both places, I initiated pilgrimage experiences for our young people and encouraged anyone and everyone who might be interested to put the Camino on their bucket list. My experience as a pilgrim, I found, had changed my approach to ministry in a fundamental way, or perhaps better, a *foundational* way. To put it as simply as possible, following my long walk to Compostela, I experienced my church far less as an institution to be "run" than as a living stream of pilgrims along their various and very personal paths to be tended. My primary job as a pastor from then on has been to *walk with* them in their joys and pains for as long as they might need me beside them. This *walking with* is an exercise of compassion, which in its Latin root means, *to suffer with*, and sympathy, *to feel with*. The *with* is the essential thing.

Despite all this, as the years passed that missing link in my grand pilgrim scheme, those last two hundred or so kilometers between Saint-Ferme and Saint-Jean-Pied-de-Port, never quite gave up gnawing at me as something yet undone. I grew increasingly itchy to close that gap in my overall pilgrimage between Leuven and Santiago de Compostela. I needed to wrap up my pilgrim life once and for all.

So I did.

Five years after my day in Finisterre, I used the occasion of a reunion of the alumni of our seminary in Leuven to get back on the pilgrim Way again. I repacked Gregory the Great, took hold of Click and Clack, slipped on my old Meindle boots and from Leuven took the train back to Bordeaux. After a night in Bordeaux, I caught another to La Reole. In Reole I hired a taxi to carry me back to Sainte-Ferme, which dropped me off in exactly the spot where I told Gene and Caroline I could walk no further.

It was a beautiful day, and by the time I arrived in Saint-Ferme, it was time for lunch so I popped into the bakery around the corner. The baker was the same man who drove me to La Reole, but did not recognize me, but why should he have? We greeted each other formally. I bought a *pain de raisin* and returned to the bench outside the old abbey church where I had taken off my boots five years earlier and there slowly consumed the circular ropes of my *pain* loaded with cream, sugar, and raisins, of course.

I hoisted Gregory to my back, stepped out onto the pavement of the highway to La Reole, took my first steps, and picked up exactly where I had agonizingly left off sixty months earlier. Over the course of three weeks I walked the rest of the Way to Saint-Jean-Pied-de-Port, the very place where I had begun my pilgrim life some ten years earlier. These final weeks on the Chemin were not without troubles or joys; as before, I was often alone and had diffiulties with tendons and blisters. At times, I enjoyed the company of other pilgrims, great characters worthy of a book all to themselves, but also had many hours ambling along wholly by myself. Always I walked with Gene and Caroline praying me down the road.

My final day was the most glorious of all my pilgrim days. I spent the night before in the Basque village of Ostabat where I and several other pilgrims were heartily entertained by our hosts, *Monsieur* Bernard and *Madame* Lucie, who served up a hearty dinner, then with his bold and beautiful voice, Bernard energetically led us in singing traditional Basque folksongs, and finally, the pilgrim hymn: *Ultreya.*

Because of on-going tendon issues in my legs, I sent Gregory ahead to Saint-Jean-Pied-de-Port and carried only a small day-pack. The morning air was cool and the sunshine brilliant across the fields of the lower slopes of the Pyrenees. I happily trailed a few of the pilgrims with whom I had lodged the night before, the sound of their voices still singing aloud the folk songs of *Monsieur* Bernard. I stopped in the next village for Sunday Mass celebrated in Basque. Then refreshed and renewed, I walked on with ease, my body in tune with Click and Clack and the ups and downs of the final stretch of the Chemin in France. My eyes were open wide to every vista spreading out before them: the green fields, the cattle, the peaks of the Pyrenees in the distance, the drop of dew on a blade of clover. Knowing this would all soon be over, I relished every thought, every prayer, every moment in this great world of ours, this gift of an earth. I felt almost as light as air as I climbed ever higher along the roads and paths leading me to Saint-Jean-Pied-de-Port. Untouched by tendonitis or blisters or even a hint of discouragement this day, I arrived in the last major town before my final destination, Saint-Jean-la-Vieux. There I took leave of the road for lunch at the entrance of the town cemetery, then stopped by the church for a quick visit before my final push upwards. I found the doors unlocked and made my entry into yet another cool and dark church interior. Alone, I dropped my small pack into a pew and took my place next to it. I knelt on the wood plank there, dropped my head, closed my eyes, and with an incredibly happy heart thanked the God of the Universe for everything: For life. For love. And for the Way.

When I looked up, my eyes fell on an ancient and life-size crucifix, not set high above an altar, but hung low on the stone wall to my right, at human level. Without much thought, I rose from my pew, went to the Christ there, placed my hands on his shoulders and leaned into him in as much of an embrace as I could manage. I then rose and looked into his open eyes: *I now know you.*

When I finally hiked up to the St. James Gate, the medieval portal that gives entry into Saint-Jean-Pied-de-Port, I did not feel a great thrill. I was not giddy. I didn't skip and jump or dance as some pilgrims do. I did not cry. I don't know why; I fully expected to, but it just didn't happen. I did experience a very full joy though: the joy that is the quiet satisfaction of completion, the joy that comes with finally finding safe harbor, the joy that is the knowledge that though I have done something very imperfectly, I have done it. After all was said and done, I had walked from the threshold of my old home in Belgium to the threshold of Saint James' old bones in Galicia. *Je suis arrivé.*

I ambled into town, visited the church, said my prayers, then spent a good night enjoying the humble hospitality of new friends at a refuge called L'Esprit du Chemin. And the following day, I made my way home.

Bye and bye, Evert never wrote me as he promised, but Marie Claire and Mary Anne did send me their promised post card from Compostela; they made it. Toni and I continue to be great friends. He and his wife, Belén, have a lovely son, Xurxo, (Galician for George). Vincent is pastor of St. Therese Parish in Albuquerque. Caroline and Gene welcome pilgrims walking through Belgium into their home and continue to pray for me. Most important of all, C. J., the young man with schizophrenia for whom I prayed late along the Chemin, continues to have his ups and downs, but is holding his own.

So, when all is said and done, or rather, walked and done, this is the thing that endures:

Tout est grâce.

Acknowledgments

I owe a great debt of gratitude to Caroline and Gene Foley, who are present throughout these pages, for their faith in me and my pilgrim ways. Their prayers and indefatigable encouragement made this pilgrimage and this book possible.

I offer a huge *abrazo* filled with *agradecimiento* to my Galician brother, Toni González Lorenzo, for his priceless friendship since we first met on the Camino so many years ago.

I will always be deeply grateful to Father Vincent Chávez for rescuing me in Tonnerre, welcoming me into his home while I recuperated, and of course, for his enduring fraternity.

I am ever so thankful to the many pilgrims and those who care for pilgrims whom I met along the Way and whose gestures of kindness and hospitality inspire me still.

I also owe an abundance of gratitude to Monsignor Michael Kujacz and the staff and seminarians of the Royal English College of Valladolid, Spain, Father Julius Rodulfa and the Seminary of St. Francis Xavier in Davao City, Philippines, and Father David Baronti and the people of Antigua Santa Catarina Ixtahuacán, Guatemala, for giving me warm and welcoming places and whatever time I needed to work on this book.

I thank my friends, Luiz Viana, Robert Schiffner, Father Edmon Benzon, and *Madame* Mimi Solvay for their ever-faithful encouragement and love.

To the parish communities which I have been privileged to serve since walking the Way of Saint James, Sacred Heart in Othello, St. Thomas More in Pullman, and now Sacred Heart in Spokane (all Washington State), I am ever so thankful for your prayers, friendship, and the opportunity you have given me to serve as your pastor.

I owe a huge debt to those who have read the manuscript of this book in its various stages of completion and offered me important suggestions for improvement, especially Gene and Caroline Foley, Ernie and Andi McGoran, Dean and Mary Duncan, Msgr. Denis Carlin, Dan Morris-Young, and Fred Sneesby.

To my own family who have persistently and patiently asked me "How's the next book coming, Kev?" or more pointedly, "When you going to finish that book, Kev?" and thereby kept me writing. Thank you.

Long after this story ended, my brother, Phillip, died suddenly while jogging through the woods near his home in Spokane. In his own way, he was a pilgrim, too. I miss him, yet cannot but look forward to embracing him anew "in that Light of Life" when as the old hymn sings, "my traveling days are done."

Lightning Source UK Ltd.
Milton Keynes UK
UKHW05f0001230418

321467UK00003B/16/P